Praise for

JAYNE ANN KRENTZ

"A master of the genre…nobody does it better!"
—*Romantic Times*

"Who writes the best romance fiction today?
No doubt it's Jayne Ann Krentz."
—*Affaire de Coeur*

THE WAITING GAME
now an original Harlequin movie on

The Waiting Game originally appeared as a
Harlequin Intrigue novel, a series of dynamic
mysteries with a thrilling combination of
breathtaking romance and heartstopping suspense.
Four new Harlequin Intrigue novels appear at your
bookseller's every month. Don't miss them!

JAYNE ANN KRENTZ

THE WAITING GAME

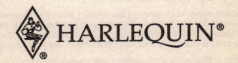

HARLEQUIN®

TORONTO • NEW YORK • LONDON
AMSTERDAM • PARIS • SYDNEY • HAMBURG
STOCKHOLM • ATHENS • TOKYO • MILAN • MADRID
PRAGUE • WARSAW • BUDAPEST • AUCKLAND

HARLEQUIN BOOKS
225 Duncan Mill Road, Don Mills,
Ontario, Canada M3B 3K9

ISBN 0-373-83351-2

THE WAITING GAME

Chapter One

Sara Frazer paused in the act of searching Adrian Saville's desk and told herself for the hundredth time that what she was doing was illegal and potentially dangerous. And while she had her faults, as her family had only recently pointed out to her in some detail, she had never, until that moment, sunk to the level of doing something of this nature.

But Sara was concerned, worried, anxious and more than a little suspicious of the stranger whose study she was going through with such haste. Besides, she told herself with her customary impulsive enthusiasm, the opportunity had been too good to let pass. The door to Saville's isolated home had not been locked when she had arrived twenty minutes earlier. And she had, after all, no intention of stealing anything. She just needed some answers.

Impatiently Sara scanned the room as she closed the drawer of the desk. The study was a clean-lined, orderly room. It was a quiet, solid, masculine room, and she couldn't help wondering how accurately it reflected its owner. Hardwood floors, simple, substantial furniture and a great deal of shelving were the main features. If the den did mirror its owner with any degree of accuracy, she would be in trouble should Saville happen to walk in the door. Something about the place seemed to resist and resent her intrusion.

A greenhouse window that overlooked the cold, dark

water of Puget Sound provided the main source of light. Dusk was settling in on Bainbridge Island, where Adrian Saville made his home, and across the expanse of water the lights of Seattle began sinking into life. Sara didn't dare turn on a lamp for fear of alerting a neighbor to her presence. The house was tucked away by itself amid a stand of fir and pine, but one never knew who might pass by on the road outside. It was late summer and she ought to have enough fading twilight to get her through the rest of the search.

She was turning away from the desk, intent on exploring the bookshelves, when she noticed the apple. Startled, Sara reached out to pick it up. In that moment she was forced to acknowledge that she might have been mistaken in her suspicions of Adrian Saville. After all, she had an apple just like this one and there was only one person who could have given it to Saville.

Sara held the object up to the fading light and studied it intently. It was not just any apple, of course. It was fashioned of heavy crystal, and the stem with its leaf was of intricately worked gold. The person who had made a gift of the apple believed in substantial things such as gold, Sara knew. Small bubbles had been captured inside the apple by the artist. They reflected the light in an intriguing manner, making anyone who held the object want to examine it more intently.

All in all, it was a very attractive paperweight, and the fact that it sat on Adrian Saville's desk put a whole new light on the situation. Sara stood still, turning the apple so that the crystal caught the light, and wondered what she was going to do next.

"Offer me a bite."

The deep, graveled voice came from the doorway. Sara chilled for an instant as fear and embarrassment washed through her. She nearly dropped the crystal apple as she spun around to face the man who was lounging calmly against the doorjamb. Frantically she struggled for self-control and a reasonable explanation of her presence in his study. Unfortunately the situation did not do wonders for her presence of mind. Sara found herself wishing very badly that she had never succumbed to the temptation his empty house had provided.

"I'm sorry," she managed, stumbling over the words. Vaguely she realized that her hands were trembling. "I didn't hear anyone. I mean, there was no one at home when I arrived, and the door was unlocked. I had no business wandering in to wait for you, but it seemed pointless to sit outside in the car and I—" She broke off abruptly as something occurred to her. "You are Adrian Saville, aren't you?"

Eyes that were either unusually colorless or else were washed of color by a trick of the dim light swept curiously over her. Sara had the feeling that the stranger had taken in every detail in that brief glance.

"If I'm not Adrian Saville, this situation is going to get even more complicated, isn't it?" he noted softly.

Sara's fingers tightened on the paperweight as she forced herself to sound reasonably cool and collected. "It would mean that there are two intruders in Mr. Saville's home instead of just one. Yes, I would say that would complicate things. But I don't think that's the case. You are Adrian Saville."

Arms folded across his chest, the man regarded her with mild interest. "What makes you so sure?"

"You're leaning much too casually in that doorway, for one thing," Sara retorted. Whatever he was thinking, he didn't seem intent on doing her any immediate harm. Actually, he really didn't look like the sort of man who would harm someone unless greatly provoked. The fear died away, leaving only the embarrassment. "Look, I can explain this, Mr. Saville."

"I can't wait to hear the explanation."

Sara felt the warm flush paint the line of her cheek-bones. Carefully she set the crystal apple back down on his desk. It was a relief to have an excuse to look away from that strangely colorless gaze. "Then you're going to acknowledge your name, at least?"

"Why not? This is my home. I might as well use my name," he murmured easily.

"I'm Sara Frazer," she said quietly, turning her head to meet his eyes once more. "Lowell Kincaid's niece. I have a paperweight just like this one at home."

"I see."

She hadn't expected the silence that followed. It made her feel uneasy and awkward. Hurriedly she tried to fill it with further explanations. "I came looking for you because I couldn't locate Uncle Lowell. I just arrived from his place in the mountains late this afternoon. I caught the ferry here to the island and by the time I found your house it was getting quite late. There was no answer when I knocked on your door, and when I tried it, it was un-locked. I'm afraid I just came on in to wait for you," she concluded with a tentative smile.

"And wound up searching my study as a means of passing the time?" He didn't return her smile but he didn't seem unduly upset.

Sara took a deep breath. "I happened to notice the pa-perweight," she lied politely. "It really is just like the one I have. Uncle Lowell gave it to me a few months ago. I assume he gave you this one?"

"Umm."

Sara decided the noncommittal sound was an affirmative. "They're quite beautiful, aren't they? I have mine on my desk at home."

He ignored her determined chattiness. "What were you looking for, Sara?"

Something about the calm manner in which he asked the question convinced her that Adrian Saville wasn't going to accept her explanation of why she happened to be in his study. Sara exhaled slowly, considering her options. This might be a clear-cut case of honesty being the best policy, she decided ruefully. Folding her arms across her small breasts in a subtle mockery of his own stance, she leaned back and propped herself against the edge of the desk. She met his gaze with a level one of her own.

"I was looking for something."

He nodded as if it were the most natural thing in the world. "For what?"

She shrugged. "That's the problem. I don't know. Anything that might give me a clue about where my uncle is."

Adrian continued to regard her with solemn interest for another long moment. This time Sara resisted the impulse to fill the silent void with attempts at explanations. She could be just as remote and laconic as Adrian Saville could, she promised herself.

"What makes you think I might have some answers for you?"

"I'm not sure you do. But Uncle Lowell once told me that if anything ever happened to him, I was to notify you. He gave me your address several months ago, shortly before he sent the apple, in fact."

"And you think something has happened to Lowell?"

"I don't know," Sara admitted. "I only know that he's not at his home up in the mountains."

"Perhaps he's taken a short trip. Was he expecting you?"

Sara swallowed uneasily. "Well, no. I just showed up on his doorstep unannounced, I'm afraid. I did try to call but all I got was his answering machine."

"Then why the concern?" Adrian pressed quietly.

Sara looked at him searchingly. "How well do you know my uncle?"

"Well enough."

Not much to go on, but she might as well see what happened when she told him the reason for her concern. "His neighbor said he went hunting."

Adrian Saville greeted that bit of information with more silence. Then he straightened away from the door. "Have you had dinner, Sara?"

Sara frowned as he turned away and started down the hall. "Wait a minute! Don't you understand?" she demanded, hurrying after him. She caught up with him just as he rounded the corner and walked into the small, rather old-fashioned kitchen. "They said he went *hunting*."

"And Lowell Kincaid doesn't go in for blood sports. Yes, I understand." Adrian opened the refrigerator door, examining the contents with a wary eye.

"It's because of his old job," Sara said quickly. "Before he retired he worked in a rather violent world, you see."

"He worked for the government, you mean." Adrian finally decided on a plastic-wrapped chunk of cheese. He removed it from the refrigerator and set it on the counter. Then he opened a cupboard and reached for a box of crackers. "I know what your uncle used to do for a living, Sara."

She blinked, watching him carefully. "Oh."

"You didn't answer my question. Did you have any

dinner?'' Adrian began slicing cheese with smooth, methodical strokes of a knife.

"Uh, no, I haven't had time," Sara said vaguely. Her mind was on other things and had been all afternoon.

"Neither have I. Cheese and crackers and some vegetables okay?"

"Look, Adrian…Mr. Saville…I'm really not very hungry. I just came here to see if you knew anything about Uncle Lowell."

"And stayed to rifle my study." He nodded. "Sorry I can't offer anything more interesting. But it's kind of late in the evening to start something more elaborate. And I'm really not that good a cook in the first place."

"I didn't rifle your study!" Sara exploded, beginning to lose her patience. She didn't have a great deal of that commodity in the first place. Life was short enough as it was, she felt. What good was an excess of patience? "Now, about Uncle Lowell…"

"There's some wine in that cupboard next to the sink. Why don't you open a bottle while I slice up a few carrots and some broccoli?"

"But I don't want any wine!"

"I do." He glanced back at her over his shoulder, a faint smile playing at the corner of his mouth. "I'm celebrating, you see."

That stopped her. "Celebrating what?"

"The sale of my first novel."

Sara stared at him, astonished. "Are you really?"

"Umm."

Again she assumed the noncommittal sound was a yes answer. Her enthusiasm sprang up, as usual, out of nowhere and rushed into her voice. "Adrian, that's fantastic! Absolutely fantastic! A once-in-a-lifetime event. I can't believe it. I've never even met an author before."

"Neither have I," Adrian said dryly. He finished slicing the cheese and opened the refrigerator to pull out a handful of carrots. "Choose whichever bottle of wine you want."

A little bemused, Sara found herself obediently reaching into the cupboard and selecting a bottle of Oregon Pinot Noir. She'd heard the Northwest wine industry was starting to flourish but she hadn't yet had much experience with the products. They hadn't yet become chic in California. "You must be very excited."

He thought about that. "Well, it was a relief to make the sale," he began consideringly.

"A relief! Why, it's marvellous! Terrific! Thrilling! What's the matter with you? I should think you'd be doing handsprings or something."

"I imagine it's easier to get excited when there's someone else around to get excited with you," he murmured, arranging raw vegetables on a platter and putting a dollop of mayonnaise in the center. "I did go out and have a beer down at a local tavern. That's where I was when you arrived, in fact."

Sara poured the wine and handed him a glass. With a smile she raised her own glass in a grand salute. "Congratulations! And here's to nice, fat royalty checks." She sipped her Pinot Noir with attention. It was good. She made a mental note of the fact. There appeared to be a future in Northwest wines. Then she remembered belatedly that she didn't have to worry so much anymore about being on top of the latest culinary trends. "Too bad you can't tell Uncle Lowell. I'm sure he'd be very happy for you."

Adrian regarded her over the rim of his glass as he took a deep swallow. "Yes, I think he would be quite satisfied."

Sara smiled at him quizzically. "Did he know you were writing a book?"

"He knew."

"Then you really are a close friend of his?" she went on doggedly.

"Umm."

Sara shot him a narrow glance. "Can't you just say yes or no?"

"Sorry. Yes."

"Then you do realize that it was odd he would tell his neighbor he was going hunting?" she continued more seriously.

"Is that exactly what his neighbor said? That Lowell said he was going hunting?" Adrian picked up the platter of vegetables and led the way into the rustic living-room. He set the plate down on a low wood-and-brass table in front of the couch and went over to the old stone fireplace. Going down on one knee, he reached for a handful of kindling. Although it was still technically summer and the day had been sunny and warm, the first hint of the coming fall was in the air tonight.

Sara sat down in the corner of the worn black leather couch, studying the man in front of her. "That's what the woman who had the cabin near his said. Her exact words."

Adrian didn't respond, his attention on constructing the fire. Sara sipped her wine and continued to watch him. There was a certain fluidity to his movements that intrigued her. There was also a definite logical precision to the way he built the fire. A coordinated, controlled man. He was dressed in a pair of faded jeans and a black denim workshirt. The clothing molded a lean, tautly built body that seemed totally balanced. On his feet he wore a pair of dusty, soft-soled canvas sport shoes. Now that she had a moment to think about it, she decided the strange eyes were really a shade between blue and gray. In the right light they might appear as silver.

He was a friend of her uncle's and that took the nervousness out of contacting him, even if he had caught her going through the contents of his desk. Although he gave the impression of being easygoing and very friendly, Lowell Kincaid was actually quite cautious in his friendships. He had worked too long in a world where few people could be trusted. If he liked Adrian Saville, then Sara knew she, in turn, could trust the stranger in front of her. Her uncle had always been an excellent judge of people. Sometimes his life had depended on those judgments. The fact that he had survived and been able to retire at the normal age was evidence of just how accurate his analyses of other people had been over the years.

Adrian set a match to the kindling and the yellow flames leaped to life. He crouched for a moment in front of the fire, making certain it had caught properly, and the flickering light illuminated the hard line of his profile.

He was far from being a handsome man, Sara reflected. The planes and angles of his face had been carved with a dull knife, not finely chiseled. But there was a primitive strength in the aggressive nose and the austere cheekbones. He wasn't the kind of man who would smile easily; the grim set of his mouth wasn't shaped for such expressions. Sara guessed his age at somewhere between thirty-five and forty; probably closer to forty. She thought she saw something of the fundamental sureness and strength in him that her uncle must have seen before he decided to make Adrian a friend. Lowell Kincaid was sure of this man and therefore Sara knew she could be sure of him, too. She relaxed even more and took another sip of her wine. She sensed she had done the right thing by seeking out Adrian Saville.

She just wished he'd show a little more interest in her concern for her uncle. But then, a man who had just sold his first book probably had a right to be thinking of other things at the moment.

"What's it called?" she asked as he got to his feet and paced back to the couch.

"My novel?" He seemed to have no trouble following her abrupt shift in the conversation. Adrian picked up a cracker with cheese on it and downed the whole thing in one gulp. *"Phantom."*

"Is it a horror tale?"

He shook his head slowly, his eyes on the fire. "Not in the sense you mean. It's what's called a thriller."

"Ah, secret things, espionage, plots and counterplots. That sort of thing. I read a lot of thrillers." She smiled. "Are you writing under your own name?"

"I'm writing under the name Adrian Saville."

"Good, then I won't have to jot down your pseudonym. You'll have to autograph a copy of your book for me when it's published. I'm sure Uncle Lowell will want one, too."

"Lowell's already seen the manuscript," Adrian said quietly. "Because of his, uh, background, I thought he might be able to give me a few ideas that would make *Phantom* sound more authentic."

"Did he?"

"Umm." Adrian stared into the fire. "He was very helpful. You're really worried about him, aren't you?"

Sara resisted the temptation to say "umm." "Yes. My uncle doesn't hunt. He doesn't even like to fish. Why would he tell his neighbor he was going hunting and then drop out of sight?"

"Beats me." Adrian swirled the wine in his glass. "But don't you think you may be overreacting? You should know your uncle can take care of himself."

"He's in his late sixties now, Adrian. And he's been out of the industry a long time."

Something close to amusement gleamed briefly in Adrian's eyes. "The industry? You sound like an insider. Lowell uses words like that."

Mildly embarrassed, Sara's mouth turned down wryly. "That's how he always referred to his government work. I guess I picked up the term."

"And some of the skills?" he asked too blandly.

She looked away, reaching for a carrot. Sara knew he was referring to the fact that he had found her prowling around his study. "Obviously I didn't pick up the skills. If I had, you would never have caught me the way you did this evening. How did you sneak up on me so quietly, anyway? Must be those sneakers you're wearing. But I was certain I'd hear any car pulling into the drive."

"I walked back from the tavern. The car is still in the garage behind the house."

"Oh." Chagrined, Sara chewed industriously on her carrot.

"You'd better practice checking out those sorts of details if you plan to follow in your uncle's footsteps."

"Don't worry, as much as I like my uncle, and in spite of the fact that I happen to be in the market for a new career, I do not intend to go into intelligence work. I can't think of anything more depressing and grim. Imagine living a life in which you couldn't trust anyone or anything. Besides, I like to limit my close association with violence to reading thrillers," she added with a small smile. "It's okay on a fantasy level but I certainly wouldn't want to make a career out of it."

"If you feel that strongly about it, you'd better give up the habit of going through other people's desks. You could have just as easily turned around and found yourself facing an irate homeowner holding a gun as a friendly, trusting soul such as myself."

She eyed him thoughtfully for a moment. "Actually, you did take the whole thing quite calmly."

"You didn't look that dangerous," he informed her gently. "In fact, you appeared rather inviting standing there in the twilight, gazing into the apple. Besides, as soon as you said you had one just like it, I knew who you were."

"You were certain I was Uncle Lowell's niece?"

"When he gave me the crystal apple he told me he'd given a second one to you. He had them made up specially for us, you know."

"No, I didn't know. That is, I didn't realize he'd had a second one made until I saw it sitting on your desk. When I spotted it, I decided I probably didn't have any reason to go on being suspicious of you," she added apologetically. "Unfortunately, I came to that brilliant conclusion a bit late. You'd already snuck up and found me in what I guess qualifies as a compromising situation. You really don't know where Uncle Lowell might have gone or why he would say he was off hunting?"

"No. But I do think Lowell can take care of himself. My guess is he'd want you to stay out of the way until he's handled whatever needs handling."

"Then you do believe something's happened to him!" she pounced.

"I didn't say that," Adrian protested mildly. "I only meant that he probably had his reasons for disappearing. Maybe he just wanted to take off by himself for a while. Maybe he's got a woman friend and didn't feel like explaining all that to his neighbor. There could be a hundred different reasons why he's not at home, none of them particularly sinister.''

''I don't like it,'' Sara muttered, feeling pressured by the logic.

''Obviously, or you wouldn't have taken the trouble to find me. So Lowell told you to look me up if you were ever worried about something having happened to him?''

''He said you'd want to know, or something like that. I wasn't exactly certain what he meant. He doesn't have a lot of close friends. I assumed you might be one of them.''

''But you weren't sure where I fit in so you decided to take a quick look around my desk drawers while you waited for me to return. Are you always that impulsive?''

''It seemed prudent, not impulsive, to take the opportunity to find out what I could about you before I confronted you,'' she said cautiously. ''Some of my uncle's old acquaintances aren't the sort with whom you want to get involved on a first-name basis.''

''You've met a lot of them?'' Adrian inquired politely.

''Well, no. But Uncle Lowell has told me about a few of them.'' Sara shuddered delicately, remembering one particular tale. ''He's got a great collection of stories and personal recollections, although he always changes names and locations to protect the guilty. I suppose he's mentioned a few of the more colorful characters to you if you used him as resource material for *Phantom*.''

''We've shared a few beers and talked on occasion,'' Adrian admitted.

''You see a lot of my uncle?''

Adrian moved his hand in a vague gesture. ''He doesn't live that far away. I get out to his place once in a while and sometimes he makes it over here. What about you? See a lot of him?''

Sara grinned. ''Not as much as I would have liked over the years. I'm afraid Uncle Lowell has always been considered the black sheep of the family. As you can imagine, though, I found him quite fascinating. He was the unconventional relative, the one who had the mysterious career, the one who showed up when you least expected him. He was unpredictable, and kids like that, I suppose. The rest of the family thought he was a bad influence on me and, of course, that made him all the more interesting.''

Adrian leaned back against the sofa, slanting her a glance. ''Why did they think he was a bad influence?''

''Because he always encouraged me to do what I wanted to do, not what my family wanted. And he had a way of understanding me, of knowing what I was thinking. He told me two years ago, for instance, that I wasn't going to be happy for long as a mid-level manager in a large corporation. Said I didn't have the proper corporate personality. He was right. I think I knew it at the time but everything seemed to be on track and running smoothly in my life. I was living the perfect yuppie life-style, and to be honest, it had its moments.''

''Yuppie? Oh, yes—'' Adrian nodded. ''—Young Urban Professional.''

Sara gave him another laughing smile. ''I was into the whole scene down in California. I had a lifetime membership in the right athletic club, dressed for success, had my apartment done in the high-tech look and kept up with the trends in food. I ground my own coffee beans for my very own imported Italian espresso machine, and I can tell you the precise moment when pasta went out and Creole cooking came in, if you're interested.''

''No, thanks. I eat a lot of macaroni and cheese. I don't

want to hear that it's 'out.' So Lowell advised you to dump the yuppie life?''

''Macaroni and cheese does not count as real pasta,'' she told him forcefully. ''Yuppie pasta is stuff such as linguini and calamari or fettuccini Alfredo. And, yes, Uncle Lowell did advise me to dump the yuppie life. Along with the yuppie males I was dating at the time,'' Sara confided cheerfully. ''I think he thought they were all wimps. He said none of the ones I introduced him to would be of any use in a crunch. I explained I didn't plan to get into any crunches but he just shook his head and told me to come visit him when I came to my senses.''

Adrian regarded her assessingly. ''And that's why you went to his place today? To tell Lowell you'd come to your senses?''

Sara stirred a little restlessly on the couch, tucking one jeaned leg under her as she shifted her focus back to the fire. ''Something like that. I quit my job last week. I think I'm going through a mid-life crisis.''

''You're a little young for that, aren't you?''

Sara ignored the underlying trace of humor in his question. ''Don't patronize me. I just turned thirty. As it happens, I've been through several mid-life crises and I know them when I see them. I'm ready to make some changes in my life again.''

''You're sure that change is what you want?'' Adrian got to his feet to throw a bigger log on the fire.

''Oh, yes,'' she whispered with great certainty, ''I'm sure.''

She sounded quite resolute, Adrian decided as he fed the flames. He'd heard that quiet certainty in Lowell's voice from time to time. Must be a family characteristic. For some reason, Sara Frazer wasn't quite what he'd expected, though, even if she did have some of Lowell's iron-hard determination. Adrian toyed with the flames a moment longer, considering the female who was curled on the couch behind him. When a man had waited nearly a year to meet a woman, it was perfectly natural that he would have developed a few preconceptions.

The few expectations he had, however, had never been fully formed. Lowell had given him some vague, odd bits of information about his niece but little that was concrete enough to build a picture in his mind. Just like Lowell to deliberately leave a great deal to the imagination. He was, after all, a man, and he knew what a man's mind could do when it went to work on a mysterious woman.

Adrian realized that he hadn't expected Sara Frazer to be a flaming beauty and in that regard he'd been correct. Taken individually, her features didn't add up to those of a beautiful woman. What surprised him was that the hazel eyes, long light-brown hair and slender figure somehow went together to create a subtly appealing combination.

On second thought, it wasn't the collection of physical characteristics that made for that appeal. There simply wasn't anything that unique about eyes that hovered between green and brown or about hair that was worn parted in the middle and clipped casually behind her ears. The red knit top she was wearing emphasized small, pert breasts rather than lush voluptuousness.

Adrian turned the matter over in his mind for an instant longer before he decided that Sara was somehow more than the sum of her parts. There was intelligence, ready laughter and more than a dash of impulsiveness in those hazel eyes. And when she had learned of the sale of his first book, her spontaneous enthusiasm had been very real even though he was a stranger to her. It was her inner animation that somehow pulled the ordinary together and made the total package strangely intriguing.

He'd been consciously and unconsciously anticipating her arrival for several months but the end result had still taken him by surprise. He simply hadn't expected to feel such an immediate and compelling attraction. He hadn't thought he'd react to the reality of Sara with such intensity. It was unsettling but he'd lay odds that Lowell would probably say "I told you so" the next time he saw him.

Satisfied with his analysis, Adrian turned and moved back toward the couch. He'd long ago accepted the fact that for some things there were no answers, but he still preferred situations that could be taken apart, analyzed and understood. He liked to have a handle on things, Adrian told himself. No, it was more than that. He liked to know he was in control of his environment. Having everything accurately assessed and properly analyzed gave him the only real sense of security one could have in this world. Sara Frazer was a new and disturbing element in his environment and it was good to know he was already beginning to comprehend her. More importantly, he was comprehending and accepting his reaction to her. He rather thought Lowell Kincaid would be pleased at the progress of the situation.

"It's getting late," Sara mused as she munched the last cracker. "I suppose I'd better be on my way. If you really don't have any idea of where Uncle Lowell is, there's no point imposing on you any longer."

"Where were you planning on going tonight?" Adrian sank back down on the couch, aware of an unexpected and totally irrational sense of disappointment. She had just arrived. It didn't seem right that she should already be planning to leave. That wasn't the way it was supposed to be. A part of him was disturbed that she seemed oblivious to the fact that things were different now. Clearly Kincaid had not given her any idea of what he'd had in mind when he'd set about engineering a meeting between Adrian and his niece.

He wondered how much to tell her about her Uncle Lowell's plans for her. He wondered how she would take the news. She might be furious or she might treat the whole thing as a joke. Women were tricky. It occurred to Adrian that in spite of being nearly forty years old he didn't know nearly as much about them as he should. It would probably be better not to bring up the subject of Lowell's plans this evening. On the other hand, Adrian found himself fiercely reluctant to let Sara go without putting the first delicate tendrils of a claim on her. Something elemental had come alive deep within him, something hard to deny.

"There's an inn on the outskirts of Winslow. It's only about a mile from here. I'll stay there tonight and be on my way tomorrow."

Adrian frowned. "You're planning on returning to California?"

Sara shook her head vigorously. "Not until I satisfy myself about Uncle Lowell. I'm worried, Adrian, even if nobody else is."

Adrian rolled his empty wineglass between his palms. "I don't think you have anything to be concerned about."

"Maybe I've got an overactive imagination. People are always accusing me of it." She lifted one shoulder in careless disregard for the fact. "But Uncle Lowell's former career must have contained some loose ends. And I know that at times he was involved with some dangerous people. There was one in particular he once told me about—" She broke off abruptly, eyes narrowing.

"What do you think you can do about the fact that he's not available at the moment?" Adrian asked reasonably.

Sara gave the matter some thought. "I think I'll go back

to his cottage in the morning and break in. Maybe he left some notes or something on his desk." Her eyes grew pensive with the plans running through her head.

Adrian looked down at the glass in his hands. "The last time you tried that trick you got caught."

She laughed. "Well, no harm done if Uncle Lowell comes home unexpectedly and catches me in his house. In fact, it will be a great relief. The mystery will be solved, won't it?"

Adrian experienced a flash of amused amazement. "You're going to do it, aren't you?"

"Why not? Maybe I'll get some answers."

"I think you'll be wasting your time."

Sara grimaced. "At the moment I have time to waste. As I explained earlier, I'm unemployed."

"There are probably more productive things you could do with your newfound time," Adrian suggested dryly.

"I know. Such as look for another job. But I think I'll see what I can find out about Uncle Lowell first."

"Are you always this impulsive and stubborn?"

"Just since I turned thirty," she told him with benign menace, her eyes mirroring an amused challenge.

Adrian found himself smiling back at her. Her gaze went to his mouth, and he realized she was very interested in his expression. Did the smile look that odd on his face? "Well, if you're intent on another act of breaking and entering, I suppose I'd better go along with you."

She was startled. "Why? There's absolutely no need for you to come with me."

"You're wrong," Adrian said gently. "There are several good reasons why I'd better tag along, not the least of which is that Lowell Kincaid would probably nail my hide to the wall if I didn't."

"Why on earth should Uncle Lowell care?"

"You're worried about him to the point where you're willing to break into not one but two private homes. Lowell would expect me to take your concerns seriously, I think. He'd also want me to make sure you didn't get into trouble. What if a neighbor saw you going through a back window and called the law? You'd have some difficult explanations to make. Messy. Lowell likes things neat and tidy." Adrian paused a moment. "So do I."

"Well, I still don't see why Uncle Lowell would expect you to take the responsibility of keeping me out of trouble," Sara declared firmly.

Adrian deliberately kept his voice casual even though he was oddly aware of the strong, steady beat of his own pulse. "Don't you? The explanation's simple enough. Lowell Kincaid has plans for you, Sara. You've arrived a little ahead of schedule. I think he was planning on you coming to visit him in a couple of months, but the timing doesn't change things."

For the first time since he had caught her in his study, a degree of genuine wariness flared in Sara's gaze. Adrian immediately wished he'd kept his mouth shut. But the strangely primitive desire to let her know she wasn't quite as free as she assumed was pushing him.

"What plans?" she demanded suspiciously.

He'd already said too much, Adrian decided. In a way it was alarming. He'd allowed his unaccustomed emotional response to push him in a direction he'd guessed would be awkward. Odd. He usually had a much better sense of discretion. Having gone this far, however, he was committed to finishing the business. He couldn't take back the words he'd already spoken. The next best thing he could do was concentrate on keeping his tone light and whimsical.

"Didn't your uncle tell you that he has decided to give you to me? You're my reward, Sara. My gift for finishing *Phantom* and a couple of other things that were hanging fire in my life."

Chapter Two

"Uncle Lowell has always had an odd sense of humor. If you're really a close friend of his, I imagine you know that by now. I've always thought he would have made a good cartoonist. Between his constant doodling and his offbeat notion of what's funny, he'd have been very successful."

An hour later Sara lay in the unfamiliar inn-room bed rerunning her response to Adrian Saville's casually outrageous remarks. She decided she'd handled the scene reasonably well. She would have suspected Saville of having a warped sense of humor except for the fact that she knew her uncle. It was entirely possible that Lowell Kincaid had "given" her to his friend. He'd told her more than once that she didn't know how to pick her men. It was Lowell who had the fractured sense of humor, Sara decided grimly. What worried her was that under that trace of whimsy, she sensed Adrian might have taken him seriously.

She turned onto her side, bunching the flat pillow into a more supportive shape, and thought about what her uncle had done. It was annoying, irritating and totally in keeping with Lowell Kincaid's somewhat bizarre way of arranging things. His affinity for the unexpected was probably some sort of survival trait. A good secret agent couldn't afford to be too predictable, Sara thought with a sigh. Normally, however, Lowell didn't allow his penchant for the unique approach to infringe too much on the lives of friends and family. He knew intuitively where to stop.

But he'd let himself go overboard this time, and Sara found herself wondering why. Couldn't he see that Saville was a man who took life seriously? You didn't play jokes on people like that. They either got mad or hurt. There was always the possibility that Lowell was deadly serious about handing her over to a man of whom he approved, of course. He'd made it clear often enough he didn't think much of her own choices in male companions. Yes, Lowell might have been very serious in his intent. In which case she would be sure to give him a piece of her mind when he showed up again.

Sara watched the shadows behind the gently blowing curtains. The window was open a few inches, allowing the fresh, crisp night air into the room. She knew a lot about her uncle's sense of humor. Over the years she'd seen enough examples of it. Strange that he was such good friends with Saville. No one would ever accuse him of having much sense of humor, warped or otherwise. The faint flashes of amusement she had seen in him that evening disappeared so quickly she might have imagined them. She had the impression that when they did appear they surprised him as much as her. Saville was a controlled, quiet man who not only seemed quite different from her uncle but who was also a perfect opposite to the kind of men who circulated in her world.

Her ex-world, Sara reminded herself. Yuppiedom was another ex-world to add to the pile of such interesting experiments. It had been fun, but she had known when she'd gone into it that it wouldn't be permanent. Sara knew she would recognize the life she wanted to live on a permanent basis when she found it. Until then she played games with the world. She wondered if she was getting a little too old for games.

Restlessly she switched to her other side and plumped the pillow again. Still, she had learned some useful skills during the past few years. For example, she knew how to slide out of a socially awkward situation such as the one that had occurred tonight. A light laugh, a wry expression and an easy comment.

Adrian had accepted her withdrawal from the topic, although he had insisted on accompanying her to the inn in her car. He'd offered her a bed at his house but had not seemed surprised when she politely declined. There was no sense complicating an already complex situation, Sara had told herself. As much as she had been intrigued by Adrian, she had been a little wary of him toward the end of the evening.

She was accustomed to men who didn't take anything except their careers, their running and their new Porsches seriously, men who knew the socially acceptable vocabulary of the new male sensitivity by heart but who didn't really know how to make commitments. Sara knew how to handle men such as that. She wasn't so sure about Adrian Saville. She sensed he took a great deal in life very seriously.

There was more age in his eyes than on his face, she thought. And there was quiet, implacable strength in that pale gray gaze. She thought she understood why her uncle liked him. But she could also picture her unpredictable uncle trying to lighten the somberness that surrounded the younger man like an aura. She could just see Lowell Kincaid laughing and telling Adrian that his niece would be good for him and that he could have her when he'd finished his novel.

Sara made a rueful face. Perhaps her easygoing uncle

hadn't realized just how seriously a man like Adrian Saville would take such an outrageous comment. Ah, well. She would do her best to keep things light and easy between herself and the budding author on the drive back into the mountains tomorrow. And when this was all over she would give Lowell a lecture on interfering in the private lives and fantasies of his friends. Assuring herself of that, Sara finally drifted off to sleep.

It was sunny and warm the next morning as Sara showered and dressed for breakfast. Accustomed to that kind of weather in San Diego, she didn't think much about it. She buttoned the wide cuffs of the oversized men's-style shirt she had chosen to wear and fastened the yellow belt that clasped the tapered olive-green trousers. Hastily she clipped her bluntly cut hair with two clips and wondered if Adrian Saville would be on time for breakfast as he'd promised. She decided he would be. Authors were entitled to be erratic in their habits, Sara felt, but Adrian was the kind of man who would be exactly where he said he would be at the specified time. Dependable.

She hurried downstairs and across the street. The coffee shop Adrian had pointed out last night when he'd escorted her back to the inn was full of people who weren't nearly so inclined as she was to take the local weather for granted. There seemed to be a kind of desperation in the air, as if everyone was determined to grab the last of summer before the Northwest winter took hold. Everyone from the hostess to the busboy commented in a dazed fashion on the fact that the Seattle area was getting another day of sunshine.

"Yes, it certainly is marvelous weather," Sara agreed politely as she was seated. Privately she thought that no one in San Diego would have even bothered to comment on it. "By the way, I'm waiting for someone." Something made her glance back toward the doorway. "Oh, there he is now. Would you show him to my table?"

The gray-haired, middle-aged hostess chuckled. "Sure." She waved energetically at the man who stood in the doorway surveying the room. "Hey, Adrian. Over here."

Not just Adrian but everyone else in the room looked around. Sara experienced an acute twinge of embarrassment. She should have guessed that in a small community like this everyone knew one another. Determinedly she smiled as Saville walked toward her.

Striving for a casual pose of polite welcome, Sara was astonished to realize that she was actually mildly fascinated with Adrian's approach. His stride was a deceptively easy, flowing movement that covered the distance between the doorway and her table very quickly. He had a coordinated, masculine grace that went beyond the kind of athletic motion her male friends developed by running or working out. Sara had a feeling Adrian's physical control and smoothness had probably been born in him, the way a cat's coordination was.

The pelt of dark hair that he obviously kept disciplined with a scissor was still damp from his shower and combed severely into place. He wore jeans and a cream-colored button-down shirt. On his feet were the usual sneakers, Sara noted in amusement. The shoes made his progress across the coffee shop quite soundless. If Sara hadn't been watching him, she would never have heard him approach the table. Just as she had never heard him come down the hall to the study last night, she reflected as he greeted the hostess.

"Good morning, Angie. How's it going today? Looks like a full house this morning."

The hostess nodded, pleased. "Give these Northwest

folks a little sunny weather and they crawl out of the woodwork in droves. We've been doing real good this past week. Real good. Have a seat with your lady friend here and I'll send Liz on over for your order.'' Beaming impartially down at Sara and Adrian, the hostess bustled off to find the waitress.

''Lady friend!'' Sara winced. ''I've always heard that in small towns people pay a lot of attention to what their neighbors are doing but I hadn't realized they were so quick to jump to conclusions! Better be careful, Adrian. When everyone finds out you've gone off to the mountains with me for the day, you'll be a compromised man.''

''I can live with it.'' He appeared unconcerned, turning his head to greet the teenage waitress as she hurried over to the table.

''Morning, Adrian. Coffee for both of you?'' Liz began filling Adrian's cup without waiting for confirmation and then glanced inquiringly at Sara.

''Please.'' Sara smiled.

''Ready to order?'' Briskly Liz whipped out her pad.

''Try the scones,'' Adrian suggested before Sara could speak.

''Scones?''

''Ummm. Homemade. They're great,'' he assured her.

''Well, I usually just have a croissant and coffee,'' Sara began uncertainly.

''You're leaving that yuppie life-style behind, remember?'' Adrian pointed out seriously.

Sara felt a wave of humor. ''All right. An order of scones and a poached egg,'' she said to the waitress.

''Got it,'' Liz responded. She glanced at Adrian. ''The usual for you? The number-three breakfast without the bacon?''

''Fine, Liz.''

Liz giggled and hurried off toward the kitchen.

Sara stirred cream into her coffee and slanted a glance at Adrian. "Okay, I give up. Why the giggle over your order of a number-three breakfast?"

Adrian's mouth twisted wryly. "Because a number three without bacon is really a number one. The first time I ate here I didn't notice the difference on the menu and just told Liz I wanted the number three minus the bacon. For some reason she's made it into a standing joke between us."

"I see. You don't like bacon?"

"I don't eat meat," he explained gently.

Sara was instantly intrigued. "Somehow you don't look like a vegetarian."

He leaned back against the cushion of the booth and picked up his coffee cup. "What do vegetarians look like?"

"Oh, I don't know. Maybe like leftovers from a sixties' commune or like a member of some exotic religious cult. Do you avoid meat for health or moral reasons?"

"I avoid it because I don't like it," Adrian said too quietly.

Feeling very much put in her place, Sara managed a faintly polite smile. She knew when she was being told to shut up. "I guess that's as good a reason as any other. So much for that topic. Let's try another one. When will you be able to leave for the mountains? I'd like to start as soon as possible, if you don't mind."

Adrian's dark lashes lowered in a thoughtful manner and then his steady gaze met Sara's. "Was I rude?"

"Of course not," she assured him lightly. "I should never have pried. What you eat is entirely your own business."

"I didn't meant to be rude," Adrian insisted.

"You weren't. Forget it. Here come the scones and they do look good." Sara flashed her best and most charming smile. The one she reserved for cocktail parties and management types.

"Don't."

She blinked and arched a brow in cool question. "I beg your pardon?"

"I said don't," Adrian muttered as his plate was set in front of him.

"Don't what?"

"Smile at me like that."

"Sorry," Sara said rather grimly. Perhaps she would go to the mountains without him.

"It looks like something left over from your yuppie days," Adrian explained carefully. "Kind of upwardly mobile. A little too flashy and not quite real. I'd rather have the real thing."

Sara couldn't resist. "Choosy, aren't you?"

"About some things. I can leave right after breakfast if you like."

"Actually," she began forbiddingly, "I'm on the verge of changing my mind."

"About breaking into your uncle's cottage?" Adrian slid a piece of egg onto a piece of toast.

"About taking you with me," Sara said sweetly.

He glanced up, surprised. "Just because I was a little short with you a few minutes ago?"

Put like that, it did sound rather trite. Sara was at a loss to explain exactly why she was vaguely reluctant to have him accompany her, but the feeling had been growing since she'd awakened that morning. She didn't really have a valid excuse for refusing his companionship, however. After all, she was the one who had sought him out and she had done so precisely because Lowell Kincaid had advised it several months ago. The sense of ambivalence she was feeling for Adrian was a new emotion for her. Sara drummed her berry-tinted nails on the table and decided to lay down a few ground rules. Normally she didn't think too highly of rules, but there were times when they represented a certain safety.

"I suppose I can't stop you from coming with me, although I'm not at all sure it's necessary. But I would appreciate it if you would keep in mind that this whole plan to get into the cottage is my idea."

"Meaning you're in charge?" Adrian munched his toast, watching her with intent eyes.

"Something like that. Forgive me if I'm jumping to conclusions, Adrian, but I have this odd feeling that you might be the type to take over and run the show." Even as she said the words, Sara realized the truth of them. Perhaps this was the source of her vague wariness regarding this man.

"Think of how nice it will be to have someone else along to share the blame in the event you get caught breaking and entering."

Sara's eyes widened. "Not a bad point," she conceded. Then her sense of humor caught up with her. "What did you do before you became a writer, Adrian? You seem to have a knack for getting what you want. Were you a businessman?"

He considered the question. "I guess you could say I was sort of a consultant."

"A consultant?"

"Umm. Someone you call in when things go wrong and have to be fixed in a hurry. You know the type."

"Sure. We used a lot of consultants in the corporation where I recently worked. What's your area of expertise? Engineering? Design? Management?"

"Management."

Sara nodded, familiar with the field. "Get tired of it?"

"More than that. I got what is casually known as burned out."

"I can understand that. I think that in a way that's what happened to me. Uncle Lowell is right. It takes a certain type of personality to be really happy in corporate management. I guess neither you nor I is the type."

A slight smile edged Adrian's hard mouth. "Maybe we have more in common than you thought. We're both in the process of changing careers and we both like Lowell Kincaid."

Sara laughed. "Do you think we can keep each other company on a long drive given those two limited things in common?"

"I think we'll make it without boring or strangling each other."

An hour and a half later Sara was inclined to agree with Adrian. The drive east of Seattle into the Cascades had passed with amazing swiftness. There had been stretches of silence, but the quiet times had not been uncomfortable. Adrian was the kind of man a woman didn't feel she had to keep entertained with bright conversation. In fact, Sara was privately convinced that Adrian would be disgusted if he thought someone was deliberately trying to entertain him with meaningless chatter. It was rather a relief to feel so at ease with him in this area, she realized. Her early-morning tinglings of ambivalence faded as Adrian guided the car deeper into the forest-darkened mountains.

When they did talk, the topics varied from the spectacular scenery to speculation on Lowell Kincaid's whereabouts. In between they discussed Adrian's fledgling career as a writer and the turning point Sara had reached in her own life.

"Are you in a hurry to find a new job?" Adrian asked at one point.

He had calmly assumed the role of driver and Sara had acquiesced primarily because she suspected he would be excellent behind the wheel. She was right. His natural coordination and skill made her feel comfortable at once. He had insisted on using his car and Sara couldn't complain about that, either. The BMW hugged the curving highway with a mechanical grace and power. Normally Sara wasn't particularly enthusiastic about being a passenger in a car being driven by someone whose driving techniques she didn't know well.

"I've got enough of a financial cushion that I can afford to take my time," she told him, her eyes on the majestic mountains that rose straight up from the edge of the highway. Small waterfalls spilled over outcroppings of granite. A crystal-clear stream followed the path of the highway on one side. Heavily timbered terrain stretched endlessly in front of the car. It was hard to believe such mountain grandeur lay so close to the heart of a cosmopolitan city. "But I'll get restless if I sit around too long trying to make up my mind about what I really want to do with my life."

"Any ideas?"

"Well…" She hesitated realizing that she hadn't discussed her tentative plans with anyone else, not even her family. "I've been thinking of going into your old line of work."

Adrian's head came around in a sudden, unexpected movement. "My old line?"

She nodded, smiling. "That probably seems odd to you, but to tell you the truth, I think I'd be a fairly good management consultant. I'd like the opportunity to be my own boss, though. I wouldn't want to work for a firm of consultants. And I'd pick and choose my contracts. I know it sounds like a contradiction in terms, Adrian, but even though I don't like working within an organization, I do have a flair for management techniques that work in an organization. It's one of the reasons I hesitated so long about quitting my last job. I was good at it in a lot of ways.''

Adrian's attention was back on the road ahead. "I don't think it sounds like a contradiction. A lot of people can give objective advice about things they wouldn't want to make a living doing.''

"It would take a long time to build a clientele," Sara said slowly.

"I know the feeling. It will take a long time to build a writing career.''

"But I do have some good contacts who would be glad to recommend me to companies looking for a consultant,'' Sara went on more enthusiastically.

"And I've sold my first book. Sounds like we both have a toehold on the future,'' Adrian said with the first hint of a smile that day.

Sara grinned. "Assuming we both don't wind up in jail because one of Uncle Lowell's neighbors sees us breaking into his cottage!''

It was shortly after noon by the time Adrian pulled into the drive of Lowell Kincaid's mountain cabin. They had stopped for lunch at a small roadside café en route.

The weatherworn house was one of a number of such cottages scattered about the forested landscape. Many were filled with summer visitors but a few, such as the one just over the next rise, were owned by permanent residents. Lowell Kincaid liked his privacy, however, and had purchased a cottage that was not within sight of the next house. Unless his nearest neighbor happened by on a casual walk, no one would notice two people jimmying the back window, Sara told herself.

"Have you ever done this before?" Adrian asked blandly as he climbed out of the BMW and stood surveying the cottage.

"I got into your place, didn't I?" Sara reminded him.

"The front door was unlocked, remember?"

"You should probably start locking it," she told him seriously. "You can't be too careful these days."

"I'll try to remember to do it," he said dryly. "Now, about this little business…"

"Well, I'll admit I have no direct experience of prying open a window, but how hard can it be? People break into houses all the time."

"And occasionally get shot doing so."

Sara gave him a bright smile. "Maybe we should knock on the front door first, just to make certain no one's home."

"Good idea."

Adrian strode to the front door of the cottage and pounded loudly. There was no response. There was also no sign of Lowell's car.

"Looks like we'll have to do this the hard way," Adrian observed morosely. "We'll probably wreck the window and Lowell will send me the bill."

Sara started around the corner of the house looking for a window at the right height and of the right size. "Don't be so pessimistic. I brought you along to help and to lend moral support, not to paint a picture of doom and gloom."

"It's just that I have this image of Lowell coming home and finding his window broken. He won't be pleased."

"I'll leave a note," Sara offered as she stopped in front of an appropriate window. "What do you think about this one?"

Adrian frowned and stepped forward to examine it more closely. ''I guess it's as good as any of the others. We'll need something to jimmy it with. Maybe the jack handle in the car. I'll go see what I can find.'' He swung around and then halted abruptly, staring at the next window on the side of the cottage. ''Well, hell.''

''What's wrong?'' Sara turned to follow his gaze. ''I don't...''

''Looks like someone else has been here ahead of us,'' Adrian said softly.

Sara peered more intently. ''Do you really think...oh.'' For the first time she felt a distinct chill of unease. It was obvious the window had been crudely but effectively forced open. The frame was badly marked from whatever instrument had been used, and the window itself was still half raised. ''Vandals?''

Adrian was examining the damage. He didn't look around. ''Surely you're not going to be satisfied with the notion that a couple of young punks broke into your uncle's house. Not after all the exotic mischief and mayhem you've been imagining.''

''Don't be sarcastic. What are you doing?''

''I'm going inside to have a look.'' Adrian shoved the window completely open and casually swung a leg over the sill.

''Wait!'' Sara grabbed for his arm. ''What if someone's still in there?'' she hissed.

He glanced inside the house and shook his head. ''The place is empty.''

''You can't be sure. It's very dangerous to corner burglars in a house. You're supposed to go call the cops before going inside.''

''Is that right?'' Adrian said vaguely. Then he swung

his other leg over the sill and dropped lightly to the floor inside.

Annoyed, Sara leaned through the window to lecture him further. But the words caught in her throat as she took in the chaos of the room. "Oh, my God."

"Umm." Adrian walked past a bookcase that had been ransacked and came to a halt in front of the old roll-top desk.

Feeling stunned, Sara followed him through the window. Inside the house she stood staring in speechless dismay as Adrian examined the desk. She remembered the desk well. She had helped Lowell select it at a junk shop in Seattle. Her uncle had spent hours refinishing it.

Now the surface was a jumble of strewn papers, books and magazines. The drawers had been unceremoniously hauled open and emptied. Folders of personal business papers had been tossed on the floor along with a notebook of Lowell Kincaid's sketches.

Infuriated more than anything else by the way the sketchbook had been dumped on the well-worn Oriental rug, Sara bent down to retrieve it. "Stupid bastards," she muttered as she tried to smooth the pages and close the cover. "Whoever it was just wanted to make a mess. I thought we had all the mental flakes down in California."

"We have a few up here in the Northwest." Adrian walked slowly through the living room into the adjoining kitchen. "Looks like someone really enjoyed himself."

"It's sick." Sara wrinkled her nose at the smell of decaying food. The contents of the refrigerator had been thrown against the walls. "Absolutely sick."

"Or else someone wanted it to look that way," Adrian murmured slowly.

Sara swung around to stare at him wide-eyed. "Good heavens, I hadn't thought of that. That's a possibility, isn't it? Whoever broke in might have deliberately tried to make it look like the work of vandals. That way no one would be able to figure out what he or she had been looking for.''

''On the other hand, it might have really been a couple of genuine vandals.'' Adrian shrugged, moving on into the single bedroom.

''Make up your mind!'' Sara hurried after him.

''How can I? I don't know what's going on here any more than you do.''

''Good point.'' Sara couldn't keep the sarcasm out of her voice. ''Given that basic fact, I guess we'd better go find the local police or sheriff or whatever passes for the law here.''

Adrian paid no attention to her. He was looking at the phone-answering machine that still sat on the table beside the bed. Whoever had gone through the room yanking open drawers and closet doors had ignored the telephone. The red light was gleaming, indicating a message had been recorded.

''The message on there is probably from me,'' Sara said quietly. ''The one I left when I called him a couple of days ago to let him know I would be arriving. There was no answer, so I just kept driving.''

Adrian pressed the button that rewound the tape. The first voice on the machine was Sara's, as she had predicted.

''Uncle Lowell? I'm driving up from California to see you. Just wanted you to know I took your advice. Mom and Dad are in a deep depression over the whole thing but I think they'll survive. Maybe they're getting used to my life-style changes. Personally, I feel great. You were right. See you tomorrow.''

Sara caught her breath when she heard the next voice

on the tape. Her uncle's easy growl was as unconcerned and laconic as ever.

"Adrian, if you and Sara are the ones listening to this, then you'll have realized I have a small problem on my hands. I can't explain everything just now but don't worry. We'll talk later. Pay attention to me. This isn't anything I can't handle but I need a little time and privacy. Some unfinished business regarding your wedding present, I'm afraid. It's tough enough to find just the right gift for a special couple like you and Sara. I didn't realize it would be even harder to protect it. Do me a favor and don't bother the local cops. This is a personal matter. Oh, and Adrian, Sara tends to have a rather vivid imagination and she doesn't handle waiting very well. A distinct lack of patience in that woman at times. I heard her message on the tape when I phoned to leave my own. I know she's on her way here and when she doesn't find me she'll probably look you up. Which, of course, explains why you're standing there listening to this tape. Aren't you impressed with my wondrous logic?" There was a rough chuckle. "Take care of her for me and keep her out of trouble until I get back. I'll see you as soon as I can."

The tape wound on into silence while Sara stood utterly still, staring at the machine in astonishment and dread. "Wedding gift?" she finally got out very weakly.

Adrian punched the stop button. "I told you Lowell had plans for us," he reminded her dryly.

"Adrian, none of this makes any sense!"

"Yes, it does." Adrian turned to look at her. His light eyes were unreadable, but the set of his harsh features was intently serious. "Lowell says that whatever's going on is private business. He'll take care of it. He doesn't want any help or he'd ask for it. And he wants me to keep you from getting involved. I'm supposed to take care of you. It all seems clear enough to me.''

"Don't be ridiculous. There is nothing clear about this mess.'' Sara spun around and stalked back into the living room. "Damn Uncle Lowell anyway. Why couldn't he have left a simple straightforward message or called you and told you exactly what was going on?'' She headed toward the rifled desk. "Just like him to leave a lot of questions lying around for us to try to answer.''

"He says it's a private matter. He doesn't want us involved. He probably didn't call because he didn't want to alarm us unnecessarily. On the other hand, he figured if we got this far he'd better leave some sort of message.'' Adrian followed her on silent feet, stopping to examine the stack of books that had been stripped from the bookcase.

"If it's such a personal matter, what was that business about protecting our wedding present?'' Sara shot him a scathing glance as she began picking up the scattered magazines that had been spilled from an end table. Lowell Kincaid was an inveterate magazine reader. Sara had frequently teased him about the number of subscriptions he maintained.

"You know your uncle. There are times when he simply can't resist throwing out a teaser.'' Adrian seemed unconcerned.

"It's his unfortunate sense of humor, I suppose.'' Sara sighed and shuffled a stack of insurance papers. "Adrian, this whole thing is going to drive me crazy. How are we going to know he's all right?''

"We won't until he gets back. But I've told you before, Sara. Your uncle can take care of himself.''

"I don't like that comment about 'unfinished business,'" she went on unhappily. "It sounds dangerous. Like something from his past coming back to haunt him."

"Lowell was right. You do have an active imagination."

"Well?" she challenged. "How would you interpret that message?"

"Like something from his past that has come back to haunt him," Adrian admitted in resigned tones. He picked up a stack of books and put them back on the shelf. "The real problem is that food on the walls in the kitchen. That's going to be a mess to clean. It's going to take quite a while, too."

"Stop changing the subject! This is important. We have to figure out what's going on." Sara frowned intently down at the papers in her hand. Predictably enough, many of them, even the most important-looking ones, contained small sketches and doodles. Lowell Kincaid was forever covering books, papers and notepads with his drawings. He did them almost unconsciously, Sara knew. He could be talking about one thing and sketching a totally unrelated subject. She remembered once having coffee with him in a restaurant and discussing her growing dissatisfaction with her latest job. Lowell had carried on a detailed and logical conversation while making comical character sketches on a napkin of the people in the next booth. "What do you suppose whoever did this was looking for?"

"That's something we can't even guess until Lowell shows up."

"Except that we know it has something to do with our so-called wedding gift," Sara muttered in growing annoyance. "What in the world could Uncle Lowell have been talking about?"

"If he'd wanted us to know, he would have told us."

"You're awfully casual about this, Adrian." Sara glared at him over her shoulder.

"I know your uncle very well, Sara," Adrian said. "He doesn't want us getting involved."

She ignored that, her sandaled foot tapping impatiently under the desk. Thoughtfully Sara stared out the window toward a stand of fir. "He said he'd already gotten the gift. Now he has to protect it."

"Something like that." Adrian reshelved another batch of books.

"So whoever did this must have been looking for whatever Uncle Lowell calls our wedding present."

"Are you going to give me a hand cleaning up the kitchen?"

"You know, Uncle Lowell once told me he believed in the old theory that the best hiding place was the one that was in full view. People really do tend to overlook the obvious. He says answers are always quite clear when you know where to look." She glanced around the room with narrowed eyes. "He'd had some experience along those lines. He ought to know what he's talking about."

Adrian went into the kitchen. "If whoever made this mess didn't find what he was looking for, the odds are you won't find it, either. It may not even be here. Or Lowell might have removed it and hidden it somewhere else. Or this chaos might really be the work of casual vandals who happened on an empty cabin. A coincidence. Sara, we don't have a clue. There's no point beating our heads against a stone wall. Let your uncle take care of his own business."

Sara heard water running in the kitchen sink. Reluctantly she put down the stack of insurance papers and got to her feet. Adrian was right. They should clean up the kitchen first.

"Uncle Lowell said he was thinking of putting in a fancy alarm system. Too bad he didn't get around to it in time to prevent this," she commented.

"I know. I was going to help him install it," Adrian said from the kitchen.

Sara took a step forward and her toe brushed a thick sheaf of papers that had been lying on the floor beside the chair. The pile of neatly typed pages was still bound with a rubber band. Automatically she leaned down to pick it up. Halfway down the first page a single word, underlined, leaped out at her. *Phantom.*

"Adrian! Here's a copy of your manuscript," she called, aware of a surging sense of interest in what she held. Curiously she flipped through a handful of pages.

"I think I mentioned that I had given a copy to Lowell," Adrian said softly from the doorway of the kitchen.

"Would you mind if I...?" Sara's request to read the manuscript died on her lips as she looked at the penciled sketch in the right-hand corner of the first page. There were other doodles at the bottom of the page, but it was the one at the top that made her grow cold.

The drawing had been done hurriedly, but Lowell Kincaid's talent lay in the quick character sketch. Strong, simple lines defined the figure in only a few brief strokes. It was the head of a wolf.

"No," Sara whispered as she stared at the drawing. "Oh, no."

"Sara? What's wrong?" Adrian tossed aside the sponge he had been holding and came toward her, his expression one of grave concern.

Feeling decidedly unnerved, Sara sank back down into the desk chair and looked up at him. "See that drawing on your manuscript?"

Adrian glanced at the page and then back at her strained face. "What about it? Your uncle is always doodling and sketching. You know that." He leaned down to flip through the rubber-band-bound stack. "Look. There are little drawings on nearly all the pages."

"I know. But this is more than just an idle sketch." She swallowed, struggling to remember details. "There was a real wolf in his past, you see. A renegade killer. Never mind, it's a long story. Uncle Lowell told me about him one night over a few drinks." Dazedly she stared down at the drawing. "Adrian, if this is the 'unfinished business' my uncle is taking care of, he's in real trouble. We've got to do something."

Adrian's mouth tightened. He reached down and picked up the manuscript. "We are going to do something. We're going to stay out of Lowell's way and let him handle his unfinished business."

"Adrian, we have a responsibility!"

"My responsibility is to take care of you. Very clear— very simple. That's what your uncle wants and that's what I'm going to do. Now, if you really want to do something useful for Lowell, come on into the kitchen and help me clean up the mess. If we don't take care of it, some helpful, foraging skunks or worse will take care of it for us."

Chapter Three

She was genuinely scared, Adrian reflected a few hours later. Tense, nervous, restless and scared. He had spent the past three hours alternately trying to reassure her that Lowell Kincaid could handle his own problems and trying to convince her that she was letting her imagination play havoc with her common sense. Neither attempt had been particularly successful. But then, he hadn't had a lot of experience attempting to soothe the fears of others.

It had been late by the time they'd finished cleaning up Lowell's cabin, and when Adrian had suggested they spend the night at a motel instead of driving all the way back to Seattle, Sara hadn't argued. He'd scrupulously booked two rooms at a charmingly rustic little lodge located just off the main highway.

Now, as he studied her across the restaurant table, it occurred to Adrian that he was going to have his hands full trying to carry out the task Kincaid had assigned him in that damned recorded phone message.

Nothing was going the way he had thought it would, and the knowledge irritated him. For the better part of the past year the unknown Sara had been hovering in the back of his mind, her nebulous image planted there by Lowell Kincaid.

"The two of you are going to be great together," Lowell had told him with vast assurance. "But you both need a little time. You've got to get *Phantom* out of your system and she has to reach a few conclusions on her own. I figure in another few months—''

"Lowell, you may be my best friend but I don't want you playing matchmaker. Understand?'' Adrian had been very firm even though he'd already downed a great deal of beer before the conversation had gotten around to the subject of Kincaid's niece.

"You're going to love her, pal. Trust me. The two of you have a lot in common.''

"That's rather doubtful, isn't it?''

"I know people, Adrian. You should realize that by now. She's perfect for you. She's intelligent and full of life. She's also fundamentally genuine and honest. She'll help you keep your life in balance. You need a dose of enthusiasm and optimism. You're too cautious. Furthermore, she's capable of making a commitment to the right man. Luckily for you, she hasn't found him yet. And she won't as long as she hangs around those wimps she's been dating for the past few years. She's smart enough to play with the dross but wait for the real gold.'' Lowell had grinned. "She's really very good at playing with life. In college she played at being pseudo-intellectual. She used to spend hours arguing about philosophical treatises. A lot of people thought she was serious, including her teachers. Got good grades. When she graduated she decided to play at being an artist for a while. Rented a genuine garret, wore her hair long and went around in paint-stained jeans. She actually sold a couple of paintings through a gallery that made the mistake of taking her seriously. Then she went through an activist phase during which she went around protesting against environmental polluters. Eventually she wound up as the epitome of the young, upwardly mobile urban professional. She always did have a good sense of timing. She also has a real flair for management. She enjoys life the way some people enjoy a game.''

''And just what am I going to be offering her in return?'' Adrian had asked roughly as he popped the top on another can of beer. The discussion was outrageous, but such conversations were allowable when you were sharing several beers with your only real friend. Besides, there was something about the unknown Sara that intrigued him more than he wanted to admit. He found himself wondering what she would think of him if Lowell ever got around to introductions.

''She needs someone strong, someone who can appreciate what she has to offer. She also needs a counterfoil for her natural enthusiasm and impulsiveness. Someone stable and steady. When she does give her heart for real, it will be completely. She'll need someone who will make the same commitment to her that she'll be making to him. A lot of men aren't capable of that. They might know several fancy names for spaghetti or how to select the right brand of running shorts but that's about the extent of their sensitivity.''

''Been reading those articles on the 'new male,' I see. I warned you about that. You should cancel some of those magazine subscriptions. Bunch of garbage and you know it.''

''Is that so? Well, how many men would you trust with your life or your wallet or your woman these days?'' Lowell had countered.

That had struck a chord, Adrian remembered. ''Not many. Maybe you. That's about it.''

''And you're the only one I would trust with anything I value. I value my niece, Adrian. Perhaps because there's something in her that reminds me of myself.''

''So you're going to give her to me? I'm not sure that

you're taking your responsibilities as her uncle seriously enough.''

''I know what I'm doing. You should be thanking me. You need a woman who can give herself completely. You also need someone who has a real understanding of loyalty. You could also use someone who occasionally shakes you up a bit. You're so damned controlled, son, that it worries me at times. It's as though you've built a carefully organized, well-defined little world for yourself and nothing gets in unless you've fully analyzed and comprehended it first.''

''I like to be sure of things, Lowell. You know that.''

The older man had grinned complacently. ''Once you get to know Sara you'll realize you can be sure of her in all the ways that count. There's a lot of love and loyalty in that woman, and the man who taps it is going to be very rich. You'll see.''

The conversation, as Adrian recalled, had gone downhill from there. The beer had flowed freely, and mercifully it had inspired Lowell Kincaid to bring up other topics for discussion. Adrian couldn't remember too many of them the next morning, but he definitely recalled the little matter of Kincaid's niece.

Phantom had absorbed most of his time and energy in the ensuing months. He hadn't seen a great deal of anyone, not even Lowell Kincaid, but the older man had known what he was doing. As usual.

The seed had been planted, and as he'd worked steadily, often painfully, on the novel, Adrian had found the presence of the mysterious Sara hovering in the corners of his mind. Sometimes late at night after he'd put in hours on the manuscript he'd dosed himself with brandy and gone to bed thinking about what he would do if he had Sara there. He'd let himself fantasize about having a woman who loved him, a woman who knew what loyalty meant. And then he'd gone to sleep with a body that still ached from the stirrings of an irrational passion.

On the rare occasions when he did talk to Kincaid, Adrian had heard himself ask after the woman with what he hoped was deceptive casualness. Lowell had supplied information readily enough, telling him about her success in her job or the latest "wimp" she was seeing.

When he'd begun to realize he didn't like hearing about the newest males in Sara's life, Adrian had finally acknowledged to himself that he might have a problem. It was ridiculous and quite asinine to start wanting a woman you'd never met, but the sense of anticipation had taken firm root. That anticipation had been followed by a curious sensation of possessiveness that was even more perplexing than the fantasy-induced desire.

Her undefined image had remained on the borders of his mind, always waiting for him. She was there when he took a break during the day from *Phantom*. She emerged to haunt him before he went to sleep at night. And she casually made herself felt when he sat by himself in front of the fire in the evenings sipping a lonely glass of wine.

Lowell had said he'd see about introducing Sara to Adrian when the book was finished. Over a period of months she had begun to seem like the prize at the end of a quest.

Last night when he'd returned from his small celebration of the sale of *Phantom* and walked home to find the lady in his study, Adrian had experienced the disorienting sensation of having met his destiny. The quest had been completed and now his gift was within reach. The fantasy hadn't diminished since the previous evening.

It should have, Adrian thought objectively as he watched Sara prod a sun-dried tomato in her pasta salad.

Fantasies were supposed to die quick deaths when reality took over. But reality was proving very interesting in this case, far more gripping than fantasy.

"So what are we going to do?" Across the table Sara finally gave up on her salad and set down her fork. Challengingly she waited for Adrian to say something brilliant.

Adrian realized he couldn't rise to the challenge. "Nothing."

"As an answer, that lacks a certain something," she muttered. "In management training I learned that you're always supposed to sound confident and in charge."

"Maybe I should take the course."

"This is not a joke, Adrian. We can't just sit around and wait."

"Why not? It's what your uncle wants us to do. We'll drive back to Seattle in the morning. You can stay with me on the island until Lowell returns."

She eyed him with abrupt wariness. "I don't think that's such a good idea."

"It sounds perfectly reasonable to me. You're certainly not going to spend the time waiting in Lowell's cottage. If you think I'd leave you there knowing that whoever went through that place once might return, you're out of your little ex-corporate skull."

He hadn't raised his voice, but Sara felt the diamond-hard determination in him more clearly than if he'd shouted the words.

"Don't worry," she said bluntly, "I'm not particularly eager to stay alone at Uncle Lowell's cottage. Not after seeing that sketch of the wolf."

Adrian glared at her and picked up his wineglass. "What the devil is all this nonsense about the wolf, anyway? You've been acting as if you'd seen a ghost ever since you saw Lowell's dumb doodle on my manuscript."

"I did. In a way." Moodily Sara stared at the tablecloth in front of her, remembering. "It's a long story, Adrian."

"We've got a long evening ahead of us," he noted grimly. "You might as well tell me the tale."

"I only know bits and pieces of it." Sara sighed and pushed aside her half-eaten meal. "Uncle Lowell never told me all the details. He probably couldn't because of security reasons, although lately my uncle has begun to demonstrate an amazing disgust for all the bureaucratic paranoia that generally controls matters of security." A brief flicker of amusement lit her eyes for a few seconds as she thought about that. She heartily approved of the trend.

"So what did he tell you about this wolf business that has you so upset tonight?"

"There was a man," she began slowly, recalling the conversation with her uncle that had taken place nearly a year ago. "A man who carried the code name of Wolf. Uncle Lowell said it suited him." Sara gave Adrian a level glance, willing him to understand the importance of what she was trying to say. "Lowell said he was so good at what he did, so dangerous, that when he walked into a room the temperature seemed to drop by twenty degrees."

Adrian considered that in silence for a moment and then murmured very distinctly, "Bull."

Sara scowled at him. "It's true."

"Your uncle's right. You do have an overactive imagination."

"It was Uncle Lowell who told me about the guy. That business of the room going cold was his description, not mine. He meant that the man could literally chill your blood. Even Uncle Lowell's blood, apparently. Now do you want to hear the rest of the story or not?"

Adrian shrugged and buttered a roll. "Go ahead."

"All right. But only if you're going to listen seriously to what I'm saying. This is not a wild tale, Adrian. Uncle Lowell meant every word the night he told me the story. He was…upset."

"Lowell was upset?"

"Yes. You see, he knew the man they called Wolf. The guy was supposed to be his replacement. Uncle Lowell had the job of grooming him to step into his shoes when he retired."

"Lowell officially retired five years ago."

Sara nodded. "But my uncle kept tabs on his replacement, I guess. He must have been very uneasy about him right from the beginning. He said this Wolf was almost frighteningly ruthless. He seemed to have no emotions, no human sensitivity. Sending him on a mission was like aiming a gun and pulling the trigger. From what Uncle Lowell said, the man would probably qualify as a sociopath. You know, someone who doesn't really function in society. No emotional equipment. Sick. Working for the intelligence group Uncle Lowell was in gave him an outlet for his antisocial tendencies and his ruthlessness. If he hadn't gotten that kind of job, he probably would have ended up as a first-class criminal."

"Lowell said all this?" Adrian seemed both skeptical and reluctantly fascinated.

"Some of it I've inferred from his description that night. My uncle was very restless about something that evening. He wanted to talk to someone, I think. I've never seen him in quite that mood. And he'd certainly never made a habit before of talking about his, uh, former business associates. Sometimes he'd tell me stories and tales but they were always deliberately vague on details. I could tell that the story wasn't being embroidered or altered for security reasons this time. Anyhow, he'd come down to spend a weekend with my family in San Diego. We had all gone out to dinner, and when we were finished he drove me over to my apartment. I knew something was bothering him, and when he started talking, I just let him go on until he'd gotten it all out of his system.''

''Did he give you any specific details on this character he calls Wolf?'' Adrian asked softly.

''You mean like a description or his real name? Of course not.'' Sara smiled wryly. ''Even when Uncle Lowell's in a chatty mood, he knows how to watch his tongue. I guess he spent too many years being cautious. All I know about Wolf is that Lowell was worried. I think he believed his protégé might be slipping over the edge. Wolf was dangerous enough when he could still be aimed by his superiors and fired like a weapon, but if he could no longer be at least minimally controlled... If he decided to go into business for himself, for example...''

''You're saying Lowell thought the guy might have gone renegade?'' Adrian demanded.

Sara took a breath. ''That's the impression I got that night. I only know that Uncle Lowell was tense and worried about what he had helped create.''

Adrian chewed meditatively on another chunk of his roll. ''Dr. Frankenstein and his monster.''

''I know it sounds melodramatic,'' Sara admitted, ''and if I hadn't seen that little drawing of a wolf's head on your manuscript, I wouldn't have thought twice about that conversation with my uncle. But after hearing the message on the telephone-answering machine and seeing the mess that cottage was in and then finding the drawing—'' She broke off, her anxiety clear in her eyes.

''Why do you suppose your uncle happened to make that little doodle on the front page of my manuscript?'' Adrian asked reflectively.

Sara lifted one shoulder negligently. "You know him. He's constantly sketching and doodling. He uses whatever's handy. I've seen him make the most intricate little drawings on cocktail napkins or paper towels or the back of his income-tax forms. Your manuscript probably happened to be nearby when he was thinking of this Wolf person. Or..." Sara's eyes widened as a thought caught her attention. "Maybe something in your manuscript reminded him of the wolf."

"Not likely. Not from the way you've described the guy," Adrian said flatly.

Sara thought about that. "Then he must have been thinking of the wolf at a time when your manuscript was lying nearby. Which means that something was making him uneasy. He tells us in that recorded message that he's going to take care of unfinished business. I think...I think Uncle Lowell always considered Wolf unfinished business."

"Because he'd trained him and then turned him loose?"

"Something like that. How would you feel if you'd been assigned to train someone and had him turn into a...a criminal or worse. Perhaps a renegade killer. Wouldn't you feel you had to do something about it?"

"Not a pleasant thought," Adrian said slowly.

"But wouldn't you feel responsible?"

"I might."

"Then maybe—"

Adrian interrupted abruptly. "But, Sara, that doesn't explain Lowell's message completely. Remember, he said he was out to protect our, er, wedding present."

"I know. I can't figure out that part," she admitted morosely.

"Face it. We don't stand a chance in hell of figuring

any of this out until your uncle gets back and tells us just what was going on. The only thing we can do is wait.'' Adrian's rare smile flickered briefly at the corners of his mouth. ''At least I got assigned a task to keep my mind off Lowell's problems.''

''What task?'' She frowned at him across the table.

''Taking care of you. I'm supposed to keep you out of mischief, remember?''

''Oh, that.'' She waved the entire matter aside. ''That was just a casual comment on my uncle's part.''

''Nevertheless, I feel obliged to take it seriously. After all, you're worried, and if someone doesn't keep an eye on you, I can envision you getting into all sorts of trouble.''

''Don't be ridiculous.''

''You might,'' Adrian concluded without any trace of amusement at all, ''even manage to make some trouble for your uncle.''

That caught her attention. ''What on earth do you mean?''

''I think that, left to your own devices, you'll convince yourself that Lowell really is in trouble. You'll start poking around, perhaps asking questions. There's no telling what small waves you might set in motion that could ripple back to Lowell.''

Sara studied him, stricken. ''You're serious, aren't you? I wouldn't do anything to jeopardize my uncle.''

''I know you wouldn't do anything deliberately, but how could you even begin to guess what might or might not have an effect?''

''Oh, come off it, Adrian, I'm hardly in a position to do anything dramatic one way or the other,'' she protested.

''No?'' He pushed aside his plate and leaned forward,

his arms folded on the table in front of him. "What if you go back to talk to that neighbor of his? What if you decide to do a little investigating on your own? Find out if anyone noticed someone hanging around your uncle's cottage recently, for example. And what if someone notices you and takes exception to your involvement? I can see you doing all sorts of little things that could blow up in Lowell's face. Or worse yet, your own face."

"That's ridiculous and you know it. Now you're the one whose imagination is running wild," she scoffed. But deep down she felt a prickle of guilt. It had occurred to her only a few minutes earlier that it might be interesting to talk to her uncle's neighbors. A vague plan to talk to some of them had been formulating in the back of her mind. She knew her flushed cheeks betrayed her.

Adrian gave her a very deliberate look. "Going to deny you were making a few plans?"

"Well, no, but I certainly don't think..." She trailed off, flustered.

"Umm. I think my little assignment is going to be the tough one," Adrian groaned. "I have a hunch Lowell knew exactly what he was doing when he asked me to keep an eye on you. If you're finished playing with your food, let's head back to the rooms. It's getting late." He stood up without bothering to wait for her agreement. The waiter hurried over with the check.

Disgruntled at the abrupt termination of the meal and the conversation, Sara got to her feet more slowly and allowed Adrian to walk her out of the small restaurant. Her head was spinning with worry, speculation and half-formed plans. In fact, her attention was focused so completely on her thoughts that she didn't notice where Adrian was guiding her until she suddenly became aware of flagstone under her strappy little sandals. He was leading her along a path that wound around the motel.

"A little late for a walk, isn't it?" she asked, glancing into the shadows of darkened stands of trees. Behind them the lights of the motel flared in the night.

"I thought a walk before turning in might calm you down a bit." Adrian took a firmer grip on her arm as she stumbled lightly on a cluster of pebbles. "Watch your step."

"That's tough to do since I don't see well in the dark," she complained.

"I'll guide you."

"You can see in the dark?" she asked very politely.

"Umm. I've always had good night vision."

"That must come in handy for this sort of thing," she allowed still more politely.

"What sort of thing?"

"Enforced midnight marches with unsuspecting females," she drawled.

"It's only nine-thirty and believe it or not I can't even remember the last time I went for an evening walk with a female, unsuspecting or otherwise." He hesitated, mulling that over. "It's very pleasant."

"Even though I'm having trouble walking in a straight line?"

"That's the best part."

"Oh." Her brief amusement vanished as suddenly as it had appeared, and Sara went back to thinking about her missing uncle.

"It won't do you any good, you know," Adrian said after a moment.

"What won't do any good?"

"Worrying."

"But I'm so good at it." She sighed.

''What you need is something to take your mind off your problems.'' Adrian came to an unexpected halt, catching hold of her with both hands as she stumbled into him. ''And I think I need the same thing,'' he added almost under his breath as he stood very close in the darkness and ran his palms down her arms.

Sara felt the strength in his hands as he pulled her close. She looked up, aware of a fierce surge of sudden awareness as she realized he was going to kiss her. For an instant she tried to read his shadowed gaze, seeking answers to questions she couldn't formulate. But in the almost nonexistent light his eyes were colorless and infinitely unintelligible. She was enthralled by her own reaction to that gaze. It lured her, promising something she wasn't sure she wanted. Before she could fathom the strange sensation, Sara felt herself pressed against him, and in the next moment Adrian's mouth was on hers.

What startled her most about his kiss was the urgency in it. It seemed to wash over her, a combination of male curiosity, hunger and carefully restrained desire. The first kiss from a man was usually tentative, polite and as practiced as he could make it. This was something else again. There was nothing tentative or polite about it. Nor was there any element of practiced seduction in the damp heat of his kiss.

Sara was tinglingly aware that it was the most honest kiss she had ever received. She wasn't sure how she knew that with such certainty but there was absolutely no doubt in her mind. It was like finding gold after years of sorting through scrap metal. The vivid realization brought forth a response from her that she'd had no intention of indulging until it flared into life. Then it could hardly be denied.

Slowly, savoring the moment of unexpected awareness, she slid her arms around his neck and found the dark pelt of his hair with questing fingertips. She was thirty years old, she thought, and not given to such episodes of instant attraction. This was something unique and she was wise enough to know it.

"Sara?"

Slowly, reluctantly, Adrian lifted his mouth from hers. He raised one hand to tangle in her hair while with the other he stroked the length of her back. She could feel the intensity in him as he urged her soft thighs against the hard planes of his lower body.

"I believe you said this was supposed to give me something else to think about?" she murmured gently.

"I don't know about you, but I may have given myself a little too much to think about tonight. Forgive me, honey, but I've been wondering what you would taste like for a long time." Once again he lowered his mouth to hers.

Sara felt her lips being parted and then he was deep in her unresisting mouth exploring her with such intimacy that she trembled. For countless moments time stood still for her there on the narrow path. She gave herself up to the intriguing, captivating touch of a man who qualified as a near-stranger and wondered why he seemed so right to all her senses.

She offered no resistance as Adrian drew her deeper and deeper into the embrace. When his palms slipped down to cup the contours of her derriere, she stood on tiptoe, nestling closer. His leaping desire made itself felt through the fabric of his jeans and her own body struggled to answer the ancient call. Sara had never known such driving urgency. When Adrian freed her mouth to seek out the sensitive place behind her ear, she heard herself murmur a throaty response. His breath was exciting and warm in her hair.

Then, slowly at first but with gathering strength the night breeze began to make itself felt. Sara became vaguely aware of the gathering chill as it swirled and eddied around her. The warmth of Adrian's body warded off some of it but not all. He seemed to realize what was happening at about the same moment and slowly lifted his head.

"I think it's time to go back," he said huskily.

"Yes." She didn't argue. He was right. It was time to go safely back to her own bed. But she felt unexpectedly weak and she found herself holding on to his arm.

For a moment longer Adrian's palms framed her upturned face. She sensed the hesitation in him and was warmed by it. He was reluctant to break the spell and that pleased her. She didn't want to be the only one caught up in the magic, Sara realized.

"If it weren't so cold out here and if you'd had a little more time to get used to the idea…" Adrian let the rest of the sentence trail off as he took her hand and started back toward the lights of the motel.

"Get used to what idea?"

"Never mind," he told her laconically. "My imagination is proving to be as vivid as yours, although it seems to be running along different lines."

Sara smiled serenely to herself in the shadows, knowing exactly what was going through his head. He wanted her, and the knowledge sent a primitive thrill through her veins. Adrian wouldn't do anything about it tonight, of course. It was much too soon. They barely knew each other and there were a great many factors that might get in the way of a relationship between them. Still, tonight she would go to sleep with a sense of anticipation that was entirely new to her.

But an hour later as she lay in bed in the room next to

Adrian's Sara realized that, anticipation or not, sleep was not going to come easily that night. Adrian had succeeded in distracting her for a while, she decided ruefully, but now that she was alone again, too many jumbled thoughts were swirling in her head. Her mind skipped around from worries about her uncle and his "unfinished business" to memories of Adrian's urgent kiss. She needed something to relax her.

"Like a good book," she decided aloud, pushing back the covers. And she knew just where to get one.

Padding barefoot across the carpet, her long cotton nightgown trailing behind her, Sara went to the suitcase in the corner. Opening it, she reached inside and removed the manuscript of *Phantom* that she had picked up off her uncle's desk. For a moment her gaze rested thoughtfully on the sketch of the wolf in the upper corner, and then she told herself to ignore it. She was after relaxation, not added worry.

A deep curiosity filled her as she climbed back into bed and started *Phantom*. Silently she admitted to herself that it was the desire to learn something more about the man she had spent the day with rather than a wish to see how the story ended that prompted the feeling. How much could you tell about a man by his writing, she wondered.

On the surface, *Phantom* was high adventure. It involved the perilous race to retrieve a cache of gold that had been smuggled out of South Vietnam during the last, chaotic days of the war. The treasure had been hidden near the Cambodian border and had been inaccessible for years because it was simply too dangerous to go after it. Only a handful of men knew the location.

As the story opened, it was learned that more than a treasure had been hidden. Secret documents that could destroy the career of a powerful government official had been buried along with the gold. Suddenly any risk was worth taking to retrieve the cache.

The action was well plotted and moved with the swiftness of an avalanche, but what held Sara's attention until nearly two in the morning was the inner conflict of the protagonist, the man called Phantom.

He was portrayed as a man who had clearly reached the limits of his emotional and physical endurance. Too many years of tension and violence had taken a savage toll. Now he had been assigned one last job by the government agency for which he worked. He was told to retrieve the gold and the documents hidden with it. At any price.

In the end the man called Phantom did the job he had been assigned to do, but it had nearly destroyed him. Then he had accidentally discovered that the incriminating documents buried with the gold constituted a shattering indictment of the man who ran the very agency for which he himself worked. The secret papers pointed at treason at the highest levels. Phantom had learned far too much. He had not been expected to survive his mission, but now that he had, his life was in jeopardy.

By the time Sara finished the harrowing and emotionally gripping tale, she felt exhausted but not at all relaxed. The writing had been lean and stark, which didn't surprise her. Adrian Saville struck her as the kind of man who wouldn't use one more word than necessary to tell his story. But she was left with the same question she'd had when she'd begun reading. How much insight could you gain into a man by reading his fiction?

Restlessly she restacked the manuscript pages and climbed back out of bed. She put *Phantom* back in the suitcase and turned to eye the rumpled sheets. She really didn't feel like climbing back into bed just yet. The book had left her far too keyed up and strangely tense.

On impulse she walked over to the sliding-glass door that opened onto the balcony and unlocked it. Taking a deep breath of the chilled mountain air, she stepped outside.

"You should have been asleep hours ago."

Sara jumped at the sound of Adrian's voice. Whirling, she saw him lounging against the railing of the balcony next to hers. He had one foot propped on the lowest rung and his elbows planted on the top one. The shadows hid the expression on his face, but she was aware of a strange tension in the atmosphere between them.

"I couldn't sleep," Sara whispered. "I've been reading."

"*Phantom?*"

"Yes."

"Learn anything?" he inquired sardonically.

Sara half smiled. "Only that I think you're going to have a very successful career as a writer of suspense novels. I couldn't put it down, Adrian."

"But did you learn anything?" he pressed softly.

She wished she could see his face. "You know I started it out of curiosity, don't you?"

"Umm."

"Well, I finished it because it was a very gripping tale. But I don't think I learned much about you in the process." She paused, thinking. "No, that's not true. I guess I did pick up a few things along the way."

"Such as?"

"You have a set of rather fundamental values, don't you? You believe in integrity and justice. Things like honor and loyalty are important to you. If they weren't you wouldn't have been able to portray the hero's emotional turmoil so well. You tore that poor man apart, Adrian. Halfway through the book I almost hated the writer for doing that to his protagonist. And then in the end, even though you pull together all the strands of the story and see that justice is done, you leave us wondering a little whether or not Phantom will survive emotionally.''

Even as she spoke Sara realized the truth of her own words. She had learned something about Adrian Saville by reading his manuscript, and what she had learned was disturbing on some levels. This was not a man who would ever understand games, let alone a lighthearted approach to life. On other levels Sara was aware of a strong feeling of respect. There were so few men who knew what it meant to have a personal code of honor and integrity. Adrian must know or he would never have been able to create Phantom. On still another level of awareness Sara experienced a sensation of compassion. Adrian must have known what it felt like to hold yourself together by sheer willpower. She wondered what he'd gone through in order to comprehend the depths of that kind of struggle.

''You wanted a miracle cure?'' Adrian turned his head to look out toward the night-shrouded forest.

''I like happy endings,'' Sara admitted with a soft smile.

''I'm not sure there are any.''

Sara leaned sideways against the rail, the chilly breeze whipping the hem of her nightgown around her ankles. ''Adrian, I swear, if you turn into one of those cynical New York-style writers I won't read your next book.''

He looked at her then and she saw the flash of a genuine grin. ''Maybe the trick is not to write endings. Just cut the story off after the main issues have been resolved and let everyone go their own way. Readers like you can assume it all ends happily.''

"You won't be able to fool me," she warned. "I know a real happy ending when I see one."

"I'll work on it," he promised so quietly she could barely hear him.

"Adrian?"

"What is it, Sara?"

"About the basic story line of *Phantom*..."

"What about it?"

"Where did you get the idea of the gold being hidden during the last days of the Vietnam war? It was very ingenious. And you made all the action so realistic."

"I got the idea from your uncle. He told me the tale of the gold."

"Really? It's a true story?"

"It's just a legend, of course. There are always a lot of tales and legends that come out of a situation like the last days of South Vietnam. Lowell told me the story one night about a year ago. Supposedly the gold was used by U.S. intelligence to buy information and finance certain clandestine operations. Your uncle told me privately that it's far more likely the gold was a payoff from some big drug deals that were going on in the south. Vietnam was a hotbed for that kind of thing toward the end of the war. At any rate the last man to actually see the gold was a U.S. agent. He arrived at his rendezvous point minus the treasure. No one really knows what happened." Adrian shrugged. "And thus are legends born."

"You added the bit about the secret incriminating documents?" Sara hazarded.

"It's called literary license. I needed an extra fillip to make the tale more than just a treasure hunt."

"You certainly accomplished that." Sara shuddered. "I

really empathized with your hero. I think I fell a little in love with him.''

There was a moment of silence from the other balcony and then Adrian said very calmly, ''I'd much rather you fell in love with me.''

Chapter Four

Perhaps it was the knowledge that she was concealed in the shadows of her balcony and that Adrian was isolated, in turn, on his own little island that made Sara feel safe enough to indulge the dangerous curiosity. Or perhaps she was still wondering just how much she had learned about him from reading his book. Then again, it might have been simply a woman's endless need to probe a man's words, searching for the real meaning. Whatever the cause, she couldn't resist asking the question.

"Why?"

"Because I think it might be very pleasant to have you fall in love with me."

The answer was straight enough, Sara had to admit to herself. Straightforward and honest. Just like the man. The bluntness of it served to wilt the small blossom of excitement within her before she'd even had a chance to fully analyze it. She stifled a small sigh of regret.

"Pleasant," she mused. "That sounds a little insipid."

He seemed surprised at her interpretation. "No. Not at all. I've learned to value the pleasant things in life," he continued slowly. "Pleasant things are civilized. They bring an element of grace and gentleness and peace into our lives. A glass of wine before dinner or a can of beer on a hot afternoon, a late-night walk on a beach, a friend you can trust with your life, a woman whose love is unshakable even if she knows you've been to hell and back. A wise man values such things.''

"It must be the writer in you that can put the love of a woman in the same category of pleasantness as a glass of wine. Don't expect a woman to be impressed, however. We like to think we're special,'' Sara said with a degree of lightness she wasn't feeling.

"You're not going to take me seriously, are you?''

"Not tonight. It's two o'clock in the morning and we've had a disturbing day. I feel a little strange after reading *Phantom;* restless in some way. And as for you, you're a man whose understanding of life's pleasures seems to be different from the way other men view them. I'm not sure I understand you. All in all, I think there are too many jumbled emotions and unknown factors hanging around tonight for me to risk taking you seriously.'' She said it all very easily but Sara believed every word she was uttering.

"You may be right,'' Adrian agreed. He paused before asking, "Are you always this cautious with a man?''

She laughed in spite of herself. "It's the only area of my life in which I am careful. Or at least that's what my family would tell you. A woman can get burned falling in love with a man who's only interested in the superficial pleasures and pleasantries life has to offer. And there are so many men out there who are only interested in the superficial things. Uncle Lowell is right. But then, he usually is when it comes to judging people.''

"I'm different, Sara,'' Adrian told her as he faced the sea. "I'm not one of your superficial wimps.''

"No, I don't think you are. But I'm a long way from figuring out just exactly what category of male to put you in, Adrian Saville. And until I do…''

"You'll be cautious?''

"I think so. Good night, Adrian." Deliberately breaking the spell, Sara turned and stepped back into her room. Resolutely she closed the sliding-glass door and pulled the curtain. She stopped for a moment, listening to the silence, trying to examine the strange emotions swirling within her. Perhaps she was only feeling the remnants of the passion Adrian had ignited with his kiss.

But that kiss had ended hours ago. Perhaps she was simply disquieted by the tale of Phantom, she thought. No, there was far more to it than the restlessness left by the powerfully told story of a man on the brink. She had to face the fact that her suspicions concerning Adrian's serious approach to life were true. In all probability he really did look upon her as the prize he'd been promised by Lowell Kincaid.

What made her deeply uneasy was that she wasn't resisting the idea of being handed over to Adrian nearly as much as she ought to. Was it because she couldn't bring herself to take the notion seriously? Or was it because she was finding herself attracted to this stranger in a way that she'd never experienced with any other man?

Pleasant! Adrian thought it would be *pleasant* to be loved completely by a woman he could trust. Sara gritted her teeth. The man had a lot to learn emotionally. Either that or he needed a new vocabulary! After having read *Phantom,* though, she couldn't believe he lacked emotions.

But after having read his novel she could believe he was the kind of man who was determined to stay in control of the emotional side of his nature. The story of Phantom told her that on some level Adrian viewed the emotional side of life as full of risk. He would want to be very certain of a woman's love before he could allow himself to trust it, Sara realized.

It was all too complicated to figure out tonight and there were so many other things to worry about. Sara took a deep breath and went back to bed.

It was the kind of conversation that neither of them would want to mention the next morning. She felt certain of that. The late hour and the inherent safety of being on separate balconies with the soft rustle of the wind in the trees as background had combined to create a strange mood that had infected both of them. The mood would be gone by morning, and she had a hunch Adrian was wise enough to let it go.

Besides, she didn't really care to be lumped into the same category as a glass of wine or a can of beer.

Out on his balcony Adrian watched the shadowy sway of a tall pine and decided that, as a writer, he really ought to pay more attention to his choice of words.

Obviously words such as "pleasant" and "pleasure" were not the right ones to use around Sara Frazer. To her they were part of the games one enjoyed in life. Not matters of seriousness. She just didn't realize how much he valued the softer things in this world, or how seriously he took everything. Well, he'd try to watch it in the future.

After all, he sure as hell didn't want to fall into the same category as all those lightweight males Kincaid claimed she dated.

Straightening away from the railing, Adrian paced back into his room and closed the door. He had been unable to sleep earlier, his body far too aware of the fact that Sara was awake next door. The glow from her room while she read had lit her balcony and had been plainly visible from his own room. Now that she'd finally turned out her light perhaps he'd be able to get some rest.

THE NEXT MORNING Sara decided to take the initiative. She would put the mood and the conversation back onto a safe track. Setting an assured, easygoing tone was second nature for her. It was a skill she'd picked up early on in the world of corporate management and perfected even more in the world of casual dating.

"I've been thinking," she said as Adrian held the car door for her the next morning, "that you never really got a chance to properly celebrate the sale of *Phantom*. You had a beer by yourself and a glass of wine with me later, and that was it. Since then, I've had you running around helping me break into a private house, clean up a nasty mess and calm my fears. This evening I think we should celebrate properly."

"How?" Adrian turned the key in the ignition.

"I'll cook dinner for you. How does that sound?" She smiled.

"It sounds very pleasant." His mouth twisted. "I mean it sounds very nice." He cleared his throat and tried again. "It sounds great." He appeared pleased with his final choice of words. "Can you cook?"

"A good yuppie can fix the current gourmet fad food at the drop of a hat," she assured him.

"How about an ex-fad food like pasta?"

"No problem, as long as it's not macaroni and cheese. Imbedded in my brain cells is a recipe for a wonderful pasta and vegetable dish that will knock your socks off."

"No meat?"

"Absolutely not. Meat would ruin the delicate flavor of the dish, anyway. We'll need a nice Chardonnay to go with it."

He nodded. "Sounds like we'd better make a stop at the Pike Place Market before we board the ferry home."

"Terrific. I'd love to see the market. I've heard about it for years. I keep meaning to go whenever I visit Uncle

Lowell, but somehow we've never had the time." Her sudden enthusiasm bubbled over.

"It's one of Seattle's main attractions. The only problem is finding a place to park. The place is usually crawling with tourists on a day like this."

They followed the highway down out of the mountains, crossed the bridge that connected Bellevue and Mercer Island to Seattle and then descended the steep streets downtown to First Avenue. Seattle's aggressive new skyline faced Elliott Bay, hugging the western coast of the continent and waiting eagerly for the daily traffic of cargo ships from around the world. The Pike Place Market, an old and honored institution, occupied prime territory a block from the waterfront. But if anyone had dared to suggest that it be razed and replaced by a high rise, he would have been lynched by the local citizens, Adrian told Sara. Seattle loved its market, with its blocks of vegetable stands, craft shops, bakeries and restaurants.

Adrian pulled off the neat coup of finding a parking space not more than a block from the busy outdoor market. He seemed quite proud of himself for being able to avoid one of the expensive parking garages. Men always seemed to see it as a challenge to find street parking, Sara realized with an inner grin. She congratulated him as he reached for her hand and led her up a flight of steps into the bustling atmosphere.

"I got lucky," he acknowledged modestly. "Stay close. I don't want to lose you."

Street musicians, a mime, a puppeteer, craftspeople and various and assorted panhandlers added noise and interest to the basic color of a working public market. Sara was fascinated by the array of intricately arranged vegetables in the produce stalls. The fish vendors hawked their wares in loud voices, waving live lobsters around to attract attention. Meat vendors offered every cut imaginable. Tourists and locals thronged the crowded aisles and spilled out onto the cobbled street that ran down the center of the market. Sara noticed that Adrian did not glance at either the fish or meat stalls.

"There's a shop where we can get the pasta at the far end of the market," Adrian advised as Sara halted to study an artistically arranged pyramid of red peppers. "And there's a wine store across the street."

"Why don't you go select the wine and pick up the pasta while I choose the vegetables?" Sara suggested. "I'll meet you back at the flower stall on the corner. That way we can save a little time. It's getting late."

Adrian hesitated. "Sure you won't get lost?"

"I'll be fine. The flower stall in fifteen minutes." She smiled up at him.

"Well, all right. You said you wanted a Chardonnay?"

"Right." Sara turned to plow through a gaggle of tourists who were trying to photograph the red peppers forming a pyramid. She was intent on finding the perfect broccoli. And she mustn't forget some Parmesan cheese, she reminded herself. There was a cheese vendor up ahead.

Somewhere between selecting the broccoli and choosing the fresh peas Sara began to lose track of time. Fifteen minutes went by very quickly and she was in the process of ordering the grated Parmesan when she happened to glance at her watch and realized she was going to be late meeting Adrian back at the flower stall. But surely he wouldn't hold her to the exact minute, she decided. He'd realize she was bound to be a little late what with all the hustle and bustle and the endless distractions around her. On the other hand, she had a hunch Adrian Saville was a man who valued punctuality. No sense kidding herself, she thought wryly. He would insist that she be where she said she would be when she said she would be there. Demanding punctuality was an element of control one could exert, and Adrian liked exerting control.

She thought about that as she ordered the cheese, realizing she had just had a strong insight into Adrian's personality. He needed to be in control of his environment. He needed to be sure of things. Maybe she'd better hurry.

She handed her money to the cheese vendor and accepted the package of Parmesan. It was as she turned away to plunge back into the stream of foot traffic that a large, male tourist careered into her.

"Excuse me," Sara said hastily, hanging on to her armful of packages. "It's so crowded here, I—" She broke off as the man gripped her arm.

"Your uncle wants to see you," the stranger grated. His fingers tightened, digging into her skin through the fabric of her shirt. He began pushing her deeply into the passing crowd.

Sara nearly dropped her parcels. Her mouth fell open in shock. "My uncle!"

"Come on, lady, we don't have time to waste."

She looked up at him, taking in the narrowed dark eyes, the gray-streaked black hair and the aquiline cast of his features. She was suddenly very scared.

"Who are you?" she managed, aware that she was being pushed toward the far end of the cobbled street. Around her the crowd ebbed and flowed. A string of cars vainly searching for the few parking spaces right next to the market stalls inched through the crowds. The flower stall was in the opposite direction. "What do you know about my uncle? And let go of my arm!"

The man didn't answer, intent on making progress through a cluster of tourists wearing name tags that declared they were all from New York. They seemed to resent his insistence.

"Hey, watch it, buddy," one of the group snapped.

"I thought folks out here were supposed to be laid back, not pushy. I coulda stayed home if I wanted this kinda treatment," muttered a heavyset woman with a huge camera strung around her neck.

The man with the face of an eagle didn't bother to respond. He simply forced his way through the grumbling tourists, pushing Sara ahead of him.

"Wait a minute," Sara gasped, beginning to panic. "I'm not going with you until you tell me who you are and what you know about my uncle! Now, unless you want me to start screaming—"

"Sara!"

She turned her head at the sound of Adrian's voice. "Adrian! Over here."

With a savage oath the man holding her arm released her. Sara spun around to watch him as he melted into the crowd. He disappeared in an instant.

"Sara, what the hell is going on?" Adrian came up beside her, pushing aside a few more New Yorkers in the process. He paid no attention to their enraged lectures on manners. "When you didn't show up at the flower stall on time, I figured you'd gotten lost. You're just lucky I spotted you when you stepped out into the street a minute ago. Who was that guy?"

"He said my uncle wanted me," she gasped. "He grabbed my arm and started pushing me along as though I were a sack of potatoes or something. Adrian, he knew who I was! How could he possibly know me? I've never seen him before in my life. And how could he know about Uncle Lowell?" She felt a wave of relief as she huddled against Adrian's side. His arm wrapped around her waist, fastening her securely as he began propelling her back toward the car.

"What did he look like? Tell me his exact words, Sara," Adrian ordered.

Sara clutched her packages and tried to think. "He looked very vicious. Sort of like a hawk, and his eyes were mean."

"Sara, that's not exactly a description, that's an emotional reaction, for heaven's sake."

"Well, I can't help it. I didn't have a lot of time," she defended herself. "He—he had dark eyes and dark hair that was turning gray. I'd say he was probably in his mid-forties. He was wearing very nondescript clothes. I can't even remember what color his jacket was. He said my uncle wanted to see me and that we didn't have a lot of time to waste."

"Those were his only words?"

"I think so. He was quite rude. Just ask those New Yorkers."

"He simply walked up to you and said that?" Adrian demanded. "Nothing else?"

She shook her head, trying to think. "No, I don't think so. I asked him who he was and what he knew about Uncle Lowell, but he didn't answer me. I was getting ready to start screaming when you showed up, Adrian, I have to tell you, I was very glad to see you! In fact I was never so happy to see anyone in my life as I was to see you a few minutes ago!" It was the truth, she realized. The sight of Adrian had meant safety.

They reached Adrian's car and he unlocked the door. His eyes narrowed as he took her arm to settle her in the front seat. "You're trembling."

"That man scared me," she said evenly. "There was something very frightening about him."

"Given the fact that it looks like he was trying to abduct you, I imagine he was somewhat scary," Adrian growled as he slipped into the seat beside her and started the car. "The bastard. I should never have left you alone."

"You know, I said he had hawklike features but you could describe them another way," she noted thoughtfully.

He slanted her a sharp glance. "How?"

"You could say that with those dark eyes and those strict features he looked a little like a wolf. Ruthless and potentially violent."

Adrian froze, his hand resting on the steering wheel. "You're letting your imagination get carried away again, Sara."

"I don't think so," she whispered, staring out the window. Behind them an impatient driver who wanted the parking space honked loudly.

With an oath Adrian put the car in gear and pulled away from the curb. He headed down toward the wharf and the ferry docks. "Sara, listen to me. I'm the writer in the crowd, remember? Leave the melodramatic touches to me."

"But I didn't get a really *cold* feeling," Sara went on, remembering her reaction. "I was scared and my palms got damp, but it wasn't like the temperature dropped twenty degrees or anything."

"For pete's sake, it's eighty-three degrees today! The meanest-looking guy in the world is hardly likely to make you feel as though the temperature dropped into the low sixties."

"True," she admitted dryly. "And I suppose Uncle Lowell only used that bit about the temperature drop for effect."

"Your uncle likes to tell a good tale and he's quite happy to embellish it for a willing audience."

Sara's mouth curved upward. "I know. I've been a willing audience since I was five years old." But there had been something different about the way her uncle had described the man called Wolf. Sara hadn't had the impression that her uncle was embroidering a story for her benefit. He had been in an oddly reflective mood the night he'd told her about the man he'd trained. Lowell Kincaid had been uncharacteristically quiet that evening. Almost morose.

"Forget your uncle's descriptive turn of phrase," Adrian said grimly as he guided the car into the line of traffic waiting for the white ferryboat. "We've got more important problems on our hands, thanks to him."

Sara shivered. "You mean the fact that someone knows who I am and managed to find me in the crowd at the market?"

"Exactly. We have to assume someone followed us. Probably from your uncle's cabin. Must have been watching it. The freeway was busy coming into Seattle today. It would have been hard to spot a tail if I'd had the sense to be looking for one."

Adrian's self-disgust was plain in his voice and it bothered Sara. "It's certainly not your fault that man found me in the market. For heaven's sake, don't blame yourself, Adrian."

"Well, he's not going to find you alone again."

"What are you talking about?"

"I'm going to start doing my job," he stated resolutely.

She smiled. "You mean keep an eye on me?"

"Umm. You'll stay at my place, not the inn, while we wait for Lowell to get in touch. I don't want you out of my sight again."

Sara absorbed the deep determination in his voice and knew he meant every word. Adrian had decided he had a job to do, so he was going to do it properly. That meant in his mind that he had to be in complete control of the situation. She would be spending the next few days with him. On the whole, she wasn't inclined to object at the moment. The man in the market had scared her. The relief of having Adrian appear at the critical moment was still with her. She wouldn't forget that sensation soon. The instinctive knowledge that he offered safety and protection was one more element to add to her growing list of things that seemed to fascinate her about Adrian Saville.

"What do we do about him?" she asked after a moment.

"The man you think is Wolf?" Adrian shrugged negligently. "Nothing right now. There isn't anything we can do except take care to keep him away from you."

"But we have no idea when Uncle Lowell will get back from wherever it is he's gone. We can't just wait indefinitely," she protested.

"Sara, honey, a long time ago I learned the value of patience. We'll wait."

"I think we ought to do something, Adrian."

"We'll wait," he repeated stonily.

"But that man seemed to know where Uncle Lowell was," she pointed out.

"If that character knew where your uncle was, why would he need you?" Adrian asked simply.

"Good point. Why *would* he need me?"

"Possibly because he intended to use you to lure your uncle out into the open."

Sara swallowed uneasily. "You have a devious turn of mind, Adrian." . . . .

"Umm. Probably an occupational hazard of being a writer of thrillers."

"So we wait?"

"It's either that or try the police—and your uncle specifically asked us not to do that."

"I doubt there's much they could do anyway," Sara said unhappily.

"No, I don't think there is."

"I guess we'll have to start locking your front door, won't we?" she offered, trying to keep her tone light.

"Lock the front door?" He glanced at her quizzically. "Oh, you mean the door you walked through so easily the other night."

"No offense, Adrian, but I got the distinct impression you haven't had to be too security conscious on your island," she said gently.

"Don't worry about it. You'll be safe. There's an alarm system installed. Lowell helped me install it a year ago."

"It wasn't on the night I walked in the front door?"

"It was on."

"But I never heard an alarm and no police came," she protested.

"My system works on a slightly different principle from most alarm setups."

"What principle?" She was deeply curious now.

Adrian parked the car inside the ferry and reached for the door handle. "The idea that it's sometimes simpler and more effective to trap an intruder inside the house than attempt to keep him out. I can set it in reverse mode, however, and keep intruders out just as easily as I can let them in. When I'm inside the house I set it that way. But when I'm gone, I use the first setting."

She blinked, not finding the idea either simple or effective sounding. But what did she know about alarm detection systems, Sara asked herself. "I see," she responded vaguely. "If I had tried to get back out of the house the other night, would I have found myself trapped?"

His mouth picked up at the corners in one of his brief flashes of humor as he helped her out of the car. "Weren't you?"

"Hardly. I mean, you just walked in and happened to find me in your study," she grumbled. He was leading her up to the passenger deck and it was hard to hear him distinctly in the noisy stairwell.

"I knew where you were in the house before I came through my own front door, Sara. I carry an electronic device that warns me when the system's been activated. The device starts working within a mile of the house."

"Really?" She was impressed.

"You never had a chance," he drawled.

She laughed. "Is that supposed to reassure me?"

"If you don't like my alarm system, blame your uncle. He's the one who helped design it."

"It sounds like something he'd come up with," Sara admitted. "It's that sense of humor of his. It would be just like him to design a system that can reverse the general principles of burglar detection. It fits in with some of his other theories, such as hiding something right out in the open where the whole world will see and overlook it. Well, if you're convinced it's safe, I'll trust your judgment."

"I'll take care of you, Sara," he said very seriously.

He meant it, Sara realized. The knowledge touched her on a very deep, perhaps primitive level. She hadn't met a lot of men who would say that sort of thing these days. And if they did say it, a woman couldn't risk believing it completely. Adrian Saville, Sara decided, meant it. And she could trust him.

She thought of something as they took a seat in the passenger section where they could watch the Seattle skyline recede into the distance. "Did you remember the pasta?"

"How could I forget the featured item in my celebration dinner?" he asked whimsically.

In spite of the unnerving scene at the public market, Sara found herself enthusiastically preparing her specialty pasta and vegetable dish later that evening. Adrian poured each of them a glass of wine and lounged in the kitchen, watching as she put the finishing touches on his dinner. He seemed to be fascinated with her every move. The kitchen took on a cozy feeling that made Sara almost forget her fear that afternoon.

"I can see you're going to expand my culinary horizons," Adrian noted as he sat down at the kitchen table he had set while Sara had fixed the Parmesan-flavored sauce for the pasta. "This sure beats macaroni and cheese."

"When did you stop eating meat?" she asked casually. Too late she remembered the last time she had asked him a question on the subject he had cut her off rather quickly.

"A little over a year ago," he answered calmly.

Relieved that he didn't seem to be taking offense over the issue, she decided to risk another question. She couldn't seem to stop wondering about every aspect of this man, Sara realized. "You don't miss it?"

"No." He plucked up a spinach leaf from the salad bowl. "Great dressing on the salad."

"Thank you." She hesitated and then tried again, delicately. "Did you just suddenly lose your taste for meat?"

"In a way." He eyed her silently as she sat down. "I

was going through my mid-life crisis at the time. When I emerged, a lot of things in my life had changed. I quit my job, moved to a new state, started a book and decided I really preferred being a vegetarian.''

"All those changes sound wonderful.'' She smiled. "I'm in the mood for some massive changes myself. Have you ever married?''

He arched his eyebrows as he forked up a mouthful of pasta.

"Sorry. I didn't mean to pry,'' Sara mumbled, lowering her eyes to her plate. It was difficult to know just how far she could push with this man.

"It's all right,'' he surprised her by saying after a moment. "I'm just not used to personal questions. No, I've never married. There's never been time. What about you?''

"No. I always seem to be changing careers and that tends to keep the available pool of men changing, too. The right one never seemed to come along.''

"You'll know him when you find him?''

"Definitely.'' Sara laughed softly. "Uncle Lowell has been telling me for two years that the right man never was going to come along in the world in which I was living. He's always been a bad influence on me. Just ask my parents. They think I get my occasional bursts of unpredictability and unconventional behavior from his side of the family.''

Adrian nodded. "He can be unpredictable and unconventional but he has a way of getting things done. He really did give you to me, Sara. I'm not making that up.''

The camaraderie she had been feeling faded into a new kind of uneasiness. "It was a joke, Adrian. I'm sure of it. Even Uncle Lowell wouldn't go that far.''

"Then why the matching gifts?''

"The crystal apples? They probably just took his fancy in some shop and he decided to buy a couple."

"He told me he had them specially made by a craftsman on the coast who works in glass," Adrian said.

"Adrian, I really don't know why he would give us a matching set of crystal apples, but I don't see that it matters one way or the other!"

"And what about that message on the tape at his cottage? The bit about protecting our wedding gift?"

"Now that," she admitted dryly, "was fairly bizarre. Your guess is as good as mine. But knowing Uncle Lowell, he was probably referring to something obvious."

"It would be just like him," Adrian agreed thoughtfully.

"When he shows up," Sara went on forcefully, "I'm going to have a few pointed remarks to make to him."

It was after dinner that Sara began to experience a strange nervousness. She knew the focus of it was the inevitable approach of bedtime and the necessity of making a dignified exit that was neither provocative nor rude. You learned to distinguish such subtle variations of behavior when you'd been through as many different careers as she had, she decided ruefully.

It wasn't that she was expecting a heavy-handed pass from Adrian. He didn't seem to do things heavy-handedly as far as she could tell. Just very deliberately. He certainly wouldn't pressure her into bed. But there was no denying the sexual tension that now existed between them, and if he alluded to it, she would find it difficult to deny.

The graceful approach was to keep things light and casual, she decided. That's the tone she would strive to maintain. After this first night it would be easier. Tonight would set the tone for the rest of her stay under his roof. She sensed it instinctively.

"Ah, a checkerboard," she exclaimed as she followed him into the living room after dinner. It struck her as the perfect answer to the question of how to spend the rest of the evening. "Are you any good?"

"At checkers? Fair, I guess. I'll give you a couple of games." Adrian poured two brandies and carried them across the room to the table where Sara was busily setting up the game. "I've played your uncle a few times."

"He prefers chess."

"So do I, usually."

"I only played it during my college years," she confided cheerfully. "It seemed to fit the academic image. Haven't played it since. I didn't really like it." She lined up the checkers in their little squares. "All that business about strategy and having to think several moves ahead was far too much like work to me. When I play games, I like to *play*."

"I see." He gave her a half-questioning, half-amused glance. "Checkers may be simpler but it's a game of strategy, too."

"You play it your way and I'll play it mine," she ordered, reaching out to make the first move.

Four games later they faced each other across the width of the table. Adrian's expression was one of wry wariness. Sara was feeling quite cheerful.

"That's two wins apiece," she pointed out. "One more game to settle the matter."

"Who the hell taught you to play?" he grumbled as he set out his pieces.

"I'm strictly self-taught," she acknowledged brightly. In truth, she was secretly pleased with her two victories. They had been achieved with wild, haphazard moves that clearly offended her opponent, who had won his two games with careful, precise strategy.

"It shows. You didn't win those two games with hard work. You got lucky on some wild moves. You have an extremely off-the-wall manner of playing, if you don't mind my saying so."

"You're just envious of my inborn talent. The way you play, a person would think the fate of the nation hinged on your next move. You're much too serious about the game, Adrian. You'd have more fun if you'd just loosen up a bit."

He looked at her, light eyes intent. "I'm afraid I tend to be a serious sort of man."

"Not given to fun and games?"

"No."

Sara caught her breath as she realized that they were suddenly inexplicably discussing more than a game of checkers. For reasons she didn't want to analyze she was afraid of the new direction. Desperately she tried to find a casual way of turning the conversation around before it strayed into the realm of the personal again. "Well, we'll see whose approach works best with this next game. I warn you, I'm going to be at my most off-the-wall!"

"In the long run, strategy and planning always succeed more often than wild luck, Sara."

"Prove it," she challenged rashly.

He shrugged and proceeded to do so. Fifteen minutes later Sara was left staring in vast annoyance at the board. She didn't have one single playing piece left on it. Adrian had beaten her with cool, deliberate ease, never relenting for a moment. Every move from first to last had been plotted and carried out with ruthless intent. Her cheerfully haphazard approach had netted her only a few of his playing pieces. Even those, she was convinced, he had deliberately sacrificed at various points to lure her into traps he had set.

"I demand a replay! You don't play fair. You play exactly like my uncle."

"What's unfair about it?" he asked, tossing the checkers back into the box.

"I don't know, but there must be something sneaky and underhanded about all that strategy," she complained. "It must be quite terrifying when you and Uncle Lowell play together."

"The games tend to last a long time," Adrian said with a faint smile.

"Who wins?"

"We're fairly evenly matched."

"You mean you win frequently?" she asked curiously.

"Umm."

"That's interesting. I don't know of anyone who can consistently beat Uncle Lowell at checkers or any other game. But sometimes I can take him," she added proudly.

"With one of your wild moves?"

"Yes." She grinned. "The thing about people who always use intense strategy is that you can occasionally upset them with my technique."

"Only occasionally. Not consistently," Adrian informed her politely. "You got lucky twice tonight, but that was about the best you could do, playing with your style."

"Something tells me that people who play with your style will never appreciate people who play my way."

And on that note, Sara decided suddenly, she had probably better make her gracious, unprovocative exit to the bedroom he had given her earlier.

Chapter Five

Adrian watched moodily as Sara went off to bed and wondered how he was going to get to sleep himself. When she had disappeared into the bedroom, he sprawled in an armchair and considered having another brandy. He needed something to squelch the restlessness that seemed to be thrumming through his veins.

This sensation was far worse than the disoriented feeling he'd had when he'd finally finished the book and put it in the mail. Then he'd felt suddenly at loose ends, as if everything had ended too quickly. But tonight's uneasiness was multiplied a hundred times by the dull ache of desire.

He could not remember the last time he'd desired a woman as intensely as he wanted Sara.

Adrian stared across the room at the waiting brandy bottle and decided against pouring himself another glass. He needed it, but this was not the night to indulge. Not when he was standing guard over a lady who had no real conception of the kind of trouble that might be waiting outside the door.

"Kincaid, you old devil, you really pulled out all the stops this time, didn't you?" he muttered, leaning his head back against the chair. "Who or what are you hunting?"

Whoever Kincaid's quarry was, Adrian didn't have any doubts about the outcome. Lowell had been out of the business for a long time, but he'd once been the best there was at what he did. He'd get his man. In the meantime, Adrian knew exactly what was required of himself. Kincaid had assigned him the task in that phone message. His responsibility was to take care of Sara.

"We also serve who only sit and wait," he paraphrased, mockingly solemn.

The fact that someone had actually approached Sara that afternoon was eating at him, fueling his unease and gnawing at his mind. His instincts were to run with her, take her as far away as he could, and hide her well. But when he left emotion out of the process and concentrated on logic, he knew she was safest here in the house. The alarm system Kincaid had helped him install was good. The best. The place was a walled fortress. Actually, when he thought about it, most of his life had become a walled fortress. Strong, secure, protected, with everything under control.

Until he'd walked into his den the other evening and found the lady with the crystal apple standing in the filtered gold of a setting sun.

He really should be trying to get some sleep, Adrian thought. He wasn't doing himself any good sitting here fantasizing about a woman with an apple. And there was no need to stay on guard all night in this chair. There would be ample warning if anyone tried to get to Sara while she was here. But somehow the thought of going off to a lonely bed was depressing. It didn't make any sense, because he was used to a lonely bed. But tonight the prospect bothered him.

Forcing his mind away from the tantalizing image of Sara undressing for bed down the hall, Adrian wondered just where Lowell Kincaid was at the moment. The older man had dropped out of sight and would probably stay out of sight until it was all over. Good, logical strategy. In the meantime all Adrian could do was wait and keep watch over the woman in his care.

Patience, he had told her that afternoon, was of great value. He wasn't sure she had believed him. The thought edged his mouth with a wry flicker of amusement. The lady did things with a certain impulsive flair. He could see why she probably wasn't cut out for the corporate world in the long run. She didn't have the patience for elaborate strategy and she didn't show any interest in restraining her impetuousness. In the short time he'd known her she'd enthusiastically broken into two private houses, comprehended and been a little shaken by the gut-level action of *Phantom,* nearly gotten herself abducted, and fixed him a celebration dinner with all the excitement of a woman who genuinely cared about his success. She'd topped that off by serenely taking herself off to bed as though she were simply a visiting relative rather than a woman who'd been subtly tantalizing him all evening.

Yes, he could see why she probably couldn't have gotten too much further in the corporate world. They liked flair in that world, it was true, but they liked it coupled with a certain amount of predictability and internalized respect for the corporate image. Adrian had a strong hunch Sara didn't have any such thing as an internalized respect for that type of image. Just as she probably hadn't had any for the academic image or the artistic image. She would play at maintaining the corporate facade the same way she played at being a yuppie. After a while, upper management would probably have figured out that she wasn't one hundred percent committed to their world. Apparently she had figured it out first and decided to make a graceful exit.

The same kind of exit she'd made tonight, Adrian concluded grimly. Did she know he was sitting here, his body in a state of semiarousal while his mind tried to anticipate the next move the guy outside in the shadows might make? He wished to hell Kincaid would call and provide some clue as to what was happening. In the meantime all he could do was sit tight and practice the virtue of patience. It was a virtue he'd learned well.

Two hours later Sara came drowsily awake and lay still in the wide bed wondering what had brought her up out of a light sleep. It had been hard enough to get to sleep in the first place. She was momentarily annoyed at the intrusion.

Then the reality of where she was and why came back and she sat up, absently rubbing her eyes. She listened for a moment but heard nothing. A wary glance at the curtained window showed no menacing shadows. Why on earth was she awake? Perhaps it was simply nerves. She certainly had a right to a severe bout of nervous tension, she assured herself. Patting a yawn, she thought about getting up for a drink of water or a glass of milk. Then she noticed that light was seeping under her bedroom door from the hall. Adrian must still be up, she realized in concern.

If he wasn't able to sleep, it was because of her. He was sitting out there in the living room, worrying. Sara was certain of it. The man took his responsibilities too much to heart. She didn't want him staying up all night to stand guard over her.

Pushing aside the covers, she climbed out of bed, found her robe and went to the door. The hall outside her room was empty and the light left on in it seemed to be the only light in the house. Perhaps she was wrong. Maybe Adrian had gone to bed after all. She would feel much better if he had.

As long as she was up she might as well see if there was any milk in the refrigerator. Stepping out into the hall, Sara walked toward the living room, intent on reaching the kitchen. It was as she left the lighted hall and moved into the shadows en route to her goal that she saw him.

"Adrian?"

He was standing near a window, his lean frame a dark silhouette amid the various dark shapes of the living room. She knew he was watching her, although the silvered eyes were lost in pools of shadow.

"Do you make a habit of running around a lot at night?" he asked gently. "This is the second evening in a row that I've found you out and about instead of tucked into bed."

She smiled. "The fact that you've been awake to observe my nocturnal habits means yours are a little odd, too. Why aren't you in bed, Adrian?"

"I wasn't sleepy," he said simply.

"I don't believe you." She took a few steps forward, her bare feet silent on the wooden floor. "You're worried, aren't you? I thought you said the house was safe."

"It is."

"Then you should be in bed, not prowling around out here."

"Is that what I was doing?" He seemed vaguely amused. "Prowling?"

Sara moved still closer. She came to a halt a foot away from him and lightly touched his arm. "I don't think I'm going to be able to sleep unless you do. I'm not used to someone fretting over me like this. It makes me feel strange, Adrian. You don't need to assume this kind of responsibility toward me."

"I don't have any choice." His tone was suddenly grim.

"You mean because of that message my uncle left on the tape?" She groaned. Her fingers tightened urgently on his arm. "Adrian, you mustn't take that too seriously. I'm not really your responsibility. There's absolutely no need to feel that you have to play bodyguard."

"After what happened this afternoon?" he asked dryly.

She shook her head resolutely. "When it comes right down to it, Adrian, that was my problem, not yours. I mean, I certainly appreciate your interest in my welfare, but I don't want you to feel you have to get so involved."

"I've already told you; I don't have any choice." He lifted his hand to touch her cheek. "And I think you know it."

Belatedly she remembered that he could see much better in the dark than she could. Sara was very much afraid he might be able to read the uncertainty in her eyes as she looked up at him. "Adrian, please..."

"What are you afraid of, Sara? That you might come to rely on me? Your uncle says you move in a world where you can't count on a man when the chips are down."

"Sometimes my uncle exaggerates," she said huskily, acutely conscious of the roughness of his fingertips. She wanted to move away from his touch and couldn't.

"Your uncle knows a lot about human nature. He learned it the hard way."

"But he's prone to sweeping generalizations," she protested. "He met a couple of the men I've dated and decided everyone in my world was like them. I don't think he approves of the 'new male,'" she added, trying for a spark of humor.

Adrian didn't respond. His hand slid down the side of her throat, resting just above the collar of her robe. "I don't think you approve of the 'new male' either, Sara, or you would have been married by now.''

''It sounds as though you're prone to sweeping generalizations, too! Actually, there's a lot to be said for the new breed of male. He acts as if he's sensitive, communicates his thoughts and feelings with all the right words; he's into things like art and gourmet cooking and he's able to handle the idea of a woman in the professional world, or says he is...''

''And he thinks in terms of relationships instead of commitments. But a woman like you needs commitment, according to your uncle. That says it all, Sara. Your uncle is right. You would never have found what you were looking for in your old world.''

''How can you know so much about me?'' she whispered, feeling confused and unsure.

''Your uncle has told me a lot about you. For nearly a year he's been feeding me bits and pieces of information about you. Enough to torment me and bait me and tease me. I've remembered everything he said. And now that I've had you with me for a couple of days I've had a chance to learn a few things on my own.''

''You're an expert on human nature, too?''

''Umm.'' The hand on her throat was warm and compelling. He traced the curve of her shoulder as if deeply intrigued by it.

''And did you gain your knowledge the hard way, also?'' she demanded, striving to maintain her sense of balance, both emotional and physical.

''There is no easy way.''

''Adrian...''

''There's nothing else to say, Sara. We're together in this. I'm going to look after you, whether you think I have the right to do so or not.''

She moved her head in a slow negative. "Because my uncle 'gave' me to you?"

"Perhaps. I haven't had a lot of gifts in my life. I've learned to take care of the ones I do get."

"Just as you've learned to value life's little pleasures?"

He muttered something under his breath, something that sounded disgusted. "You misinterpreted what I meant last night."

"Did I?"

"And now you're using that misinterpretation as an excuse to withdraw from me tonight, aren't you?"

"Yes," she acknowledged, aware of an ache of pain and regret because of her own defensive behavior. She wanted to toss it aside and give into the promise of the moment. Feeling torn in a way she had never known before, she couldn't bring herself to release her grip on his arm and walk back to the bedroom. It should have been a simple enough action. She knew it would certainly be the wisest thing to do under the circumstances.

"Sara, you don't have to be afraid of me," he said so softly she almost didn't hear him. It was the urgent need in his voice that got through to her.

"I know that." The bluntly honest words were out before she could halt them, a response to the urgency in him. Hastily she tried to retreat. "It's not that I'm afraid of you, I simply don't want you assuming so much responsibility toward me."

"I know. Because you're afraid that if you give me that right, you'll come to rely on me and at some point in the future that could be dangerous, couldn't it?"

"Dangerous?"

"You're afraid that one day you'll turn around and I won't be there or I won't be the man you think I am at the moment you need me most."

Sara took a deep breath and tried to control the trembling in her fingers where they rested on his sleeve. "That's quite an analysis."

"I told you; I've been studying you. Between your uncle's observations and my own, I've got a fair amount of data," he murmured.

"So you think you know a great deal about me now, is that it? What about you, Adrian? What do you need?"

"You."

The single word was a monolith between them. Sara knew there was no way around or over the starkness of his answer. She could only retreat or accept it. It was not possible to ignore it.

Intellectually she knew she should retreat. But her intense emotional reaction anchored her to the spot. She could not move. In that moment she knew she wanted him, too. The one element of caution that she had always practiced in an otherwise playful approach to life seemed to be disintegrating. The strange swirl of emotions she experienced around this man was blowing into a full-scale storm. Sara was no longer certain she could resist the impact.

"Adrian," she heard herself whisper, "are you sure?"

"Do you have to ask?"

"No." She looked up at him wonderingly. "No, I don't think I do. I've never met anyone like you."

"I know. I've never met anyone like you, either." The hand on her throat held her very still as he brought his mouth down to hers.

Sara trembled a little beneath the warm onslaught of his kiss, and there was a soft sound far back in her throat that was lost against his lips. She felt the need in him and the leashed hunger and knew that the honesty of his desire was going to be overwhelming.

Slowly her palms lifted to rest against his strong shoulders as her mouth flowered open.

"Sara…"

Her name was a husky groan uttered deep in his chest and then he was tasting the damp warmth behind her lips. The aggressive intimacy of the kiss seemed to swamp her, making her sway against him. Adrian steadied her, holding her with a kind of fierce gentleness that provided all the strength she needed.

Slowly he lifted his head until he could look questioningly down into her face. His eyes gleamed with a silvery brilliance that captivated her, and she knew in that moment that she was lost. Or found. She couldn't be sure which. Nothing seemed normal or totally rational. But one fact seemed to emerge from the shimmering world of her emotions. If Adrian wanted her tonight, she was his.

He must have read the vulnerable response behind her lowered lashes because he let out a long sigh and lifted her into his arms.

"It's all right, Sara." His voice was a dark and passionate stroke along her nerves. "It's all right, honey. I'll take care of you. I'll take care of everything. I've waited and wondered so long. I didn't even realize how much I needed you until you finally walked into my life."

Sara felt the easy power in him and rested her head against his shoulder. Unconsciously she surrendered the last remnants of her caution. She didn't care where he was taking her or what would happen when they arrived. Never had she been so certain that it was safe to abandon the future for the moment. There was no longer a distinction between the two in her mind. In fact, it seemed to her that there could be no real future without this timeless interlude. Adrian needed her and she needed him.

She was vaguely aware that he carried her into his own

bedroom, not hers. Carefully he stood her on her feet while he turned back the covers. His eyes never left her face. When he'd finished the small task, he stood in front of her and put his hands at the base of her throat. There was more than passion in his touch, Sara realized. There was that sense of need and urgency she had responded to last night on the balcony of her motel room. Once more it enthralled her and this time there was no barrier to keep her from tumbling into the glittering net.

"Don't think about anything else except us," he whispered as he slowly slid his hands inside the robe and pushed it off her shoulders. "Please, Sara. Just us."

"I don't think I could concentrate on anything else even if I wanted to," she said truthfully. Again she shivered. The light robe fell to the floor at her feet.

"Are you afraid of me?"

Sara shook her head. "No."

"You're trembling." He seemed incredibly concerned over the fact. His fingertips stroked her bare arms and then he touched the rising swell of her breast just above the edge of the nightgown.

"I know, but not because I'm afraid." She smiled a little as she covered one of his hands with her own. "You're trembling a bit, too."

"I'm shaking like a leaf. I want you, Sara. I've been wanting you all evening. No, longer than that. I've been wanting you for months." The words were raw with honesty.

"Adrian, it's probably much too soon—"

"No," he interrupted roughly. "It couldn't possibly be too soon. Not for us."

His hands moved down over her breasts and she felt the tantalizing heat of his palms through the thin material of the nightgown. She knew he must realize that her body was already responding. Sara could feel the tautness of her nipples as they came tinglingly alive. She caught her breath and began to fumble with the buttons of his shirt.

"Please, Sara," he breathed into her hair. "Yes, please."

His need filled her with a longing to satisfy and comfort him. Slowly she made her way down the front of his shirt until it parted, exposing the dark hair on his chest. So entranced with the vivid sensuality of the moment was she that Sara was hardly even aware of her nightgown floating to the floor.

But when Adrian's hands slid down her back to the full curve of her hips, she moaned softly and stumbled a little against him. She glanced up into his face and read the masculine anticipation there.

"You're so soft," he murmured in tones of wonder. His fingers sank luxuriously into the flesh of her derriere and he pulled her tightly against him.

"You're not soft at all," Sara said unthinkingly and then buried her flushed face against his chest as he growled his amused response.

"No, I don't suppose I am. I feel as though I'm made up of angles and rough edges. You, on the other hand, are composed of curves and gentle valleys. Places where a man can lose himself."

He let his fingers trail into the cleft between her buttocks and Sara's nails dug lightly into his skin as he followed the path to the dampening juncture of her thighs.

"Adrian..."

"Say my name like that again," he demanded hoarsely as he picked her up and settled her on the bed. "It sounds different when you say it."

"Does it?" She lay watching as he yanked off his shirt, stepped out of his shoes and unclasped his jeans. A moment later he stood nude beside the bed, the light from the hall emphasizing his lean, hard body. He was wonderful, she thought dazedly. Everything she could ever want in a man. It was strange to be so certain of that, because until now she hadn't been quite sure just what she had wanted in a man. She had only known that she hadn't found it.

"Oh, Adrian," she whispered as he came down beside her. "Adrian, I didn't know..."

"Didn't know what?" He flattened his palm on her stomach and smoothed her skin down to the curling hair that veiled the heart of her femininity.

"Never mind. I don't think I can explain it just now." She curled into him, shifting languidly under his touch. "I can't even think right now."

"There's nothing to think about." He leaned down to kiss the peak of her breast. His tongue teased the firm bud of her nipple until she cried out and pulled him closer. "That's all you have to do right now," he told her approvingly, the words heavy with desire. "Just give yourself to me. Let me open my present. I've been waiting so long for you, sweetheart."

She obeyed, wrapping her arms around his neck as he touched her with growing intimacy. When his prowling fingers found the hot damp center of her need she said his name again, this time with an urgency that matched his own.

"Sara, my sweet, Sara." He pinned one of her legs with his strong thigh and probed her deeply with a deliciously questing touch. When she shuddered, he muttered hot, dark words of encouragement into her ear.

She lifted herself against his hand, unable to resist the caress. Never had she responded so completely and so readily. Her senses seemed inflamed, thoroughly alive and aware in a way that was new to her. Fascinated by the world of sensation that was beginning to spin around her, she stroked his smoothly muscled frame. Her palms slipped over the sleek contours of his back, down to the hard planes of his thigh. Then, with gentle boldness she moved her fingertips around to find the flat terrain of his stomach. For an instant longer she hesitated. Then her hand went lower.

"Yes," he grated with harsh need when she dared to tease his male hardness. "Take me inside, sweetheart. Let me have all of you. I need you so."

She couldn't find words but he seemed to know she was ready. With passionate aggression Adrian pushed her into the pillows and lowered himself down along the length of her.

"Put your arms around me, Sara, and never let go," he commanded. "Never let go...."

She did as he instructed, pulling him to her until she felt the blunt hardness of him waiting at the gate. The knowledge that he was on the verge of entering her fully and completely brought a brief, startling flicker of alarm. For an instant Sara had a vision of the reality that lay beyond tonight. *This man was unique. After tonight nothing would ever be the same.*

The fleeting glimpse of the future was gone an instant later as Adrian moved heavily against her. All of Sara's senses returned to the moment, lost once more in the pulsating excitement.

"Oh, *Adrian...*" The words were torn from her as she felt the full impact of his body taking possession of hers.

"Hold me, Sara."

Instinctively she obeyed as she adjusted to his sensual invasion. Then he began to move within her, slow, tantalizing strokes that pushed her senses into tighter and tighter bundles of energy that strove for release.

The end was a revelation to Sara, a new understanding of her body and its responses. She found herself clinging to the man above her with an abandon that she would never have believed if she hadn't experienced it firsthand.

''That's it, honey,'' he rasped as she cried out his name once more. ''Let go. Just let go. I'll take you with me all the way.''

Willingly, unable to do anything else, Sara gave herself to him completely and gloried in the knowledge that he was returning the gift in full measure. She heard the sound of her name as it was wrenched from him and then he was pushing deeply into her one last time. His hard body shuddered for a long moment and then collapsed. Outside the window the night breeze briefly stirred a stand of fir and then all was silent.

It was a long while before Sara became aware of the sprawled weight that still trapped her in the depths of the bedding. She opened her eyes to find Adrian lying on top of her, his head on the pillow beside hers. He was watching her from behind half-closed lashes.

''Am I too heavy for you?'' he asked lazily.

''Umm.''

His mouth flickered in brief amusement as he recognized her deliberate imitation of his characteristic response. ''What does 'umm' mean?''

''I don't know. You're the expert. You tell me.''

''It means 'uh-huh.''' He sighed regretfully and slowly rolled onto his side. Then he gathered her close. ''Too bad. You're very comfortable.''

''Am I?''

His head inclined downward once in a short nod. ''Incredibly comfortable. I can't recall when I've been this comfortable. Or this relaxed. Or this content.''

"Neither can I," she said honestly. It was the truth. Tonight there were no pretenses or games or caution. Her fingertips worked small, idle patterns on his chest. "Adrian, I've never felt quite like this before in my life.''

"You don't sound as if you're sure you like feeling this way.'' He touched her cheek.

Nothing will ever be the same. "It feels strange.''

"We'll get used to it,'' he assured her.

"Will we?''

"You're nervous all of a sudden, aren't you?''

"No,'' she denied quickly.

"Sara, honey, don't try to fool me now. You can't do it,'' he told her gently.

"Well, maybe I am a little nervous. It was too soon, Adrian.''

"It was inevitable, so the timing doesn't really matter.''

"We hardly know each other.''

"You were a gift to me, remember? I was bound to open you as soon as I could.''

She flushed. "I thought you were a great believer in patience.''

"Only when it's the best option.''

"You don't think we should have waited awhile longer? Made certain of our feelings?'' she asked anxiously.

"I am certain of my feelings,'' he told her roughly.

"I don't want you confusing your feelings of responsibility for me with...with your, uh, more personal feelings.''

He looked down at her in mocking pity. "Believe me, I'm not mistaking a sense of responsibility for raw passion. From my point of view the two are quite distinct. You're the one who sounds confused.''

''You're not?''

''Not at all, Sara. If anything, tonight just makes everything even simpler and more straightforward.''

She eyed him curiously. ''What does that mean?''

''It means we don't have to have any more arguments about my right to take care of you, for one thing.'' He brushed her parted lips and then drew back to study her expression. ''You belong to me now. That gives me all the rights I need.''

''I've never met a man so anxious to assume responsibility,'' she tried to say lightly. But she was very much afraid her voice cracked a little on the last word.

''I've never been particularly anxious to assume responsibility for anyone else,'' he told her seriously. ''With you, it's different.''

''And what do you want from me in return?'' she asked carefully.

''I've already told you, remember?'' He pushed a strand of hair back behind his ear. ''I want you to love me. I like the idea of having you love me. I like it very much.''

''You think it would be 'pleasant,''' she couldn't resist saying somewhat tartly.

''You said you fell a little in love with the hero in *Phantom*.''

''So?'' she challenged softly.

''How do you think he would treat a woman whose love he wanted?''

The question startled her. She frowned. ''I think he would take care of her. She could trust him.''

''I want you to trust me the same way.''

She half smiled. ''You're not Phantom.''

"I created him. There must be something of me in him and vice versa."

Sara studied his intent features. She had asked herself so many questions about the similarities between Adrian and his hero the previous night when she'd read the manuscript. "Yes, I think there might be."

"Trust me, sweet Sara," he grated, rolling onto his back and pulling her down on top of him. "Trust me with your love. Like your uncle, I know what has value in life. I'll take good care of you."

"Aren't you worried about how well I'll take care of you?" she parried, aware of the renewing tautness in body.

"You won't play games with me."

"What makes you so sure?" she demanded, rather irritated with the certainty in his voice.

"Because it would tear me apart if you did," he said simply. "You wouldn't do that to me, would you, Sara?"

Horrified at the thought, Sara cradled his face between her palms. "No, Adrian. Never that," she vowed.

Unaware of how deeply she had just committed herself, Sara kissed him, translating the verbal promise into a physical one. His hands came up to wrap around her waist and he arched his lower body demandingly into hers.

"Adrian?"

"Umm."

She didn't bother to ask him what he meant. It was becoming very obvious. Sara parted her legs for him and her mouth locked with his as he began the spiraling climb to passion.

THE FIRST HINT OF DAWN was in the sky the next time Sara came awake. There was a moment of lazy curiosity as she opened her eyes and absorbed her surroundings.

Adrian's room was a thoroughly masculine affair, with its warm cedar walls and heavy, clean-lined furniture. It was as orderly and controlled-looking as the rest of his house. She was finding it interesting until she became aware of the weight of his arm across her stomach. Then she awoke completely.

Memories of the night filtered back in a haze of lingering passion and midnight promises. She turned to look at Adrian and was grateful to discover he was still sound asleep. What exactly had she agreed to last night, she wondered with a sudden feeling of panic.

There had been talk of love and responsibility and a promise not to play games. But it seemed to her that most of the dangerous, reckless promises had come from her. The only thing he had vowed in return was to take care of her.

It was crazy, Sara chided herself as she cautiously slipped out from under his arm. She hadn't intended to let things go so far. She had never meant to wind up in bed with him, at least not so soon. She had barely met the man. This was exactly the sort of behavior she had instinctively avoided in the world she had just left. What on earth was the matter with her?

Adrian stirred restlessly when she slid off the bed but he didn't awaken. On silent feet Sara fled down the hall to her own room and scrambled about for her jeans and a shirt. She badly needed to get out of the house for a while. She needed time to think and reevaluate the whole situation. Her family had often warned her that her periodic bouts of impulsiveness would land her in real trouble someday. Even Uncle Lowell had felt obliged to point out that there were some risks involved in playing games with life.

But last night had been no game. Last night had been for real. Twenty-four-karat real.

Shoving her feet into a pair of sandals, Sara yanked a lightweight Windbreaker out of her suitcase and hurried down the hall to the living room. She let herself out the front door and stood on the porch, inhaling deeply of the sea-sharpened morning air.

For a moment she hesitated, unable to think clearly enough to decide on a destination. Then she remembered the car she had left parked in the inn parking lot. With a small sigh of relief at having provided herself with a focus for the morning walk, she hurried down the steps and out to the road. She would walk back toward town and pick up her car. Wonderful. It would give her something useful to do while she tried to sort out her future, she thought. Sara patted her jeans pocket to make certain she had the keys.

Behind her she was unaware of the house purring to life with news of the unauthorized exit. Adrian came instantly awake as the nearly silent vibration in the headboard jolted him. The alarm-clock radio beside the bed was blinking in a fashion that had nothing to do with its normal function. The message was quiet but clear.

The house was doing its duty. Faithfully it undertook to warn its owner that Sara was gone.

With an oath that was half rage and half pain, Adrian threw off the covers and reached for his clothes.

Chapter Six

The flash of rage and pain gave way to another emotion even as Adrian slipped out the front door. Fear began to claw at his insides, and in that moment he could not have said whether it was fear for Sara's safety or fear that she was leaving him. The two seemed to combine in the bottom of his stomach, forming a knot of tension that increased as he realized she was already out of sight. He was at a loss to explain how he could have been so sound asleep that he hadn't even felt her leave the bed. Normally he never slept that deeply. Last night had altered something as fundamental as his sleeping patterns and that was unnerving in some ways.

The truth was he hadn't handled last night all that well. He'd practically pushed her into bed, Adrian berated himself. He should have waited. He'd known it was much too soon. She hadn't spent nearly a year with a fantasy nibbling at the edge of her mind the way he had. She couldn't know what it was like to have a fantasy become reality. As far as Sara was concerned she'd only known him a couple of days. She must have awakened this morning with a head full of doubts and anger aimed at him.

So she'd taken off without bothering to say good-bye.

Damn it, he thought furiously, where the hell could she have gone? There had been no sound of a car. She must be on foot and that meant she couldn't have gone far.

The car. Hers was still at the inn and it probably represented escape to her. The road would seem the fastest way into town to her, Adrian decided. Without hesitating a second longer, he loped down the steps and started up the drive toward the winding road that led into the Winslow.

He saw her just as he reached the pavement. She was walking briskly along, her light-brown hair catching a sheen of gold from the dawn light. It complemented the faint gleam of gold from the little chain on her wrist. He remembered the way the tiny little bracelet had glittered last night against her skin. She had told him that her uncle had given it to her a long time ago. Her slender, soft body moved with an ease that seemed to emphasize the intriguing roundness of her hips and the subtle, feminine strength he recalled so vividly that morning. Adrian watched her in silence, remembering the sweet passion he had tapped during the night.

The year's wait had been worth it, he acknowledged to himself as he began to pace silently a few yards behind her. He had not set himself up for disappointment by allowing Lowell to build an image in his head. In his wildest imaginings, though, he could not have envisioned that she would wrap her arms around him with such abandoned demand. Nor could he have dreamed up the clean, womanly scent of the real Sara Frazer. It was unique to her and he would never forget it. There was no way his fantasies could have created the exact feel of her soft thighs as she opened herself to him and there was nothing in fantasy that approached the real-life sensation of sinking himself deep into her soft, clinging warmth.

But it was the words he remembered with such stark clarity that morning. Her soft words of need and the promises he had coaxed from her lips. He had thought the words would hold her even if the lovemaking could not.

She had told him she would not play games with him and she had said she wanted him.

But this morning she was running from him.

It would be easy enough to catch her. She wasn't even aware of him prowling along behind her on the empty road. Her mind seemed focused on her destination, whatever that was. Was she planning to take the car and head back to San Diego? Or would she go to Kincaid's house and wait there for her uncle?

Not that it mattered, Adrian thought grimly. His hand curled and uncurled briefly in a subtle act of tension. He couldn't let her leave.

He ought to just catch up with her and explain very succinctly why he couldn't let her off the island. Perhaps she would be rational about the matter. Or he could simply overtake her, scoop her up and carry her back to the house. She'd probably start screaming. Then again maybe it would be simplest if he caught her and swore never to touch her again as long as she did as she was told. And just how would he manage to keep a promise like that?

None of the alternatives seemed viable. With a savagely stifled oath, Adrian continued to trail her along the narrow road. It was ridiculous following her like this, unable to make up his mind about how to handle her. Kincaid would collapse in laughter if he could see him now. The Adrian Saville he knew had never been prone to indecision or uncertainty.

Several yards ahead Sara walked toward town with an energy that was fueled by a sense of impending fate. She couldn't explain the feeling of being caught in a trap, but the sensation was strong in her mind. A part of her could not regret last night no matter how hard she tried. But another side of her warned that everything had happened much too quickly. It was so completely alien for her to catapult herself into a situation like that. She shook her head morosely, unable to comprehend her own emotions. Throwing herself into bed with a virtual stranger was one game she had never played.

There was no denying that the unfamiliar blend of emotions she had experienced around Adrian had taken her by surprise. In a way, it seemed almost logical, almost inevitable that they had culminated in last night's sensual conclusion. That sense of inevitability, however, was new and disturbing. What irony that Adrian had been worried about her playing games with him! Nothing had ever seemed less like a game than her own fierce response in his arms. Perhaps if it had seemed more like a game, she would be feeling far more comfortable this morning.

Of course, Sara decided caustically, she could always reassure herself that Adrian wasn't exactly a stranger. Hadn't Uncle Lowell apparently chosen him for her? Dear outrageous, unpredictable and not infrequently brilliant Uncle Lowell. The man should be dangled over hot coals for creating this mess.

Uncle Lowell.

Her uncle's name brought a dose of common sense. This whole mess had been precipitated by Lowell Kincaid. Where was he and when would he return?

Sara's brows were shaping a thoughtful line above her hazel eyes when she finally reached the inn on the outskirts of the small town. Her car was still waiting patiently for her in the parking lot. She hoped the inn management wasn't upset about her tardiness in picking up the vehicle. Digging into her pockets for the keys, Sara started forward.

She had her hand on the door handle, absently trying to identify the slip of paper she noticed resting on the front seat when the shock of Adrian's voice behind her spun her around.

"You can't just disappear into the mists, you know. Only fantasies can evaporate like that and you're not a fantasy any longer." The remark was made in a cool, conversational tone that completely belied the shimmering intensity of his gaze. He stood a few steps behind her, his hands thrust into the back pockets of his jeans. The familiar canvas shoes were on his feet and Sara dimly realized that he must have followed her for nearly a mile without making a sound in those shoes.

For an instant the unlikely combination of the easy tone and the fierce demand of the silver eyes caused Sara to feel as though she had somehow lost her balance. Her hand closed tightly around the door handle behind her as she steadied herself.

"I didn't realize you were behind me," she finally managed, pulling herself together quickly. It was ridiculous to let him throw her like this. "You should have said something."

"If you'd wanted company, you probably would have mentioned it before you decided to sneak out of the house."

She was taken aback by the tightly reined emotion she sensed in his voice. Was it anger or pain? In that moment she couldn't be certain. But she knew she'd prefer that it was anger. Even in her uncertain state of mind this morning she realized that the last thing she wanted to do was hurt Adrian Saville. On the other hand there was such a thing as self-preservation. Sara acknowledged that she felt more than a little on the defensive.

"I didn't sneak out of the house. I simply went for a walk and decided to pick up my car while I was out.

You're the one who was sneaking around! You and those sneaky shoes you wear!''

''The last time I let you go off by yourself you nearly disappeared, remember? It's my job to keep you out of trouble until your uncle gets back.''

''Is that what you were doing last night?'' she challenged, goaded by the accusing tone of his voice. ''Keeping me out of trouble?''

''If we're going to talk about last night, let's do it somewhere else besides this damn parking lot,'' he growled. He stepped forward and closed his fingers around her upper arm. ''We can get a cup of coffee down at the wharf.''

''Adrian,'' she began firmly, and then decided against an argument. Uneasily Sara acknowledged that she couldn't tell what he was thinking this morning. Nor could she be sure of the state of his emotions. Given the uncertainty in his mood and her own odd feelings, it seemed wisest to avoid an outright confrontation.

He led her down the hill from the inn to a pier that thrust out into the beautiful, sheltered cove that was called Eagle Harbor. A marina full of peacefully tethered boats of all shapes and sizes extended out from the pier. On the other side of the cove Sara could see private homes tucked away above the water's edge. At this early hour there were several people lounging on the rail, or working on their boats. Fishing rods and tackle were in evidence as folks came and went from the marina to the small wharf buildings. Near the entrance to the short pier a small shop featured coffee and fresh pastries. Adrian bought two containers of coffee to go and wordlessly handed one to Sara.

''Thank you,'' she murmured with exaggerated politeness.

He didn't bother to respond to her comment. Instead he

seemed to be deep in thought as though he were struggling to find the right words. The idea that he was having trouble made Sara relax a bit. She had the impression Adrian was not accustomed to dealing with this morning's sort of situation. She was glad.

"I wasn't exactly going to disappear into the mists," she tried tentatively.

"No?" He sounded skeptical.

She shook her head, sipping at her coffee as they walked out onto the pier. "No. I only intended to pick up my car and drive it back to the house. If I'd been planning to duck out, I would have taken my suitcase. Or at the very least, my purse."

"Umm."

She slanted him a glance. "What is that supposed to mean?"

"That you've got a point," he said grudgingly. "I should have thought of it. I just figured you were so upset about last night that you raced out of the house without bothering to pack or say good-bye."

Sara focused on the far end of the pier. "I was upset about last night." She felt him examine her profile but she didn't turn her head to look at him.

"I rushed you into bed," he said finally.

"*We* rushed into bed," she corrected firmly.

"You're not going to let me take all the blame?"

"Do you want all the blame?"

Adrian took another sip of coffee. "No. I'd like to think you had a hand in the final decision. I don't have much interest in playing the role of seducer of unwilling females."

The response that came to Sara's lips was cut off abruptly as a fisherman who had been unloading his morning's catch walked past with a bucket of water in which two fish swam lethargically. The man turned to wave to a comrade who hailed him from a nearby yacht. Quite suddenly he stumbled over a fishing-tackle box that someone had left on the pier. In the next instant the bucket of fish tilted precariously and one of the silvery, wriggling creatures fell out. It landed right in front of Adrian's foot and lay shuddering as it began to die.

"Whoooeee, look at that sucker!" a young boy exclaimed excitedly.

"Must be six pounds if it's an ounce," another man said approvingly. "Nice catch, Fred."

The man named Fred grinned proudly as he caught his balance. "Thanks, Sam. Thought I'd do 'er over a mesquite fire tonight. The wife's having the neighbors in for cards."

Sara was aware of a familiar pang of regret at the sight of life going out of the fish. She understood about the food chain and that humans were inclined to be carnivores but she preferred her fish neatly filleted and packaged in plastic in a supermarket.

She glanced away from the fish before realizing that Adrian had come to a halt and was staring down at the creature that lay dying at his feet. There was no expression on his face. He simply stood silently watching the wriggling, flopping fish. The man who had caught it leaned forward to retrieve it.

Without stopping to think, Sara reached out and grabbed Adrian's wrist. He glanced up as she pulled him firmly around and led him toward the pier entrance. He followed her lead, not saying anything as they walked away from the sight of the now-dead fish.

"That sort of thing is hard enough on us supermarket carnivores," Sara heard herself say casually. "I imagine it's rather sickening for a vegetarian."

"Don't worry, I'm not going to be sick out here in public," he said dryly.

She cast him a quick, assessing glance. "No, you're not, are you?"

"I'm a realist, Sara. I don't eat meat but I understand how the world works," he said quietly.

"Yes, I suppose you do." She dropped his hand, feeling foolish at having made the vain effort to protect him.

"That doesn't mean I don't appreciate the thought," he told her softly.

"What thought?"

His mouth was edged with quiet amusement and a hint of satisfaction. "You were trying to shield me from a bit of reality back there. It was very—" he hesitated, hunting the word "—very compassionate of you."

"Forget it," she said sturdily. "Now about our plans for the immediate future…"

"Does this mean we've finished our discussion of the immediate past?" he inquired politely.

"There's nothing to talk about. We've both agreed that we were equally to blame for rushing into the situation." She straightened her shoulders. "We're adults and we should be able to analyze our actions and learn from our mistakes. We are stuck here together until my crazy uncle sees fit to get in touch, so we will have to conduct ourselves in an intelligent manner. Now, I suggest we both put last night behind us instead of trying to rehash it."

Adrian shrugged. "Suits me."

"I'm so glad," she muttered too sweetly.

"You weren't running away this morning?" he confirmed quietly.

"No, I was not running away. I just wanted a little time by myself. I felt as if I needed some fresh air."

He nodded and then said calmly, "I think I can under-stand that."

"Kind of you," she drawled.

"Just make damn sure you don't do it again."

A faint trickle of unease went through her at the cool way he spoke. "I beg your pardon?"

"I said, don't do it again."

They were back in the inn parking lot, approaching Sara's car. She had the keys in her hand but her mind was on his quiet command. "Adrian, one of the reasons I decided to get out of the corporate world is that I don't take orders well. We'll get along much better if you don't get carried away with your sense of responsibility."

"I hear you," he said agreeably.

"Good." She reached down to open the car door and slid into the front seat.

"Just don't go running off again without me," he con-cluded as he settled smoothly on the seat beside her. He held out his hand for the keys.

Sara felt goaded. "The next time I try it I'll be sure to look back over my shoulder to see if I'm being followed."

He lounged into the corner of the seat, never taking his eyes from her stormy gaze. "I thought we were going to act like adults about this."

She drew a deep breath, aware of feeling extremely childish. "Sorry," she mumbled. "You're right, of course. I should never have left the house alone this morn-ing. I wasn't thinking. I was feeling rather, er, emotional. I assume you don't have that problem frequently your-self?"

He didn't smile at her sarcasm. "Wasn't I emotional enough for you last night?"

Sara felt a flush suffuse her face. "What you appeared

to be feeling last night is often referred to by an entirely different name.''

''Passion?''

''Try lust,'' she bit out.

''I thought we just got through agreeing that we're adults. If that's the case, then I think it's safe to say both of us know the difference between lust and...'' He hesitated. ''And other feelings.''

She stared at him in silence for a long, troubled moment. She knew the difference, she thought. She just wasn't quite ready to admit that what she had felt last night went by a very dangerous name of its own. It was called love.

Instinctively Sara moved a bit farther over in her seat, seeking to put some distance between herself and Adrian. The car seemed filled with him, she thought. As she slid across the upholstery something crackled beneath her thigh. Belatedly she remembered the slip of paper she had noticed earlier on the car seat. Grateful for the minor distraction, she reached for it.

''You'll give me your word you won't take off alone again?'' Adrian asked in a neutral tone as he switched on the ignition. He glanced at the paper in her hand as she unfolded it.

''Oh, I'm nothing if not cooperative.''

''I appreciate it. What's that?'' He put the car in gear, ignoring her sharp tone.

''I don't know. Just a piece of paper that was lying on the seat. I don't remember...'' Sara's voice trailed off in stunned amazement as she read the short message she held.

Adrian frowned at her, his foot on the brake. ''I said, what is it, Sara?''

"A problem. A very big problem." Mutely she held the typed message out to him.

Adrian stared at her wide eyes for a second longer before switching off the ignition again and reaching out to take the note from her hand.

It wasn't a long note. Sara had it memorized after reading it through twice.

The one-fifteen ferry to Seattle. Come alone.
You'll be safe.

"Well, hell," Adrian said thoughtfully.

TWO HOURS LATER he was still acting and sounding very thoughtful. It infuriated Sara because she had argued herself hoarse in the meantime. She no longer felt in the least thoughtful. She felt quite desperate in fact. For the hundredth time she paced to the far end of the living room and whipped around to glare at Adrian, who was lounging quietly on the sofa. He had one foot on the coffee table in front of him and was flipping through a magazine with absent attention.

"Listen to me, damn it!" Sara was sure her voice would give out at any moment. It seemed to her she had been yelling at him for hours. "I haven't got any choice! I have to be on board that ferry at one."

"You don't have to be anywhere at one." Adrian's responses had been quiet and reasonable for two solid hours. They were driving Sara up a wall. How could anyone remain quiet and reasonable and totally inflexible for two solid hours?

"How else are we going to discover what this is all about?"

"People who leave notes in cars are no doubt creative

enough to think of alternatives when Plan A doesn't work.'' Adrian turned the page of his magazine. ''Under the circumstances I think it would be better to make them resort to whatever it is they didn't want to do first. No sense letting them have the easiest option. Gives them an advantage.''

''Adrian, I don't want to wait around for Plan B!''

''That's what the guy is probably counting on. Be patient, Sara.''

Sara swung away, striding restlessly back to the other end of the room. Anger and nervous dread alternated relentlessly in her head. She was furious at Adrian's refusal to even consider letting her go alone on board the one-fifteen ferry. The nervousness was a growing fear that whatever her uncle was involved in was proving to be more than he would be able to handle. She braced a hand against the window frame and stared out at the stand of trees that guarded the drive.

''Uncle Lowell must be in very big trouble,'' she forced herself to say carefully.

''Or someone wants you to think he is.''

''Since when are you the expert on how people such as that man Wolf think and operate?'' she snapped. ''You've only written one thriller, for heaven's sake. That hardly qualifies you as an authority on the real thing.''

Adrian put down the magazine. ''Sara, I'm only doing what your uncle asked me to do.''

''I understand,'' she said, trying to be patient. ''But you're taking his instructions much too literally. The situation calls for a little improvising. Something's gone wrong, don't you see?''

''No.''

Her fingers closed into a futile fist and she leaned her

forehead against the window. She was rigid with exasperation. "Adrian, please listen to me."

He came up behind her, moving soundlessly across the floor to rest his hands on her shoulders. "Honey, if I let you go on board that ferry by yourself, we wouldn't be exactly improvising. We'd be following someone else's plan. Surely you spent enough time playing corporate manager to know that following the opposition's game plan is usually not to your advantage."

"We've got to find out what he wants!"

"What he wants," Adrian said distinctly, "is to use you."

"We don't know that. Maybe he has news. Maybe he wants to give us some information. For heaven's sake, Adrian, whoever left that note might not even be what you call the 'opposition.' He might be a friend of my uncle's trying to get a message to me."

"Sara, your uncle has a strange sense of humor but I don't see him pulling a stunt like this."

"Whoever is going to be on that ferry is someone who knows something about Uncle Lowell. I'm going to find out who it is and what he knows." Sara lifted her head away from the window, aware of Adrian's fingers sinking heavily into her shoulders.

"Sara…"

She shook her head, tired of arguing, her mind made up. "No, Adrian. I'm through discussing the matter. I'm going to be on the ferry. Be reasonable. What can happen to me on the boat? It will be full of people commuting to Seattle. Whoever is going to meet me will be trapped on there, just as I will be until the ferry docks. He can hardly pull a gun and shoot me, can he? After all, he'd be stuck with the body until he gets to Seattle."

He turned her around beneath his hands, his face drawn

and grim. "Sara, this isn't a game like corporate management or checkers. You can't handle it with your casual off-the-wall style. You don't know what you're getting into."

"I'm already into it," she pointed out stiffly. "And I can't stand the waiting, Adrian."

He searched her face. "I can force you to stay here."

"Not unless you tie me up and throw me in a closet," she retorted.

"That's a possibility."

"Don't be ridiculous!"

He dropped his hands to his sides and turned to walk back toward the sofa. "You can't go alone," he finally said flatly.

She frowned, trying to decide if she'd just won part of the battle. "But the note said—"

"Damn the note!" He glanced at her over his shoulder. "You can't go alone."

"Are you saying you're going to come with me?"

"If you're refusing to listen to my advice, then I don't have much choice, do I?" he asked, sounding bleakly resigned.

"Not unless you really do tie me up and throw me in a closet." Sara tried for a tremulous smile, hoping to lighten his mood now that she appeared to have won the confrontation.

Adrian just looked at her. "The temptation is almost overwhelming."

Sara let the smile fade abruptly. "You're not a good loser, Adrian."

"No. I never was."

She'd won half of the concessions she needed, Sara realized. It shouldn't be tough to get him to agree to the rest. The note had specified that she be on the ferry alone.

"I'm glad you've decided to be logical about this, Adrian," she began cautiously.

"I generally am logical and reasonable."

"Then you can understand why I have to go alone today."

"Forget it, Sara. I'm not that logical and reasonable. Try to get out of this house alone and you'll find me standing in the way. Think you can walk over me?"

At ten minutes to one, Sara was sitting beside Adrian as he drove down the ramp onto the ferry. The crowd was a small one for the afternoon crossing and they easily found seats in the main lounge. Scanning every face that went past her, Sara suddenly realized that her palms had grown damp around the strap of her shoulder bag. She wasn't accustomed to this kind of tension, she decided unhappily. Her body felt unnaturally alert, poised for the unknown. There had been no sign of the wolf-faced man in the ferry terminal.

"It's very stressful, isn't it?" she muttered to Adrian, who was sitting across from her in the booth they had chosen by a wide window.

"Very," he agreed wryly.

"You can jot down your feelings and put them in your next book," she suggested with false lightness. "It'll add a note of realism."

"I'll do that."

Sara twisted the shoulder strap. "What if he doesn't show because you're with me?"

"Frankly, I'll be relieved."

She glowered at him. "Are you going to drag this little incident out every time we quarrel in the future? Throw it at me and use it to illustrate how headstrong and foolish I am?"

"I doubt I'll need any additional evidence. You seem

to provide enough on a day-to-day basis.'' He paused, thinking, and then asked interestedly, ''Will we be doing it a lot?''

''Doing what?'' she grumbled, watching people as they filed past to the snack counter.

''Quarreling.''

''I hope not,'' she said feelingly. ''It's wearing. I feel as though I've been through the wringer today and the main event hasn't even taken place.''

''Umm.''

The ferry moved out of its slip, beginning its crossing to Seattle. In the distance a giant freighter loaded with containers of cargo headed toward the bustling port of Seattle. Sea gulls hoping for tidbits kept pace with the ferry, wheeling and gliding alongside.

''You know, Adrian, there's something to be said for living in this area,'' Sara remarked wistfully. ''It's beautiful country.''

''Umm.''

Sara was about to demand an explanation of his monosyllable response when she caught sight of the man who was walking into the lounge from the outside deck. She went very still as she recognized the grimly handsome aquiline features. He looked at her down the length of the passenger lounge.

''Adrian,'' Sara whispered tightly, ''it's him. The man who tried to grab me in the market.''

With a casual movement that Sara couldn't help but admire, Adrian turned calmly to stare at the hawk-faced man. He examined him in silence for a moment and then swung his gaze back to Sara. ''Looks like he's going to go ahead with Plan A, even though some of the details have been changed.''

''You mean the fact that you're with me?'' She

watched the stranger make his decision and walk firmly down the aisle of window seats. "If you want to know the truth, Adrian, I've changed my mind. I'm glad you're here. Very glad."

"It's always nice to be appreciated," he muttered just as the other man came to a halt beside Sara.

"Miss Frazer?" His voice was quiet and unruffled.

Sara swallowed, trying to keep her face unemotional. "Yes."

"I'm Brady Vaughn. I'd like to talk to you."

"We assumed that from the rather melodramatic note you left in her car," Adrian said before Sara could respond. "Why don't you sit down and tell us what this is all about."

Brady Vaughn coolly examined Adrian and then appeared to dismiss him. He returned his attention to Sara. "This concerns your uncle, Miss Frazer. It's a very private matter."

Sara stared up into the darkest eyes she had ever seen. The man was towering over her, and if Adrian hadn't been sitting quietly across from her, she would have felt terribly vulnerable. As it was she instinctively took her cue from Adrian and gestured at the seat beside her. "Whatever you have to say can be said in front of my friend. He is as concerned about my uncle as I am. Please sit down, Mr. Vaughn."

"For your own sake, Miss Frazer, I think the fewer people involved in this, the better."

"I'm already involved," Adrian growled softly. "Sit down, Vaughn, or leave us alone."

Sara held her breath as the tall man flicked another assessing glance at Adrian, who returned the look expressionlessly. Then the aquiline-faced Vaughn shrugged and sat down beside Sara. When he spoke he ignored Adrian.

"This is rather a long story, Miss Frazer."

"Perhaps you could summarize?" Adrian suggested easily. "We've got short attention spans."

Sara saw the flare of impatience in Vaughn's eyes. "Please, Mr. Vaughn. Tell us what's going on."

Vaughn rubbed the side of his jaw with an air of contemplation. Then he nodded slowly. "To put it simply, Lowell Kincaid is in trouble."

Sara caught her breath. "Do you know where my uncle is at the moment?"

"We think he's in Southeast Asia."

"Southeast Asia!" Sara glanced in astonishment at Adrian, who kept his gaze on Brady Vaughn. "What on earth would he be doing there?"

Vaughn sighed. "I told you this was a long story. The truth is it goes all the way back to the last days of the Vietnam war."

Sara went still. "Go on."

"Your uncle was working for the government in those days, Miss Frazer. He was assigned to the embassy in Saigon but he spent a lot of time in the countryside. He knew his way around South Vietnam as very few Americans did. He had friends in the oddest places." Vaughn looked a little pained. "If you remember the news reports, you'll recall that things were very chaotic toward the end. Panicked crowds from the city tried to overrun the embassy walls in Saigon. Everyone wanted a seat on one of the evacuation helicopters. Things were in turmoil. A lot of men such as your uncle had to play it by ear when some of the normal chains of command broke down."

With a disturbing sense of déjà vu, Sara listened to the tale. She never once looked at Adrian to see how he was reacting. Something told her she should respond to Brady Vaughn as though she were hearing the story for the first time. Not as if she had read the nucleus of it in a manuscript called *Phantom*.

''There was a lot of valuable material that had to be salvaged during the U.S. evacuation of the country,'' Vaughn was saying quietly. ''Some of it was taken out by helicopter but some of it was sent out through less obvious routes. Your uncle was in charge of handling a particularly valuable shipment. He was to take it across a border. To be blunt, Kincaid reached his rendezvous point in Cambodia but the shipment he was assigned to safeguard never made it.''

''I see.'' Sara's throat felt constricted.

Vaughn looked at her with a cold, even glance. ''We think he's decided to go back and bring out the shipment he left behind, Miss Frazer.''

''Who's 'we'?'' Adrian inquired politely.

Vaughn frowned. ''The people for whom Kincaid used to work.''

''The government?'' Sara pressed.

Vaughn inhaled slowly. ''Yes and no.''

''That's a little vague, isn't it?'' Sara asked tartly.

Vaughn's handsome features twisted ruefully. ''I should make it clear, Miss Frazer, that while I have ties to the same agency for which your uncle worked, this is something of a personal matter for me. I am not representing the government in this.''

''You want that shipment for yourself?'' Adrian drawled.

Vaughn shook his head tiredly. ''There's no chance of getting that shipment out of Southeast Asia. Kincaid will only get himself killed trying. I'd like to prevent that. Your uncle and I go back a long way together, Miss Frazer. I owe him. He was my friend.''

"Who would kill him if he went back?" Sara whispered.

"The story of that lost shipment of, uh, material, is not exactly a secret, Miss Frazer. There have been rumors and speculation for years. A couple of very dangerous people are aware of its existence and of the fact that only your uncle knows where it is. They've dropped out of sight since Lowell Kincaid did. I have reason to believe they've gone after him. I want to get to Kincaid before those others do."

"And just where do I fit into all this?" Sara demanded urgently.

"Your uncle is a very independent man. Especially now when he no longer has any ties to his former employers. He probably won't listen to me but I think he might listen to you. I want you to come with me, Miss Frazer."

"Come with you where?" she asked dazedly.

Vaughn slid a speculative glance at Adrian and then refocused intently on Sara. "I'd rather not say our destination. But it will be in Southeast Asia. There are ways of getting a message to your uncle once we're in contact with certain local people."

"I don't have a passport," she heard herself say.

"That detail can be handled. Leave it to me."

Adrian stepped in, his voice remote and restrained. "She needs time to think it over, Vaughn."

"How much time?" Vaughn kept his gaze on Sara. "We haven't got a lot to spare."

"Forty-eight hours," Adrian answered for her.

Sara glanced at him and once again instinct made her follow his lead. "Forty-eight hours, Mr. Vaughn. Please. I have to think about this."

Brady Vaughn got to his feet. The Seattle waterfront

was rapidly filling the horizon. He touched Sara lightly on the shoulder. "Forty-eight hours, Miss Frazer. For Kincaid's sake, please don't take any longer." He turned and walked away.

Sara sat staring at Adrian as the ferry bumped gently into the dock. She ran her damp palm over her shoulder where Brady Vaughn had touched her. "Does it feel as if it's gotten colder in here?" she asked vaguely.

Chapter Seven

Sara concentrated on another bite of the chocolate-chip ice cream she was eating as she strolled along the Seattle waterfront. Beside her Adrian neatly devoured the pecan-flavored cone he had chosen. The ferry wouldn't be leaving for another half hour. It had been Adrian who had suggested they take a walk on the picturesque wharf before they caught the boat. Neither had said much until after they bought the ice cream at one of the many fast-food stalls that dotted the wharf.

Sara knew the reason for her silence was probably the same as Adrian's. They were both lost in contemplation of the scene on the ferry with the man who called himself Brady Vaughn. Finally Sara polished off the last of her cone and flipped the napkin into a trash container outside the entrance to the aquarium.

"You know what I think?" she announced, thrusting her hands into her pockets.

"What?" Adrian seemed fascinated with his disappearing ice cream.

"I think that legend Uncle Lowell told you about the gold is not pure fiction."

"Brilliant deduction."

She slanted him a disgusted glance. "Either it's for real or else—"

"Or else other people such as Brady Vaughn believe

it's for real, which amounts to the same thing," he concluded grimly.

"Know what else I think?" Sara went on determinedly.

"Let me guess. Your uncle's idea of the perfect wedding gift is a cache of gold buried somewhere in Southeast Asia." Adrian swore softly.

Sara sighed. "He always did like gold. Said it was the only real hedge against an uncertain world. I can imagine him thinking gold would be the perfect present for me. Whenever he's given me a gift, it's usually been made out of gold." She extended her wrist briefly, displaying the thin gold chain. "And he did say something about going off to protect our, uh, wedding gift."

"Does chronic idiocy run in your family?"

"My uncle is not an idiot!"

"I know," Adrian agreed derisively. "He just has a bizarre sense of humor. You'd think I'd realize that by now."

Aware of Adrian's irritation, Sara felt obliged to turn the conversation away from a defense of Lowell Kincaid's odd actions. There would be time enough to defend her uncle later. With any luck he would return to take up his own defense. Heaven knew it had always been a little tricky making excuses for him. Sara decided to go on the offensive.

"Are you quite certain that Uncle Lowell didn't say anything about the legend being for real when he told you the story?" she demanded.

"He told me it was only a tale. There are others like it that came out of the war, you know. I turned up a lot of them while doing research for *Phantom*. It certainly isn't unique."

"Really?" Momentarily distracted, Sara stared up at him, her eyes widening. "Tell me some of them."

Adrian lifted one shoulder in a heedless shrug and tossed away the end of his cone. A trolley car designed to carry tourists from one end of the waterfront to the other clanged past along tracks that paralleled the street. Adrian didn't speak until the sound of the whistle had faded. "Well, there's a story about the CIA agent assigned to destroy vital documents in the hours before the embassy was overrun."

"And?" Sara prompted.

"According to the legend he kept some of the more interesting ones, such as a list of agents and their covers operating in Asia. Then he tried to hold an auction."

"He was going to sell the list to the highest bidder?"

"That was the plan, I gather."

"Did he?" she demanded interestedly. "Hold the auction, I mean?"

"Sara, it's just a legend. How should I know what happened?"

"Oh." Disappointed, Sara pushed for more information. "What other tales did you hear?"

"Leftover legends from that particular war?" Adrian's heavy brows came together in thought. "I think there was a story or two about businessmen who were supposedly hired by the U.S. government to supervise construction projects in Saigon and the surrounding area. Apparently they used their visits to South Vietnam to establish heroin connections that continued long after the war ended, making them very rich men. Then there are the tales of gold deals made in the north. The list of such stories is endless, Sara. Wars breed them. Just think of all the stories and legends that came out of World War II. People still write novels based on them."

"I see what you mean. So when Uncle Lowell told you

the story of the gold, you assumed it was just that: a story."

"Umm." Adrian appeared lost in thought. "It still might be just that."

"I don't know," Sara mused. "I can see Uncle Lowell doing something like this—hiding a cache of gold in a bizarre location and then telling me it's supposed to be my wedding gift."

"*Our* wedding gift," Adrian corrected. "Don't forget he gave me the story first."

Sara ignored that. "What I can't see is him stealing the gold in the first place."

"We don't know that he did. At this point all we've got is Vaughn's version of things."

Sara shivered. "Creepy guy, isn't he?"

Adrian looked at her with a wry expression. "That's one way of putting it."

Sara came to a halt and leaned over the railing to stare out across Elliott Bay. Several long piers on either side of her, many full of import shops and souvenir stands, poked fingerlike out into the water. Around her, children ate popcorn and other assorted goodies while their parents browsed around the shops and enjoyed the sun. Another large ship was making its way into port flanked by tugs. Its deck was stacked high with containerized cargo. The ship carried a strange name and a foreign flag. A sailing yacht skirted the tip of a pier, seeking a place to tie up so that its passengers could come ashore for a meal at one of the many restaurants featuring fish. The sight of all the seagoing traffic made Sara think of places she had never been to and which, under normal circumstances, she would probably never go to, places that had bloody histories stretching back a thousand years.

"Have you ever been to Southeast Asia, Adrian?"

There was silence for a moment and then Adrian moved to lounge against the rail beside her, his eyes following her gaze. "Why do you ask?"

"Just curious. I was wondering what it's like."

"You're not going to find out in the company of Brady Vaughn," he told her roughly.

Her head came around, her face mirroring her serious mood. "I may not have a choice, Adrian."

His fingers tightened on the railing. "You think I'm going to let you get on a plane with him forty-eight hours from now?"

Sara moved restlessly, not quite certain how to handle the harshness in him. "That reminds me," she said, not answering his question. "What made you think of asking for a couple of days' leeway?"

"I didn't ask."

"That's right." She nodded, remembering. "You just told him that we were going to take that much time, didn't you? That was very quick thinking, Adrian."

"I try," he murmured sardonically.

She frowned. "Maybe writing thrillers helps you think fast on your feet in situations such as this."

"I was sitting down at the time."

She peered suspiciously at his profile, wondering if he'd actually attempted a small joke. "Well, I'm just glad you were there. I'm not sure that he wouldn't have been able to pressure me into going with him if I'd been alone."

"You're not accustomed to dealing with people like him. They can be very convincing, especially when they're using the fate of someone you love as bait."

"You really think Vaughn is lying?"

"There's a hell of a lot we don't know about this mess, Sara."

She was silent for another moment or two as she turned things over in her mind. "He must be who he says he is, Adrian."

"Who? Vaughn? What makes you think he's telling the truth?"

"Well, there was that business about being able to get me a passport on two days' notice, for one thing. I mean, no one but a real government agent could accomplish that."

"Money and the right connections can buy just about anything in this world."

"Oh, yeah?" She was beginning to resent his calm, cynical superiority. "And just where would someone like Vaughn go to buy a fake passport?"

There was a slight pause and then Adrian said quietly, "He might try Mexico City."

"Mexico City!"

"Umm. It's huge, Sara. One of the largest metropolitan areas in the world. Here in the western hemisphere it's one of the places frequented by a certain kind of 'in crowd.' A man can shop for anything, including a fake passport. He can also get lost there and reappear on the other side of the globe without bothering to answer a lot of inconvenient questions."

She stared at him. "More lore you've picked up from writing thrillers?"

Adrian watched the sailing yacht make another pass along the piers. "Legends and tales, honey. A writer of thrillers collects them."

"Which is probably why Uncle Lowell couldn't resist feeding you that story of the gold."

"Probably. Lowell knows a sucker when he sees one."

"Well, we'll deal with him later," Sara vowed. "In the meantime, we have to deal with Vaughn."

"Sara, we can't trust that guy one quarter of an inch," Adrian said evenly. "You said yourself he's a, uh, creep."

"But he knows where Uncle Lowell is," she protested.

"He *says* he knows where he is. But if we go on the assumption that we can't trust Vaughn, we have to assume we can't trust anything he tells us, right?"

"It's very confusing, isn't it?" she groaned. "And in the meantime Uncle Lowell could be in real trouble."

"I think we're the ones in real trouble, thanks to good old Uncle Lowell," Adrian said, pushing himself away from the rail. "Come on, honey. The ferry will be leaving soon. We'd better get going."

"Forty-eight hours isn't a very long time, Adrian."

"I know."

"What if my uncle doesn't get in touch before the deadline?"

"I didn't set the deadline because I hoped Lowell would have sense enough to contact us. I set it to give myself some time."

Sara glanced at him in astonishment. "Time to do what?"

Adrian wasn't looking at her. He appeared to be concentrating on the brightly dressed crowds of casual strollers who were ambling along the waterfront. "Sara, I'm going to leave you alone for a while tomorrow." He spoke slowly, as though measuring each word.

"Why?" she demanded, utterly startled.

He hesitated. "There's something I want to check out. A man I want to see."

"Are you going to try contacting that government agency my uncle used to work for?" she demanded.

"No. I'm not sure we could trust any answers we got from that source," he told her honestly. "Look who we're dealing with from that department now."

She wrinkled her nose. "Vaughn. I see what you mean. So who are you going to contact?"

"Somebody who may know for certain whether or not Lowell really is in Southeast Asia."

"But if we don't know it for certain, who would?"

"Sara..." Adrian reached out and threaded his fingers through hers. His tone was low and urgent. "Sara, would you please not ask any more questions? Your uncle and I have talked a great deal during the past year. He's told me things I don't think he's told anyone else."

"But, Adrian..."

"Please, Sara. Just trust me, okay?"

She wanted to scream that no, it was not okay. She wanted to tell him it had nothing to do with trust, that she simply deserved some explanations. Sara was infuriated and frightened and she felt like lashing out but she realized with an instinct that went to the bone that it wouldn't do any good. Her uncle had apparently shared some confidence with Adrian that neither of them had seen fit to share with her. Adrian would not tell her anything else at this point. She was certain of it.

"If you've known someone we could contact all along, why haven't you already done it?" she asked in a carefully controlled voice.

"Because your uncle wouldn't want me doing it unless I thought we had a full-fledged crisis on our hands. Up until now I've been going by what he said in that taped message."

"You've been assuming he could handle his 'old business.'"

"Yes."

Sara pulled her hand free from his, putting a small distance between them. "All right. There's not much I can say if you won't tell me what's going on. Go ahead and contact whoever it is you think can give us some information."

"You're angry, aren't you?"

"I'm feeling a little annoyed at the moment, yes," she bit out. "I don't like being kept in the dark."

"I'm sorry, Sara," he began but she cut him off.

"Forget it. Just don't ever again accuse me of playing games. You're turning out to be a real pro at the art."

That stilled him for a moment. He said nothing until they were back at the ferry terminal and walking on board the boat. Then Adrian told her the rest of his decision. "It will take me most of tomorrow to do what I have to do. You'll be alone at the house."

Sara threw herself down on a seat, her arms folded across her breasts in cool disgust. "Why? Or is that part of the game?"

He sat down beside her, his hands clasped loosely in front of him. He studied his linked fingers. "I'm not playing games, Sara. I have to leave you alone because I wouldn't dare risk using the phone to contact your uncle's friend, even if I thought I could get through to him."

She watched his profile through suddenly narrowed eyes. "You think the phone's tapped?"

"After meeting Vaughn, I'd say we have to assume the worst, wouldn't you?"

"Probably. What do you mean, you aren't sure you could reach this man on the phone even if you did dare use it?"

"From what your uncle says, this guy isn't the sort who trusts people over the phone. I'll have to see him in person."

"Where is he?"

"Not far," Adrian answered evasively. "I can catch a plane and reach him in a few hours. I'll leave as soon as

I can book a flight in the morning. I should be home by late tomorrow afternoon.''

''And in the meantime I just sit patiently waiting, is that it?'' Sara muttered.

''Sara, you'll be safe in the house,'' he told her quietly.

''I'd rather go with you.''

He shook his head, staring down at his clasped hands.

''Can't you at least tell me why I can't accompany you?''

''Sara, please—''

She interrupted whatever it was he intended to say with an exclamation of impatience. ''Forget I asked.''

They were politely remote with each other for the rest of the day. They walked up the street from the ferry docks and into Winslow so that Adrian could make his plane reservations at a pay phone. Sara was too proud even to attempt to overhear his conversation with the airline clerk. Later she berated herself for not having tried to eavesdrop. At least she could have found out where he was going. When he rejoined her to walk back to the cottage, she asked only if everything was settled.

''I can't get a flight out until nearly seven tomorrow morning.''

''I see.''

''That means I'll have to take the first morning ferry to Seattle.''

''Yes.''

His mouth thinned as he listened to her aloof responses. ''Sara, there's one thing I want to make very clear.''

''That would be a change.''

He ignored that. ''You're not to leave the house for any reason after I've gone.''

''I understand.'' She didn't look at him, her gaze fixed stonily ahead.

"Good. You're safe in the house after I've set the alarms. No one can get in unless he decides to use explosives."

"What a pleasant thought."

"Don't worry about it," Adrian said dryly. "Just give me your word of honor you won't leave the house until I get back."

"Or until Uncle Lowell gets back," she amended smoothly.

He nodded. "Promise?"

She wondered briefly what would happen if she didn't promise and decided not to push the matter. "All right. Word of honor."

"I swear I'll return within a few hours, Sara. I'll be back on the five-fifty-five ferry."

"I believe you."

"Then can't you stop giving me the ice treatment for a while?" he asked gently.

"Speaking of cold," she drawled slowly.

He gave her a sharp glance as they walked down the drive and opened the door of the house. "Is that your imagination I hear cranking up again?"

"I think Vaughn might really be the one they called Wolf," Sara told him in a low voice. "It would make sense, wouldn't it? He was once very close to my uncle, so he might know about the gold."

"There's no sense speculating about it, Sara."

"Why not? Maybe if we speculate long enough and hard enough, we'll come up with some answers."

"Not on that subject." He stood in the hall for a moment, listening. Then he ushered her inside.

"Just think, Adrian. That creep is probably the renegade. Uncle Lowell might have gone to Southeast Asia thinking he could hunt him down and remove him before he got the gold.''

"Sara, all we've got at the moment are a lot of questions. Not answers.''

"But why would Vaughn be hanging around here if he was after Uncle Lowell's gold?''

"How the hell should I know?'' Adrian stalked into the kitchen and put a kettle of water on the stove.

Sara trailed after him. "Adrian, I think we're missing something. Something crucial.''

"Like your uncle?'' he suggested bluntly.

"I mean a clue!'' she gritted. "Listen to me, Adrian. Let's assume Uncle Lowell really does have some connection with that gold and that he had some fantastic notion of giving it to us as a…a wedding gift.''

Adrian leaned against the stove waiting for the water to boil. He crossed his arms on his chest and eyed Sara deliberately. "All right, for the sake of argument, let's assume it. Now what?''

Sara tried to construct her thoughts into a logical sequence. Frowning intently, she began to pace the kitchen. "Okay, he knows where that gold is but he hasn't made any attempt to date to retrieve it. At least no attempt that we know of. In that taped message he didn't say he was going to *fetch* our wedding gift. He only said he was going to *protect* it.''

"True.'' Adrian watched her closely.

"Now if he suddenly decided he had to protect it for us, it must be because he got word that someone was out to steal it. We have to assume that very few people would even know for certain that the tale was anything more than a legend. The most logical person my uncle might have confided in besides you or me is his ex-protégé.''

"We're back to Wolfie?''

"This is not a joke!" she hissed.

Adrian exhaled heavily and turned around to pour the boiling water into two cups. "I know. Go on."

She glared at his broad shoulders. "Not only is Wolf or Vaughn or whoever he is the one man who might know about the gold and might even know its approximate location but we have the evidence that Uncle Lowell was definitely thinking about him before he left for parts unknown."

"You mean that sketch on my manuscript. Sara, that's pretty damn slim evidence."

She shook her head. "I don't think so. I think it means that the man called Wolf was on Uncle Lowell's mind recently and that could easily be because he had reason to fear the guy was going to make a move on the gold. Something or someone we don't even know might have tipped him off. Who knows how many mysterious contacts my uncle has left around the world? You yourself are going to try to find one of them tomorrow!" She flung her hands outward in a sweeping gesture. "Don't you see? Uncle Lowell is trying to protect our so-called wedding gift from the one man who might be able to steal it."

"Then what's Vaughn doing hanging around the Northwest?" Adrian asked logically. "Why isn't he in Southeast Asia?"

"Because he doesn't know where exactly in Southeast Asia the gold is hidden. No one knows except Uncle Lowell. Vaughn is probably looking for my uncle. Maybe he thinks he can use me somehow." Sara nibbled on her lower lip while she considered that. "My uncle has dropped out of sight. He told the neighbor he'd gone hunting. Guess who the quarry is?"

"Wolfman?" Adrian asked mockingly.

"Go ahead and laugh if you want, but I think I'm getting a handle on this."

"I'm not laughing at you, Sara." Adrian handed her a cup of tea. "You may be right for all I know. But I think the first thing to establish is whether or not your uncle is where Vaughn says he is. And I only know one way to do that."

"Find that man whom Uncle Lowell mentioned. I know. I'm not going to argue with you any more on that score, Adrian. I can see your mind is made up," she said wearily.

It was over a rather strained dinner a couple of hours later that Adrian brought up the subject again. Sara was poking idly at the roasted red pepper salad she had made when, after a long silence, Adrian spoke.

"There's one other thing," he began thoughtfully.

She glanced up. "What's that?"

"Lowell told me the story of the gold for a reason. He knows it forms the kernel of the plot in *Phantom*."

"That's right." Sara set down her fork.

"If you're right about the wedding gift being that cache of gold, then what he was really doing was—"

"Giving you the first clues about what your wedding gift actually was and where it was located," Sara finished on a note of excitement. "I can see him doing something like that."

"So can I. Damn it, I may pound the man into the ground if and when he finally does show up," Adrian growled. "He knows I don't like games."

THE SPARSE CONVERSATION at dinner faded into a very long silence by mid-evening. The strain in the atmosphere grew stronger as bedtime approached. Adrian watched the clock move slowly toward ten and knew from the remote expression in Sara's eyes that he would be sleeping alone tonight.

He'd been expecting to find himself in a cold bed, of course, ever since he'd awakened that morning and realized that for Sara everything was happening much too quickly. She had a right to some time to adjust to the idea of having him as a lover. After all, she didn't have all those months of fleshing out a fantasy that he'd had. He was too much of a stranger yet, too much of an unknown quantity.

Adrian inclined his head politely when she excused herself and disappeared down the hall to her own room shortly after ten. He sat in his chair, legs stretched out in front of him, and repeated the admonitions he'd been giving himself all evening.

Not enough time.

Too much of a stranger.

Too many other problems at the moment. Big problems.

And she was mad as hell because he wouldn't take her with him tomorrow.

All in all, a formidable list, he thought wryly. But the logic and the rationalizations didn't seem to be making much of an impact on the pulsing desire that was going to keep him awake tonight.

He thought about what he had to do in the morning and told himself that he needed sleep, not a night spent brooding in an armchair. He'd already had enough of those during the past year.

No doubt about it. He needed sleep; he could do without the brooding and he had no right at all to go to Sara's room. All three things were perfectly clear and logical in his head. But, as he'd learned the hard way, clear logic didn't always chase away the shadows of emotions. Adrian wondered briefly at that. Emotions were odd things.

There had been a time when others had sworn he didn't have any. Adrian knew better.

Slowly he got to his feet and began a silent tour of the house. Sara would be safe here. The house could keep out intruders. And he would be back for her as soon as possible. Quietly he checked and double-checked the hidden alarms and the exotic barriers Kincaid had helped him install. Lowell, with his skillful hands and his crafty, convoluted mind. *Where are you tonight, my friend?*

His soft-soled shoes making no sound on the hardwood floor, Adrian walked from one checkpoint to another, reassuring himself that the gift from Lowell Kincaid would be safe. Keeping Sara secure was the most important priority in his world, Adrian realized. It was a strange feeling to accept such total responsibility for another human being. Almost primitive in a way. He considered just how completely she had infiltrated his thoughts and then he headed down the hall toward his bedroom.

He would not pause in front of Sara's door. He would not listen for a moment to see if she was restless in her bed. He would not stand in the hall and let himself think about what she would do if he opened her door. He was a disciplined man and he could deal with his body's hungers.

It was the hunger in his mind he wasn't sure about, Adrian admitted as he approached Sara's closed door. How did you discipline the need for another person? Especially when you'd spent a lifetime not really needing anyone?

His steps slowed in spite of all the logic and discipline, and Adrian was vaguely aware of his hand curling tightly against his thigh. She would be asleep by now.

Sara lay very still in the wide bed, her hair fanned out on the pillow, and watched the shifting light under her door. She couldn't hear him but she knew he was standing there. She sensed the tension in her body and realized she was waiting for the door to open. She'd been lying there waiting for it since the moment she'd turned out the light and climbed into bed.

Because, Sara thought grimly, there was no way she could allow him to leave in the morning without letting him know that he had a right to be in her bed tonight.

The knowledge was sure and complete in her mind. She couldn't account for the certainty, but it was there.

Sara threw back the covers and sat up on the edge of the bed. She was reaching for her robe when the door of her room opened soundlessly. Adrian stood framed in the doorway, his face in deep shadow. Sara's fingers froze around the fabric of the robe as she looked up at him.

"You're not asleep." His voice was low and gritty; the words a statement, not a question.

"Neither are you." Sara let the robe drop from her hand. The wave of longing that swept through her was startling in its intensity. She was afraid that if she tried to stand up she wouldn't have the strength.

"You should have been asleep," he told her very seriously.

"Should I?"

"It would have made things…easier." He didn't move in the doorway.

"Easier for whom?"

"For me."

Sara drew a deep breath. "But not for me," she whispered, and held out her hand in an ancient gesture of feminine invitation.

"Sara?" Adrian's voice was raw with the question.

"Come to bed, Adrian. Please."

He hesitated for a timeless moment. Then he moved

forward in a dark, silent glide that swept her up and bore
her back onto the bed.

"Adrian…"

"Hush, Sara. There's no way on earth I could let you
change your mind now." He was sprawling heavily on
top of her, his hands pinning her passionately against the
pillows as he sought her mouth with his own.

She wanted to tell him that she had no intention of
changing her mind, that she wanted him, needed him, that
she had never felt like this about a man before in her life.
But the words seemed to be locked in her throat as he
began to make love to her.

Adrian pushed the canvas shoes off his feet without
even bothering to sit up on the bed. Sara heard them thud
softly to the floor. She felt him fumble with the fastening
of his jeans and then the buttons of his shirt. And all the
while he kept her achingly close to him, deliciously
trapped under his strength.

"I told myself I shouldn't stop at your door," he grated
as he kicked his clothing to the floor.

Sara's head moved from one side to the other on the
pillow. "No, this is where you belong." She circled his
neck with her arms, pulling him close.

"Sara, my sweet Sara." He tugged at the nightgown,
pushing it off her shoulders and down to her waist. Flattening the palms of his hands across her breasts, he grazed
her nipples with a rasping, tantalizing touch that brought
them to taut peaks.

Sara uttered a soft sigh into his mouth and dared him
with the tip of her tongue. He responded instantly, thrusting deeply behind her teeth. She traced the contours of
his sleek back with her fingertips until he groaned heavily.

Lifting himself for an instant, Adrian pulled the nightgown down over her hips and let the garment fall to the

floor beside his jeans. Then he came back down beside her and Sara felt the demanding hardness of him against her thigh. She could feel the almost violently taut need in him and her own body reacted to it with fierce awareness.

Slowly, with deliberate provocative strokes, Adrian caressed her. His fingers played an enticing game on the inside of her leg until Sara thought she would go out of her mind with excitement. When he moved his hand upward, she cried out against his mouth.

Then she was struggling passionately to return the heady thrill and the throbbing anticipation. She slid her hand down his back to the slope of his thigh, feeling the crisp curling hair. Then she explored him more and more intimately until she cupped the heavy evidence of his desire.

"Sara, you're driving me wild," he groaned out.

"Yes, please," she whispered breathlessly.

"Sara, are you sure?"

"I've never been more certain of anything in my life." She used her nails with excruciating delicacy, and he muttered something soft and savage against her throat.

"Adrian?"

"I couldn't stop now if all the forces in hell got in the way," he said, and then he was parting her legs with his own, sliding toward her warmth until he was only a pulse beat away from possessing her completely.

Sara whispered his name again and again, lifting herself with undisguised longing.

"That's it, sweetheart. Give yourself to me. Just give yourself to me. I need you so."

She gasped as he entered her, the shock of his passionate invasion ricocheting through her whole system. Then she tightened her arms and legs around him, wrapping him as close as possible.

Lost in the embrace, Adrian knew only that he wanted Sara to cling to him forever. There was nothing else besides this shattering moment and Adrian seized it with all of his strength. There would be time enough tomorrow to wonder at the intensity of her need, time enough to worry that she was only reacting to the drama of the situation, time enough to reconsider the wisdom of letting himself be swept up in her hot, damp warmth. There was always time enough to regret the past. But he was living for the moment tonight, he told himself, and for this hour he would revel in it. He would allow himself to believe it was all for real.

When he felt the telltale tightening of her body, it precipitated an echo in his own. For an instant he forced himself to raise his head so that he could watch her face during the fiery release. He had a few seconds to wonder at the compelling possessiveness he felt for the woman in his arms and then he was trapped in the vortex of their combined desire. It swept them both to a violent, throbbing climax, left them hanging for a sweet moment and then slowly, slowly ebbed.

The moment in which he had been living was already becoming the past, Adrian thought distantly as he lay beside Sara. Soon the morning would arrive and with it another slice of the past. Perhaps there was some sense of balance in nature. Perhaps one piece of the past could offset another. He would have the memory of Sara's warmth tonight to carry with him as a talisman against the chill of tomorrow.

She stirred in his arms. "Adrian?"

"I'm here, Sara."

"Good," she murmured drowsily. "See that you're here tomorrow night, too."

When tomorrow night comes will you really want me here, my darling Sara, he wondered silently.

HE LEFT AT DAWN and Sara was at the door to watch him go. She had awakened the instant he did, her senses aware of his every movement. He'd lain quietly for a long moment looking down into her face and then he'd brushed his lips lightly against hers. Words flooded his head but he couldn't find a way to say them aloud. There wasn't time now to say the things that should be said. Perhaps it was better this way.

Pushing aside the covers, he'd climbed out of bed and headed for the bath. Without a word she'd fixed coffee for him while he dressed and then she'd stood on tiptoe to kiss him good-bye.

"Be careful, Adrian. Please be careful."

"Hey, I'm only going to talk to a friend of your uncle's," he protested gently. He was afraid of the intensity he saw in her gaze. He liked it better when she was laughing up at him with her eyes or watching him with passion. Adrian realized just how much he had come to value the impulsive warmth that was so much a part of Sara. Life would be very cold without it. "I'll be home by sundown."

"Yes." She didn't argue.

"You won't leave the house," he said again, making it an order.

She shook her head. "Not unless you or Uncle Lowell tell me to leave the house," she answered obediently.

"Sara..." He hesitated on the porch, turning back to her one last time.

"Just hurry, Adrian. I'll be here when you return."

He looked at her, nodded once and left without glancing back again.

Chapter Eight

The house seemed incredibly lonely after Adrian left. Sara wandered around from room to room, wondering if doing a little housekeeping might help her deal with the strange mood in which she found herself. The thought brought to mind the question of who actually did Adrian's house-cleaning. Something told her he probably took care of the chores himself. Certainly no one had been in during the few days she had known him to sweep the hardwood floors or dust. But everything seemed orderly and reasonably clean. Keeping his environment neat and precise was undoubtedly a part of his nature. It fit with what she knew of his preference for being in control of his world.

Sara wondered if Adrian had ever felt out of control. When had the need to be in command of everything around him come into existence? Perhaps he had been born that way. Or perhaps something in his past had made him so cautious and controlled. Surely the average person didn't install the kind of sophisticated electronic gadgetry that protected this house unless some event had instilled a raging desire for security. Adrian was definitely not the type of man to let his imagination make him paranoid. He must have his reasons for his self-control and the controls he had imposed on his surroundings. The only time she sensed that he slipped his own leash was when he made love to her.

The images engraved on her mind from the previous

night rose to warm her now. She remembered the passion and intensity of the man who had held her. And she recalled her own ungoverned responses.

She drifted into the library and drew a finger along the top shelf of the bookcase. There was a smudge on her hand afterward but nothing really terrible. Just a normal amount of dust. The kind she herself collected on the top shelf of her bookcase. The kind people living alone tended to collect. She wondered how long Adrian had lived alone. Most of his life, apparently.

Finding the thought depressing, she turned away from the bookcase and walked over to his desk. Having been through it once, she felt there was no point amusing herself by browsing through it again. She sat down in the swivel chair and remembered the way Adrian had caught her here a few nights ago. She hadn't heard his approach, she recalled. You hardly ever heard the man. He moved very quietly in those well-worn sneakers.

A shaft of morning light caught the crystal-and-gold apple, making the trapped bubbles come alive for a moment. Sara leaned forward and studied the shimmering effect. She liked the notion of Adrian having sat here at his desk for months, the apple in front of him, while he worked. How many times had he glanced up idly and found himself studying the apple? Perhaps as many times as she had.

But she hadn't known there was a duplicate crystal apple in existence, Sara reminded herself. While Adrian had known all along that there was another apple and that someday he would encounter its owner. She wondered what he had expected her to be like. What picture had her uncle sketched for him? It was suddenly very important to Sara that Adrian had found his gift satisfactory. She wanted to be sure he would return to collect it this evening.

"Adrian," she whispered aloud, "remember what I said about taking care of yourself. I don't think I should have let you go alone." As if she'd had a choice.

Uneasily Sara stood up and walked slowly back out of the study. She'd make herself another cup of coffee and see if she couldn't find something to read. It was going to be a very long day.

She was pouring the coffee when she realized that what she wanted to read was *Phantom*. Perhaps if she went through it a second time, this time knowing her uncle had deliberately been planting information, she might pick up something useful. Digging the manuscript out of her suitcase, she carried it back to Adrian's study and sat down to read it with the cup of coffee at her elbow.

She wrinkled her nose at the sketch of the wolf on the first page and then deliberately set herself to go through the manuscript with an alert eye. There must be something in it. Didn't Lowell believe in hiding things in plain view? He certainly had doodled a great deal on the pages. But then, that was standard operating procedure for Lowell Kincaid whenever he found himself with a pencil in hand and a sheet of paper nearby. The man should have been an artist instead of a secret agent.

Just as had happened the first time through *Phantom*, Sara once again found herself caught up not in the intricacies of the plot but in the hero's pain and savage determination to survive. The feelings of protectiveness she had experienced the first time she read it returned anew. She longed to comfort the hero even as she told herself that only he could endure his own survival both emotionally and physically. In the end she knew she would again be left wanting to know for certain that there really was going to be a happy ending. And once more the question of how much of Adrian existed in the guise of *Phantom* returned to haunt her. This was a first novel. Somewhere she had read that they tended to be the most autobiographical.

Sara was into chapter three when the phone on the desk rang shrilly. The unexpected sound startled her. In the time she had been staying at Adrian's home, the thing had never rung. She hesitated a few seconds before reaching out to pick up the receiver. Then the thought that it might be Adrian calling for some reason made her fumble with the instrument.

"Hello?"

"Sara."

"Uncle Lowell!" Sara sat stunned as she heard her uncle's distinctive growl of a voice. "Uncle Lowell, where are you? I've been absolutely frantic. This whole thing is—"

"Sara, don't talk, just listen to me," Lowell Kincaid said quickly. "Come back to my place as soon as you can."

"But Uncle Lowell—"

"As soon as you can, Sara. I can't explain. I'll be waiting."

He hung the phone up in her ear before she could get in another question.

Her first instinct, Sara realized, was to panic. She had no way to reach Adrian to tell him what was happening, no way to find out if her uncle needed immediate help such as an ambulance, no way even to begin to figure out what might be wrong. All she could do was obey Lowell Kincaid's summons as swiftly as possible. Desperately she tried to reassure herself with Adrian's words about her uncle's competence. *He can take care of himself.*

Whatever else was happening, at least she knew he wasn't in Southeast Asia! If only she could get in touch with Adrian to call him off that wild-goose chase. Frantically Sara tried to think. It took her a moment to break through the paralysis engendered by her uncle's phone call. Then she was on her feet and running toward the bedroom. Her purse was where she had left it, slung on the bed. She grabbed it and scrabbled around inside for her car keys.

Sara was almost to the front door when she remembered the elaborate warning devices built into Adrian's house. Forcing herself to slow down and concentrate, she went into Adrian's bedroom and programmed the alarms as he had taught her so that she could leave without causing a disturbance. Almost as an afterthought she pushed the reset button so that the house would be able to detect intruders. Adrian wouldn't thank her for leaving the exotic alarm system completely turned off. She was afraid to set it to keep out intruders because Adrian hadn't told her now to bypass the alarms if she were to leave and then try to reenter. There was always the chance that she might be coming back here this evening with her uncle. This way the house would recognize that it had been entered, but she would be able to get back inside if she wished. When she was finished, the alarms were set just as they had been the night she'd walked so easily into Adrian's study to search it. She'd better leave a note, too, just in case Adrian returned before she got back.

She dashed back down the hall to the study and found a pen and a piece of paper. Hastily she jotted down the facts about the phone call and Lowell's summons. Then she glanced around for a means of anchoring the slip of paper. The crystal apple caught her eye. She picked it up and a shaft of morning light broke into a rainbow as it passed through the apple and touched the frozen bubbles inside. Sara found herself staring into the depths of the crystal for a split second. The apple had been the start of this whole mess, she realized. And it had provided the first link between herself and Adrian.

Shaking off the momentary sense of distraction, she plunked the crystal apple down on top of her note. Time enough later to figure out whether the apple was more significant than it seemed.

Finished with the task, she flung herself out the door and down the steps to where her car was parked in the drive. She was furious with her own nervous tension and her anger just served to make her more nervous. It seemed an incredible chore to get the key into the ignition. The wait at the ferry dock was interminable. The Interstate was jammed through the heart of Seattle and over the bridge to Mercer Island. Everything seemed to be conspiring to keep her from making good time out of town.

When at last she was free of the city's congestion, she found it difficult to keep within shouting distance of the speed limit. Every instinct was to hurry. Uncle Lowell's words had sounded extremely urgent. But there had been an oddly flat quality to his voice, she thought as she drove. She'd never heard him sound quite that way.

On the other hand, she had never been around him when he was "working." For her he had always been the laughing, witty man who had seemed to understand her even when the rest of the family hadn't. There had been an affinity between her and her uncle since she was a small girl. Her parents tolerated it good-naturedly most of the time. But there had been occasions when she had been warned that it wasn't right to play games with life. The black sheep of the family might be a lot of fun but he didn't set a responsible example for a young person.

With every passing mile Sara wondered what had gone wrong with Lowell Kincaid's latest game.

It wasn't until nearly two hours later when she was turning off onto the narrow road that led toward the cottage that Sara remembered to wonder why her uncle hadn't mentioned Adrian. If there was anything really wrong, would Lowell have asked her to come alone?

Impatiently she slowed to take the twists and turns of the old road. Quite suddenly she was furious with both her uncle and Adrian. Men and their little macho schemes. And they had the nerve to say she played games! When this was all over, Sara decided as she braked for a sharp curve, she would give them both a piece of her mind. More than that. She'd tear a wide strip off each of them.

The car that blocked the road on the far side of the curve came as a distinct shock. It was sitting across both lanes, making it utterly impossible to get past. Sara, who had her foot on the accelerator again as she came out of the curve, hurriedly slammed on the brakes.

"Damn it to hell!" It was the last straw, Sara told herself as she came to a halt. Well, at least she could walk to the cottage from here. Angrily, her mood fueled by a firestorm of mounting concern, she pulled over to the side of the road, pushed open the door and climbed out. There was no one in the other car as far as she could tell. Who on earth would be stupid enough to leave a vehicle in the middle of the road? Probably some drunk driver who hadn't made it home from a local tavern.

Leaning down, Sara reached inside her own car to yank her purse off the front seat and remove the keys from the ignition. It couldn't be more than a mile now to her uncle's house. Luckily she'd worn comfortable sandals. She straightened up, stepped back to slam the car door, spun around and found herself staring straight into Brady Vaughn's hawklike face.

"Congratulations, Miss Frazer. You made excellent time." He motioned almost negligently with the compact, snub-nosed gun he held in his right hand. "I just put the car across the road fifteen minutes ago. Thought you'd take a little longer to get here."

"I shouldn't have hurried, apparently," Sara managed in a tight little voice. She couldn't take her eyes off the gun. The casually efficient way Vaughn held it seemed as frightening as anything else that was happening. A man who held a gun that coolly must have had plenty of practice. "Who are you, Mr. Vaughn?"

"Let's just say I'm an old acquaintance of your uncle's." He nodded toward his vehicle as he spoke. "Now I think we'd better get these cars off the road. This isn't a well-traveled area but I wouldn't want some stranger coming along and starting to ask silly questions."

"Such as why you're holding a gun on a woman?" Sara didn't move. She wasn't certain she could.

Vaughn's smile was an odd travesty of humor. "Take it as a compliment, Miss Frazer. I learned long ago that the female of the species can be just as dangerous as the male. I don't take chances. Get in the car. You'll drive."

When he stepped toward her, Sara discovered that she could, indeed, move. She edged back toward the nondescript compact that was lodged across the road. "Drive where?"

"To your uncle's cabin, of course. That's as good a place to wait for him as any."

"I thought you said he was in Southeast Asia!"

"I lied. I do that quite well. You should start getting used to it. A lot of men in your life lie to you. Now move,

Miss Frazer. And please, for both our sakes, don't try anything too tricky, okay?''

There was no opportunity to try anything clever even if she had been able to think of something truly brilliant, Sara discovered. At the point of the gun she slid into the driver's seat. Her fingers trembled as she took the wheel. Her red shirt was turning dark under her arms from nervous perspiration. Vaughn got in beside her, his eyes never leaving her for an instant.

The drive to Lowell Kincaid's cabin was a short one. Sara fantasized briefly about stomping down on the accelerator and trying some wild maneuver that might dislodge the weapon from Vaughn's hand but common sense warned her it wouldn't work. There was no way she could get the car up to a fast rate of speed before he could put a bullet in her. There would be plenty of time for him to kill her and grab the wheel.

The cottage appeared exactly as she and Adrian had left it. When Sara obediently switched off the ignition, Vaughn ordered her out of the car.

''Now we'll walk back and get the other one.'' He stood aside and waited for her to start back down the road ahead of him.

''Why the stunt with the car across the road? Why didn't you simply wait for me in the cabin?''

''I was afraid you might be suspicious about entering the house when you noticed the strange car in the drive. And there wasn't any convenient place to hide it and still have it readily available.'' He indicated the clear area that extended from the drive to the front of the house. ''I also didn't know if you and your uncle might have some particular signal.''

''You're giving me a lot more credit for caution and observation than I deserve,'' Sara told him dryly. ''I doubt that I would have thought twice about the car. I would have assumed it was my uncle's. And we don't have any special greeting signal! Good grief, I'm his niece, not a secret agent.''

''Oh, I'm aware of who you are, Sara Frazer. Very much aware. I'm counting on your identity to lure your uncle out into the open, you see.''

She turned to glance back at him over her shoulder. The gun was still pointed unwaveringly at her back. ''But that was my uncle's voice on the phone. I don't understand. Where is he?''

Vaughn arched an eyebrow. ''It was your uncle's voice, all right. Right off the tape on his answering machine.''

''His answering machine! But he didn't say those things on the machine,'' Sara gasped, startled.

''Sure he did,'' Vaughn told her with a soft chuckle. ''He just didn't say them in quite that order.''

''You mixed his words from the tape into different sentences?''

''And recorded them onto another tape. It takes a little work and the right equipment, but it can be done. I had both his recorded message to callers and the message to your friend Adrian with which to work. Plenty of material from which to get a few simple sentences.''

Sara stared unseeingly at her car as she rounded the bend. ''You appear to be very professional at this sort of thing, Mr. Vaughn,'' she whispered dully.

''Very,'' he assured her. ''It would be best if you didn't forget it.''

She drove the second car back to the cottage under the same circumstances as she had driven the first. When she finally parked it beside Vaughn's compact, he motioned her into the house.

''What now?'' she asked quietly as she stepped inside.

"Now we wait. Make some coffee if you like. It's probably going to take a while." Vaughn appeared unconcerned.

"But what exactly are we going to wait for?"

"Your uncle should be contacting us in the near future."

"But why would he do that? How would he even know where I am or that I'm with you?" The shock of the situation was affecting her mind, Sara thought vaguely. She couldn't seem to think properly. Perhaps she ought to take Vaughn's advice and make some coffee. At least it would give her something to do. She was very much afraid that if she sat down or stood still she would begin to tremble uncontrollably.

"Your uncle is looking for me. It's only a matter of time before he figures out I'm waiting patiently right here on his home stomping grounds. And when he does, he'll discover I have you with me."

Sara turned on the tap in the kitchen sink, aware of Vaughn watching her from the doorway. "You're going to use me?"

"I'm going to trade you to your uncle for the information I want," Vaughn confirmed. "I see it all as a business deal."

"And what information is it that you want, Mr. Vaughn?" she demanded softly.

"Don't you think you should start calling me Brady?"

"I don't see us ever getting together on a social basis," she gritted out as she set the pot into place in the drip machine.

"But we are together, Sara," he drawled smoothly. "Perhaps for some time. You made it very easy, really. I was a little worried about how to get rid of the boyfriend. I wasn't sure until yesterday where he fit into the scene.

I had a couple of plans I thought would work but he simplified matters considerably when he obligingly left on the morning plane to Mexico City. His leaving for Mexico also confirmed his part in all this."

"Mexico City!"

"I got the clerk at the airline counter to verify that he bought a one-way ticked to Mexico. What's the matter, Sara? Didn't he tell you where he was going?"

"Yes, but I...I just don't see how you could find out that sort of information." Sara was surprised that she could get the lie fairly glibly past her lips. Mexico City! It didn't make any sense. You didn't pop down to Mexico City for the day and return by early evening. And just yesterday Adrian had been telling her tales of how a man could disappear into Mexico City and reappear on the other side of the world.

"You can get all sorts of information out of people if you flash the right badges at them," Vaughn informed her. "Poor little Sara. You still don't realize what he's done, do you? You've been had, lady. In more ways than one."

"He's a writer," she explained, struggling for something logical to say. "He does a lot of research and he's had this trip planned for some time. My showing up got in the way of his schedule, I'm afraid. He's setting the next book in Mexico." Did that sound reasonable? "I didn't have the time to go with him."

"Is that a fact?" Vaughn said musingly. "So he just left you up here all by yourself to worry about your uncle? After asking for forty-eight hours to think over your problem?"

"I...yes." It was probably better not to weave any more strands into the story. She wouldn't be able to keep it straight in her own head.

"Not terribly gallant of him, was it?"

Sara said nothing. She focused on the pot filling with coffee.

"You're a fool, Sara," Vaughn finally said calmly. "You've been dumped. As long as Saville figured you were the easiest way to get at the gold, he was willing to play lover. But yesterday when I let him know that others were getting close to the prize, he panicked and decided you were no longer the quickest or safest means to an end. I know better. I know that you still are the best means to this particular end. I'm a patient man, Sara."

She cast him a quick, frightened glance. He smiled again. "Want me to tell you the real reason he's gone south?"

"What's your explanation, Mr. Vaughn?"

"Oh, it's simple enough. Mexico City is a wide-open town. It has a certain reputation in the industry. Among other things it's a jumping-off point for people who want to head for such places as Cambodia without letting the U.S. government know where they're going. You can buy anything in Mexico City, including alterations on your passport. Your boyfriend has skipped out on you. He's probably heading for Southeast Asia."

"I thought," she said weakly, "that the stories about Mexico City were just the product of espionage fiction. Legends and tales."

"Fact, I'm afraid. Your lover has skipped." Vaughn seemed amused.

Sara lowered her lashes. "Why would he do that?"

"Because he's decided to risk going after the gold on his own instead of waiting for your uncle to return. As I said, he got nervous yesterday when he realized others were closing in on it. He's obviously a friend of your uncle's and Kincaid made the mistake of trusting him, both with his niece and with the information about the gold. Kincaid never used to make mistakes like that, but he's getting old. He's trusted the wrong man with the details of what was probably intended to be your dowry. The race is on, Sara, but I'm the one with the inside track. I've got you. I'm not worried that Saville tried to buy himself forty-eight hours for a head start. It won't do him any good because he's obviously an amateur. A greedy amateur, but an amateur nonetheless.''

"Why do you say he's an amateur?"

"Because a professional would have realized that you're the most useful key around. And that I'm the biggest threat. A professional would have made a try for me before leaving town, if for no other reason than to find out just how much I know. Southeast Asia is a big and dangerous place to go hunting without specific directions and a few contacts. Saville will probably just succeed in getting himself killed trying for your uncle's gold. And it does nothing to change my plans. One way or another I wound up with you, and ever since you appeared on the scene so conveniently, that's been my goal. I'm a highly adaptable man. Before you came along I was using a different approach. I'd been through this cabin with a fine-tooth comb. I was just realizing how useless that method was going to be when you showed up out of the blue. Couldn't figure out who you were at first, but after you'd left the first time I remembered seeing the phone-answering machine. I played it back to see if I could pick up any information about Kincaid's unexpected female guest, and sure enough, all the news I needed was on that tape. That's how I found out you're Kincaid's niece.''

"You want that gold, don't you?" Sara reached for a cup and poured coffee with exaggerated care. She was afraid that if she wasn't extremely cautious she would spill the hot liquid all over her feet. "The gold you said my uncle left behind in Southeast Asia."

"Yes, Sara. I want the gold. Pour me a cup, too. Just set it on the counter. I'll get it. Wouldn't want you trying to throw it in my face with a grand, heroic gesture."

"So you're going to use me to force my uncle to tell you exactly where he hid the stuff?" Sara persisted, standing back so that Vaughn could pick up his coffee.

"Precisely."

"You said Uncle Lowell thinks you're in Hawaii," she began with a frown as she tried frantically to put the pieces of the puzzle together.

"I made certain he got information to that effect. Rumors are very effective in our crowd, even among the, uh, golden-agers. I wanted him sidetracked for a while so that I could try getting the data I needed the easy way."

"You searched this place," she whispered, remembering the chaos she and Adrian had discovered.

"Unfortunately, as I said, my search didn't turn up anything so convenient as a map or a set of coordinates that would have made my task a straightforward one. I really thought I'd have a chance of finding what I wanted because I knew your uncle rather well at one time, Sara. I know his theories on hiding important data, for example. He always got a kick out of concealing things right in front of someone's nose. Kincaid had a sense of humor, you can say that for the man. When I didn't turn up anything, I realized matters were going to get complicated. I made the search look like the work of punks and decided to keep watch on the cabin for a while. It paid off. You happened along and greatly simplified my life."

Sara leaned back against the counter, her hands braced against the cool ties. "Why would my uncle go tearing off to Hawaii just because he thought you were there, Mr. Vaughn?''

''He thinks that after all these years I've decided to go after the gold. He's got a couple of other reasons for following my trail, too. He and a few others, I believe, have some private suspicions about me.'' Vaughn sipped tentatively at his coffee. ''Not bad,'' he declared. ''I enjoy good coffee.''

Sara took a deep breath before plunging in with the next question. ''My uncle has other reasons for hunting you down?''

''''Hunting' sounds a bit melodramatic, don't you think? Let's just say he couldn't resist the hint that I might have surfaced and that he might be able to find me.''

Sara met his gaze unflinchingly. ''Do you by any chance go under the code name of...of Wolf?''

Vaughn went still, the coffee halfway to his mouth. Slowly he lowered the cup, his dark eyes narrowing speculatively. ''Now what would you know about the man called Wolf?''

Her fingers tightened around the counter's edge. Sara was beginning to wish she hadn't brought up the subject. ''Not much. My uncle mentioned him once. That's all.''

''And you've been assuming I might be...Wolf?''

She didn't like the cold amusement that was suddenly in his eyes. ''The thought occurred to me.''

''Fascinating.''

''Well?'' she challenged bravely.

Vaughn's mouth drew back in a humorless smile. ''Your uncle always could tell a good story.''

''Is that all Wolf is? A Lowell Kincaid tale?'' she breathed. It was getting difficult to tell legends from reality, she realized.

Vaughn chuckled, shaking his head. ''No. As usual

with your uncle, there's a germ of truth in the story. There really was a man called Wolf. I never met him. Few people did and survived to tell about it. His cover was very deep and he protected it. They said he had a thing about maintaining his cover.''

A man who liked to be in total control of his surroundings. Sara shivered. ''What do you mean his cover *was* deep?''

''He's a legend, Sara. Just like the gold that never made it out of Vietnam. But he was real like the gold, too. Lethally real, from what I understand. In my business legends can be real.'' His mouth twisted ironically.

''But you're not him?''

''Hell, no.'' Vaughn grimaced. ''Give me some credit. The guy cracked up completely, according to the old gossip. Went bonkers on his last mission. He never returned.''

Sara was very still. ''What do you mean, he cracked up?''

''Just what I said. The story goes that he broke like a fine-tuned violin string. Came apart. Went crazy. Cracked. Couldn't handle what he was paid to handle. Got himself killed on his last assignment. Why the interest? Because you've been assuming I'm him?''

''The thought had crossed my mind,'' she admitted softly.

''I'm not especially flattered. The guy may once have been good, the best there was, in fact, but I sure as hell don't intend to lose my nerve the way he did.''

''What are you going to do with the gold if you get it?'' she pressed, desperate to keep the conversation moving. She had no particular wish to chat the afternoon away with Brady Vaughn, but she somehow felt safer when he was talking.

"I'm going to retire, Sara. Somewhere far, far away. Some nice island, perhaps where a lot of gold will buy a lot of silence and a lot of what I want out of life. I've been living under a great deal of tension for the past couple of years. And you know what they say about the dangers of too much tension. I've done well financially, but as the magazines say, stress takes its toll."

"Like it did on the man called Wolf?" she flung back.

Vaughn shook his head. "That was an entirely different sort of situation. According to the story, he simply broke. With me, dropping out is more of a reasonable, strictly pragmatic business decision. You see, I've been working very hard lately. And I'm a little tired. Holding down two jobs will do that to a man."

"Two jobs?" she questioned, confused.

"Never mind." Vaughn shifted his position in the doorway. "I really don't feel like discussing it any further at the moment. Let's go into the living room and sit down. We might have a long wait ahead of us. But have no fear. Sooner or later your uncle will figure out that he's been sent on a wild-goose chase. When he does he'll rush back here. We'll be waiting for him. I bought some food. Enough to last us a couple of days, if necessary. But I doubt we'll have to put up with each other's company for that long. Your uncle is a smart man."

What did you talk about when you found yourself whiling away the hours with a man who kept a gun in his hand while he conversed with you?

Sara was still asking herself that sometime later as she sat almost immobile on the sofa in front of the cold fireplace. She hadn't moved in so long that she was afraid her foot might have grown numb. When she did move it cautiously, Vaughn glanced at her sharply.

"Going somewhere, Sara?"

''The bathroom, unless you have any objections,'' she muttered, rising slowly to her feet. There was a tingling sensation in her left foot but it wasn't completely numb.

Vaughn eyed her thoughtfully. ''None. There's no way out of that room. I've checked. Try to resist the temptation to forage for a pair of scissors or a razor blade. You'd only wind up cutting yourself.''

Sara didn't respond. She turned away and went down the hall to the bathroom. When the door closed behind her, she sagged against the sink and stared at her drawn face in the mirror.

She had to do something. She couldn't bear this endless waiting. What was it Adrian had said about the value of patience? In her case it bought nothing but anxiety. It didn't seem to bother Vaughn particularly, she reflected. He was very professional about the whole thing. Or at least he seemed professional. Hard to judge, given her limited experience in this kind of business. Sara winced.

Vaughn had the ability to wait but would he bother with that route if he thought there might be a shortcut to his goal, she asked herself as she splashed her face with cold water. He'd tried a shortcut once before when he created the diversion that had sent her uncle off to Hawaii. If she could make him think there was an alternative to this interminable waiting, perhaps he would go for it. She dried her flushed face and thought of Adrian's promise to return by early evening.

There was no way he could make it back tonight if he'd actually gone to Mexico and Vaughn seemed convinced he'd gone.

But Adrian had promised her he'd be back. And the house was set on its alarm status. If she were inside the house with Vaughn, Adrian would know as soon as he returned that there was trouble. His small signaling device would warn him there had been an unauthorized intrusion when he came within a couple of blocks of his home.

That scenario would only work if Adrian really was planning to return tonight. If he was even now en route to Mexico City, she was in very bad trouble. Heaven only knew where her uncle was.

Sara wrenched herself away from the mirror. It was an incredible disaster, and if she didn't act, it was going to get worse. She didn't have any illusions about the man in the next room. He was quite capable of casually raping her tonight and killing her later after he had what he wanted from her uncle.

Her only real chance was to bank on the fact that Adrian had told her the truth about returning this evening.

Legends and reality. How could a woman be sure of the difference, she asked herself.

A few minutes later Sara opened the bathroom door and went down the hall to the living room. She saw the fleeting spark of interest in Vaughn's eyes as she resumed her seat on the couch. No, the last thing she wanted to risk was spending the night here with him.

"In another couple of hours we'll have to discuss the sleeping arrangements, Sara," Vaughn mused, tossing a magazine into the bin beside the chair. "I think that could be interesting."

"Really? Do you sleep with your gun in your hand, Mr. Vaughn?"

He chuckled. "I think I can dispense with the gun once I've tied you up for the night. You'd look interesting spread-eagled on a bed."

Sara shuddered and nerved herself for the next bit. "I'm not interested in sharing a bed with you."

"Perhaps I will find it a challenge to see if I can create a little interest," he suggested coolly.

"I doubt it. I'm going to be married soon."

"Are you?" he murmured blandly. "To the boyfriend who just skipped town? You'll have to catch him first, won't you?"

Sara chose her next words carefully. "That gold you're after is supposed to be my wedding gift from my uncle."

Vaughn's eyes narrowed thoughtfully. "Just how much do you know about your uncle's little social-security cache?"

She tried for a mild shrug, her arms wrapped around her drawn-up knees as she sat on the couch. "About as much as you do. You know my uncle. He's fond of dropping little, uh, hints."

"Kincaid never does anything without a reason. And in spite of that easygoing facade, I worked with him long enough to know he's a shrewd and careful man. If he was dropping hints to you about the gold, then he must have truly believed it was safe for you to know about it. No reason he shouldn't think it was safe after all these years, I suppose."

"In addition to being shrewd and careful, my uncle also likes to plan for the future," she added deliberately. "He wanted Adrian and me to know enough about the gold to be able to find it someday in the event something happened to him."

Vaughn leaned forward on his chair, the gun cradled loosely in his fist. "That's very interesting, Sara. Very interesting. It puts a whole new light on the situation. Up until now I've assumed that no one except Kincaid knew the truth about the gold. It's a fact that your uncle tries not to leave much to chance, though. Tell me more, little Sara. Tell me what made Saville think he's got a shot at the gold. I've been wondering who he plans to contact after Mexico City."

She caught her lower lip between her teeth, watching him the way a small mouse probably watched a hovering eagle. *Adrian, where are you?* "Mr. Vaughn, I'll make a deal with you."

He smiled and she could almost hear the way he must be laughing inwardly at her naiveté. The knowledge made her grit her teeth.

"I'm listening, little Sara."

"If I...if I show you where I think the information is hidden, will you take it and go away?"

"I'd have no reason to hang around any longer if I had a map showing the location of the gold," he murmured.

Sara wanted to cringe, but she managed to project a hopeful expression. "It's at Adrian's."

"Your boyfriend's house?"

"He's the man I'm going to marry. Uncle Lowell gave us each a copy of the map. If what you say is true about Adrian being in Mexico, then he must have taken his copy with him. But I have my own. Or at least I have information that will lead me to the gold. I'm not sure that it's exactly a map."

"I can't quite decide whether or not to believe you, little Sara," Vaughn finally said.

She clenched her fingers tightly together. "I can show you."

"But first we have to drive all the way back to that damn island? I don't like islands, Sara. A man can get trapped on islands. So few ways off, you see."

"I thought you were going to retire to an island," she shot back.

"Ah, but that will be different. Much different. There I will have my own means of transportation."

She let out her breath. "Then you're not interested in

getting your hands on the information my uncle gave to me?''

Vaughn was quiet for a long while and then he suddenly seemed to come to a decision. ''It would make things much simpler if it turned out that you're telling the truth, although I have a few doubts. Still, your boyfriend is several thousand miles away by now following some lead. I'd give a lot to know exactly what kind of lead he thinks he has. Who knows when your uncle will show up.'' He drummed his fingers on the arm of the chair, his eyes hooded and speculative. ''I suppose there's no harm in checking out your story. We could be into the city and over to that damn island within a couple of hours.''

''Yes.'' She could hardly breathe as she waited for the final decision. Was greed finally going to swamp this man's patience?

He nodded once. ''All right, Sara. We'll go. But I warn you that if you've lied to me, I will make things most unpleasant for both you and your uncle. And probably your boyfriend, too.''

''I'm not lying,'' she said with great conviction. ''I know where my copy of the information is hidden. I had finally realized it just before you made that fake phone call this morning.''

''I do believe you're telling the truth,'' Vaughn mused as he studied the certainty in her expression. ''Fascinating. Remind me to thank you later.''

Sure, thought Sara as she got to her feet. *I'll remind you. Just before you pull that trigger.*

Chapter Nine

The drive back into Seattle was the longest and most exhausting traveling Sara had ever done in her life. She decided that the normal stresses and strains of rush-hour traffic are not enhanced by the fact that your passenger is casually holding a gun in his lap.

Brady Vaughn didn't say much during the drive. He was undoubtedly contemplating his imminent retirement, Sara thought as she navigated the off ramp from the interstate and found the street that led down to the ferry docks. He kept the gun discreetly shielded under a jacket but he kept it aimed in her direction. She had a hunch that once she had parked her car on the ferry Vaughn wouldn't allow her to go up onto the passenger decks. The thought of sitting on the car deck for the entire length of the ferry ride was depressing.

She was right, of course. Vaughn simply lounged in his corner of the car and watched her speculatively. Unobtrusively Sara glanced at her watch. Her timing, at least, was good. If Adrian had told the truth this morning, he would be catching the ferry that would be leaving Seattle forty minutes from now. She would have forty minutes to entertain Brady Vaughn. Her fingers flexed uneasily on the wheel.

The whole exercise would be extremely pointless if Adrian didn't show up on the right ferry. Halfway across the bay Sara had a wild thought or two about flinging herself from the car and making a dash to the passenger decks. It would be a futile move and she knew it. Even if he chose not to use the gun, Vaughn could probably run her down easily in the close confines of the parked cars. Besides, she reminded herself, that wasn't the plan. She had a much better one in mind.

If it worked. *Legends and reality.* Where did the truth stop and the legend begin? Perhaps in some cases there was no difference. Perhaps a woman just had to make the leap to faith.

"You look nervous, Sara," Vaughn observed politely. "I trust you're not wasting my time with this little chase? It won't do any good, if you are. I know what I'm doing."

She shook her head. "All I want is for you to take the information about the gold and leave."

"Sounds simple enough. I do like simple plans; don't you?"

"Yes." How simple was hers?

"Will you dream about the gold you could have had, Sara? Will you think about it occasionally in the future? Wonder what it might have been like to have your hands on your uncle's cache?"

Again she shook her head. "Even if the gold is still there, I don't see how I could get it out. How are you going to accomplish that little feat, Vaughn? Just walk into that part of the world and tell the current government officials you'd like to do a little digging on their borders?"

He chuckled. She was learning to hate that poor excuse of a laugh. "Nothing that obvious. I prefer quieter techniques. I have contacts and I'll have cash with which to grease the way. I'll be going in through Cambodia. That gold must be somewhere near the Cambodia-Vietnam border.''

''Gold is heavy. You won't be able to simply hoist it over your shoulder and hike out of the country with it. Not if there's as much there as you seem to think.''

''I'll have help,'' he explained absently.

Sara slanted him a curious glance. ''Help?''

''There are men who will undertake a great many risks for a promise of a split of the profits.'' He shrugged.

''You'll find some mercenaries to help you get the gold out?''

''They undoubtedly think of themselves as entrepreneurs,'' Vaughn murmured.

Sara closed her eyes and willed the ferry to a faster speed. She couldn't take much more of this unremitting tension. Whether her scheme worked or not, all she wanted to do at the moment was get it over and done with. She didn't see how anyone could live constantly under the stress of genuine danger. It was easy to see how a man or a woman might crack.

The ferry docked eventually and Sara turned the key in the ignition with a sense of fatalism. Forty minutes from now, if she was very, very lucky, Adrian would be driving off a similar ferry. If she was not so fortunate... Sara pushed the thought aside. There wasn't much point dwelling on that possibility. She would deal with it when the time came.

She drove slowly along the narrow road that wound around the island's perimeter, more slowly than was really necessary. Any time she could eat up this way was that much less that had to be used up at the house waiting for Adrian.

For the first time since she had arrived in the Seattle

area the weather was finally beginning to live up to its reputation. The day was rapidly turning gray and overcast. A light mist began to fall.

"Come on, let's get going." With one of his first hints of impatience Vaughn moved the gun in an ugly gesture.

Sara tried to think of something calming to say. "You don't have to use the ferry to get back off the island, you know. You can drive across a bridge on the far side. It's the long way around if you're trying to get back to the airport or Seattle, but—"

"Just shut up. I know my way around."

Of course he did. He was, after all, a *professional*. He wouldn't trap himself on an island. Sara pulled into the driveway in front of Adrian's house. The windows were still dark, so that removed the possibility that by some miracle Adrian had actually arrived home ahead of her. *Forty minutes.*

"Is it true?" she began tentatively as she slowly opened her car door.

"Is what true?" Vaughn reached out and snapped the keys from her hand. He pocketed them.

"That you really have a chance of getting that gold out of Southeast Asia?"

"Believe me, I wouldn't be going to all this trouble if I didn't think it was possible." Vaughn made a careful outside inspection of the house, reassuring himself that no one was around. Then he cast an amused glance at Sara. "What's the matter, honey? Having second thoughts about giving me that map?"

She stopped at the top of the steps and looked back at him. "I admit that until now I assumed the gold was completely inaccessible."

He chuckled. "For years I believed it probably didn't

exist at all! Kincaid hid the truth well behind the legend.
He made everyone think it really was just one more wild
tale set in the last days of the war. There were a hundred
other similar stories and there was no real reason to think
this one was for real. But a year ago I came across an old
file that had been sealed since shortly after Saigon fell.
The one thing that damned war generated was paperwork.
Files and memos and reports will probably still be turning
up twenty years from now. At any rate this one contained
some notes by a journalist who claimed he'd interviewed
some villagers in the south. He said they told him a story
about an American agent who had worked with them toward the end of the war. They described him as a man
who knew how to laugh and how to hold his whiskey. A
man who was always telling stories. A man who could
sketch your face before you even realized he was holding
a pencil.''

Sara caught her breath.

"Exactly." Vaughn nodded grimly. "A perfect description of Lowell Kincaid. The reporter's notes went on
to tell a fascinating story. It culminated in Kincaid's de-
parture for the Cambodian border with a jeep full of gold.
The villagers didn't actually see the gold in Kincaid's jeep
but they did see the share of it he left for them. He apparently stashed it in the village well and told the elders
to wait until the North Vietnamese had passed through
before digging it back out. Just like Kincaid to make a
grand gesture like that. He was a brilliant agent, but he
had some definite weaknesses. When I put that report together with the legend I'd first heard back in 1972, I began
to believe I might be dealing with more than just another
war tale. It's taken me months to piece together some idea
of what might have happened and where. The file with

the journalist's notes led to other files. Eventually I knew I was onto the real thing.''

''What happened to the journalist?'' Sara heard herself ask.

''He died,'' Vaughn said carelessly. ''An accident down in South America earlier this year, I believe.''

''I see.'' She wondered how much Vaughn had had to do with the ''accident.''

His mouth twisted wryly. ''I do believe I recognize that look in your eyes, little Sara.''

''What look?''

''Greed, love. Pure unadulterated greed. I saw it in your boyfriend's eyes yesterday and it's in yours today.''

She feigned a nonchalant movement of her shoulders and turned to open the front door. There was no sound from within. The house was as quiet and innocent-looking as it had been that first night when she'd arrived and searched Adrian's study.

''Doesn't your boyfriend believe in locking his front door?'' Vaughn drawled as he followed Sara into the house. He held the gun at the ready while he verified that the place was empty.

''He says there's virtually no crime around here.''

''A trusting soul.'' Vaughn smirked. He took in his surroundings with a quick, professional eye. ''I take it back. It goes beyond trusting. I think we can safely say your friend Saville is probably a fool.''

''And what about me?'' She slung her purse down on the sofa and turned to face him.

''Oh, you're very smart, Sara. Very smart indeed, if you're telling the truth.'' Vaughn's eyes hardened. ''Where's the map?''

She grabbed for her courage, using all of her willpower

to keep her expression cool. "I've tried to tell you, it's not exactly a map," she began carefully.

"What the hell are you talking about?" The violence in Vaughn was very close to the surface.

"My uncle has his own unique way of doing things. You know that. He made sure I'd have the information I needed but he hid it in an unique manner. I don't know how he gave Adrian his information, but I think I know where my copy is." Her fingernails dug into her palms. She wondered if Vaughn realized just how scared she was.

"Sara, let's not play any games. You'll lose, believe me. Where's the map?"

"It's not a map. I'm trying to explain. It's a sort of…of code."

Vaughn stared at her. "A code? You told me you and your uncle didn't go in for codes."

"I said we didn't have any prearranged greeting signals."

"Then what are you saying?"

"I'll show you." Moving cautiously so as not to alarm him, Sara turned and started down the hall toward the study. This business of trying to think two steps ahead of a man with a gun was tricky. The ferry that might or might not be bringing Adrian to the rescue had left Seattle by now. Her fate was in the hands of the Washington state ferry system. They claimed to have an excellent safety record.

Vaughn was close behind her as she stepped into the study. The crystal apple gleamed on Adrian's desk, still pinning her note. Beyond it the manuscript of *Phantom* waited.

"There," she whispered, indicating the pile of typed pages. "Everything you want to know about that gold is in that manuscript. My uncle has jotted down little doodles and notes all over the margins, you see.''

Vaughn stared first at the stack of papers and then gestured viciously at her with the nose of the gun. ''You little bitch. What kind of game do you think you're playing?''

She hugged herself, trying to master the faint trembling that threatened to weaken her limbs. Her head bent forward and a sweep of her hair hid her expression. ''It's there. I promise you. And I know how to get at the information you want. It's in code and my uncle once taught me the code. It will take a while, but I can do it.''

''Why you little fool!'' he snarled. ''Stalling isn't going to get you anywhere. There's no one around to come to your rescue. If there was any likelihood of that, I'd never have agreed to let you drag me here.''

''No.'' She shook her head and lifted her chin defiantly. ''I'm not trying to stall. I'm…I'm trying to make a deal. You said you were going to be hiring professional help to assist you in getting the gold out of Southeast Asia. Well, I want you to consider me as hired help, too. I can decode Uncle Lowell's doodles on that manuscript. I can do it here and now, in fact, and prove that what I'm saying is true. In return, I want you to cut me in for a piece of the action.''

He studied her derisively. ''You've got your uncle's nerve, little Sara, I'll say that for you. Decode the manuscript. What a crock of—''

''It's true,'' she insisted. ''You know Uncle Lowell. It would be just like him to hide the information so I would be sitting right on top of it all the time. That manuscript was waiting for me at his cabin the other day. It was right out in the open. You'd overlooked it, naturally. He says people always overlook the obvious. But I recognized the doodles on the margins. It's the code he taught me when I was a little girl. It was a game we used to play together. Give me half an hour and I'll have the information you need to find that gold.''

Vaughn was clearly and dangerously undecided. His eyes slid from the manuscript to her face and back again. "Half an hour?"

She nodded quickly. "Is it a deal?"

"I can afford half an hour's wait. I was prepared to wait for much longer than that for Kincaid to return. And your boyfriend is no doubt getting ready to land in Mexico City so there's plenty of time on that end. All right, my greedy little Sara. You've got yourself a deal.''

"You'll cut me in for a slice of the profit?'' She had to make it sound real, Sara told herself. She tried to inject just the right note of hopeful greed.

"Sure. Why not?'' He threw himself down into a chair in the corner. "Half an hour. And if it turns out that you're lying, little Sara—''

"I'm not lying.'' She sat down slowly behind the desk. From there she was looking through the study door and into the hall beyond. Brady Vaughn would be able to see anyone who came through the door but from his seat in the corner he could not see into the hall as she could. Sara figured she would have a couple of seconds' advance notice if and when Adrian arrived. Nervously she reached out and pulled the manuscript toward her.

She found herself staring down at the sketch of the wolf. For an instant it almost paralyzed her. Then, with excessive care, she turned over the first page of *Phantom* and picked up a pencil.

Time ticked past with a slowness that made Sara think she was waiting for eternity to end. She would have no way of knowing until the last moment whether or not Adrian would arrive. He would have the warning about the invasion of his house shortly after he drove off the ferry. He would probably leave the car down the road and walk the final few yards, she decided. Neither she nor Vaughn would have the sound of a vehicle to alert them.

Carefully she went through the manuscript, occasionally stopping to jot down a meaningless number or word on the notepad beside her. It would be particularly ironic if there really was a code imbedded in her uncle's margin doodles, Sara decided at one point. A real joke on her. As far as she knew she was looking at nothing more than meaningless notes and drawings.

Time crept past. Outside the window the mist turned to rain. Sara turned on the desk lamp. Vaughn's eyes never left her as she went page by page through the manuscript. His patience was as amazing to her as Adrian's had been. Where did they learn that kind of skill? Perhaps some people were just born with it. It was a cinch she wasn't one of those lucky souls. She shuddered and turned over another page. She would force herself not to sneak another glance at the clock or her watch for at least ten minutes, Sara decided resolutely at one point. The last thing she wanted to do was give Vaughn the idea that she was waiting for someone. She kept her head bent over the manuscript for what she estimated must surely be at least ten minutes if not more and then, unable to resist, she slid her gaze upward to the clock on the wall near the door.

She almost didn't see Adrian standing in the shadows of the hall. When she did, she thought her breath had stopped permanently. He was simply waiting there, watching her in absolute silence. It was as if a ghost had materialized out of thin air and in her odd, light-headed state of mind she might have believed just that if it hadn't been for the rain-dampened Windbreaker he wore. It took her another instant to see the gun in his hand.

"Something wrong, Sara?" Vaughn asked conversationally from the corner. He lifted his gun in an easy threat. "You seem a little tense."

Sara swallowed and dropped her eyes from Adrian's still, shadowed figure to the crystal apple in front of her. "I've just realized that I made a mistake."

"Did you?" Vaughn seemed only politely interested. "Just what kind of mistake would that be, little Sara?"

She picked up the apple and held it so that it caught the light from the desk lamp. "The information you want isn't in the manuscript."

"Then you have a problem, don't you, Sara," he said with brutal emphasis.

She shook her head. "No. I don't think so. Not anymore." She tossed the apple up in the air and caught it again. "Here's what you want, Mr. Vaughn." She tossed the crystal object once more and caught it easily. Beyond the door Adrian did not move. He was as still as midnight waiting to descend. She couldn't see his eyes but she knew they would be quite colorless.

"I think," Vaughn said abruptly, "that I've had enough of your games, bitch."

"Ah, but I'm so good at them," she protested gently. "What you want is right out here in front of your very eyes, Mr. Vaughn. As clear as crystal. Just the sort of trick my uncle would pull, don't you think?" With sudden decision she hurled the apple toward the window.

"What the hell...I've had it with you, lady. I'm going to kill you for this!" Without warning, Vaughn's patience snapped. He surged out of the chair, his gun trained on

Sara but his eyes following the apple as it crashed against the tempered glass.

The sound of the crystal striking the window and falling to the floor was lost beneath Brady Vaughn's scream of pain and rage as Adrian floated through the doorway and brought the base of the gun down in the direction of the other man's skull. In the split second before the butt of the gun would have made contact with his head, however, some instinct must have warned Vaughn. He threw himself to one side, tumbling across the desk. Adrian's gun struck him violently on the shoulder but it didn't stun him. The weapon Vaughn had been holding, however, fell to the floor and skidded along the hardwood surface until it struck the edge of a rug.

On the other side of the desk, Sara screamed. She was trapped against the wall as the momentum of Vaughn's panicked, sliding rush across the desk threw him toward her. An instant later he seized her even as he stumbled wildly to his feet. Sharp steel blossomed in his hand. He held the knife to Sara's throat, his arm locking her against his body.

"Hold it right there, Saville. Come one step closer and I swear I'll kill her."

Sara couldn't take her eyes off Adrian. The temperature in the study seemed to have suddenly dropped by about twenty degrees.

His face was utterly without emotion. It reminded her of the way he had watched the fish dying at his feet the other morning on the pier but it was a thousand times more remote. He didn't look at Sara. His whole attention was on the heavily breathing man who was holding the knife to her throat.

"Let her go, Vaughn."

"You think I'm crazy? She's my ticket out of here. Drop the gun." He jerked his arm more tightly around Sara's neck. "I said, drop it, damn you! Think I'm playing games?"

"No, I don't think you're playing games." Moving slowly and deliberately, Adrian took a step forward and set his handgun down on the floor at his feet. The blue steel gleamed savagely in the light of the desk lamp.

"Come on, you bitch." Vaughn tugged Sara around the edge of the desk, clearly heading toward the spot where his own weapon had landed when it had been jolted from his hand. "Move, damn you!"

Sara tried to make her body as limp and heavy as possible but the feel of the steel at the base of her throat kept her from refusing to cooperate entirely. Vaughn would use that knife, she knew. Just as he would use the gun when he got his hands on it.

Across the room Adrian stood balanced a step away from his own weapon. If push came to shove, Sara didn't doubt but that he'd make a grab for it. He watched Vaughn the way a wolf might watch a circling hyena.

"Your best bet is to make a run for it, Vaughn. Hanging on to Sara will only slow you down."

Sara felt the tension in her captor's body as he pulled her toward his gun. "I've come too far in search of that gold, Saville. I'm not leaving without getting what I want."

"Sara doesn't know where it is."

"Maybe. Maybe not. I can't quite figure sweet Sara. But Kincaid knows where it is, and when he finds out I've got his niece, he'll bargain."

"You think so? I've never known Kincaid to bargain

for anything without coming out on top," Adrian said thoughtfully.

"You don't know him as well as I do," Vaughn assured the other man. He stopped beside the gun on the floor and his fingers bit abruptly into Sara's shoulder. "Bend down very slowly, Sara, and pick up the gun, muzzle first. And keep in mind that I'll have this knife at the nape of your neck."

Sara realized that it would be dangerously awkward for him to try scooping up the gun while still retaining a stranglehold on her. The action might give Adrian the opening for which he was clearly waiting. So Vaughn was going to make her pick up the lethal chunk of steel and hand it over politely to replace the knife.

Sara glanced down at the gun and then up at Adrian's still, unreadable face. If she gave the gun to Vaughn, he would surely use it against the one thing that stood between him and the door: Adrian.

"Do as I say!"

Slowly Sara knelt, aware of the tip of the knife following her nape. Adrian didn't move, his eyes never leaving Vaughn's face. She went all the way down on her knees and reached out reluctantly for the muzzle of the gun.

"Hurry up," Vaughn snarled, forced to bend over slightly in order to keep the knife within striking distance of her neck. "Pick it up and give it to me!"

She wasn't going to get a better opportunity, Sara realized. It was now or never. Handing the gun to Vaughn was the equivalent of signing Adrian's death warrant. She took a deep breath.

Then she threw herself full-length on the floor and rolled to one side, straight into Vaughn's legs. Her falling body covered the gun.

"Damn you!"

The knife flashed as Vaughn was forced to step backward in order to regain his balance. The blade arced downward, scoring Sara's shoulder. She felt the icy sting of the steel even as she struck his left leg. The pain brought a startled cry to her lips.

"Sara!"

Her name was the only sound Adrian made. In the next instant he launched himself across the room in a deadly rush.

But Vaughn was already moving. He hurled the blade straight at Adrian, who must have guessed what was going to happen next. Sara opened her eyes in time to see Adrian throw himself to one side. The blade whipped harmlessly past and imbedded itself deep into the far wall. The rushing assault had served to draw the snake's fangs.

In the small space of time he had bought for himself, Vaughn glanced down and seemed to realize he didn't stand a chance if he took another moment to push Sara off his gun. He raced for the door even as Adrian dived for his own gun.

Sara gasped in pain, her fingers going to the wound on her shoulder just as Adrian leaped for the door. Her cry of anguish stopped him as effectively as a steel cable. He whirled and came back to her even as the sound of Vaughn's running footsteps disappeared down the hall.

"My God, Sara." Adrian went down on his knees beside her. "How bad is it? Let me see." Carefully he guided her to a sitting position, pulling her face into his shoulder as he pushed aside her shirt.

"I...I don't think it's all that bad," she managed, inhaling sharply as she leaned into him. She was trembling. "It just hurts."

"I know, Sara," he soothed in a soft growl as he examined the shoulder. "I know. But you're right. It isn't very deep. Do you think you can handle it yourself?"

"Myself?" She lifted her head in astonishment and then realized what he meant. "Adrian, you're not going after him!"

"I've got to, Sara. You know that."

"No, I do *not* know that," she retorted. "Let the police worry about him. It's not your job—"

"Sara, it is my job." Adrian's face was a cold mask, his light eyes frozen, crystal pools. "After what he's done to you, I don't have any choice."

"No, damn it!" she raged, grabbing at him as he rose to his feet. "You'll never catch him, anyway. He'll take my car. He's got the keys." But even as she argued she realized there was no sound of a car leaving the drive.

"I took care of the car before I came into the house. A precaution." Adrian moved away from her, scooping up the gun and started for the door. "He'll be on foot and unarmed. This is easy hunting, Sara. Don't worry about it."

"I don't want you going hunting! Please, Adrian, wait...."

But she was calling to no one. Adrian had already disappeared down the hall after his quarry.

Easy hunting. Sara's eyes filled with tears. She didn't want Adrian going hunting. In that moment she would have given her soul to keep him from pursuing Vaughn.

Once again she remembered the way Adrian had watched the fish dying on the pier.

Outside the house Adrian paused briefly on the porch, listening. He shoved the gun back into the leather holster he wore at the base of his spine. The rain was coming down heavily now, obscuring visibility. Sara's car stood silently in the drive, unable to function since he'd clipped two strategic wires.

He'd really made a mess of this, Adrian told himself grimly as he started down the porch steps at a long, loping run. Everything was coming apart in his hands, and to top it all off, he'd nearly gotten Sara killed. The fury and fear he had felt when he'd realized what was happening inside the study were unlike anything he'd ever experienced in his life. The combination of the two had risen up to choke him, causing him to mishandle the situation badly.

But Sara was safe now. The knife had drawn blood but it hadn't gone deep. She had been too close to the floor, depriving Vaughn of an easy target.

Vaughn. Adrian shook his head as his sense of logic returned. There were only two ways off the island, the ferry from Winslow and the bridge at the far end of Bainbridge. Vaughn would head for the highway and try to commandeer a car to go for the bridge. The ferry was already pulling out of its slip on the return run to Seattle. There would be no chance for Vaughn to catch it.

His hunting instincts told Adrian that Vaughn would stick as much as possible to the wooded terrain until he spotted a car that could be hailed. And he would want to keep moving in the general direction of his goal, the bridge. Panicked quarry didn't think to backtrack or race off along a route that would seem to be in the opposite direction. When you were trying to escape, the sense of urgency effectively destroyed a good portion of natural logic.

With grave certainty, Adrian started toward the woods that bounded the road. He moved silently on the wet ground, oblivious to the rain that was soaking his hair and clothing. He knew he was heading in the right direction when he found the scrap of cloth Vaughn had apparently lost when he'd blundered into a thick cluster of blackberry bushes. After that, the trail became increasingly easy to follow.

Just like old times, Adrian thought with a chill that did not come from the rain. Maybe you could never really leave the past behind. Maybe it stayed with you forever.

He had told himself a year ago that a good, solid, iron-tight cover was the answer. A good cover had saved his life often enough in the past. Logically it should be able to provide him with a new life in the future. He'd had it all worked out, every detail in place, every aspect of his new world under control. He was a writer now, a slightly eccentric vegetarian, a man who could fall in love and marry just as other men did. If asked, he could have supplied a complete life history that would have satisfied any inquiring reporter.

The cover had been letter perfect until this afternoon when he'd walked into his study and seen the truth in Sara's eyes. That's when Adrian had learned that there was no such thing as a perfect cover.

She knew who he was. He'd blown it all when he'd stood in the hall with a gun in his hand.

A good cover, it seemed, couldn't quite cover up the past.

Vaughn was moving with increasing carelessness. Probably because there hadn't been any traffic on the quiet road. Maybe he was beginning to realize that making his way to the other end of the island was going to be very difficult.

Not difficult, Adrian thought savagely. Impossible. Vaughn wasn't going to drive, walk or fly off Bainbridge

Island. At least not under his own power. Adrian quick-
ened his pace, gliding silently through the rain-wet trees,
skirting the berry bushes and listening with every nerve
in his body.

In another couple of minutes he heard the first faint
sounds of his quarry. Vaughn might be good but he obviously didn't know much about this kind of fieldwork.
He was probably more accustomed to the streets of foreign cities. Most likely he'd never done a lot of real fieldwork in Vietnam or South America. An office spy. A man
who worked embassies and cocktail parties.

Easy hunting.

Adrian could hear him clearly now. Vaughn wasn't far
ahead of him. What lead he'd had had been chewed into
by berry bushes, a driving rain and a woodsy terrain with
which he wasn't familiar.

Adrian, on the other hand, knew every inch of the
woods around his house. He'd walked them often enough,
head bent against a cold drizzle, hands stuffed into his
jacket. He'd thought about *Phantom* during those long
walks. And he'd thought about the mysterious Sara.

Sara. My passionate, impulsive, loving Sara. Sara, from
whom he would have done anything to keep the truth.
Too late now. The cover was blown.

A rough, hastily bitten-off oath from the man ahead
blended with the steady beat of the rain but Adrian heard
it. He slipped forward, starting to reach for the gun in his
holster at his back. And then he caught sight of the muted,
striped shirt Vaughn was wearing. Vaughn was having to
swerve in order to go around another thicket of blackberry
bushes. Adrian changed his mind about the gun. *Easy
hunting. Easy prey.*

You should never have touched her, Vaughn. You

should never have gone near Sara. It's going to cost you everything.

Vaughn trotted to the left, searching for a way around the thorny bushes. He heard nothing as Adrian made his silent rush through the trees. In the last second, though, Vaughn felt the movement behind him. He whirled, clawing at his pocket to withdraw a switchblade.

But he was too late. Adrian's body catapulted into his quarry's, bearing both men to the soggy ground. Adrian had his hands locked around the fist that held the knife. He crushed with all his strength, hearing something snap. Vaughn yelled. The knife fell into a pile of leaves.

It was all over in less than a minute. Adrian had the advantage and he used it. With brutal efficiency he used his hands to stun his opponent. In a startlingly short period of time Vaughn lay limp and dazed beneath his attacker.

should never have gone near Sara. It's going to cost you
everything.

Vaughn turned to the left, searching for a way around
the thorny bushes the night now ... Adrian made his
other tools through ... as a ... his second thought,
Vaughn felt the first ... of... He would have slowed
and ... his passage over ... if it weren't...

He was too late. A thick rope ... around him like
... as Vaughn took his ...

Chapter Ten

Sara adjusted the bandage on her shoulder for the twen-
tieth time, using the bathroom mirror to guide her. It had
been exceedingly awkward trying to bandage the wound
without help but at last she'd gotten the bleeding stopped.
She had been right. It hurt like hell, but the slicing cut
wasn't all that deep. Her gaze went to the watch on her
wrist. It had been over two hours since Adrian had left
the house in pursuit of Vaughn.

Too much time. She was growing increasingly frightened as the minutes ticked past. But she felt incredibly
helpless. Not because she thought for a moment that
Vaughn would succeed in ambushing Adrian, though. Her
mouth twisted in response to another stab of pain from
her shoulder. No, Adrian would get his man. The wolf
was on the hunt and he always did what had to be done.

Just as Phantom always did what must be done.

What truly frightened her was the thought of Adrian
being thrown back into the life he had left behind. She
would have given anything to keep him from having to
resurrect the past. Because now she knew just how hard
he had worked to put it behind him. But there was nothing
she could do.

Adrian was the man they had once called Wolf, the
legend who had been only too real. She had been coming

slowly to that conclusion all day as bits and pieces of evidence came together in her mind.

When she had realized that her only hope of escaping Vaughn lay with Adrian, Sara had acknowledged the truth. Her life had depended on the man code-named Wolf, the man she had once imagined was a renegade killer.

And she had known on some instinctive level that Adrian would save her. That was why she had lured Vaughn back to the island house.

It was her love for Adrian that had enabled her to view the evidence of his past with different eyes. That love had begun from almost the first moment she had turned to find him watching her going through his study. She had known in that first glimpse that this man was different. He was her uncle's friend. The kind of man you could count on when the chips were down.

She had known for certain she was in love last night when she'd lain in Adrian's arms and prayed he wouldn't leave in the morning.

It was all so clear now. Crystal-clear, in fact. She probably should have been suspicious from the start about his identity. He was a man who needed to control his environment, to maintain a cover. It was the way he had built a new life.

Sara shuddered and tears filmed her eyes as she wondered how Adrian had felt when he'd realized his carefully structured world was crumbling around him. She ached to be able to comfort him but she was terribly afraid he wouldn't want the comfort. He had depended on no one but himself for too long.

The knock on the door shocked her into dropping the roll of tape she had been using. Sara frowned into the mirror. Adrian wouldn't knock on his own door, surely. Nervously she held a square of gauze to her shoulder and adjusted her shirt as best she could. Then she went cautiously down the hall to the front door. Standing on tiptoe, she peered through the tiny viewing port.

A man dressed in a wildly patterned aloha shirt and holding a festive-striped umbrella stood on the porch.

"Uncle Lowell!" Sara flung open the door and rushed into his arms. "My God, Uncle Lowell, are you all right? We've been so worried. Adrian's gone after Vaughn and it's been over two hours! I've been going out of my mind. How did you get here? Where have you been?"

"Easy, Sara," Kincaid said, smiling down at her. "One question at a time. Where did you say Adrian was?"

Sara stepped back into the house and held the door. "He's gone after Vaughn." She shook her head, trying to sort it all out for him. "Vaughn was holding me prisoner. He was going to trade me to you for information about that damned gold. Adrian rescued me but in the process Vaughn got away."

Kincaid arched shaggy eyebrows. "He did?" He followed his niece through the door, shaking out the umbrella as he did so. "That doesn't sound like Adrian."

"Well, it was all very chaotic, believe me." Sara sighed. "Vaughn was holding a knife at my throat and he'd made Adrian throw down his gun. Oh, it's a long story. But the end result is that Vaughn got clear and Adrian went after him. I've been worrying myself sick, Uncle Lowell."

"What's wrong with your shoulder?" Kincaid leaned forward, thick brows drawing into a solid line.

"Vaughn scratched it with the knife." She turned her

head, trying to look at the gauze-covered wound. "It's not really that bad but it hurts so."

"Knife wounds generally feel like fire. Here, let me see if you've got it properly bandaged."

"The wound is all right, Uncle Lowell. It's Adrian I'm getting frantic about." But she stood still while Lowell glanced at the slice in her shoulder and then taped down the gauze.

"Adrian can take care of himself."

"You two keep saying that about each other but, personally, I'm having severe doubts! And I didn't want Adrian having to…to go back to his old business!"

Lowell tilted his head to one side, studying her speculatively. "So you've figured out what the old business was?"

Sara nodded grimly. "And I mean to have a heart-to-heart chat with you about that. But we can do it later. I've got other things on my mind just now."

"So have I. Got any coffee? After a few days in sunny Hawaii, it's a bit of a shock to come back to Seattle." Lowell started in the direction of the kitchen.

"But what about Adrian?" Helplessly Sara followed in her uncle's wake.

Lowell Kincaid was the same as ever, she decided. You'd never know that behind the laughing blue eyes was a brain that could function in the most convoluted patterns. He was nearing seventy now and had gone quite bald except for a fringe of well-trimmed gray hair. Kincaid had never gone to fat; his body was still whipcord lean. In addition to the aloha shirt, he was wearing sandals and a pair of white cotton slacks that were spotted with rain. On his wrist was a gold watch. It went nicely with the thin gold chain around his neck. Sara knew the gold was real. Her uncle never wore fake gold.

"Adrian will be back when he's taken care of things." With the familiarity of a man who has frequently been a guest in the house, Lowell began making coffee. "Damn sorry he had to clean up my mess, though."

"Uncle Lowell," Sara said with forced patience. "Why don't you tell me what the hell has been happening?"

Lowell stretched and lifted a hand to rub the point between his shoulder blades. "Well, to put it in simple terms, I've just spent the last few days following a false trail in Hawaii. Came back today when I realized it was a dead end. Vaughn really had me running around the countryside," he added ruefully. "I feel like an idiot."

"Who is Vaughn, anyway?"

"Old business."

"Oh, yes." She nodded, remembering the taped message. "You said something about taking care of old business."

"Look, when Adrian gets back, he's going to want some explanations, too. Why don't we wait until we're all sitting cozily around a nice warm fire. And what about dinner?"

"Dinner," Sara said vengefully, "is the last thing on my mind at the moment. What are we going to do about Adrian?"

"Absolutely nothing. Never was much anyone could do about Adrian," her uncle said reflectively as he poured boiling water over instant coffee. "Just aim him and pull the trigger."

Sara felt sick to her stomach.

SARA KNEW who he was. *She knew who he was.* Adrian couldn't forget the memory of her description of the man she knew as Wolf. Her words still rang in his head. A renegade killer or something equally picturesque. A man who, when he walked into a room, chilled everything and everyone. He'd seen the expression in her eyes when he'd stood in the hall just outside the study early this evening. She had looked up from the manuscript and he'd known that for her the room had grown very cold.

It was all over.

He drove back to the cabin with a sense of deep foreboding. There was a good chance she wouldn't even be there. Then what? When he pulled into the drive and saw the familiar green Toyota, he felt some sense of relief. Lowell was back. And that meant Sara was probably still around. Her car was still there but that didn't mean much since he'd disabled it earlier.

It was nice that Kincaid was home safe and sound, of course, Adrian told himself as he opened the car door. But the real benefit to his return was that it meant Adrian wouldn't have to face Sara alone. He still hadn't figured out what to say to her and he was beginning to accept the fact that he might never figure it out. He'd never been very good with words around Sara. In any event, she would probably be gone from his life soon, anyway.

She wouldn't want to hang around a wolf.

He walked slowly up the porch steps. The wet night had descended completely now and the warm lights of the house beckoned. But Adrian wasn't fooled. He knew the warmth was an illusion. Without Sara, there could be no real warmth in his life. He tried to dredge up some polite greetings, the sort of thing a man might say in this situation. He should be a gentleman about it. Give her an out. But deep inside he wasn't sure he could do it. He wanted her so and he'd begun to believe lately that he could have her. The thought of letting her walk out now filled him with a tight, gnawing tension.

There were a lot of things a man could take in this world but a woman's love was not among them. It had to be given willingly and it had to be for real. He had spent the last few days realizing the truth of that. The wonder of having Sara for himself couldn't be pushed back into the corners of his mind where he now kept other things that were better forgotten. He couldn't give her up.

But she hated and feared the man called Wolf.

The mechanical-sounding words Adrian had been practicing as he climbed the steps were wiped out of his head as the front door was thrown open.

"It's about time you got back!" Sara cried as she flew across the porch. "Adrian, it's been hours!"

He felt the soft impact as she hurled herself against him. Automatically his arms went around her. He was dazed by the greeting.

"Sara?"

"You said you'd be back on the five-fifty-five ferry," she whispered into his wet shirt. "I knew you'd get back on time. I knew all I had to do was have Vaughn here and you'd take care of everything."

He held her fiercely, absorbing the warmth of her. "Yes." He stroked her hair wonderingly. "I got the read-out from the house alarm system right after I drove off the ferry." His fingers tightened abruptly in her hair. "I've never been so scared in my life, Sara."

"Hi, Adrian, sorry about all this. Everything okay?"

Adrian gazed over Sara's head, his eyes meeting those of his friend. "Everything's taken care of." He felt Sara shiver in his arms.

Kincaid nodded. "Figured it would be."

"You may have a few questions to answer from your old pals at the agency in the morning, though."

Kincaid's eyes gleamed. "How's that?"

"I left Vaughn tied up in a neat package a few yards off I-90. Then I called the West Coast agency office and left a message telling them where they could find him. When the guy who took the call demanded to know who was leaving the message—"

"You gave him my name." Kincaid grinned ruefully. "Thanks a lot, pal. Well, I guess I can't complain. I deserved it. Lord knows I owe you for taking care of Sara. Besides, maybe Gilkirk and his boys will be so delighted to have their hands on Vaughn they won't want to ask too many questions."

Sara lifted her head, her hands moving upward to frame Adrian's face. "You didn't kill him."

"No."

She smiled. "Of course not. Supper's ready. Go and take a hot shower. I'll pour you a glass of wine." She pulled free and disappeared back into the house.

Adrian stared after her, aware of a gnawing uncertainty. The uncertainty was painful but it was better than the cold, dead certainty of loss he'd been feeling earlier. Uncertainty contained hope. He followed Lowell into the house and headed for the bathroom, stripping off the wet Windbreaker as he moved.

ADRIAN HAD BEEN WATCHING Sara since he'd emerged from the shower, trying to second-guess her thoughts. She'd chattered about the gold while she'd prepared a hearty rice and vegetable salad, making a joke out of her uncle's idea of a wedding gift. She'd poured him and

Lowell a glass of wine and put the sourdough rolls in the oven while discussing Lowell's unplanned vacation in Hawaii. Then she'd kept up a running monologue on Kincaid's new aloha shirt and how typical it was of him to bring something like that back from Hawaii.

Lowell had talked easily, too, leaning against the kitchen counter while responding to her teasing about his new shirt.

"Glad you like it. Got three more in the suitcase. Picked 'em up while I waited for the flight back this morning." He'd glanced down at the front of the splashy shirt with obvious pleasure.

Adrian had felt left out of the conversation but he hadn't known how to get into it. Sara and her uncle kept up a bright dialogue that covered everything under the sun except the subject of the man called Wolf. Adrian told himself morosely that it was probably because they were both too polite to talk about someone when the object of the conversation was within hearing distance brooding over a glass of wine.

During dinner Sara finally pounced on her uncle, demanding answers. Adrian surreptitiously kept an eye on her lively hazel eyes while she quizzed Lowell Kincaid. He searched for signs of disgust or fear or rejection in her expressive features. The stranger inner anxiety was eating him alive, demanding assurances and explanations and at the same time preparing him for the worst. Surely, after everything she had believed about the man named Wolf, she couldn't possibly be this warm and nonchalant now.

Adrian's fingers crumpled the napkin in his lap and he glanced down, vaguely astonished at the outward show of tension.

"All right, Uncle Lowell, let's have it," Sara demanded

as the meal came to a close. She leaned back in her chair, her fingertips steepled beneath her chin as she regarded Kincaid with a gleaming gaze.

"Well," Lowell began with an easy grin, "I had to go to about three shops before I found just the right selection of shirts but when I saw this one with the pineapples on it, I knew—"

"Lowell Kincaid, I am not talking about the aloha shirts and you know it. I want to know about the gold."

"Ah, the gold," he echoed softly. "I figure that you may not be able to get at it until sometime around your twenty-fifth wedding anniversary, or you may have let your children inherit the treasure map, but either way it makes an interesting wedding present, don't you think? Even if you never actually see the gold itself, you'll have it to talk about and laugh about and tell stories about. I can just hear the tales you'll be telling your kids."

"I think," Sara interrupted firmly, "that we're getting a little ahead of ourselves. I'm not interested in what I may be telling my kids, especially since I don't have any."

"Yet," Lowell interjected wisely.

Sara raised her eyebrows but Adrian noticed she didn't look at him. She kept her attention on Kincaid. "I'm more concerned with the past at the moment. Did you or did you not steal CIA gold and stash it near the Cambodian border?"

Kincaid grinned at Adrian. "She's rather aggressively direct when she wants an answer."

"Umm." Adrian sipped the last of his wine and wondered why Sara hadn't been aggressively direct in pinning him down about Wolf. Maybe she didn't want to know the full truth. He set down the wineglass with grim care.

"Okay, Sara, here's the story," Kincaid began. "For starters, it wasn't CIA gold. It wasn't U.S. gold in any sense of the word, really. It belonged to some very astute gentlemen who were doing an active drug business under the guise of working in a civilian capacity for the U.S. government. I accidentally stumbled across them while working with some friends of mine."

"Friends?"

Lowell nodded. "I had spent a lot of time with the people of a particular village. They had been very useful during the war, supplying information and some very brave young men and women. At any rate, I was in the village when rumors came of the two drug runners being killed. The business career of a drug runner is precarious, to say the least. I was near the scene of the killing and, through a series of, uh, arranged coincidences, managed to get my hands on the gold."

"Uh-huh." Sara sounded distinctly skeptical. "'Arranged' being the operative word, I imagine."

"I then had myself a problem. I knew things were deteriorating rapidly. Saigon was about to go under, and everyone who had any sense was aware of it. I was several miles away and there was no way I could make it back to the embassy with the gold. I would have been lucky to make it back with my life. So I decided on another route out of the situation."

"A route that would allow you to take some of the gold with you?"

Kincaid chuckled. "You know me and gold, Sara. I couldn't bring myself to just toss it away."

"Vaughn said he uncovered a file that indicated you left some of it behind with your friends in that village."

Kincaid's shaggy brows lifted. "A file, hmm? I wondered how he got curious enough about the gold after all these years to make a try for it. Well, Sara, let me tell you a fact of life. There's nothing quite as useful as gold when you're trying to survive in a country that's recently been overrun by a conquering army. And I owed those villagers. As for myself, I'd been making some friends near the Cambodian border and decided to call in a few favors. I loaded my share of the gold on a jeep and drove to the border. There was no way I could get it out of the country, so I buried it, made a map and then rendezvoused with my contacts. They got me out of the country.''

"Where does Brady Vaughn fit into all this?" Sara demanded.

"Vaughn has been a thorn in the agency's side for some time. We all knew he was working both sides of the street.''

"He said something about working two jobs," Sara said dryly. "Was that what he meant? He was selling information to the other side?''

"Information we wanted him to sell, although he didn't know it. We used him after we'd learned he'd been turned." Lowell smiled. "But his usefulness was becoming limited from what my former associates have told me. Apparently the other side felt the same. Vaughn was smart enough to sense that something was going wrong and wisely decided to disappear. Apparently he wanted a little nest egg to cushion his sudden retirement.''

"And he chose your cache of gold.''

"He'd been assigned to Saigon during that last six months. We'd worked together on a couple of jobs. But I never did fully trust the man. I tried to plant my own rumors about the gold whenever I heard it mentioned after the war. I knew it would be almost impossible to keep the whole thing absolutely secret. There were all those villagers who knew about it, for one thing. And Lord knows who the drug dealers knew. But I made sure most of the gossip about the missing gold implied the stuff was government material kept at the embassy and used for clandestine operations. I sort of left the impression that the two drug dealers were really agents. And of course I kept my own name out of it. You never know. I didn't want to implicate myself. If someone knew the drug story or got too friendly with the villagers, he might be able to track down more of the tale.''

"Apparently some journalist did get friendly with the villagers," Sara said. "And his notes somehow ended up in an old file that Vaughn came across."

Lowell sighed. "I thought after all these years the story of the gold really had become nothing more than a legend."

"Vaughn said he deliberately planted a rumor about him being in Hawaii recruiting mercenaries to help him get your treasure," Sara said.

Kincaid shook his head. "I'm embarrassed to admit it worked. I got wind of the plan and did exactly as he anticipated. I took off for Hawaii." He glanced at Adrian. "I honestly thought I'd have everything taken care of within forty-eight hours or so. Didn't think you'd be bothered with cleaning up my mess."

Adrian couldn't think of anything to say. He just nodded austerely and continued to watch Sara's face through narrowed eyes. Why didn't she say something about what had happened that afternoon. The suspense was going to shred him. A part of him wanted to get the confrontation over and done with. Another part wanted to pretend nothing devastating had occurred. Abruptly he pushed his chair away from the table and went over to where he kept the brandy.

"Can I pour you some, Lowell?" His voice felt thick and scratchy in his throat.

"Sounds great." The older man beamed.

Sara focused on her uncle again. "Vaughn is definitely out of the way? He won't be bothering us again?"

Lowell Kincaid smiled. "You don't have to worry about him. I'll talk to Gilkirk in the morning. But from what I hear the agency's tired of using him, anyway. Even if he got turned loose tomorrow, he realizes everyone knows who he is and what he's been doing. He'd disappear in a hurry."

"He had plans, you know," Sara mused.

Adrian could feel her watching him as he poured the brandy. "What plans?" he managed to ask, although he couldn't have cared less. Vaughn, as Kincaid had just said, was no longer an issue. He'd made sure of that when he'd left the sullen man bound and gagged in the rain beside the freeway. Vaughn was smart enough to know that everything had fallen apart. Vaughn, too, knew what it meant to have his cover completely blown.

"He thought that, given the map and a few carefully selected mercenaries, he could get into Cambodia and get at the gold. He told me all about his scheme," she finished blithely. "Aren't you going to pour me some brandy, too?"

Adrian turned back to the counter and poured another glass. "Sorry," he muttered shortly. When he handed it to her, she raised it cheerfully.

"Here's to finally getting some answers." She downed a healthy swallow.

Lowell grinned. "Haven't I always told you that answers are always crystal-clear once you know where to look?''

With a snap, Sara set down the brandy snifter. ''Speaking of crystal-clear answers,'' she began. And then she was on her feet, hurrying down the hall toward the study.

Kincaid traded glances with Adrian. It was the first time they'd been alone together without Sara in the room. ''Everything's under control?''

Adrian nodded. ''Yeah. The agency will handle it. I really did lead them to believe you were the one who'd wrapped Vaughn up for Christmas. I guess if Vaughn says too much, though, Gilkirk may figure out I'm still around.''

Kincaid chuckled. ''Even if he does, you'll be all right. You're old news now, I'm afraid. The last time I talked to Gilkirk I casually brought up your name just to see what he'd say. He wasn't terribly interested, frankly. You'd be a minor curiosity and that's it. Gilkirk won't push it. He owes you and he knows it. He's a good man. Pays his debts.''

''I like being old news.'' Adrian thought about that. ''But Sara...''

''Don't worry about Sara,'' Kincaid said softly. ''She's my niece. I know her.''

''She's a woman,'' Adrian countered. ''And she had a wild image of Wolf built up in her mind. What did you tell her about me, Kincaid?''

''Only bits and pieces. I was very concerned about you a year ago, my friend. I wasn't sure if this book was going to be the therapy you needed. I guess I had a few drinks with Sara one evening and talked. More than I should have, probably. She took the information and embroidered it a bit with her rather active imagination.''

"Did you really give her some idiotic story about the temperature, uh, dropping in a room when I walked in?" Adrian demanded.

Kincaid blinked. "I suppose I did. There are times when it's perfectly true."

Adrian winced. "No wonder I don't get many invitations to cocktail parties."

Lowell Kincaid howled with laughter. "Don't worry. The description only applies when you're working. If you're not getting party invitations, it's because people suspect you're not the party type. Not because they don't need an extra ice bucket."

"What about telling her I was a...a renegade?"

Kincaid looked surprised. "I never said that. I'm afraid she came to that conclusion on her own. I told her that I had trained a man who wound up with the code name of Wolf and that I was now worried about him. I guess she assumed—" He was about to say something else and stopped as Sara trotted back down the hall, tossing the crystal apple in her hands. "Ah, the apple."

"Yes, the apple." She pinned him with a mock-ferocious glance. "This is where the answer is, right Uncle Lowell? Clear as crystal?"

He nodded genially. "It's a microdot masquerading as one of the bubbles captured in the crystal. Pretty little apple, isn't it? I had one made especially for both you and Adrian. You each have half of the map. That's the wedding present, you see. Not the gold itself but the adventure of having a treasure map of your very own. And someday, someone in your family will be able to go after the gold. Maybe twenty years from now, when the politics and violence in that part of the world have changed.

Maybe the next generation will get it. Who knows? In the meantime you'll have the fantasy.''

''It was a brilliant gift idea,'' Sara said with a warm smile.

''I thought so. Just the thing for a woman with an over-active imagination. When did you figure out that the apple was the key?''

''While I was talking to Vaughn. I knew the answer wasn't in the manuscript.'' She slid a quick glance at Adrian. ''*Phantom* answers some other questions, but it doesn't tell where the gold is hidden. I just used that as an excuse to get Vaughn back here to the house. I figured out the role of the apple, though, when I put everything I knew together. The gold, you implied, was a wedding gift. Something to be shared. And you had given both Adrian and me an apple. It was a link between us. The key. Then there was your penchant for hiding things out in the open, the way you always say answers are crystal-clear. The apple itself has a gold stem and leaf and that was another clue. The gold on the apple was meant to be a connection to the gold in Southeast Asia, right? And you'd given us the basic clue when you told Adrian the legend. Last but not least, I knew you always like to cover your bases. You would have wanted the information available to both Adrian and me just in case something ever happened to you. It made sense that you had given us the answers. And you would have given them to us jointly. All we had to do was look around.''

''And you realized that the only thing I had given both of you was the apple.'' Kincaid nodded. ''Not bad, Sara. Not bad at all.''

''Games,'' Adrian heard himself mutter.

"Better get used to them if you're going to marry into the family," Lowell advised lightly.

"I've played enough for one day. If you both will excuse me, I'm going to go to bed. Lowell, you can have the couch. Your niece has the spare bedroom." Adrian got to his feet.

Sara's head came up quickly. "Adrian..."

He stood still, looking down at her. "What is it, Sara?"

"I...I just wondered about your trip this morning." She chewed on her lower lip, obviously searching for the right words. "I mean, Vaughn seemed to think you'd gone to Mexico."

"That's what I wanted him to think."

"But..."

"I bought the ticket. But the plane made a few stops between here and Mexico City. I got off in L.A."

"I see," she said quietly. "You planned it that way to make Vaughn think you'd left the country to go after the gold yourself."

"I thought my leaving would draw him out into the open," Adrian explained very patiently. "I figured he'd make his try at night, thinking you'd be alone. I'd planned to circle back and be waiting for him. I had it all worked out. But you rewrote the rules."

"He tricked me," she protested. "I had a phone call from Uncle Lowell. Or at least I thought it was from him. Vaughn made a tape from the answering-machine recordings in Lowell's cottage and mixed up the words into whole new sentences."

"I know," Adrian said. "Vaughn told me."

Sara eyed him curiously. "Did he?"

"He told me a great many things," Adrian said. "Good night, Lowell. Sara." He left the room.

Sara watched him go, the smile fading from her eyes and being replaced by a wistful yearning. Slowly she lowered the apple into her lap as she sat down beside her uncle.

"He has a nerve accusing us of playing games," she whispered. "What does he think he was doing today when he fed me that song and dance about going off to find a mysterious contact who might know where you were?"

Kincaid swirled the brandy in his glass. "He wasn't playing games. Adrian never plays games. He simply didn't want you to know the truth."

"What truth?"

"That he didn't have any magic man to contact. The only one around he could depend on to protect you was himself. He had to make Vaughn believe he had really left town and the only way to do that was to actually get on the plane. Mexico City was the logical choice because it has a reputation in the industry. Vaughn made all the assumptions he was supposed to make when he discovered that was Adrian's destination."

"But why didn't Adrian tell me?" She sighed.

"He wanted to keep you from finding out the truth about him. In the end there was no way he could accomplish that. Not and save your life, too."

"What did you mean about Adrian never playing games?"

"Just that." Lowell took a long swallow of brandy and gazed up at the beamed ceiling for a moment. "You and I, Sara, we have a capacity for stepping back emotionally from a situation we don't like. You did it all the time in the corporate world. You treated it as a game when it threatened to get too serious or intense. I saw you do it in the academic world and when you played at being an artist. It was a survival mechanism for you. It works very well. I should know. I've used it myself. I could frequently put my work into that kind of perspective when things got too grim. I would detach myself and instinctively try to see all the moves and countermoves as just part of a great big chess game."

"And Adrian couldn't do that?"

"No. For him it was very real. He gave everything he had to his work and it finally took its toll."

"Phantom." Sara stared down at the crystal-and-gold apple. "The real truth in the manuscript isn't the hint about the gold that you put in, is it? It's the part Adrian put into the story. The reality of what he faced."

"When he finally realized the job would eventually break him, he turned in his resignation. It wasn't accepted. They told him there was one last mission."

"And he went on it." Sara shuddered. "I think he just barely survived, Uncle Lowell."

"He did what he had to do. Adrian always does what has to be done. He was quite lethally serious about his work and that attitude made him the best there was in the industry."

"Better than you, Uncle Lowell?"

"Better than me. But the violence and the frustration of that last job were the end for him. When it was over he simply disappeared. He showed up on my doorstep three months later, calling himself Adrian Saville."

"That's not his real name?" Sara asked in astonishment.

Lowell Kincaid smiled. "It is now. I told you, Adrian doesn't play games. Everything is for real. He took another name and started a new life. He would have done anything to keep it real."

"Well, it is real," Sara protested. "Nothing's changed."

"Now you know the truth about him," her uncle pointed out quietly.

"But I don't feel any differently about him," she breathed. "How could he think——"

"Apparently you gave him quite a horror story about Wolf."

"That was all your fault. You're the one who told me the tale!"

"I was a little drunk that night as I recall. And I was genuinely worried about Adrian. I wasn't certain writing the book was going to work for him."

"That's no excuse. You told me things——"

"They were all true," Lowell Kincaid said, giving her a level glance. "But I will not assume responsibility for what you did to the facts with your imagination."

Sara grimaced. "When I found myself realizing this afternoon that my only chance for surviving lay with Adrian, I knew who he was. I also knew that whatever he had been, he was now the man I loved. You were right about him. He's the kind of man you can count on when the chips are down. Why did you sketch that wolf's head on the manuscript?"

"I was just doodling. It was natural that I'd be thinking about Wolf when I read the tale of Phantom."

"I suppose so. It put me on the wrong track altogether, though. I thought it was Wolf you had gone after." Sara fell silent for a moment. "I guess I'll go to bed, too."

"You do that," her uncle murmured blandly.

She shot him a half-humorous, half-rueful glance. "Going to throw your favorite niece to the wolf?"

"Wolves take care of their own." Lowell got up and

headed across the room to the brandy bottle. "Good night, Sara."

She went over to him and hugged him affectionately. "Good night, Uncle Lowell. I'm so glad you're safe."

"Not half as glad as I am that you're okay. Guess I owe Adrian for that."

Sara said nothing. She merely smiled and walked down the hall toward Adrian's bedroom with a deep sense of certainty.

Lying in bed, his arms folded behind his head, Adrian stared into the darkness and listened to the sound of Sara's footsteps. He waited for them to stop outside her bedroom door, and when she didn't even pause he tensed.

It would be best if she stayed in her own room, he told himself. Quickly, silently, he ran down a list of why she shouldn't open his door tonight. Too much had happened today and she was inclined to be emotional. She was also inclined to be impulsive. She needed time to sort out her feelings. He didn't want her coming to him without having had time to absorb the full implications of what she had learned about him today. She might be feeling sorry for him. She might have convinced herself he needed her and she was too compassionate to deny him comfort. He didn't want her pity.

So many reasons, he thought savagely. So many excellent reasons why he should send her back to her own room if she dared to open the door.

She turned the doorknob and stepped inside. Adrian looked at her as she stood silhouetted against the light and knew that he could never find the willpower to send her back. He needed her warmth too badly tonight. It had been so cold today.

"Asleep, Adrian?" she asked softly, shutting the door and coming forward into the shadowed room.

"No."

"You must be exhausted."

"Umm."

There was a rustle of clothing as she undressed. He saw the pale gleam of her bare shoulder and then the lighter area of her hip as she stepped out of the jeans.

"I'm a little tired myself," she admitted softly as she walked naked to the bed.

"Sara…" He tried to say the words that should be said, tried to explain why she shouldn't be there. But she was pulling back the comforter and slipping in beside him and the logical phrases disintegrated in his throat. The warmth and softness of her as she reached out to hold him were a temptation and that was far more difficult to resist than all the gold in Southeast Asia.

"Don't worry," she whispered huskily. "I won't be making any demands on you tonight. We've both had a hard day." She stroked her fingers through his hair, soothing the nape of his neck.

"Sara, it's not that, it's just… Oh, Sara, hold me. Put your arms around me and hold me."

She did, cradling him even as he pulled her tightly into the curve of his body. Adrian inhaled the familiar, enticing scent that was uniquely hers, knew the incredible comfort of her touch, felt the shape of her locked securely in his arms and relaxed for the first time since the day had dawned. Now he would be able to sleep.

Hours later he awoke to the light of dawn and the knowledge of what he must do. A part of him resisted the knowledge even though another side of him realized it was the only sure way. It was best to do things the sure way, he reminded himself. Careful, cautious, certain. He had spent the past year carefully, cautiously, certainly pulling himself back together. He knew about patience. He knew about being sure.

It would be tricky trying to teach those skills to the warm, frequently impulsive woman who lay curled so contentedly in his arms. But it was the only way. Above all else he wanted her to know exactly how she felt about him.

No games. Not even the kind played out of pity or compassion. Especially not those.

Adrian didn't move as he lay beside Sara. He was almost afraid of disturbing her because once she came awake he would have to explain his decision. He preferred to steal these last few minutes of closeness and warmth, make them last as long as possible. A wolf, he thought wryly, took whatever he could get.

Sara opened her eyes slowly, aware of Adrian's arm around her, his hand resting possessively on her breast. She lay still for a moment, letting herself realize fully just how good it felt to lie next to him. It felt right. A sense of deep certainty settled on her. It was unlike any emotion she had ever known. She was in love with Adrian Saville. She had known it since yesterday.

It didn't surprise her that love would arrive like this. Such an emotion, when it finally came into her life, was bound to happen in just this manner. For someone like her there was no other way. Quick, impulsive, but absolutely right. She knew real gold when she found it. Lazily she stretched, a serene, confident expression in her eyes as she turned to meet Adrian's steady gaze.

"Good morning," she murmured, touching her mouth lightly to his. "How did you sleep?"

He blinked, his features holding a trace of surprise as he thought about the question. "Solidly." His hand moved on her, following the curve of her thigh. "Thanks to you."

"Good." Feeling vastly pleased with herself, Sara stretched again, this time bringing her body quite deliberately against his. "I'm glad I'm useful for something. I felt like such a fool yesterday when I walked straight into Vaughn's hands."

Adrian didn't respond to the invitation of her languid stretch. In fact, she decided, he seemed almost tense. Not at all like a man who'd had a good night's sleep.

"It wasn't your fault," he told her. "Anyone would have been fooled by the recording. I've heard tapes scrambled from other tapes. They can sound very real. But you kept your head. You got him back here."

"I knew you would be coming back and that you could handle everything," she said.

"How long have you known?" He watched her with cool eyes.

Sara knew the coolness was deceptive. She also knew the real question he was asking. She knew him very well now, Sara decided. Reading *Phantom* had filled in many of the blanks a person normally encountered when learning about another human being. Her heart ached to replace what had originally occupied those blanks in his life.

"How long have I known that you were the man they used to call Wolf?" There was no point in not being totally honest. "Since yesterday for certain. When Vaughn told me that Wolf had been a legend at one time but had not made it back from his last assignment—"

"Because I'd cracked," Adrian put in bluntly.

Sara refused to acknowledge his interruption. "I began

to think about Phantom. About a man who had been to the brink and hung on instead of going completely over the edge. A man who had forced himself to survive when by all logic he should have been crushed. And then I thought about the way I feel safe around you...''

"Safe?"

She nodded. "I realized it that day at the Pike Place Market when you showed up just as Vaughn was about to coerce me into his car. And yesterday when I found myself trying to think of a way to deal with Vaughn. Something told me I only had to get him back here. When you arrived I knew I would be safe again. There were lots of other little clues, of course. Your concern with the security of this house. The way you move. That sketch of my uncle's. Even the way you play checkers. So intense and cool. Then there was your recent conversion to vegetarianism. Somehow that seemed symbolic. Something a carnivore might do if he were trying to put aside that aspect of his life. It all fit. Especially once I knew for certain that Vaughn wasn't Wolf.''

"You had such a terrible image of Wolf," Adrian began heavily.

"By the time I realized you had once been Wolf, I was ready to throw the image out the window. I knew the real you by then." She smiled dreamily, loving him with her eyes.

Adrian's face became remote. "I'm not so sure, Sara."

"Not so sure of what?"

"That you know the real me." He stilled the protest that rose instantly to her lips by putting his fingers against her mouth. "Listen to me, Sara. I rushed you into bed that first time. The second time was too intense, too emotional because you knew I was leaving and you weren't sure what was going to happen. We've been living in the eye of a storm ever since I walked into this house and found you in my study. There's been no chance for you to get to know me in a normal fashion.''

Alarm flickered into life. Sara watched him intently. ''Are you trying to tell me you aren't sure how you feel about me, after all?''

He shook his head once, a quick, violent negative movement. ''I know how I feel about you. I've been wanting you for months. You've been growing in my mind every day, taking shape, tantalizing me, until I knew I had to have you. But your uncle was right. There was something else I needed to do first.''

''Write *Phantom*.''

''That book was a final step in freeing myself, Sara.''

''I understand.'' And she did. Completely now.

''You were a goal, a treasure waiting for me after I had put the past behind me. I feel as though I've been getting to know you for months. Your uncle saw to that. But it didn't work that way for you. You've only known me a few days and that time has been too intense, too dangerous and too emotional.''

''Falling in love is bound to be emotional!'' she put in quickly.

''Are you saying you think you're in love with me?'' He searched her face.

''Yes.'' She spoke the single word with gentle assurance.

''Sara, you can't know that!''

''You told me once that you would like me to love you,'' she reminded him.

His fingers tightened on her. ''I want that very badly.

But you have to be certain. You have to be sure. No games, Sara.''

"I've never played games with you.''

"How about with your own mind? Honey, it's just too soon. You can't possibly know how you feel. Not yet. Hell, up until yesterday, you've been thinking of Wolf as some kind of psychotic killer. Now you've learned that Wolf and I are one and the same. You can't tell me you've managed to adjust to that kind of news overnight!''

"I get the feeling I can't tell you much of anything,'' she tossed back. "You're not ready to listen to me. You've already decided the way things have to be, haven't you?'' The alarm was coiling tightly in her as she began to see where his words were leading.

"Sara, I want you to have time to get to know me,'' he told her urgently. "This time around we'll do it right.''

"I don't understand!'' But she did and the realization panicked her.

Adrian continued forcefully, his certainty clear in every word. "Yes, you do, honey. We're going to do it right. I want you to have a chance to make absolutely certain of your feelings. The next time you tell me you love me I want you to have had plenty of opportunity to think through just what you're saying.''

Sara pulled free of him, sitting up with the sheet held to her breast. Her hair swung in a soft tangle around her shoulders as she stared at him. "Are you sending me away?'' Her voice sounded odd. She was clinging to more than the sheet. She was hanging on to her control with both hands.

Slowly Adrian sat up beside her, his eyes almost colorless. He was committed to finishing what he had started,

Sara realized. She would not be able to reason with him this morning.

"We're going to start a normal relationship," he said.

"What's normal? Adrian, you of all people should know by now that life is short and highly uncertain. We've found something wonderful together. Why should we waste time? Please don't do this." The plea was all wrong, she thought. She was letting her emotions rule her tongue. Adrian wouldn't trust her to know her own feelings if she did that. He didn't trust emotions.

"I'm not sending you to Outer Mongolia," he said.

"No? Then where are you sending me?"

"I think it would be best if you went back to San Diego."

"San Diego! But I don't even have a job there!"

"You've got your apartment, don't you? It's still your home."

She groped for an argument. "What about you? Are you just going to sit around here until you figure I've had enough time to know my own mind? Adrian, that doesn't make any sense. I'm an adult. I already know how I feel."

"I'm going to come and see you. Call you. Sara, I'm going to court you, don't you understand? I'm going to give you plenty of time—"

"How much?" she challenged.

He looked blank. "How much what?"

"How much time, damn it!"

"I don't know." He frowned. "However long it takes, I suppose."

"That's not fair, Adrian. If you're going to sentence me to exile, you have to at least put a time limit on it. Give me a date. One week? One year? I want a date."

"Sara, you're getting hysterical."

The worst part was that she knew he was right. She was losing her self-control. It was the shock, Sara decided. The shock of waking up in love and being told by Adrian that he wasn't ready for her love. Sara gulped air, swallowing sobs of anger and panic. The more emotional she became, the less Adrian would trust her to know what she really wanted. For the sake of their future, she had to get hold of herself.

"Yes," she whispered, sliding off the edge of the bed. She looked around a little frantically for something to wear and finally saw her shirt on the floor where she had left it last night. "Yes, you're quite right. I'm getting emotional." Her fingers fumbled with the buttons but she managed to get the shirt on. Then she picked up her jeans with hands that still trembled. Adrian never took his eyes off of her.

"Sara, honey, listen to me."

She shook her head. "No, no, I'm all right. I understand. You don't fully trust intense emotions because you learned once that they can take you to the edge of the disaster. I should have realized that after reading *Phantom*. That was the lesson you learned when you went through with that last mission and then disappeared, wasn't it? Your emotional response to your work nearly got you killed. You kept yourself so tightly leashed and under such control for so long that in the end you almost came apart when the explosion occurred. That's why you talk in terms of appreciating life's pleasures. Anything stronger than pleasure might be dangerous."

Adrian got slowly to his feet, completely unconcerned with his nakedness. "I just want you to be sure of how you feel," he repeated stubbornly.

She got her jeans zipped and lifted her head to meet

his eyes. "You want to be sure of everything. Sure of the security of your house, sure of me, sure of your own self-control. Well, go ahead and make sure, Adrian. Being absolutely sure of things seems to be one of the few *pleasures* you get out of life. Who am I to deny you?"

Whirling, Sara fled from the room.

Chapter Eleven

Adrian's version of a courtship, Sara decided a month later, was going to drive her slowly insane.

Over and over again she told herself that he was the one who needed the time. Time to be sure of her. She would give him that. After all, she loved him; she would give him anything he asked. But how long would the farce continue, she wondered dismally.

"Farce" was hardly the most respectful term for Adrian's courtship, but it was the one that came to Sara's mind most often during the torturous, contrived, carefully choreographed weekends. True to his word Adrian flew down to San Diego every Friday evening. He spent Saturday and Sunday with her and then flew home to his island.

Sara's hopes for the first weekend were dashed when he checked into a motel near her apartment and continued to retreat to it every evening of his stay. The other weekends were no different. He took her to dinner, shows, the zoo and the beach. But he never took her to bed.

In fact, he rarely touched her with any intimacy at all. That was the part that was beginning to drive her out of her mind, Sara realized. She was left with a feeling of genuine panic every Sunday evening when she saw him off at the airport. Perhaps he wasn't capable of making the final step of total commitment. She knew he wanted her, knew he took pleasure in her company but he had convinced himself that she didn't understand her own feelings.

What she really feared, Sara decided, was that he didn't understand the depths of his own feelings for her. He was afraid to surrender completely to the force of his emotions.

They would be fierce and intense, the emotions of a strong man who had much to give once he had accepted the power of his own nature. But he had learned the hard way that there was a risk in losing some of his self-control. She yearned to set him completely free, to urge him to take a risk both on her and on himself but there was no way to break through the controlled facade. On Monday morning after the fourth weekend Sara acknowledged that Adrian had established the rules and he was going to force her to play by them.

Bad analogy, she told herself wryly as she fixed coffee with her imported Italian espresso machine. Adrian didn't like anything that smacked of game playing. She stared morosely out at the palm tree in front of her kitchen window and thought of the carefully restrained kiss she had received at the airport the previous evening.

Uneasily she tried to brush aside the worry that perhaps Adrian would never be able to relax and let himself trust both of them completely.

He did love her, she told herself with some violence. He hadn't said the words but that was all right. She knew him, understood him. She had complete confidence in his love. Her only fear was that he would never have the same confidence.

Somehow he had to learn that the iron control he held over himself wasn't necessary any longer. He was a whole human being now. He'd healed himself. He must learn to have faith in the health of his emotions and in those of the woman who loved him. He could live safely now without a perfect cover.

And she did love him, Sara knew. With every fiber of her being. One month of the stilted courtship hadn't changed that. Nothing on earth could change it. She had never been so certain of anything in her life.

She was at home that evening when he called. She was always at home these days. Not because she didn't have friends or invitations but because she was terrified that Adrian might phone and find her out. She wanted nothing to upset him or alarm him. She wanted him to know that she was simply waiting for him.

The conversation followed by its now predictable path.

"How was the flight back to Seattle?" she asked politely.

"Fine." He hesitated. "Have you eaten?"

"Oh, yes. I fixed myself a salad." Sara searched mentally for something to add to the careful conversation. "And I had a glass of wine."

"I went down to the tavern and had a beer."

At least you got to get out of the house, Sara thought irritably. *I'm forced to sit here from five o'clock on because I can't be sure when you'll call. And I'm terrified you'd use the evidence of my not being at home as an indication that you were right not to trust me.* "Sounds good," she said brightly. "How's the plotting going on the new book?"

"Okay. I'm trying to figure out how to untwist some things in chapter four without giving away too much information. This book is going to be a lot easier to write, though, than *Phantom* was."

Not surprising, Sara thought. This second book wouldn't be nearly so autobiographical. *Phantom* had been a form of catharsis. The next book would truly be fiction. She didn't have any doubt that it would be as good in its own way as its predecessor, however. The bottom line was that Adrian really could write. "Speaking of giving away information, Adrian," Sara heard herself begin quite firmly.

He paused before inquiring cautiously, "Yes?"

She floundered. "Well, I was wondering. I mean, it's been a month now and I was just thinking that you might have come to some, er, decision."

"About what?"

Sara very nearly lost her temper. "About us!"

"Oh. You still want a date when everything's going to be settled, don't you?"

"Adrian," she tried reasonably, "this is getting us nowhere. I've tried to be patient—"

"You don't know much about patience, honey."

"Don't be condescending. Just because people like you know all about patience, doesn't meant the rest of us—"

"What do you mean, people like me?"

Sara wanted to cry for having used all the wrong words. The forbidding cold was back in his voice. "I just meant that you seem to have developed a great deal of patience during your life. I, uh, I haven't been quite that fortunate, Adrian, I'm trying to give you the time you need, but—"

"I'm not the one who needs the time," he interrupted quietly.

"Well, I sure as hell don't need it! I know what I want. I'm in love with you, and this past month has been awful. I feel like I've been in exile. You don't touch me, you're so polite I could spit, and you won't tell me how long it's going to go on. There are times when I really begin to wonder if you—'' She halted the flow of words abruptly.

True to form, Adrian refused to be left hanging. ''You wonder if I what?''

''Nothing,'' she mumbled.

''Sara, tell me what you were about to say.''

She sighed. ''I wonder if you will ever really trust yourself or me enough to love me.'' There. It was said. She hadn't dared anything that intimate before and she wasn't at all certain how he would react. She had been assuming a great deal, Sara thought bleakly.

Silence on the other end of the line greeted her statement. Then Adrian's voice came with rock-hard certainty.

''I love you, Sara.''

She caught her breath, her fingers clutching the receiver. ''You do?''

''You've been a part of me for months. I can't imagine life without you.''

The simple words were devastating to her. ''You never said anything quite that explicit before,'' she finally got out rather weakly.

''I don't think I've thought it out quite that explicitly until now,'' he admitted slowly. ''You've just been there, a part of me.''

She closed her eyes in relief. It was finally over. It must be over. ''Oh, Adrian, Adrian, thank you. I love you so much and I've been going crazy down here waiting for you to be sure.''

''I've been sure all along.'' He sounded vaguely surprised. ''It's you who needed the time.''

Sara's eyes narrowed as she picked up the first inkling that her waiting might not be ended after all. ''I don't need any more time, Adrian. Please. I've been very patient. I could wait forever if there was a real need, but there isn't. There's no need for us to be apart.''

His voice hardened. ''I want you to have more time.''

She heard the finality in his words and fury mingled with despair. ''You think I'm playing a game with you.''

''No, Sara, it's not that. I just—''

She didn't let him finish. ''Adrian Saville, you don't know what real game playing is!'' Quite precisely and quite definitely, Sara hung up the phone. Then she walked to the hall closet and found her shoulder bag. There was a chic, cheerful little tavern down the street and around the corner. If Adrian could have a beer in the evenings, so could she. Come to think of it, she needed it a lot more than he did tonight.

The phone rang insistently behind her but Sara ignored it. She walked to the door, opened it as the phone continued to ring, and then she stepped outside. It was a wonderful, balmy Southern California evening. The scent of the sea hovered in the air and the row of palm trees lining her street rustled lazily in the evening breeze. Sara walked briskly down the sidewalk, wondering what the trees looked like in Southeast Asia.

The tavern was only half full, with a crowd of people in their late twenties and early thirties. The women, with their cleverly casual hairstyles, their silk shirts and jeans, chatted vivaciously with men in equally expensive hairstyles and designer jeans. Several heads nodded familiarly as Sara took a lone seat in the shadows at the back of the room. She ordered an imported beer and sipped it thoughtfully when it arrived.

The trees in Southeast Asia. Images of menacing jungles and treacherous swamps came to mind. Not really her kind of place. Adrian had learned caution the hard way in such places around the world. Caution and patience.

But there was a time and place for caution and patience. Surely they shouldn't be allowed to stand in the way of a loving commitment. Love was so rare and so valuable it was a shame to make it wait on caution and patience. Sara took another taste of the expensive import and thought about Adrian's reluctance to release himself completely from the reins of his self-control.

He had let those reins slip on a couple of occasions, she reminded herself. The first time he had made love to her, for example. The second time as well. Of course, on those occasions he had been assuming that he could keep his past hidden from her. He'd had no need to fear her reactions to learning his full identity because he'd assumed she never would know of it.

But even that last night at his home he had been unable to send her away although he had already made up his mind to give her time. He had needed her that night, not in a sexual way, but in the way a man sometimes needs comfort from a woman. He'd let her comfort him to some extent, she reminded herself on a note of hope. He'd held her very tightly that night, even in his sleep. She'd been aware of the tension gradually leaving him. She seriously doubted that Adrian had ever risked taking much comfort from others.

Sara turned the matter over in her mind. He loved her and she loved him. And as she had told him, life could be short and precarious. Love was too important to risk losing because of too much caution and patience. She needed to find a way to make Adrian understand that. She needed to yank him out of his cautious, patient, controlled world.

An hour later she walked home alone, opened the door and saw the gleam of the crystal apple as it sat reflecting the light of her desk lamp. She stared at it for a long moment, thinking of Vaughn's plans to retrieve the gold. Then, very slowly and very thoughtfully, she closed her door.

The phone rang just as she was about to get into bed an hour later.

"Hello, Adrian."

"Have you calmed down?"

"I've calmed down."

"I love you," he said quietly.

"I know. I love you."

"Just give it a little more time, sweetheart," he urged. "The waiting isn't easy for me, either."

"I think it's easier for you than it is for me," she told him.

"No," he said in a raw tone. "It isn't. Good night, Sara. Sleep well."

"Good night, Adrian."

She hung up the phone and trailed slowly out into the living room. Once more her eyes fell on the crystal apple. There must be a way to break the impasse. The apple held the key to the gold. Perhaps it held the key to unlocking Adrian's emotions.

Again she wondered what the trees looked like in Southeast Asia.

ADRIAN ANSWERED his phone on Friday morning with a sense of anticipation that he couldn't deny. Very few people in the world had his unlisted number. Sara was one of those people.

"Hello?"

"She's gone crazy, Adrian. I warned you this would happen. Don't say I didn't warn you!" Lowell Kincaid was one of the few other people who had the number.

"You didn't warn me," Adrian said patiently. Determinedly he squelched his disappointment that the caller wasn't Sara. After all, he would be seeing her this evening. He could wait. "Calm down and tell me what you're talking about, Lowell."

"You think it's a joke, but I can tell you from past experience, it isn't."

"Okay, it's not a joke. Now tell me what it is that isn't a joke."

Kincaid spoke grimly. "She's applied for a passport."

Adrian paused, absorbing that. "A passport?"

"And she called me up to see what I knew about getting in and out of Cambodia."

"That is a joke, right? You and she both have a very strange sense of humor, Kincaid. I've told you that on previous occasions." But Adrian's hand was like a vise on the telephone receiver.

"Believe me, I'm not finding this funny. Applying for a passport isn't the end of it, either."

Adrian sucked in his breath. "All right. Let me have it."

"She asked me for a second copy of your half of the map and she's put an ad in the L.A. *Times*. Want to hear it?"

"No. But I think I'd better."

"Listen to this." There was a rustle of newspaper on the other end of the line and then Lowell began to read: "'Danger, adventure, financial reward for the right person. Applicant must be willing to travel out of the country, able to take care of himself and willing to follow employer's orders. Personal interviews only, no phone. Three o'clock on Friday.' That's today, Adrian.''

''I know it's today.''

''She goes on to name the hotel down in San Diego where she'll be interviewing applicants. You know as well as I do that every California bozo who's into fantasy violence is likely to show up. Adrian, this is all your fault. I'm holding you personally responsible.''

''My fault? You're the one who gave her half a map and a legend, for pete's sake!''

''And then I gave her and the map to you, damn it! I thought you would now how to take care of both!'' Lowell hung up the phone with a crashing noise that made his listener's ear hurt.

Adrian stood silently staring at the receiver for a very long moment. The lady was playing games again. In her usual impulsive, off-the-wall style she was issuing a full-blown challenge.

She appeared to have absolutely no fear of him. Sara must know that he would be furious when he found out what she had planned. Everything she had done was quite deliberate, of course. She'd notified her uncle just to make certain Adrian would find out immediately what was happening.

A challenge, Adrian thought as he yanked his canvas overnight bag down from the closet shelf. She had one hell of a nerve. He recalled the way he had walked into his home that first night and found her casually searching his study. She'd had no fear of him then, not after she'd found the apple. And she obviously had no fear of him now.

But she had shuddered and gone cold whenever she had

mentioned the man called Wolf. And she knew he had been Wolf.

He had wanted to give her plenty of time to accept him completely once she'd learned the whole truth. He'd wanted to be certain she could handle the idea of what he had once been. He loved her. It would tear him apart if deep down she was unable to accept him and his past. A few more weeks or months and he would have been more certain she knew what she was doing.

But Sara had no patience for strategy. She had applied for a passport and put an ad in the papers. She was going to force his hand.

Adrian zipped the bag closed, checked for his keys and set the house alarms. It would take him several hours to get to San Diego and he didn't want to waste any time. There was a midmorning flight that he just might make if he moved quickly.

He was astonished to find himself suddenly very impatient.

THE LINE BEGAN FORMING outside the hotel room at two o'clock. Sara watched in growing trepidation from the lobby, trying not to be obvious. If any of the wildly varied assortment of men in the line realized that the potential employer was the lady in jeans who was hanging around the front desk, she would be mobbed.

She had never dreamed so many people would show up in response to that ad. What really alarmed her was that Adrian was not among the thirty-plus males lounging in line. Nervously Sara wiped her hands on her denim pants. In a few minutes she was going to have to start dealing with that motley crew. Several of them looked rather tough. One or two appeared to be ex-bikers. A few were probably ex-military and some appeared merely curious. None of them was an ex-wolf.

Reaching for a pad of hotel paper and a pen Sara tried to jot down a few interview-type questions. What did one ask a mercenary? Especially when one had absolutely no intention of hiring him? She needed a question or two that would definitely exclude everyone in that line. Desperately she searched her brain for something that would make each of the waiting men ineligible.

At five minutes to three Sara steeled herself for the task ahead. Adrian was nowhere in sight. She was going to have to start the interviews or risk a very discontented line of applicants. The hotel management would not thank her for starting a riot.

Chin high, she took hold of her jangled nerves and swept down the line of rather scrungy-looking males. Without glancing at any of them she opened the hotel-room door and said over her shoulder, "I'll see the first man in line now."

Five seconds later she found herself alone in the room with a swaggering young man who was wearing a much-abused military fatigue shirt. He took one look at her and grinned arrogantly.

"You the lady who wants to hire me?"

"I'm the lady who is looking for the right man," Sara said coolly. "Now, if you don't mind, I'm going to ask you a few pertinent questions."

"Go right ahead, ma'am," he retorted with mock courtesy. "I'm at your service."

The swaggering young man's grin was gone when he stomped out of the room five minutes later. He was grumbling fiercely under his breath. Sara beckoned for the next applicant.

She had sent fifteen of the men packing when there was a loud commotion in the hallway outside the room. Angry voices rose in protest and a second later the door was shoved violently open. Sara looked up from interviewing candidate number sixteen and saw Adrian filling the doorway. Anger, a seething impatience and a vast masculine annoyance burned in his eyes when he looked at her.

But the room didn't go cold.

Adrian pinned her for an instant, then his gaze flicked to candidate number sixteen, a middle-aged ex-military type running to fat.

"Out."

The ex-military type examined the newcomer for a few taut seconds, then shrugged and got to his feet. "I was just leaving. Seems I don't fit the profile of the successful applicant," he drawled. He used the words Sara had just spoken a second before the door had been flung open. He sauntered past Adrian, a flicker of amusement in his expression. "A very interesting lady. Good luck, buddy. I think you're going to have your hands full."

Adrian ignored him and turned to confront the remaining candidates. "Everyone can go home. Interview time is over. The lady has already hired a man. Me."

"Now wait just a damn minute, pal...."

Adrian glanced over his shoulder at Sara. "Tell them, Sara."

She got to her feet and realized her knees were slightly shaky. She had seen Adrian in a lot of different moods, including the one that could chill a room. She had never seen him thoroughly annoyed. She summoned a polite smile as she nodded at the men in the hall.

"I'm afraid he's right. Mr. Saville is the perfect candidate. Thank you all for showing up today."

There were a few growls of protest but the cluster of men dissolved. A moment later the hall was empty and Sara was left to face Adrian alone.

He leaned back against the doorjamb, his arms folded across his chest. "What the hell kind of game do you think you're playing, Sara Frazer?"

She sighed and sat down again. It was easier than standing. "I didn't know so many people would actually answer an ad like that."

"This is California, remember? Put an ad like that in the paper and you're bound to lure a lot of nuts out into the open." He came away from the wall and stalked over to the desk, flattening his palms on its surface as he leaned down to glare at her. "Did you think I'd let you get away with a stunt like this?"

She smiled tremulously. "No."

He narrowed his eyes. "I'd have been here earlier but the flight was delayed. I've been amusing myself for the past several hours thinking of what I was going to do to you when I finally did get to San Diego."

"I can imagine."

"I ought to take a belt to your sweet backside."

"Sounds kinky."

"Damn it, Sara, what the devil do you think you're doing?" He straightened away from the desk and paced to the window. "I'm furious with you."

"Yes. I'm sorry about that part, but I—"

"Sorry about it!" He whipped around to stare at her. "Sorry about it!"

"I couldn't think of any other way to force you into realizing that this stupid courtship has to end. It's driving me crazy, Adrian." She sprang to her feet to confront him.

"We're wasting time and love, and everyone knows those are commodities that are too valuable to waste."

"What makes you think you've achieved anything other than annoying the hell out of me?"

She faced him determinedly. "There's only one way you can keep me from going to Southeast Asia."

"Really?" he asked with soft menace. "And what's that?"

"You're going to have to marry me. If you don't, I'll be on my way as soon as my passport arrives."

He looked dumbfounded. "Marry you!"

"This is blackmail, Adrian. Pure and simple. I'm giving you an ultimatum. Marry me or I'll go off on my own in search of that gold."

Adrian continued to stare at her as if she'd taken leave of her senses. "You're serious, aren't you?"

"I'm serious. This isn't a game, Adrian. I don't play games with the really important things in life."

"And I'm one of those things?"

"Adrian, you are the most important thing in my life," she said with simple honesty.

There was a moment of profound tension as he regarded her with an unwavering gaze. Sara had the impression he was seeking the proper words to express his feelings. She waited in an agony of suspense.

"Sara," he finally said carefully, "I'm very angry. I can't ever remember being quite this angry."

"I know," she whispered. "And I regret that, but—"

"But you're not afraid of me, are you?" he finished.

"Are you kidding? I've crossed all my fingers and toes." Her mouth curved in wry humor.

"But you're not terrified, are you?" he pressed.

"Not the way you mean, Adrian. The room hasn't gone

cold. The only time it ever did was the time you rescued me from Vaughn. And I knew at the time that the chill was my protection, not something I had to fear. I love you and you love me. How could I be truly terrified of you?"

He ran a hand through his hair and turned back to the window. "I've been scared to death," Adrian admitted starkly.

"Of loving me?"

He shook his head. "Of worrying that you couldn't really love me knowing who I am."

Sara stepped around the desk and walked slowly toward him. "I love you, Adrian. I love you so much that I'll do whatever I have to do to stay with you. I know all the important things about you. I read *Phantom,* remember? I told you after I read it that I'd fallen in love with the hero."

"And I told you that I'd rather you fell in love with me."

"You thought it would be pleasant." She nodded.

"I think," Adrian said huskily as he turned toward her, "that it would be more than pleasant. I think it's absolutely essential."

"Oh, Adrian," she breathed, throwing herself into his arms. "I love you so much. Don't send me away again. I couldn't bear it." She buried her face against his shirt, clinging to him.

"You do tend to dramatize, don't you? I never sent you away. This past month was supposed to be a courtship."

"It was a test and I hate tests. I trust you, Adrian. All I want is for you to trust me."

"Or else you'll blackmail me into marriage?"

Her nails bit into the muscled back beneath his shirt.

"I've told you, I'll do whatever I have to do in order to keep you."

He stroked her hair, tangling his fingers possessively in the golden-brown strands. "I believe you, honey. After this fiasco today, how could I not believe you? I have to admit you're not exactly looking for a way out of our relationship. But I thought I had to offer you that escape if you wanted it."

"So that you could be sure of me. Well, I'm not looking for an escape, Adrian Saville."

"I love you, Sara."

She lifted her head, eyes shimmering with emotion. "I love you."

He smiled and wrapped her close. "Can we go home now?" Adrian asked.

"Yes."

"We can stop in Vegas on the way back to Washington," he went on thoughtfully.

"You really are going to marry me?"

"I thought I didn't have a choice."

"You don't," she assured him.

Adrian thought about being wanted so badly by Sara that she'd do anything to keep him. It was a novel idea. He discovered he liked it. He was suddenly very sure she wasn't playing games.

The phone was ringing in Sara's apartment when they walked in the door a few minutes later. Adrian reached for it.

"It'll be your uncle," he explained as Sara glanced at him in surprise. Then he spoke into the receiver. "Hello, Lowell. You can stop panicking."

"I knew you'd handle things once you got there,"

Lowell said in tones of great satisfaction. "What happens now?"

"We're going to get married in Vegas on the way up to Washington."

"The hell you are! Whose idea was that?"

"Sara is blackmailing me into it," Adrian explained, watching her as he talked.

"Blackmail, hmm? I always knew the two of you had a lot in common. You both know what's important in life and you'll both do whatever it takes to get the job done. You just approach things in a slightly different style, that's all."

"Umm."

"But that doesn't mean I'm going to let you two get away with a Las Vegas wedding. I've been waiting for years for Sara to find the right man. I demand a real wedding. With me there." Lowell paused and then said in tones of satisfaction. "I won't have to worry about shopping, will I? I've already given you your gift. That reminds me, I'll be expecting a thank-you note." Lowell Kincaid hung up the phone.

Adrian stood looking at Sara. "Your uncle wants a thank-you note."

"Don't worry, I'll write one."

"He's also demanding what he calls a real wedding. He doesn't approve of the Vegas idea."

Sara grinned. "He just wants an excuse to wear one of those dumb aloha shirts."

"Lowell always did like parties."

Sara smiled. "Well, much as I hate to admit it, we may have to accommodate him. I'm extremely grateful to him. But not for the map."

"I know what you mean. I feel the same way." Adrian

moved, sweeping her up into his arms. "You're the real treasure. I will take very good care of you, my sweet Sara."

She nestled trustingly against him. "I know. And I will take very, very good care of you."

It was a long time later that Adrian stirred in the depths of the tangled sheets of Sara's bed and remembered the question he had wanted to ask earlier. He drew a hand playfully down her spine until he arrived at her derriere.

"Sara?"

"Umm?" She was rapidly adopting his characteristic response.

"What did you tell all those candidates before I arrived at the hotel? How did you get rid of them?"

"I told them that there was one important requirement the successful candidate had to meet."

"What requirement?"

"The successful applicant had to be a vegetarian."

There were a few seconds of startled silence. Sara turned over onto her back in time to see the laughter dawn in Adrian's eyes. A moment later it consumed him completely and she was left to marvel at the first full-throated laugh she had ever heard from him.

She decided that a laughing wolf was a very enthralling sight. She would make certain Adrian laughed a lot more in the years ahead.

THE WEDDING RECEPTION, held on the ocean-front terrace of the home of Sara's parents, was a loud and exuberant success. Mr. and Mrs. Frazer were pleased with their new son-in-law. For them, Adrian's cover was still nicely intact. They thought he would have a steadying influence on their beloved but often unpredictable daughter. They had several qualms about allowing Lowell Kincaid to act as best man, however.

"I knew he'd wear something ridiculous," Mrs. Frazer said with a resigned groan as she stood with her daughter near the punch bowl. "Just look at him in that silly shirt. Everyone else is in formal wear! I should have put my foot down right at the beginning and made it clear he would not be allowed to participate in this wedding unless he was willing to conform!"

"You wouldn't have had much to say about it, Mom." Sara laughed at her attractive, worried mother. "The best man was the groom's choice, not yours."

"It's not that I don't love my brother dearly, it's just that he's so...so..." Mrs. Frazer waved her hand helplessly.

"Have some more punch, Mother." Sara leaned over to pick up a fresh glass of the frothy red concoction.

"And that's another thing," her mother went on a little grimly. "Does this punch taste funny to you?"

"Spiked to the hilt, I'm afraid," Sara admitted cheerfully. She was watching her new husband as he stood talking to her father. The two men appeared to be involved in a very serious discussion.

"I knew it," Mrs. Frazer exclaimed. "I thought I saw Lowell fooling around near the punch bowl an hour ago! The champagne wasn't enough for him, I suppose!"

"Excuse me, Mom, I think I'd better go rescue Adrian before Dad sells him on the idea of investing all his royalties in long-term certificates of deposit."

"Adrian is a very stable, very intelligent man, dear. I'm sure he'll want to hear your father's advice. He's a man who will want to plan for the future."

"Adrian has me to help him plan his future." Sara

swept up another glass of punch for herself and went off to join her husband.

The look in Adrian's eyes as she went to stand beside him warmed her from head to toe. He loved her. Above all else, he loved her. His was a total commitment. Just as hers was to him.

"Your father's been telling me about the advantages of long-term investments," Adrian said, putting his arm around his wife's waist.

"I'll just bet he has." Sara smiled at her father.

"I'll go over some more details with you later, Adrian. So glad Sara found herself a man who has his feet on the ground," Frazer said easily. He nodded in a friendly fashion, leaned down to kiss his daughter and went off to have some more of the heavily spiked punch.

"Feet on the ground, hmm?" Sara tipped her head up so that Adrian could brush his mouth against hers.

"That's not where they're going to be in a couple of hours," he warned.

"No?"

"Nope. Unless we decide to try something really unusual in the way of wedding nights, I plan to spend the evening horizontally."

"Adrian, I must tell you that lately you've begun to develop an odd sense of humor."

"Any sense of humor is better than none," Lowell Kincaid declared jovially as he sauntered up to join them. He was holding a glass of champagne in one hand and a glass of punch in the other. "Nice party, Sara. Your mother can throw a decent bash when she sets her mind to it." He took a sip out of each glass.

"Glad you're enjoying yourself, Uncle Lowell."

"I always enjoy parties. Say, I'm glad I finally caught

the two of you alone. I've been wanting to talk to you all day.''

Adrian looked at him warily. ''Is that right?''

''Yeah, you know, I've been thinking.''

''I'm getting nervous already.''

Lowell shook his head. ''No, no, this is serious. I've been giving some thought to Vaughn's little plan for getting the gold out through Cambodia. After Sara put that ad in the paper—''

''Don't remind me of that ad,'' Adrian warned.

''I'm telling you, Adrian, it's given me pause. There just might be a way to do it.'' Lowell leaned forward conspiratorially. ''If we put together the right team—and you know we've got some good contacts—we could slip in and out of the country without anyone even knowing we were there.''

''Uncle Lowell!'' Sara's eyes widened excitedly. ''Do you really think so?''

''Well, it would be risky, of course. But it just might be feasible.''

Adrian's gaze narrowed. ''The only reason it sounds feasible to you, Kincaid, is because you've been drinking too much of that damn punch. Forget it.''

Sara turned to him eagerly. ''But, Adrian, just think. What an adventure it would be!''

''I said forget it and I meant it.'' Adrian lifted his champagne glass and swallowed deeply.

''But, Adrian, darling…''

''Don't 'Adrian, darling' me. I said no. That's the end of it.''

Lowell chuckled. ''How about this. Your first marital quarrel.''

''And you started it,'' Adrian shot back.

"You know what I think?" Sara demanded, glaring up at her husband. "I think Adrian is taking his new sense of husbandly duties a little too seriously. He's starting to lay down the law and we haven't even left the reception."

"Start as you mean to go on," Adrian quoted blandly. "And speaking of going on, I think it's time we said good-bye to all these nice folks. We've got a wedding night waiting for us. Are you ready to leave, Mrs. Saville?"

"Yes, Adrian."

"I've never seen her quite so amenable," Lowell marveled.

Adrian grinned suddenly. "It won't last. I intend to take advantage of it while I can. Let's go, honey."

Sara caught her uncle's eye as she obediently turned to leave on her husband's arm. Kincaid winked. Sara laughed silently back at him. The gold could wait for a while. After all, legends lasted a long time.

Lowell Kincaid's sister drifted up to stand beside him. She smiled maternally after her daughter. "Well, Lowell, in spite of that idiotic shirt you're wearing, I have to admit that this time you really came through. I was beginning to wonder if my daughter was ever going to fall in love. But you seem to have found just the right man for her."

Kincaid raised one of the glasses he was holding and grinned. "The best. A legend in his own time."

MEN at WORK

All work and no play?
Not these men!

July 1998
MACKENZIE'S LADY by Dallas Schulze

Undercover agent Mackenzie Donahue's
lazy smile and deep blue eyes were his best
weapons. But after rescuing—and kissing!—
damsel in distress Holly Reynolds, how could
he betray her by spying on her brother?

August 1998
MISS LIZ'S PASSION by Sherryl Woods

Todd Lewis could put up a building with ease,
but quailed at the sight of a classroom! Still,
Liz Gentry, his son's teacher, was no battle-ax,
and soon Todd started planning some
extracurricular activities of his own....

September 1998
A CLASSIC ENCOUNTER
by Emilie Richards

Doctor Chris Matthews was intelligent, sexy
and *very* good with his hands—which made
him all the more dangerous to single mom
Lizette St. Hilaire. So how long could she
resist Chris's special brand of TLC?

Available at your favorite retail outlet!

MEN AT WORK™

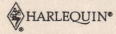 

Look us up on-line at: http://www.romance.net   PMAW2

Take 2 bestselling love stories FREE

Plus get a FREE surprise gift!

Special Limited-Time Offer

Mail to Harlequin Reader Service®

3010 Walden Avenue
P.O. Box 1867
Buffalo, N.Y. 14240-1867

YES! Please send me 2 free Harlequin Superromance® novels and my free surprise gift. Then send me 4 brand-new novels every month, which I will receive before they appear in bookstores. Bill me at the low price of $3.57 each plus 25¢ delivery and applicable sales tax, if any.* That's the complete price, and a saving of over 10% off the cover prices—quite a bargain! I understand that accepting the books and gift places me under no obligation ever to buy any books. I can always return a shipment and cancel at any time. Even if I never buy another book from Harlequin, the 2 free books and the surprise gift are mine to keep forever.

134 HEN CH7C

Name	(PLEASE PRINT)	
Address		Apt. No.
City	State	Zip

This offer is limited to one order per household and not valid to present Harlequin Superromance® subscribers. *Terms and prices are subject to change without notice. Sales tax applicable in N.Y.

USUP-98

Glamorous, hot, seductive...

THE AUSTRALIANS

Stories of romance Australian-style guaranteed to
fulfill that sense of adventure!

September 1998, look for
Playboy Lover
by **Lindsay Armstrong**

When Rory and Dominique met at a party the attraction was
magnetic, but all Dominique's instincts told her to resist him.
Not easy as they'd be working together in the steamy tropics
of Australia's Gold Coast. When they were thrown together in
a wild and reckless experience, obsessive passion flared—but
had she found her Mr. Right, or had she fallen for yet another
playboy?

*The Wonder from Down Under: where spirited women win
the hearts of Australia's most independent men!*

Available September 1998 at your favorite retail outlet.

HARLEQUIN®
Makes any time special ™

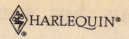

Not The Same Old Story!

 Exciting, glamorous romance stories that take readers around the world.

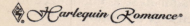 Sparkling, fresh and tender love stories that bring you pure romance.

 Bold and adventurous— Temptation is strong women, bad boys, great sex!

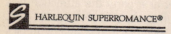 Provocative and realistic stories that celebrate life and love.

 Contemporary fairy tales—where anything is possible and where dreams come true.

 Heart-stopping, suspenseful adventures that combine the best of romance and mystery.

 Humorous and romantic stories that capture the lighter side of love.

Quitting Smoking & Vaping

by Charles H. Elliott, PhD, and
Laura L. Smith, PhD

A Wiley Brand

Quitting Smoking & Vaping For Dummies®

Published by: **John Wiley & Sons, Inc.,** 111 River Street, Hoboken, NJ 07030-5774, www.wiley.com

Copyright © 2020 by John Wiley & Sons, Inc., Hoboken, New Jersey

Published simultaneously in Canada

For general information on our other products and services, please contact our Customer Care Department within the U.S. at 877-762-2974, outside the U.S. at 317-572-3993, or fax 317-572-4002. For technical support, please visit https://hub.wiley.com/community/support/dummies.

Wiley publishes in a variety of print and electronic formats and by print-on-demand. Some material included with standard print versions of this book may not be included in e-books or in print-on-demand. If this book refers to media such as a CD or DVD that is not included in the version you purchased, you may download this material at http://booksupport.wiley.com. For more information about Wiley products, visit www.wiley.com.

Library of Congress Control Number: 2019954890

ISBN 978-1-119-61691-7 (pbk); ISBN 978-1-119-61692-4 (ebk); ISBN 978-1-119-61695-5 (ebk)

Manufactured in the United States of America

V10016341_121619

Contents at a Glance

Table of Contents

Introduction

Quitting Smoking & Vaping For Dummies, is a comprehensive toolkit for anyone struggling with an addiction to nicotine. If you or someone you care about wants to give up a habit, this book provides a complete recipe for quitting.

Many stop-smoking books and programs are highly limited in what they recommend. Some give you a long list of tips and not much more. Others promise that you'll have an absurdly easy time quitting with virtually no effort (that is, if you buy their products).

We aren't promising you anything magical. And we suggest your efforts to stop smoking or vaping will be difficult. You may not even succeed on the first try. That's okay — we tell you how to deal with relapses.

You can count on us to give you the straight scoop about the best approaches to quitting smoking, using smokeless tobacco, and/or vaping. Guess what? You probably won't use them all and that's why we give you choices. If what you try at first doesn't work for you, there's a whole lot more you can try.

About This Book

Our number-one goal is to help as many people as possible give up the costly, unhealthy habits of nicotine and tobacco consumption. In order to accomplish that goal, we describe the various methods of smoking-cessation strategies. These include medications, rethinking your relationship to urges and smoking, increasing motivation, finding alternatives to fight urges, and more.

Tobacco can be consumed in a variety of ways. In addition, vaping devices are another way of obtaining nicotine. A second goal of this book is to let you know that these different delivery systems all have distinct risks associated with them. We describe those risks and the controversies surrounding each system in some detail. This information is particularly valuable for parents and teachers who may be worried about teens who could be experimenting with or thinking about vaping.

Throughout the book we give you examples to illustrate the points we're making. These examples are based on real experiences; however, they're based on composites of several people we've known or interviewed. Any resemblance to a specific person is entirely coincidental.

Sidebars in various chapters contain interesting information. However, they are not essential reading to the main goals of this book. Feel free to read them or not. Similarly, anything marked with the Technical Stuff icon can be skipped.

Throughout the book, the strategies we give you can be used for quitting vaping, smoking regular cigarettes, or smokeless tobacco. For simplicity and convenience, we don't repeat all the tobacco and nicotine forms each time we bring up a quitting strategy. All our suggested techniques can be applied to any form of tobacco or nicotine addiction.

Within this book, you may note that some web addresses break across two lines of text. If you're reading this book in print and want to visit one of these web pages, simply key in the web address exactly as it's noted in the text, pretending as though the line break doesn't exist. If you're reading this as an e-book, you've got it easy — just click the web address to be taken directly to the web page.

Foolish Assumptions

We assume that if you're reading this book, you want to quit smoking or vaping. Or perhaps you know or care about someone who does. Some people may pick this book up because it gives them a lot of information about the new phenomenon of vaping. If you're one of them, welcome!

Icons Used in This Book

Look for the little pictures in the margins. Those are called *icons* and they're intended to get your attention in some specific way. We use the following icons:

REMEMBER

This book is a reference which means you don't have to commit it to memory. But sometimes we tell you something so important that you really should remember it. And when that happens, we use the Remember icon.

TIP

Whenever we give you a practical idea for quitting smoking or vaping, improving your health, sticking with your program, carrying out suggestions more efficiently, and improving long term gains, we mark it with the Tip icon.

WARNING

When we alert you to potential risks, things not to do, or other important considerations you don't want to miss, we use the Warning icon.

EXAMPLE

As we mention earlier, we use examples based on real people's stories. When we do, we mark them with the Example icon.

TECHNICAL STUFF

Every once in a while, we dig deeper into more technical information that isn't essential to your understanding of the subject at hand. When we do that, we use the Technical Stuff icon. If you're the sort who likes to know *everything* about a subject, read these paragraphs. If you just want to know what you *need* to know, you can safely skip these paragraphs.

Beyond the Book

In addition to the material in the print or e-book you're reading right now, this product also comes with a free Cheat Sheet available on the web. The Cheat Sheet provides tips for dealing with cravings, affirmations to motivate you, tips on boosting your metabolism, and more. To access the Cheat Sheet, go to www.dummies.com and type **Quitting Smoking & Vaping For Dummies Cheat Sheet** in the Search box.

Where to Go from Here

You don't have to read this book from start to finish. Each chapter stands on its own, so you can dip into the book wherever you want. You can use the Table of Contents or Index to find the information you're most interested in right now.

Not sure where to start? If you're a parent scared to death about vaping and your teenager, head straight to Chapter 7. If you're a smoker or vaper, and you just want to get a plan for quitting now, head to Part 4. If you've already quit (good for you!), and you're struggling to stay a nonsmoker, Part 5 is for you.

1

Lifting the Fog on Smoking and Vaping

IN THIS PART . . .

Understand how to quit smoking and vaping.

Dive into tobacco and addiction.

Uncover the health effects of tobacco in its various forms.

Recognize the other costs of smoking for families and communities.

» **Knowing the enemy: addiction**

» **Accepting yourself**

» **Going for the long game**

Chapter 1

A Matter of Life

magine taking up a truly enjoyable hobby. It's a little costly, but it feels good. Unfortunately, there's a downside: About half of the people who practice this hobby regularly end up dead due to the riskiness of the hobby.

Now, we're not talking about climbing Mt. Everest or *BASE jumping* (jumping off cliffs and using a parachute at the last minute). No, those hobbies are relatively "safe" by comparison to what we're talking about. The hobby of smoking kills about half of long-term enthusiasts.

That fact probably accounts for why most smokers actually want to quit smoking: They know what's in store for them down the road. Yet, giving up jumping off cliffs as a hobby is easier than giving up smoking. Wanting to quit is a start, but not enough by itself.

However, progress is happening. Today, the combined effects of regulated advertising, greater restrictions on locations that allow smoking, and changes in societal norms have culminated in substantial reductions in overall tobacco use. In 2000, no state in the United States banned smoking in bars, restaurants, or the workplace. By 2018, 38 states had passed at least partial bans on public smoking.

These changes have contributed to a dramatic reduction in overall smoking rates from a high of almost half of all adults to a rate of just under 14 percent today. Some experts have even declared that the war on tobacco has almost been won.

But just before victory could be declared, another formidable threat appeared on the horizon: vaping. Many experts have expressed the opinion that vaping may pose many of the same risks as smoking combustible cigarettes. Surprisingly, other leading authorities contend that vaping nicotine may be a useful tool in finally winning the war on tobacco. The jury is still out on this issue, but we give you the latest analysis in this book.

We contend that smoking, vaping, or chewing tobacco are all basically unhealthy pursuits. So, in this book, we offer you the best, evidence-based methods for quitting smoking, vaping, or using smokeless tobacco. Essentially the same change techniques can be applied to all these related addictions.

REMEMBER

It won't be a cake walk, and you may stumble. But we give you ways to pick yourself up and go at it again. Keep trying and you're likely to kick the habit for good.

Accepting the Consequences of Being Human

Becoming addicted to nicotine is not something that people choose to do. When people take a few puffs of a cigarette or a vaping device, they don't intend to become dependent on a drug that costs money and time, while taking a serious toll on their health.

The brain's wiring makes addiction virtually inevitable for most people when certain substances, such as nicotine, are ingested repeatedly. Over time, the brain powerfully associates good feelings with those substances and unpleasant sensations of cravings when denied them.

An addicted brain offers a seductive promise: Keep supplying the drug and you won't ever have to deal fully with pain, suffering, or hardship. Unfortunately, it's a false promise. As addiction takes hold, it enslaves the mind. The addict is almost doomed to a life of finding ways to satisfy never-ending cravings. Luckily, there are ways to beat an addiction, and this book helps you accomplish that goal.

REMEMBER

Addiction is not a moral failure, a character flaw, or a sign of weakness. Addiction happens to people. When you're caught in its grip, fighting off an addiction takes courage, effort, and persistence. Don't worry — we lead you through the process and hold your hand every step of the way.

TIP

If you struggle with smoking, don't become mired in self-loathing, blame, and shame. You did *not* choose to become addicted to nicotine. Blaming yourself makes it tougher to move forward. You need all the resolve you've got to fight this — don't add more baggage to your load.

In addition to being vulnerable to addiction, humans have considerable tenacity and resilience. We help you build on your strengths in order to overcome addiction to nicotine.

Tabulating the Health Costs of Smoking

Almost a half a million people die from smoking-related illnesses each year in the United States alone. Thousands of young people start to smoke or vape every day. Left unchecked, it's assumed that about 5.6 million of today's teenagers will die prematurely from smoking.

Smoking costs more than $300 billion a year in both lost productivity and direct healthcare services. Smokers routinely die of lung cancer, cardiac disease, and strokes, among other smoking-related maladies.

We give you these facts not with the purpose of scaring you. You already know smoking causes life-threatening illnesses and wreaks havoc. Just consider using this information to inspire your efforts and realize you're contributing to a healthier society when you stop smoking. See Chapter 3 for more about tobacco and health.

Summing Up a Financial Spreadsheet

What could possibly be worth spending one million dollars each and every hour of each and every day? Tobacco companies spend that amount of money on promotion and advertising in order to get your business and pump up their profits. What's more important to you is what it's costing you. Above and beyond the "mere" price of cigarettes themselves, smoking costs much more. For example:

>> Smokers pay more for health and life insurance.

>> Smokers earn about 80 percent of the earnings of nonsmokers.

>> Some employers, especially in the healthcare industry, refuse to hire smokers.

>> Smokers pay more out of pocket for medical care.

>> Smokers use more sick days than nonsmokers.

>> Smokers spend more time and money on washing and cleaning their smelly clothes, homes, and cars.

Comparing costs with vaping

Direct comparisons of the cost of vaping with that of smoking regular cigarettes is difficult. That's because different vaping devices have quite variable costs and e-liquids come in an array of types and container sizes with their own unique costs (see Chapter 5 for descriptions of vaping devices and e-liquids). Nonetheless, if consumers shop carefully, they're likely to discover that vaping costs considerably less than smoking combustible cigarettes.

The issue of health and life insurance policy costs is completely up in the air. Given that vaping is a relatively new phenomena and few studies have been conducted on its long-term safety, insurance companies have not clarified their rules and fixed different premium prices for vaping versus smoking policyholders.

TECHNICAL STUFF

Some insurance companies require a physical exam before offering a policy. Many health and life insurance companies charge a higher premium to smokers. The way insurance companies test for whether you smoke or not is to check nicotine levels. Because most vaping e-liquids contain nicotine, vapers will test positively for nicotine. Thus, smokers who turn to vaping for their reputedly lower risk profile will still face higher premiums (see Chapter 6 for more information about the risks of vaping and Chapter 12 for information about vaping and harm reduction).

Calculating the ways you want to spend your windfall

Savings you accrue from not buying endless packs of cigarettes (or other tobacco or nicotine products) mount up rapidly over time — even if you ignore all the considerable funds that aren't spent on insurance, lost work, and other indirect costs. We strongly recommend that you start putting aside what you would've spent on tobacco or nicotine. Watch it grow!

Make a list of spending priorities when it reaches a tidy sum. Post that list in a visible place and look at it often for inspiration. Let's say that an average cost of a pack of cigarettes in your state runs about $7. If you smoke a pack a day, that comes to about $2,555 per year. The ten-year total accumulates $25,550. You could buy a car with that! There are lots of other things you could do with just one year's savings, like:

>> Buy a new computer.

>> Buy an amazing TV.

>> Buy a bunch of new clothes.

>> Pay off a credit card.

>> Buy a terrific new appliance.

>> Pay for gym dues for a long time.

>> Take an amazing weekend getaway or a nice vacation.

>> Make a nice donation to the charity of your choice.

The really great thing about these expenditures is that you can almost think of them as free money. It's money you absolutely would not have accumulated without quitting. Stop burning your money! Give it back to yourself. You've earned the right to splurge a bit!

Some people prefer to invest their smoking savings. You can do that in an ultra-safe savings account or go a little wilder and invest in a specific stock or in a mutual fund. It's amazing how much more that money can grow to if you put it in and let your gains compound over time. Consider reading *Personal Finance For Dummies*, 9th Edition, by Eric Tyson (Wiley) for more ideas.

TIP

Investing for the long term will only work if you find it highly rewarding to watch those returns grow slowly over time. If you're someone who prefers more immediate gratification, we recommend that you go ahead and be a bit self-indulgent for the highly worthy goal of quitting smoking or vaping.

Breaking Up Is Hard to Do

Well, not always. If you ever broke up with an abusive partner, then you know that breaking up may feel temporarily tough, but afterward there is a tremendous sense of relief. That's what breaking up with smoking is like. Smoking is a toxic partner. Walking away from it is hard at first, but soon you'll find yourself feeling tremendous relief.

Life is full of hard-to-accomplish goals. Think back; ponder what you've done in your life that took guts, time, and hard work. Those are the things that you feel incredibly proud of when you look back. Quitting smoking will be an accomplishment you can be proud of. But don't get discouraged and defeat yourself before you start by thinking it's *too* hard.

REMEMBER

You've faced and conquered a few (or more) grueling challenges in your life. You can get through this too with a little help from this book, support from friends, and the same grit and determination that you've mustered in the past!

Seeing that a little help goes a long way

Many paths lead to a smoke-free life. We cover them in detail in Parts 3 and 4. Before you quit, you may want to consider reading about the techniques offered throughout those chapters. To get a sense of what's available for your quitting endeavor, here's a list of most of the techniques we have to offer you:

>> Nicotine replacement therapy (NRT)

>> Medications

>> Rethinking your relationship to cravings and urges

>> Planning alternative actions to counter urges

>> Support from smoking cessation apps

>> Quitlines

>> Support groups

>> Websites for quitting smoking

>> Mindfulness

>> Rewarding your progress

>> Developing a healthy lifestyle

>> Managing your weight

>> Dealing with lapses and relapses

>> Strategies for enhancing long-term success

You can see you have lots of strategies to choose from. Don't let the length of this list scare you. See Chapter 15 for figuring out how to pick what's best for you to start with. You won't have to use all these techniques. And if what you start with doesn't work, there's more standing by ready to help.

Making a plan and checking it twice

Most people find that developing a detailed quit plan *before* quitting will increase the odds of success. Therefore, we suggest that you don't go cold turkey until you've done some preparation. We detail how to make a plan in Chapter 15 and help you get through the first day in Chapter 16.

Chapters 17 and 18 prepare you for dealing with the first month of quitting and throughout the next five months. We tell you how to deal with sleep problems, cravings, and the crabbiness that often accompanies your quitting journey.

IT'S A SMALL WORLD

When a friend of ours heard that we were writing a book about quitting smoking, she said, "You've got to talk to Frank."

"Frank who?" we asked.

"Frank Etscorn, your neighbor. He got the first patent for a nicotine patch designed to deliver nicotine through the skin."

So, we invited him out for a beer. Frank, a behavioral psychologist, told us that in the 1980s he was carrying out experiments on flavor aversion and nausea. During his experiments, he used nicotine, which is a stimulator of the vomiting center. One day, he accidentally spilled some liquid nicotine on his arm and immediately became dizzy, nauseous, and unable to stand. Frank had a significant case of nicotine poisoning. He replicated his so-called "experiment," by re-exposing himself to liquid nicotine (not a practice we recommend). He quickly realized the implications of his finding. He worked on the development of a skin patch that could deliver nicotine to smokers. His goal was to help smokers give up smoking cigarettes. He obtained a patent in 1986, which earned him and his school, the New Mexico Institute of Mining and Technology, millions of dollars.

Remember: If you vape and refill your own vaping device, make sure that you don't get nicotine on your hands. Although most e-liquids are not pure nicotine, exposure can still cause undesirable effects. And you probably won't be able to get a patent that generates millions of dollars.

Life After the Breakup

Many quitters assume that if they've quit for six months or so, their battle has been won. And indeed, they've made great, substantial progress! But some vigilance is still advisable.

Let your guard down and nicotine can crawl back through the door unnoticed. So, we recommend you stay on the lookout for high-risk situations such as the following:

>> **Places that you associate with smoking:** These could include a certain area of your own home, your car, or a neighbor's porch.

>> **Times when you're easily angered or frustrated:** When you're angry, it's easy to say, "To heck with it," or "I just don't care," but those are simply reactions to your anger. Expect urges at such times and have an alternative to caving in ready to go (see Chapter 17, 18, and 19 for tips on dealing with cravings).

>> **Socializing with people you associate with smoking:** This situation is dangerous. Others may tempt you with offers of a cigarette. Have a reply ready such as, "Thanks, but I'm doing the toughest thing I've done in a long time — quitting. And I know that one cigarette will lead to another."

>> **Celebrations:** This high-risk situation may surprise you. Celebrations are good, right? Yep. But good times are also often powerfully associated with smoking. Be prepared.

Slipping and tripping insurance

Regular smokers are often jealous of so-called casual smokers, those who claim that they can go for months without a cigarette and only smoke occasionally during parties or other social gatherings. Wouldn't it be nice to be a casual smoker, able to just have one cigarette here and there? Well, for almost all cigarette smokers, there is no casual opportunity. When a smoking habit begins, it quickly escalates into a regular, frequent pattern of smoking.

After quitting, the mind tries to trick former smokers into believing that they can have just one cigarette. But like potato chip advertisers know, one is never enough. A lapse of just one or two cigarettes can quickly morph into a full pack-a-day habit again.

TIP

If you do slip, pay attention. Go on high alert. Review your quit plan and get support. People who take lapses like these seriously can often get right back on track. You need to reach out. Consider calling the national quitline at 800-QUIT NOW (800-784-8669). People who "blow off" the importance of a few cigarettes often relapse completely.

REMEMBER

For most smokers, when they quit, there should be no puffs, not one. It's just not worth the risk.

Lighting the way to a new, nonsmoking lifestyle

We're here to support your efforts for the long run. Our ultimate goal for you at the end of the day is that you find a lifestyle as a nonsmoker that gives you more satisfaction than you had as a smoker. That may sound impossible, but it's not. Assuming that you share the objective of finding a better nonsmoking lifestyle, there are a few things you need to do.

Deserving and seeking healthy pleasures

People report greater life satisfaction when they reward themselves with healthy pleasures. But if you're going to do that, you have to believe you deserve to have more pleasure in your life to begin with.

Let's face it, you quit smoking. That took a lot of work. You deserve a break! And putting pleasure into your life will help keep you smoke free.

Practicing self-compassion

Hey, it's tough being human. You have huge responsibilities — whether that's work or family or friends or pets or some combination of these. Along the way, you're going to make mistakes as everyone does. Start being your own best friend. When you slip up, forgive yourself unconditionally. Be kind to your body and your mind. People who practice self-compassion are happier and have greater life satisfaction. See Chapter 22 for more information about self-compassion.

Reaching for resilience

It takes resilience to make it through today's challenging world. In order to get up after a fall, it's important to have strong social connections. Nurture your friendships and spend time with people you care about. Connections provide a buffer from the unanticipated obstacles that come out of the blue. You can also strengthen your inner resources through practicing mindfulness strategies. See Chapter 21 for more information about mindfulness and meditation.

Chapter **2**

Talking about Tobacco

D o you remember your first cigarette? If you're like most people, you were probably a teenager hanging out with one or more friends — no adults to be found. You may remember a fit of coughing as you awkwardly struggled to inhale. You and your friends may have nervously choked and giggled while hoping not to be caught. It may have seemed delightfully rebellious.

Perhaps you wonder how you, as well as millions of others, took that first irritating, disgusting drag and continued to smoke. And, amazingly, you kept doing it despite the revolting smell, filthy cigarette butts, money, and risks to your health. You didn't fear addiction because you'd never get addicted to something so vile as smoking. However, if you ask most long-term smokers whether they'd take that first cigarette again, most would say never, no way, no how.

Yet, over time, that disgusting smell morphed into a smoker's perfume. The cigarette butts became mere nuisances. The money seemed justifiable. And health risks appeared to lie in the distant future.

In this chapter, we report on the numerous physical, emotional, and social causes of smoking addiction. We give you a tool for helping you understand just to what extent you're "hooked" on smoking. We also review the various ways people manage to get their tobacco fix and note how tobacco has created so much pleasure, pain, profit, and problems.

TIP

Although this chapter focuses on addiction to cigarettes, this information applies to all addictions to tobacco products whether they're smoked, chewed, vaped, or snuffed.

Analyzing Addiction

Most smokers want to know *why* they smoke. No one starts smoking wanting to become addicted, and most new tobacco users think it won't happen to them. But for those who continue to smoke after those first early packs, addiction powerfully contributes to why they keep smoking.

Experts don't have a universally agreed upon definition of *addiction*. That's because it's a complex concept that defies easy explanations. Nevertheless, most people have notions as to what they think it is. And perhaps you'll find it helpful if we describe *our* way of looking at the phenomenon.

An addiction involves powerful feelings that come about from ingesting certain types of drugs or substances. The hallmark of an addiction is using a substance chronically despite harmful effects on a person's life now and in the future. Using addictive substances generally feels good, and bad feelings abate for a while. Unfortunately, negative feelings return, and the craving for positive feelings increases, culminating in a vicious cycle of addiction.

TECHNICAL STUFF

Tolerance is another important aspect of addiction. Tolerance occurs when a substance is used over and over again, and it begins to have a reduced impact. More is, therefore, needed to get the same effects. Tolerance develops quickly for most regular smokers — 1 or 2 cigarettes a day quickly turns into 10, 20, or more. Of course, at some point, smokers usually reach a stable level of intake (after all, there are only so many hours in a day!).

There are many myths and misconceptions about what an addiction is and isn't. The following points explain some of these myths:

>> **Myth: Addiction is unfixable.** Actually, considerable data suggests that many people ultimately *are* able to break their addiction, whether it's tobacco, drugs, or alcohol.

>> **Myth: All addicts must reach rock bottom before they can break their addiction.** *Rock bottom* is hard to define — it varies from person to person. However, lots of people stop using addictive substances well before hitting anything like a true rock bottom.

>> **Myth: Willpower is all you need.** Psychologists don't even fully agree on what exactly willpower is. If you think of yourself as lacking something fundamentally necessary, such as willpower, you'll never succeed. If you want to quit, it's worth taking a shot, no matter how much willpower you think you do or don't have.

» **Myth: Addicts are weak people.** People become addicted for a variety of reasons as we explain in the following sections on biological, psychological, and social factors. Being strong or weak has nothing to do with it.

» **Myth: Addiction is simply a choice.** Sure, there's an aspect of choice involved with starting to smoke. However, most addicts would truly not choose to be addicted.

» **Myth: I could never become addicted.** Thinking like that could make you more vulnerable to becoming addicted. No one is immune.

» **Myth: Addicts always suffer considerably when they try to quit.** Surprisingly, there are a few, lucky people who manage to quit a substance like cigarettes without struggle. But for most people, the more they develop a plan and garner support and help from others, the easier they'll find quitting.

» **Myth: After you're detoxed, you're done with your addiction.** Your system clears itself of nicotine in a few days, but cravings are another matter. Those may continue for weeks, months, or sometimes forever (though almost always they lessen over time).

» **Myth: Taking medication to help with addiction is cheating by substituting one drug for another:** Medications used to treat addiction (see Chapter 9), are always safer than the original substance. Even nicotine replacement therapy avoids tars and toxic chemicals that come from burning cigarettes. Furthermore, most people use these medications as a bridge to quit entirely at some point. Does it help to call it cheating? No.

» **Myth: Addicts are bad people.** We can't deny that those who are addicted to almost anything are often shamed and stigmatized by others. But so-called addicts are people just like everyone else. They start out using substances as recreation, response to pressure, or a variety of other reasons. What they don't do is start out with the intention of becoming addicted.

TECHNICAL STUFF

When we use the term *addiction* in this book, we're referring only to the response people have to certain *substances* such as opioids, alcohol, and nicotine. This approach avoids applying the term addiction to behavioral issues such as aberrant sexuality, Internet addiction, and kleptomania, which may actually belong in another category of mental dysfunction that lies beyond the scope of this book.

REMEMBER

To further understand addiction to tobacco, it's important to appreciate how an addictive substance affects the body. In addition, it's useful to recognize that addiction interacts with powerful feelings and emotions. Finally, addiction affects relationships while relationships simultaneously impact addiction. In other words, addiction is driven by biological, psychological, and social forces as explained in the following sections.

Burrowing briefly into biology

Imagine taking a drag on a cigarette. Smoke pours into your lungs while dumping a stew of chemicals into your bloodstream. These chemicals quickly breach the blood–brain barrier and deliver a jolt to the brain, most of which comes from nicotine. It takes less than ten seconds to go from drawing in that first puff of smoke to the brain starting to respond.

Nicotine stimulates the effects of *dopamine,* a brain chemical that increases feelings of pleasure. Dopamine levels also rise after ingesting cocaine, eating a favorite food, and having sex; in other words, stuff that feels good.

Nicotine also increases *adrenaline,* a neurochemical that stimulates the body to increase blood pressure, increase heart rate, and restrict blood flow to the heart. Adrenaline prepares the body for threat — the well-known fight-or-flight syndrome that prepares you to either stand and fight or flee from danger. It also increases focus and causes calories to burn at a faster rate.

In addition, nicotine causes the body to dump more *glucose* (blood sugar) into the blood stream. Normally, when blood sugar rises, insulin is secreted, which enables blood sugar levels to come back to normal. However, nicotine inhibits that process, which leads to higher levels of blood sugar and decreased appetite.

So, in ten seconds or less, nicotine delivers pleasurable feelings, increases focus, decreases appetite, and increases energy. What could possibly go wrong?

Well, within a few minutes, nicotine levels begin to decline rapidly. Lower nicotine levels elicit feelings of reduced pleasure, increased nervousness and anxiety, diminished energy, a lack of focus, and the emergence of cravings. That's why most long-term smokers report immediate decreases of anxiety and a sense of great relief when they light the next cigarette. No wonder, the pattern continues throughout the day.

But oddly, not through the night. Very few smokers wake up every hour to have another cigarette. And most smokers manage to get through work, movies, and airplane flights without intense distress. So, something more than mere biology must be contributing to the addiction of smoking.

TECHNICAL STUFF

Some experts contend that any addiction is a disease of the brain. Although biological factors clearly form part of the picture, that's not the whole story. Thinking of smoking as a disease minimizes the importance of psychological and social contributors to the problem.

Inspecting psychological factors

We now turn to psychology to further clarify smoking addiction. People struggle with how to explain why they do things that they know are not in their best interests — smokers are no exception. The following three sections explain. First, a popular metaphor reveals how the mind works. Next, we show you how distorted thinking contributes to difficulty quitting smoking. Finally, we help you see how common associations become triggers for turning to tobacco.

Discovering elephants and their riders

Think of yourself as having two minds. The first you can think of as your elephant mind, and the second, as the elephant *rider* part of your mind. To a casual observer, the rider is in charge. The rider directs the elephant to go right, and the elephant usually obeys. However, if a hungry elephant spots its favorite meal on the left (consisting of luscious tree bark dripping with sap), who do you think will win?

Think of addiction as the elephant part of your mind, commanded by intense feelings of pleasure, pain, and/or fear. Yet the elephant isn't that smart and mostly responds to what's right in front of its trunk. The elephant does a poor job of forecasting the future or learning from the past. Immediate pleasures, temptations, and fears dominate the elephant's decisions.

By contrast, the rider "knows" exactly what to do and is controlled by logic, reasoning, and critical thinking. The rider is no match for the brute strength of the elephant. The elephant part of the mind wants what it wants when it wants it. And the elephant truly does not like to feel one bit of discomfort.

So, how do the elephant and the rider parts of your mind dictate whether you'll smoke? The elephant just wants to have fun. It can't process and reason about long-term threats to health such as lung and cardiovascular diseases (see Chapter 3 for more information). The rider knows better but can't seem to control the elephant. The rider tries reasoning, bribes, and persuasion, but the elephant feels bad when it doesn't smoke and feels better when it does. It's that simple.

Your rider mind can slowly but surely train the elephant to obey commands more often, but the training involves considerable skill, persistence, and patience. See Parts 4 and 5 for ideas about how to gain greater control over your elephant mind.

REMEMBER

If you're trying to quit smoking or vaping and you experience a relapse (see Chapter 19), remember that you're dealing with a very, very large elephant. It takes time to train the elephant. Be patient with your elephant, and yourself!

Adding up addictive thoughts

From a psychological standpoint, one of the most problematic factors driving both addiction and emotional distress can be found in the realm of distorted thinking. Distorted thinking causes you to make unwarranted assumptions and inaccurately portrays reality, usually in negative ways. Such thinking can be seen in these examples related to smoking:

>> "I smoke because I'm so nervous. If I quit, I'd be a wreck and never be able to do my job. I'd get fired, for sure."

>> "I'll probably gain a hundred pounds if I quit smoking."

>> If I want another cigarette this badly, I must need it."

>> "I smoked when I shouldn't have today. Might as well give up."

>> "My grandfather smoked two packs a day and died in his sleep at 92. It worked for him; it should work for me."

>> "Just because countless others have learned to quit smoking, doesn't mean I can do it."

>> "I can't function without a cigarette."

>> "I've tried to quit before and failed, so I might as well give up and enjoy smoking."

These thoughts all contain distortions of reality. And they wreak havoc on people's attempts to quit. They sabotage quitting efforts by making mountains out of mole hills, ignoring positive evidence, increasing feelings of helplessness, and decreasing confidence. Not exactly a recipe for success. See Chapter 10 for help with problematic, distorted thinking.

Behavioral associations turn into smoking triggers

Do you remember getting thoroughly sick to your stomach after eating something? If so, you probably felt queasy or disgusted when you next encountered that food. Maybe you avoided that food for years or never ate it again. That's because your mind connected the food with getting sick. The food became a potent trigger for nausea. However, that food might be both tasty and nutritious. You might spend a lifetime not eating a perfectly good, healthy food because of one association.

Associations are also formed to protect us. For example, when you smell badly spoiled food, you probably also feel nauseous. That's a good thing, because the feelings prevent you from eating food that might make you sick.

On the other hand, the smell of freshly baked peanut butter cookies might take you back to a pleasant childhood memory. And if it doesn't lead to binge-eating peanut butter cookies, that's great. The brain tries to connect experiences that way so that it knows how to make you feel good and avoid feeling bad. And that can be a good or a bad thing.

With addictions, these brain connections or associations can work against you. They make you anticipate something very pleasant (we're talking tobacco here) when thinking about or encountering certain settings, people, activities, or events. Associations can also bring on unpleasant emotions that make you want to smoke in order to feel better. These associations become triggers for smoking. Here's a list of particularly common triggers that push many smokers to smoke.

>> The first cup of coffee in the morning

>> The sound and smell of someone opening a fresh pack of cigarettes

>> Coffee after dinner

>> Boredom

>> Driving to work

>> After lunch

>> Eating out

>> Driving in traffic

>> Before a job interview

>> After a job interview

>> Break time at work

>> Having a drink

>> After sex

>> Playing cards

>> Getting in trouble

>> After an argument

>> At a party

>> Talking on the phone

>> With certain friends

Good grief. What's a smoker to do? Avoid everything in life? No. But you can see how powerful associations can lead you straight to the next cigarette. Whether it's to feel good or avoid feeling bad, the influence can be hard to escape. See Chapters 10 and 15 for ideas on how to deal with triggers.

THE DOUBLE WHAMMY OF ADDICTION

Addiction involves two powerful types of learning that psychologists refer to as *positive reinforcement* and *negative reinforcement*. No doubt you've heard of positive reinforcement. We train our dog, Sadie, with positive reinforcement. We give her a small treat when she sits on command or comes when called.

Negative reinforcement is another matter. This type of learning is not punishment although many people misunderstand that fact. With negative reinforcement, you remove or take away something unpleasant. Sadie trains us with negative reinforcement! She doesn't know it, but she does. How? She puts her nose in our laps when we're typing and scratches at our legs. She stops when we pet her. We've learned to pet her a lot. That's negative reinforcement — removing something unpleasant like scratching to get something she wants (petting).

It's really hard not to do something that results in both positive and negative reinforcement. That's what smoking gives you — a positive jolt of pleasure (positive reinforcement) and relief from unpleasant cravings (negative reinforcement). Smokers begin smoking to seek positive reinforcement. As their addiction takes hold, they continue smoking in order to avoid negative feelings (negative reinforcement).

Searching for social contributors to addiction

Kids who hang out with smokers are more likely to smoke. Research suggests that adolescents are influenced to smoke by their friends or family who smoke, including parents, siblings, and extended family. That influence happens for three reasons:

>> **Modeling:** Modeling is referred to as observational learning or imitation. People readily pick up on behaviors demonstrated by important people they relate with. See the nearby sidebar, "Monkey see, monkey do," for an example.

>> **Predisposition:** Secondhand smoke from household members may create a biological predisposition for acquiring an addiction to nicotine. Animal studies support that connection. See the nearby sidebar, "Secondhand smoke: Priming kids to smoke," for an example.

>> **Peer pressure:** Peers not only model smoking behavior, but also sometimes exert pressure on their friends to do the same. The pressured friends cave in so that they can fit in better and be liked. Adolescents are particularly vulnerable to peer pressure. See the nearby sidebar, "All the cool kids are doing it . . . ," for an example.

EXAMPLE

MONKEY SEE, MONKEY DO

Jackson, a 14-year-old middle-school student excels at his studies. He has many good friends, none of whom smoke. He has a close-knit family and relatives whom he admires greatly. His father is a construction worker who chews tobacco to improve his focus and productivity. His dad warns Jackson not to turn to tobacco because it's highly addictive. But his dad doesn't seem like a junkie to Jackson.

One day, Jackson experiments with his dad's stash and hates the taste. He can't believe his dad finds chewing tobacco pleasurable, so he tries it again just to see if he missed something. He finds it a bit disgusting, but not as bad as the first time. And he does feel just a slight buzz from the tobacco. His experimentation continues in that manner. Each time he tries it, it's a little less awful and a bit more enjoyable. Soon, Jackson can't stop. He turns to cigarettes because they seem to give him a quicker jolt and are less messy than chewing tobacco. Jackson falls under the influence of *modeling*.

The degree to which these influences impact any given person varies greatly. And for some people, all three influences come into play. The following three stories illustrate how modeling, addiction vulnerability due to secondhand smoke, and peer pressure lead to trouble.

EXAMPLE

SECONDHAND SMOKE: PRIMING KIDS TO SMOKE

For Daniela, secondhand smoke plays a big role in her spiraling smoking addiction. She grew up in a home with a small living room where her family gathered most nights. Unfortunately, both her parents smoked — a lot. Daniela didn't think much about her parents' smoking and never saw herself as likely to become addicted to such a disgusting habit.

Her parents warned her to never take up the practice, and she was always sure she never would. Nonetheless, after she turns 15, Daniela is curious. How bad could her parents' smoking be? She thinks she'll try smoking for a day just to see what it would be like. From her third cigarette on, she feels like she'd been born to smoke — it seems to make her troubles go away.

No doubt, modeling is influencing Daniela, but it's also likely that secondhand smoke prepared her brain to be ready for developing a smoking addiction.

EXAMPLE

ALL THE COOL KIDS ARE DOING IT . . .

Larry is a sixth-grader attending a Catholic school. One day, Sister Maria lines up all the boys in his class. The boys know they're about to hear yet another lecture. Today the sister is particularly passionate about her topic. As she shakes her finger in their faces, she strides from one end of the line to another, "Don't you *dare* go over to that corner store where they play pinball and smoke cigarettes!" Larry has the immediate thought, "Wow, there's a store nearby with pinball! Awesome!"

The next day, Larry and six of his good friends sneak out at lunch so that they can play pinball. A couple of his friends buy a pack of cigarettes, but Larry refuses to join them — at first. The friends keep buying cigarettes during the lunch hour, and Larry eventually feels pressure to participate. Peer pressure and rebellion both work to create a group of smokers.

TIP

If you're a smoker, try to remember your earliest cigarettes. Ask yourself if modeling, secondhand smoke, or peer pressure may have played a role in your becoming hooked on cigarettes.

TIP

According to the U.S. Surgeon General, the younger you start, the more likely you are to become addicted. Out of every four high school smokers, three will become adult smokers. Sadly, out of those three, only one will quit and another will die early from the health consequences of smoking.

EXAMPLE

THE EXCEPTION TO THE RULE

Riley's parents smoke a lot. Both smoke two packs a day. Riley has been exposed to secondhand smoke since she was born. Her parents modeled smoking and didn't tell her that smoking was something to avoid. When she turns 13, her best friend takes up smoking and suggests that she try it, too. Riley wants to and can't see much reason not to. She's eager to indulge. Her first cigarette causes some throat irritation and coughing. But her friend reassures her that's normal and will lessen with practice. So, practice she does. After a couple of days, she decides to swear off cigarettes forever. Why? She totally hates the taste, especially because the taste lingers in her mouth for hours after a single cigarette.

Despite modeling, likely genetic influences, exposure to secondhand smoke, and peer pressure, Riley doesn't become addicted to smoking. Does this mean she was a stronger, better person than those who succumbed to addiction? Not at all. It came down to her good luck that she hated the taste of tobacco.

On the other hand, not every person with biological, psychological, and social risk factors becomes addicted to tobacco or nicotine. See the nearby sidebar, "The exception to the rule," for an example.

Assessing your tobacco addiction

It's easy to deny the idea that you're addicted or teetering on the edge of addiction to something like cigarettes. If you deny it, you're likely to fool yourself into minimizing the damage it's causing in your life. We have a quiz for you that may help you decide if your smoking really is a problematic addiction.

How bad is your addiction or how hooked are you? Ponder the following list of questions (our dirty dozen) to help you know.

» Do you smoke every day?

» Do you smoke to feel better?

» Do you have physical withdrawal symptoms such as agitation, restlessness, and increased appetite when you're not smoking?

» Do you have emotional symptoms of withdrawal such as depressed mood, anxiety, lack of concentration, or stress when you're not smoking?

» Would you buy cigarettes even if you couldn't afford them?

» Do you avoid places that don't allow smoking?

» Have you tried and failed to quit smoking numerous times?

» Do you have health problems from smoking?

» Do you crave a cigarette immediately after waking up in the morning?

» Do you plan for your next cigarette?

» Do you sometimes smoke instead of doing something else you need or want to do?

» Do you continue to smoke even though you know you're harming others (your kids, spouse, or friends) through secondhand smoke?

» Do you worry when you're about to run out of cigarettes?

There is no specific cutoff score for this quiz. But obviously, the more questions that apply to you, the more you're hooked. Even answering yes to two or three of these questions suggests you have significant trouble with smoking. At the end of the day, it doesn't matter to what extent your addiction is based on biological, psychological, or social factors. Either way, smoking kills, and it's tough to quit.

TOBACCO'S GLORY DAYS

Indigenous people of the Americas enjoyed tobacco for many generations before Columbus. Tobacco smoking was particularly partaken by religious figures, chiefs, and medicine men. Smoke from tobacco was thought to bridge the gap between mortals and the spirit world. Tobacco was recommended for a variety of ailments and medical uses such as

- Colds
- Fatigue
- Pain relief
- Headaches
- Toothaches
- Earaches
- Diarrhea
- Burns and injuries (in the form of an ointment)
- Anesthesia

After Columbus brought tobacco back to Spain, the practice of consuming tobacco in various forms caught on rapidly. At first, it was largely used to treat a variety of medical conditions. By the end of the 16th century, most of Europe had been introduced to tobacco.

Tobacco quickly circled the globe and became wildly popular. It was used for loan collateral during the Revolutionary War. It was also used as currency throughout the colonies because gold and silver were scarce. Tobacco was seen as a highly valued commodity.

But change was coming.

The power of smoking addiction can't be overstated. Ask any hospital nurse about patients' desperate attempts to smoke while hospitalized. You're likely to hear stories of people suffering from end-stage lung cancer still craving the very thing that's killing them. One nurse we spoke to remembered a lung cancer patient, too weak to walk, who wanted to be wheeled outside to smoke. When the nurse turned down the request, the patient called 911 to report that he was being abused by the uncaring staff. After the patient's third phone call to the police, an officer was dispatched to the hospital. Upon hearing his complaint, the officer was less than sympathetic to the patient. No charges were filed. To be clear, we have no intent to disparage this patient. Consider the anguish he must have been feeling over his overwhelming compulsion to smoke. Under such circumstances, all reasoning and common sense are drowned by the intense cravings for a cigarette.

TIP

About half of all smokers try to quit each year, but only a very few do it without help. See Parts 3 and 4 for more information about quitting successfully.

Dissecting Tobacco

Tobacco is a plant found across the world. Tobacco leaves are cultivated and then cured before conversion into products like cigarettes, cigars, snuff, and such. Like any plant, tobacco contains a variety of ingredients. Nicotine is the most addictive constituent.

Before it's burned, tobacco contains about 4,000 chemicals, dozens of which have been demonstrated to have carcinogenic effects. (See Chapter 3 for additional, specific health effects of these and other chemicals.) Just a few of the ingredients in this toxic stew include

>> Formaldehyde (also used in embalming)

>> Acetone (used in nail polish remover and dissolving Super Glue)

>> Arsenic (need we say more?)

>> Cadmium (a poisonous metal used in batteries)

>> Lead (a highly toxic metal that causes damage to the entire body, especially the nervous system)

>> Hydrogen cyanide (used in chemical warfare, it blocks the body's ability to use oxygen)

>> Radioactive elements (which over time can deposit in the lungs)

WARNING

No matter how you ingest tobacco, these chemicals come along for the ride. Don't be fooled by promises of "safety" because the tobacco is consumed orally or not inhaled as is generally the case with cigar or pipe smoking.

Different tobacco delivery systems (for example, cigarettes, snuff, pipes, and so on) have different combinations of these and other toxic chemicals. However, in a nutshell, burning makes everything even worse, and that's what happens when you smoke cigarettes.

THE DEVIL MADE ME SMOKE

Indigenous people believed that tobacco use promoted physical, emotional, and spiritual well-being. Tobacco was offered as a gift and a sign of respect. In 1492, upon arrival to the New World, Columbus was greeted by native people. He wrote in his journal, "The natives brought fruit, wooden spears, and certain dried leaves, which gave off a distinct fragrance."

Not knowing what the leaves were for, Columbus discarded them. However, one of his crewmen, Rodrigo de Jerez, was reportedly fascinated to see locals burning the leaves and "drinking" the smoke. He tried it himself and quickly became an addicted smoker.

When Rodrigo returned to Spain, he ostensibly brought tobacco with him and continued to smoke. Big mistake. The villagers were frightened by a man with smoke coming out of his nose and mouth. That's because anything out of the ordinary in 15th-century Spain was thought to be the work of the devil.

Sure enough, the Spanish Inquisition had him thrown into jail (where presumably he was able to quit smoking, surprisingly without the help of this book). He was released after seven years and by then, Queen Catherine de Medici had been prescribed snuff to cure her migraines. She and the rest of the Royal Court of Spain were happily sniffing snuff. So much for the devil.

Delivering Tobacco to the Body

Humans have shown considerable creativity when figuring out ways to ingest tobacco. Choices abound. In this section, we review some of the most common methods of tobacco consumption. New strategies come out all the time. Various tobacco delivery systems have different health implications (see Chapter 3 for a discussion of effects of tobacco on health).

Burning tobacco

Burning does more than heat tobacco prior to inhaling. It also changes the chemical composition and adds new toxins to the mix. Here are some of the popular ways of burning tobacco:

>> **Cigarettes:** About 34 million adults in the United States smoke cigarettes, which represents a new low of about 14 percent of the adult population. Most cigarettes are commercially manufactured, although a few people roll their own. Manufactured cigarettes include filtered, nonfiltered, low tar, all natural,

menthol, and so-called "light" versions. See Chapter 3 for information about the health risks associated with various types of cigarettes.

>> **Cigars and cigarillos:** These products come in a variety of sizes. Cigars and cigarillos are wrapped in either leaf tobacco or another material that contains tobacco, which contrasts with cigarettes (which are wrapped in paper). Cigarillos differ from cigars in that the former are generally smaller and thinner than cigars. Fewer than 10 million adults in the United States smoke cigars or cigarillos. Alarmingly, cigars may be becoming more popular with adolescents because they can be sold individually and now have desirable flavorings available.

>> **Pipes:** Pipe smokers generally place loose tobacco in a bowl with an attached stem for inhaling the smoke produced by burning the tobacco. Although pipes are considered a symbol of affluence and sophistication in some circles, tobacco smoke from pipes is also toxic. Pipe tobacco flavors appeal to teens and young adults. Who wouldn't want to try Grandpa's, Cherry Smash, Cupcake, Vanilla Cream, or Log Cabin pipe tobacco? However, very few people (about 1 percent in the United States) smoke pipes frequently.

>> **Waterpipe tobacco (similar products include hookah, bong, shisha, maassel, and so on):** Waterpipes are used as a way of filtering and/or cooling burning tobacco by running the smoke through water prior to inhaling. Well under 1 percent of American adults smoke tobacco with some type of water pipe. Of note, hookah lounges are popular with adolescents and young adults. These lounges are often seen as particularly enticing due to their use of flavored tobaccos.

Heating tobacco without burning

Touted by merchants of tobacco as far safer than burning tobacco, some devices vaporize tobacco by heating it without actually burning it. Also known as heated tobacco products (HTPs) or heat not burn (HNB), proponents of this delivery method claim that the subjective experience closely resembles that derived from smoking cigarettes.

TECHNICAL STUFF

HTPs contain nicotine (which is highly addictive), additives, and flavors. They are not considered e-cigarettes because they heat *tobacco* whereas e-cigarettes heat *liquid nicotine*. See Chapter 3 for a discussion about the relative safety (or lack thereof) of heated tobacco products.

HTPs were around in the 1980s but failed to catch on. They were reintroduced around 2013 and have been heavily marketed by major tobacco companies since then. In 2016, sales totaled about $2.1 billion and are expected to reach $18 billion by 2021. HTPs are far more profitable than traditional cigarettes.

CLEARING OUT THE SMOKE

EXAMPLE

Lilly opens her birthday gift and finds a slick case with what looks like a vaping pen. Her roommate tells her it's the newest way to smoke without smoking. She had complained about Lilly's cigarette smoking for months because of the smell and filthy mess of smoking. Lilly agrees to try the cleaner, smoke-free HTP device for two weeks, and then she'll see about switching permanently.

Lilly brings the heat stick to her mouth and inhales. She notices that the vapor smells sort of like cigarette smoke, but not as powerful. After a day of using her HTP, she doesn't notice her typical cigarette cravings.

What she doesn't like is having to recharge and clean her device. She also complains about the relatively high initial cost as compared to her cigarettes. On the other hand, her roommate is delighted by the absence of filthy ashtrays and barely detectable tobacco smell. After two weeks, Lilly isn't entirely convinced, but she agrees to stop smoking in the apartment. That's a big win for her roommate.

TECHNICAL STUFF

Facing a decline in cigarette sales, it's no wonder that the largest tobacco company in the world sought an alternative, profitable product. They developed a type of HTP that their marketing team branded as an IQOS device. Urban legend has it that IQOS cleverly stands for "I Quit Ordinary Smoking." The manufacturer of the IQOS denies this suggestion and contends that IQOS is meaningless.

Ingesting tobacco without burning or heating

Smokeless tobacco can be sucked, chewed, sniffed through the nostrils, or dissolved in the mouth. Smokeless tobacco usage pales in comparison to cigarettes, but it's significant and it has been increasing. Smokeless tobacco is fairly popular among American males, of whom, about 7 percent indulge in the practice (which compares to only about 0.5 percent of American women).

Around a million American high school students and a quarter million middle school students report current use of smokeless tobacco. Manufacturers have been incorporating kid-friendly flavorings to many of these products. Here are the most common forms of smokeless tobacco:

>> **Chewing tobacco:** This product comes in the form of loose leaves, leaves pressed into a plug form, or leaves twisted together like a rope. Frequent spitting is required, thereby limiting where you can consume it. On the other hand, there are those who don't seem to care where or when they spit.

Chewing tobacco comes in a variety of teen-friendly flavors such as berry blend, citrus blend, cinnamon, peach blend, wintergreen, apple blend, and grape.

>> **Snuff:** Snuff can be moist or dry tobacco and comes finely ground. Moist snuff is placed in the mouth on the gums and requires spitting. Dry snuff is either put in the mouth or inhaled through the nose. Snuff has enjoyed increased popularity around the world as more locations have been designated as nonsmoking areas.

>> **Snus:** This product originated in Sweden. It's advertised as safer than other forms of smokeless tobacco because the manufacturing process appears to involve lower toxic levels of chemicals in the curing process. The tobacco comes in a teabag-like container, which is held in the mouth and easily disposed of. In fact, the U.S. Food and Drug Administration (FDA) has recently allowed a Swedish tobacco company to advertise snus as safer than smoking regular tobacco cigarettes.

>> **Dissolvable tobacco:** This product is highly desirable to kids because it looks like candy or mints and often comes in interesting flavors. The tobacco is sometimes made into lozenges or a toothpick-like stick or thin sheets that look like dissolvable breath strips. No spitting required.

TIP

To spit or not to spit? To sniff or not to sniff? Those are the questions. Dipping, chewing, snuffing, or snussing. The language of smokeless tobacco can be confusing. One reason is that different countries have different terminology for similar products. For example, *snus* is Swedish for a type of snuff. But the bottom line is that, however you ingest, it's all smokeless tobacco. The choice is yours.

REMEMBER

The best choice of all is to quit consuming all forms of tobacco. See Chapter 3 for information about the health risks of various types of tobacco, including the smokeless variety.

RUINING TOBACCO'S REPUTATION

Since early in the 20th century, a series of discoveries began to emerge in the scientific literature that gradually eroded the public's faith in the safety of cigarette smoking, including the following:

- In 1930, scientists from Cologne, Germany, reported that there appeared to be a relationship between smoking and cancer.

(continued)

(continued)

- In 1944, the American Cancer Society stated that, although there was no definitive evidence, smoking appeared to cause health issues.

- In 1950, scientists published a stunning report. They found that 96.5 percent of all lung cancer patients were moderate to heavy smokers.

For the most part, smoking rates remained stubbornly high despite this emerging data. Smokers were more influenced by a highly popular piece in a 1952 issue of *Reader's Digest* titled, "Cancer by the Carton." For the first time since cigarettes were introduced, smoking rates began to decline.

The powerful tobacco industry fought back and published full-page ads in hundreds of the nation's newspapers on January 4,1954. The ad attempted to dissuade smokers from believing that cigarettes caused health problems, stating, "We believe the products we make are not injurious to health. For more than 300 years, tobacco has given solace, relaxation, and enjoyment to mankind. At one time or another, during those years, critics have held it responsible for practically every disease of the human body. One by one, these charges have been abandoned for lack of evidence."

But the real evidence continued to accumulate:

- In 1962, Surgeon General Luther Terry, convened a group of experts to look at all evidence related to health and smoking. The panel included ten esteemed scientists, half of whom were smokers.

- In 1964, the Surgeon General's report proclaimed that cigarette smoking causes lung cancer. This report splashed the front pages of the nation's newspapers.

- In 1982, the Surgeon General reported that secondhand smoke may cause lung cancer.

- In 1990, cigarettes were banned from short airplane flights and all interstate buses.

- In 1992, the Marlboro man died.

Despite mounting evidence, seven of the top executives of America's largest tobacco companies sat before Congress in 1994 and, one after another, testified that nicotine was not addictive. However, their testimony was sharply contradicted by several whistleblowers who had access to the scientific data, which clearly verified the addictive nature of nicotine.

By 1998, chief executives from five of the largest tobacco companies returned to testify before Congress. This time, they admitted that nicotine was addictive and settled a lawsuit for damages of $368.5 billion. Much of this money and other settlements have been used in smoking prevention and treatment efforts by the states.

Chapter 3

Taking Tobacco's Health Costs into Account

A group of friends, camping together, join around the campfire after the sun sets and the night turns cooler. The group finishes eating their s'mores, sings a couple of folk songs, and relaxes around the brightly burning fire. The hostess reaches into her backpack and brings out paper straws that she passes to her guests.

Most guests take a straw, lean into the fire and then suck up the gritty smoke, breathing deeply in and out. Plumes of smoke rise through the trees into the star-filled sky. A couple of guests pluck bunches of leaves from nearby plants and start chewing them — while spitting out the residue. Others gather dead leaves, crush them into a powder and snuff it up their noses. A satisfying end to a lovely evening.

Does this sound like your vision of an idyllic camping adventure? Yuck. Probably not. But ask yourself how different this scene is from what people do when they smoke, chew, or sniff tobacco, whether indoors or out. Why would anyone do that? As Chapter 2 notes, it's largely about addiction, of which nicotine is a prime culprit.

In this chapter, we review the consequences of smoking or ingesting tobacco products. First, we describe how consuming tobacco affects a person's life. Then, we delve into the longer-term consequences of smoking cigarettes, pipes, and cigars, or using smokeless tobacco products.

WARNING

Research tells us that scare messages about tobacco just don't work very well to help people stop smoking. For some, such messages seem to even make things worse. We report this information not with the intent of scaring you. Just realize that in order to make good decisions, it helps to know the truth about the risks of tobacco.

How Smoking Affects Everyday Life

In this section, we primarily address how smoking affects day-to-day living. That's because, to date, more people smoke than use smokeless methods of tobacco ingestion. Plus, a vast body of research on the effects of smoking exists for us to draw upon.

There are limited studies on pipe smoking, cigar smoking, low-tar and low-nicotine cigarettes, so-called "all-natural cigarettes," and filtered versus unfiltered cigarettes. Smokeless tobacco (such as chewing tobacco and snuff) has also been researched. We note this information when it's available and where it's applicable.

However, there is much less research to draw upon regarding heated tobacco products (HTPs). In fact, to date, research on HTPs has been done primarily by the very companies that are selling the devices — and that's not exactly unbiased research. It will take multiple long-term studies to answer the questions about the safety of HTPs.

WARNING

There is no verifiably safe tobacco product available today. You may hear claims to the contrary, but the evidence fails to support that idea. Whether you smoke, inhale, chew, or sniff, tobacco is hazardous to your health.

Examining exercise

Smoking makes it much harder to exercise. That's unfortunate because the benefits of exercise on overall physical health and well-being are hard to deny. The following is just a partial list of health benefits you can expect from frequent, consistent exercise, whether you smoke or not. Specifically, exercise

>> Normalizes blood pressure

>> Improves overall cardiovascular health

>> Decreases the risk of diabetes

>> Reduces some cancer risks

>> Improves muscle and joint function

>> Reduces inflammation

>> Strengthens bones

>> Improves memory and brain functioning

Regular exercise also improves mental health. Frequent exercisers have less depression and anxiety. They also have better focus and handle stress more effectively. Find a drug that can do all that for both mental and physical health, and you'll become rich and famous!

So, if you smoke, it's even *more* important to exercise. That's because smoking damages many of the things that exercise at least ameliorates. Unfortunately, smoking also makes exercise more challenging because smoking

>> Narrows the arteries, reducing blood flow

>> Increases resting heart rate

>> Decreases lung capacity

>> Increases carbon monoxide in the bloodstream

>> Increases the body's production of phlegm

>> Decreases the body's ability to use oxygen

These effects of smoking obviously decrease your stamina and aerobic capacity. Smoking also damages muscles and their capacity for growth because of impaired circulation. That doesn't mean you shouldn't exercise, but you need to proceed with care. Exercise seems to mitigate *some*, but not by any means all, of the risks from smoking. Quitting is best.

WARNING

If you smoke and plan to start an exercise routine, be sure to check with your primary-care provider first. Your health may already be compromised, and you may have to adhere to a graduated, careful regimen.

The nearby sidebar, "Getting moving," illustrates how a smoker can benefit from exercise.

TIP

Some regular smokers who exercise claim that smoking doesn't impact their health. This belief involves denial and wishful thinking. Smoking may not have fully caught up with them or, more likely, they're experiencing some effects that will worsen with time.

GETTING MOVING

Liam, a freelance writer who works at home, has a two-pack-a-day smoking habit. Now in his early forties, he notices that he's losing muscle tone and feeling out of breath. He asks his doctor about joining a gym and starting an exercise program. His doctor fully endorses the idea, but also strongly recommends that Liam stop or at least cut back on his smoking, something Liam feels little desire to do right now. He can't imagine his life without smoking.

Nonetheless, Liam is cleared for takeoff. He begins an exercise regimen at his local gym. He signs up for three months with a personal trainer and soon makes some gym friends.

Liam thinks he'll die the first day; he's breathless and can barely keep up with the trainer's directions. Yet, slowly but surely, he notices increased stamina. Strangely, without intending to, Liam finds himself cutting back a bit on smoking. He just doesn't feel like smoking for a while after working out. After going down to less than a pack a day, Liam decides to quit. He even discovers that he can use exercise both at home and at the gym to counteract cravings to smoke. After four months, Liam declares himself a nonsmoker.

Many smokers report that they don't enjoy smoking immediately after aerobic exercise. In Liam's case, this spurred him on to cutting back and eventually quitting a habit that had already begun to negatively impact his health. You should also know that exercise alone rarely leads to successful smoking cessation, but many smokers find that exercise does provide some help with cravings.

But how about *smokeless* tobacco? See Chapter 2 for information about the types of smokeless tobacco. Given that it's not inhaled, you could be tempted to think it's benign. In fact, smokeless tobacco has been widely used in sports. Because of the stimulant effects of nicotine, many athletes have believed that chewing or snuffing tobacco could improve their performance.

Indeed, smokeless tobacco does appear to have a few short-term, positive effects on athletic performance. It seems to improve concentration, decrease performance anxiety, and temporarily improve aerobic capacity.

But what may help a bit in the short run, can bite you in the long run. Data tell us that smokeless tobacco has been associated with increased rates of mouth, tongue, gum, and cheek cancer. Caffeine has many of the positive effects of nicotine and much less downside risk. Consider having a cup of coffee instead.

SPORTS AND CHEWING

It's widely known that athletes will go to considerable lengths to enhance their performance. Some even risk becoming disqualified for using banned substances. Others put their long-term health at great peril in order to win. For those athletes, the financial rewards are considerable and feel irresistible.

For decades, nicotine has been a favorite performance enhancer, especially among baseball players. In 2014, it was estimated that a little over a third of all Major League Baseball (MLB) players used some form of smokeless tobacco, down from 50 percent in the past. This practice appears to be decreasing due to multiple municipal laws, as well as policies enacted by MLB.

A Hall of Fame baseball player, Tony Gwynn, blamed his salivary cancer on consumption of smokeless tobacco. Sadly, he died at the age of 54. In 2016, MLB finalized an agreement with the players banning smokeless tobacco use for all new players. It's only a matter of time now before smokeless tobacco will be eliminated from the game.

When it comes to other sports, the World Anti-Doping Agency (WADA) monitors nicotine (the addictive component of tobacco) use but has yet to ban the substance. WADA appears to focus less on negative long-term effects and more on what could artificially enhance athletic performance.

Eating and smoking

Many teens, especially girls, start smoking because they want to lose weight. In fact, merely *desiring to diet* increases the chances that a teen will turn to smoking. And, perhaps unfortunately, there is some truth that smoking, and nicotine help control weight. Nicotine appears to have many impacts on the body, including increasing metabolism and suppressing appetite. In addition, smokers sometimes claim that they reach for a cigarette rather than a cookie or a donut.

However, smoking negatively affects nutrition. For example, tobacco smoke has the potential to decrease absorption of calcium and vitamins C, B, and E. Furthermore, smokers are less likely to eat a healthy diet full of fruits and vegetables.

Smokers who quit tend to gain weight. The amounts are typically moderate, but significant. Sometimes smokers who previously had normal body mass indexes move into the overweight category after quitting smoking.

TECHNICAL STUFF

The body mass index (BMI) is a measure of body fat that is based on your height and weight. Your BMI indicates to what degree your weight is on target, underweight, or overweight. You can find your BMI at `www.nhlbi.nih.gov/health/educational/lose_wt/BMI/bmicalc.htm`.

WARNING

Concerns about weight gain are important. However, it's important to remember that the negative health effects of smoking far outweigh the costs of gaining weight. See Chapter 20 for dealing with weight gain when trying to quit smoking.

Smelling and smoking

When it comes to the sense of smell, you get hit with two problems from smoking:

» **Smokers are six times more likely to have a diminished sense of smell than nonsmokers.** Those who smoke more lose even more of their sense of smell. Loss of smell can make food less appetizing. Loss of smell even poses some danger: You may not be able to detect gas leaks or smoke and fire. You may not know your house has some horrible odor — not a good thing when having company over.

» **Smokers, well, um, they tend to smell like disgusting smoke and cigarettes to nonsmokers.** Cigarette smell is notorious for permeating curtains, furniture, bedding, cars, clothes, and even your hair. You may wonder why you don't smell it. Did we mention you lose your sense of smell?

Perhaps surprisingly, smokeless tobacco appears to affect sense of smell and taste as well. No easy out here.

Looking in the mirror

Smoking affects the youthfulness and health of your skin. Several studies have been conducted in which identical twins (one a smoker and one not) were evaluated by researchers who did not know their smoking history. Overall, nonsmoking twins were judged as more attractive and had fewer signs of facial aging than their smoking counterparts.

So, if you want healthier, more vibrant skin, giving up smoking may be your next miracle beauty cream. And instead of having to pay over $100 an ounce for it, you get paid by not having to buy cigarettes!

Smoking also affects appearance by causing

» Yellowing of the fingers and fingernails

» Thinning hair and hair loss

- » Acne breakouts
- » Stained teeth
- » Patches on the tongue (especially ugly if your tongue is pierced)
- » Belly fat
- » Increased risk of psoriasis
- » Sagging skin

TIP

Smokeless tobacco products don't cause as many of these problems, although they aren't entirely benign, as evidenced particularly by oral effects such as stained teeth and periodontal disease.

Reproducing and smoking

If you're thinking about having a baby, there's no better time than now to stop smoking. Fertility in both men and women decreases with smoking. Sperm quality, density, count, and motility decline. Eggs are exposed to the toxins and appear to be damaged by smoking.

WARNING

Men who smoke are at risk for erectile dysfunction. We're pretty sure that could make getting pregnant a bit more challenging and possibly less rewarding.

Worse are the effects of smoke on the unborn child. Smoke, whether from the mother, or secondhand, goes directly to the developing fetus. Smoking is associated with

- » Increased rate of miscarriages and stillbirths
- » Increased incidence of birth defects
- » Prematurity
- » Sudden infant death syndrome (SIDS)
- » Low birth weight
- » Lung and respiratory problems

In effect, the baby becomes a smoker right along with both mom and dad. Most advice in books and on the Internet implore you to stop smoking if you're planning to become pregnant. Prospective parents already know that. We simply suggest that this is a time future parents don't go it alone. See your healthcare provider to coordinate your pregnancy, or your partner's pregnancy, with an effective stop-smoking plan such as the one outlined in this book. You don't need to try harder, just smarter.

Khloe's story (in the nearby sidebar, "Getting the help you need") describes how a healthcare provider can help or hinder a pregnant woman's desire to quit smoking.

TIP

If you're a smoker and become pregnant, beating yourself up will not help. We know you care about your baby, and feeling guilty won't make things better. You need to find someone who can support you and help you develop a solid game plan for quitting and preparing yourself for the birth of your baby.

EXAMPLE

GETTING THE HELP YOU NEED

Khloe had smoked half a pack a day for 20 years and hadn't expected to get pregnant. But, of course, that's what happened. She was already into her third month when she realized she was pregnant.

She and her fiancé have mixed feelings about the pregnancy. Khloe has a successful career and doesn't know how she can afford the additional costs and time a baby would need. They also worry about the effects both of their smoking habits might have on the unborn baby.

Khloe and her fiancé know she needs to get prenatal care and she makes an appointment with an OB-GYN. After her exam and interview, the doctor reviews all the ways Khloe is harming her baby and admonishes her for continuing to smoke. She declares that Khloe must quit smoking immediately, no matter what.

Khloe, stressed about the pregnancy to begin with, starts to cry. She can't see herself as a mother, much less a nonsmoker. Not a good way to start a pregnancy or to stop smoking. She feels lost and alone and leaves the office unsure what to do.

Fortunately, after talking to a friend about her unhappy experience, Khloe decides to find another doctor. Luckily, she finds a more sympathetic healthcare provider who helps her develop a stop-smoking plan that works for her. The doctor gives Khloe and her fiancé considerable credit for facing the daunting difficulty of stopping smoking for the baby's sake. The doctor also congratulates them and reassures them that even stopping now will benefit the baby.

Khloe was fortunate to find a healthcare provider that was not judgmental and used encouragement to help her quit. Khloe, like most pregnant women felt terrible about smoking. She needed support and kindness from her healthcare provider, not heavy-handed criticism.

Getting Seriously Sick from Smoking

Unfortunately, ingesting poison into your system daily for many years takes a toll. We say that not to shame or scare you. Mercifully, we're keeping some of the gory details limited. The reason it's important to know about these issues is that it may help give you additional motivation for quitting.

TIP

If you feel you grasp the overall health risks of smoking or just find the information too gruesome and upsetting, you can certainly skip right to Parts 3 and 4. Those parts focus on quitting strategies and developing your personal plan for doing so.

The good news is that quitting smoking confers substantial health benefits no matter when you do it. The bad news is that you actually have to quit to get these benefits.

So, exactly what can you expect in the relatively near term when you quit smoking? Here are a few of the benefits:

>> If you're an exerciser, your lung function starts to improve after just a few weeks of not smoking.

>> Fertility returns to normal quickly after quitting.

>> The risk of babies born with low birth weight is the same as nonsmokers upon quitting.

>> Your smell and taste will gradually return after six months or less.

>> You won't cough as much in the first year or so.

>> Your heart disease risk reduces after the first year and improves to that of a nonsmoker after 15 years.

>> Cancer risk reduction takes longer but declines after five years.

>> Your risk of a stroke declines substantially after five years.

In the following sections, we detail the major health risks of smoking. Smoking continues to be the most preventable cause of death in the United States and most of the world.

Examining the vascular system

The circulatory system includes the heart, arteries and veins and is responsible for delivering oxygen-rich nutrients and removing waste from all areas in the body. In a healthy body, the process of circulation is effortless. Smoking interferes with that process.

Cardiovascular disease

Heart disease is the leading cause of death for men and women in the United States. About 20 percent of all deaths from heart disease can be directly attributed to smoking. In addition, smokers who have heart disease are more likely to die younger than nonsmokers.

WARNING

Every single cigarette a smoker consumes increases the risk of heart disease. In other words, the more you smoke, the more likely you'll die of heart disease.

What does smoking do to the cardiovascular system? If your health care provider tells you that you suffer from one of the following health issues, you can bet that smoking has contributed to these interrelated diseases:

>> **Hypertension (high blood pressure):** Smoking increases blood pressure immediately and over the long term. Hypertension causes the heart to pump harder. It damages blood vessels, causing them to narrow, weaken, or rupture. That damage, in turn, can lead to stroke or heart attack.

>> **Arteriosclerosis:** This disease involves plaque buildup in the arteries, which can result in a serious blockage resulting in stroke or heart attack.

>> **Heart disease:** When the plaque buildup affects the blood supply to the heart or the coronary arteries, it can cause chest pain, shortness of breath, or a heart attack. When a heart is weakened, it can lead to what's known as *heart failure.* Heart failure occurs gradually, and symptoms include shortness of breath, weakness, fatigue, wheezing, and retention of fluids, resulting in swollen feet and ankles.

WARNING

Although many pipe and cigar smokers claim that they don't inhale, some do, and all of them ingest secondhand smoke close up. Smoking cigars and pipes increases both the risk of heart disease and stroke.

Cerebrovascular disease

Strokes occur when the blood supply to the brain is impeded by a blockage or leakage. The more you smoke, the higher your risk for stroke. In fact, strokes are the top cause of serious long-term disability in the United States. The acronym FAST can help you remember the symptoms of a stroke. Here's what the acronym stands for:

>> **Face:** Numbness or weakness as evidenced by a droopy or asymmetrical smile.

>> **Arms:** Weakness or paralysis on one side of the body, which can be determined by trying to raise both arms at the same time. With a stroke, one arm may not function the way the other one does.

HEART ATTACKS: KNOW THE SIGNS FOR MEN AND WOMEN

If you haven't seen a heart attack in person, you've seen it in a movie. In the movies, someone, almost always a man, clutches his chest, cries out in pain, and topples over. In real life, those symptoms sometimes happen. Here are the most common symptoms of heart attacks for both men and women:

- Chest pain, feeling of pressure or tightness
- Shortness of breath
- Nausea, indigestion, or heartburn
- Pain that radiates to the shoulders, neck, arm, or jaw
- Sweating
- Dizziness or loss of consciousness

Women present somewhat differently. They may have the symptoms listed above, but they're often more subtle. Women more often describe discomfort rather than pain; indigestion and vomiting are more common; they more often feel an overwhelming weakness or fatigue; and women are more likely to report anxiety or a sense of impending doom.

A heart attack is always a medical emergency. Get immediate help. Call 911. Far too many people are afraid of looking stupid for making a possible "false alarm," or think their symptoms will merely fade away. In fact, emergency rooms report that more than half of heart attack victims ask a friend, relative, or neighbor to drive them to the emergency room rather than calling 911. Time is of the essence. Don't delay. It's a life-or-death matter.

>> **Speech:** Confusion or difficulty speaking, or understanding may show themselves.

>> **Time:** If these symptoms appear, call a doctor immediately. Urgent, prompt attention can improve the outcome greatly.

Smoking leads to a host of cerebrovascular problems. It also hijacks the mind, body, and soul. Ted's story, in the nearby sidebar, "Dying for a smoke," shows how powerfully addiction leads to deterioration in health, but also impedes recovery.

EXAMPLE

DYING FOR A SMOKE

Ted, age 62, has been a two-plus-pack-a-day smoker for 50 years. He is transferred to a rehabilitation facility following his hospitalization for a stroke. Ted suffers from weakness on his left side that requires him to use a wheelchair. He hopes that following physical therapy, he'll regain his ability to walk and return to working on his ranch. He also has no intention of quitting smoking, saying, "I'd rather die with a cigarette in my mouth than give it up."

Ted is angry about the indoor no-smoking policy at the rehab center. He also doesn't have a way to get to the store to buy cigarettes. He wheels his chair outside and tries to bum cigarettes from some of the other patients. No dice. Desperate for a smoke, he spots a mostly smoked cigarette butt on the ground. He wheels himself over to it but can't quite reach it. He locks the wheels of his chair and tries to tilt it so he can retrieve the prized butt.

Unfortunately, Ted tips his chair over and lands on his face. Multiple broken bones and lacerations are now another challenge for him to deal with.

Poor Ted. His story illustrates the terrible toll smoking extracts on its victims. His addiction was literally so strong that he was willing to die for it.

Checking for peripheral artery disease

With peripheral artery disease (PAD), plaque builds up in the arteries of the outer (or peripheral) part of the body, most commonly the legs. PAD results in pain, cramping, weakness, and numbness in the extremities. If the blood flow is sufficiently restricted, it can also lead to a high risk of infection, which is difficult to treat. Those with severe PAD, can develop gangrene in the affected tissues, which can lead to amputation or even death. Smoking and diabetes are both risk factors for PAD.

Looking at lungs even if you don't want to

From the moment a smoker inhales for the first time, the lungs rebel. Most first-timers choke and cough as part of this rebellion. But the lungs adapt after a while and seem just fine again — until they're not so fine.

WARNING

In addition to lung problems directly caused by smoking, smoking exacerbates preexisting asthma, makes recovery from colds or flu slower, and can increase the risk of pneumonia.

WARNING

See your doctor for any cough that lasts for three weeks or more or immediately if you're coughing up blood.

Confronting coughs

Most smokers develop a smokers' cough. It's caused by toxins setting up shop in your lungs, which the body tries to eliminate by coughing. In the beginning, it's a dry, unproductive cough without phlegm. As time passes, it becomes more frequent, gets worse in the morning, and starts producing phlegm. Treatments designed for typical coughs are not particularly effective for smoker's cough. Eventually, smoker's cough often leads to more serious conditions.

Taking a turn for the worse

Many people fear lung cancer as the worst outcome of long-term smoking, and for good reason. However, chronic obstructive pulmonary disease (COPD) ranks pretty high on the list, too. In fact, the U.S. Centers for Disease Control and Prevention (CDC) ranks COPD the fourth leading cause of death in the United States. As COPD progresses, the lungs struggle to function properly. The lung tissues thicken, which makes it more difficult to inhale and exhale. More mucus is also produced as the disease progresses.

Again, our intention is not to scare you, but people with end-stage COPD have great difficult breathing and become cognitively impaired due to the lack of oxygen. Most experience substantial anxiety because of being unable to catch their breath, which can turn into feelings of drowning. Although there are medications for easing symptoms for a while, there is no cure for COPD. Smoking causes at least 75 percent of all cases of COPD.

TECHNICAL STUFF

COPD is often used as an umbrella term encompassing both chronic bronchitis and emphysema. *Chronic bronchitis* is bronchitis that persists for months, often recurring over years. Symptoms of chronic bronchitis include

>> Shortness of breath

>> Unusually low energy

>> Cough

>> Overproduction of mucus or phlegm

>> Sometimes fever

The most severe symptom of *emphysema* is shortness of breath. That shortness of breath may appear when going for a long walk at first. However, as the disease progresses, shortness of breath becomes much worse and can be evoked by almost doing nothing, even when sitting. Also, people with advanced emphysema suffer chronic fatigue, poor alertness, and blue or gray fingernails.

Confronting lung cancer

Eighty percent to 90 percent of all lung cancers appear to be caused by smoking. Most lung cancers are not diagnosed in the early stages, which is why about half of all patients die in the first year following diagnosis. The five-year survival rate is just under 20 percent. We should note that a few new, targeted medications and immunotherapy hold some promise for future improvements in these outcomes.

WARNING

Smoking light or menthol cigarettes does *not* reduce a smoker's risk of lung cancer compared to regular cigarettes. However, smoking unfiltered cigarettes doubles the risk of lung cancer for smokers. Filters do *not* make cigarettes safe in any way, shape, or form. But if you're going to smoke something, come hell or high water, at least consider avoiding unfiltered cigarettes.

TIP

Early detection greatly improves survival rates. If you're a smoker, consider going to www.lung.org for a free quiz that you can use to determine if you're eligible for a low-dose CT screening exam that could save your life.

Normally, the first sign of lung cancer is a cough that doesn't go away. Hoarseness, shortness of breath, chest pain, coughing up blood, weight loss, and frequent lung infections represent more concerning symptoms. Don't wait; if you think you're at high risk or you have some of these symptoms, see your healthcare professional right away.

WARNING

When it comes to your risk of heart disease, stroke, and especially COPD and lung cancer, you may think you've succeeded at dodging the bullet if you use smokeless tobacco. Although your risk of lung cancer and COPD may be lower as a smokeless tobacco user, that's not necessarily the case for many other forms of cancer. In the next section, we look at some of the health risks faced by smokeless tobacco users.

WARNING

HTPs have not yet been linked to lung cancer. And tobacco companies claim that they're safer than cigarettes. We have two problems with this claim:

>> There have not been any long-term studies of the safety of HTPs compared to cigarettes.

>> You're inhaling the vapor of the entire tobacco product. Indeed, HTPs don't involve the range of carcinogenic materials and chemicals of burned tobacco, but they do contain some of the same toxins.

Scanning for other cancers

Smoking not only devastates the lungs and circulatory system but also is responsible for many otherwise preventable cancers. Cancer involves cells going wild dividing and invading healthy tissue. Cancer cells move stealthily through the blood and lymphatic system. Toxic chemicals from tobacco make emerging cancer cells more likely and stopping cancer cells more difficult. Warning signs of cancer include

>> Unexplained weight loss

>> Persistent cough or hoarseness

>> Sores that take too long to heal

>> Unexplained lumps that appear anywhere on the body

>> Bleeding or discharge

>> Fatigue

WARNING

If you have any of the troubling signs above, or significant changes in appetite, bowel or bladder routine, or unexplained pain, see your healthcare provider for a checkup.

The more cigarettes you smoke and the more years you smoke them, the greater your risk of cancer of most types. Sending toxic chemicals throughout your body has consequences including a higher risk of the following:

>> Mouth and throat cancer

>> Esophageal cancer

>> Cancer of the larynx

>> Cancer of the trachea

>> Pancreatic cancer

>> Stomach cancer

>> Bladder cancer

>> Kidney cancer

>> Liver cancer

>> Cervical cancer

>> Colon and rectum cancer

>> Leukemia

WARNING

Whether smoky or smokeless, using tobacco causes cancer. For those who smoke pipes or cigars, chew tobacco, or use snuff, the resulting cancer is mainly found in areas that have been directly exposed to the tobacco, such as the mouth, throat, nose, and sinuses. In addition, smokeless tobacco is associated with a higher risk of pancreatic cancer.

Eroding overall health

Ingesting poison into your body day after day, not only causes cancer, heart disease, and stroke, but a whole lot of other heartache. Smoking negatively impacts every part of your body. Smoking increases the risk for a variety of disorders, from loss of hearing to loss of bone mass. The following problems have been linked to smoking:

» **Hearing loss:** Smoking decreases oxygen levels, which negatively effects the blood vessels that keep the critical hair cells in the inner ear healthy.

» **Cataracts and macular degeneration:** Smoking tobacco substantially increases the risk of eye problems. Some studies have found that smokeless tobacco also increases risk.

» **Crohn's disease:** Crohn's disease is a type of inflammatory bowel disease that causes pain, diarrhea, weight loss, and malnutrition. Smoking is a risk factor, and it can lead to more disease.

» **Periodontal disease:** This disease involves chronic infections of the gums around the teeth. Tobacco use makes it worse, and chewing tobacco is a particular risk.

» **Type 2 diabetes:** This chronic disease impacts health negatively across a variety of domains and is 30 percent to 40 percent more likely to occur for smokers as compared to nonsmokers.

» **Rheumatoid arthritis (RA):** RA is a chronic, autoimmune disease, and smoking has been shown to increase its risk and severity.

» **Osteoarthritis:** It's unknown exactly why, but smoking actually seems to confer some small benefit for reducing this disease of the cartilage that protects the ends of bones. Given all the other problems smoking causes, it hardly seems worth going for this mild benefit.

» **Osteoporosis:** This disease involves a deterioration of bone density. The more cigarettes you smoke, the more likely you'll have osteoporosis and break bones. And if you do break a few bones, they'll heal more slowly.

» **Ulcers:** Evidence suggests that ingesting tobacco increases the risk of stomach ulcers and slows healing.

You could almost get the impression that the human body just isn't designed to handle cigarette smoke or tobacco products.

Chapter 4

Looking at the Impact of Smoking on Families and Communities

Smoking is not an individual sport. Even if you're completely alone every time you light up, you add a bit of contamination to your environment. Trivial? Maybe. But the truth is, small amounts of pollutants release into the air but the poisonous debris left from smoking is much more noticeable. It adds up if you consider the billions of butts discarded every year. Animals and sea life ingest this toxic material indiscriminately.

And that's just a small amount of the environmental pollution that occurs directly from smoking. When others are around a smoker, second- and thirdhand smoke also can cause problems. *Secondhand smoke* is what's emitted from the end of lit cigarettes and the smoke that's exhaled. *Thirdhand smoke* comes from the tobacco pollutants — the dust and smell that permeates clothes, hair, carpets, and eventually, all the people who encounter it. Surprisingly, even thirdhand smoke is not benign.

In this chapter, we describe the effects of smoking on the family, the community, and the environment. We also look at the role of legislation in preventing people from starting smoking and decreasing the rate of smoking overall.

Smoking at Home

If you smoke, *even if you don't smoke in your house,* you're exposing your family to cancer-causing toxins. That's because thirdhand smoke on clothes and hair lingers long after you've blown smoke into the air.

TIP

We don't want to shame you or make you feel even more guilty by talking about the effects of second- and thirdhand smoke. We know how difficult it is to quit smoking. But it's important to be aware of the impact you're having. Sometimes it's easier to do something hard when you're doing it for someone else. If you don't quit for yourself, consider quitting for those you care about.

Whether you have kids or not, if you smoke around children, you're harming them. Not a pleasant thought we know. Babies exposed to smoke are at greater risk for dying of Sudden Infant Death Syndrome (SIDS). Furthermore, children exposed to secondhand smoke have more severe and frequent ear infections, asthma attacks, and respiratory infections. And kids who grow up around smokers are at higher risk of becoming smokers themselves.

There is an absence of studies to date that have followed the kids of smokers into their adult years to see whether they're at increased risk for cancer and heart disease. But studies *have* shown that *spouses* of smokers are at increased risk for cancer and heart disease. Bottom line: Roommates, family members, partners, and spouses who live with smokers run a high risk for a host of serious health problems.

WARNING

Many people believe that by not smoking in front of family members, they're protecting them from harm. Unfortunately, that's just not true. Thirdhand smoke builds up over time on all your furniture, clothes, and belongings — and it lingers for months and months. Studies document that even thirdhand smoke exposure produces many of the same health risks as secondhand smoke. Infants and toddlers are at the greatest risk when it comes to thirdhand smoke exposure, because they have less-developed immune systems, put things in their mouths, crawl on the floors, and even breathe at a faster rate than adults do. Madison's story (see the nearby sidebar) illuminates how thirdhand smoke exerts its insidious effects outside of a smoker's awareness.

TIP

Here are a few things you can do to protect your family from second- or thirdhand smoke:

>> Don't allow people to smoke in your house.

>> Don't allow people to smoke in your car.

THIRDHAND SMOKE AND KIDS

EXAMPLE

Madison, age two and a half, whimpers in her mother's arms. The pediatrician remarks that this is her fourth visit in the last six weeks. He explains that she has chronic ear infections and she's been having respiratory problems as well. He asks, "Is Madison exposed to smoking by anyone in the family?"

Her mother responds that neither she nor Madison's father smokes. The pediatrician then asks if any of Madison's caregivers smoke. Her mom replies, "Well, her grandmother smokes like a chimney, but she says she doesn't do it around Madison, and we believe her."

The pediatrician tells Madison about the dangers of thirdhand smoke. He explains that toxins are transferred from the grandmother's clothing, her car, her furniture, and carpet directly into Madison's system. He concludes, "This could explain Madison's sicknesses this year. We need to have a talk with Grandma."

» If one of your childcare providers (even a relative) is a smoker, consider getting someone else because thirdhand smoke cannot be eliminated from a smoker.

» Be supportive of any family member who tries to quit smoking. (See Chapter 23 for ways to help someone you care about quit.)

Looking at the Environmental Impact of Smoking

Most people know that smoking negatively impacts both smokers and those around them. But did you know that tobacco also inflicts a great cost on the environment? You may look at a cigarette and think, "Just how bad can this little thing be?" Here are a few of the costs that accumulate over trillions of cigarettes consumed every year:

» **Pollution:** Many of the roughly six trillion cigarette butts thrown away each year end up on beaches and waterfronts. In fact, the number-one waste product found on international beaches is not plastic, but cigarette butts. Butts are not biodegradable, and they're deadly to fish and sea life. Plus, who wants to spend time on a beach, at a park, or in any outdoor area when it's littered with thousands of cigarette butts?

In terms of air pollution, it is estimated that putting the tobacco industry out of business would be like taking 16 million cars off the roads and highways. It's amazing how those small cigarettes can add up, isn't it?

» **Depletion:** Cigarette smoking doesn't just add to pollution, it takes away from the environment. Deforestation increases greenhouse gases and, most scientists believe, contributes to climate change. One tree is required to make approximately 300 cigarettes. That comes to about 20 billion trees cut down in order to manufacture a worldwide supply of cigarettes for one year — trees that won't be there to pull carbon dioxide out of the atmosphere, thus exacerbating climate change. In addition, because tobacco is often grown on the same soil, season after season, soils become depleted of important nutrients that must be replaced with chemical fertilizers.

Tobacco cultivation also depletes available land that could be used for traditional food crops. Because tobacco is often grown in poor, developing countries, this leads to more worldwide hunger.

» **Pesticides:** Profitable tobacco production requires the use of copious amounts of pesticides. These pesticides are among the most toxic used on crops. Workers exposed to pesticides have higher rates of cancer, nervous system damage, and birth defects.

» **Poison:** Poison control centers across the United States report thousands of calls each year regarding small children and animals that have consumed cigarettes or cigarette butts. Serious problems are rare but can occur due to nicotine's high toxicity. However, concerns have been raised due to the trend toward flavoring tobacco products, which could appeal more to infants and kids.

Combatting Smoking through Legislation

Maybe you're old enough to remember that as recently as the early '90s you could smoke almost anywhere — restaurants, bars, even the cancer ward in most hospitals. Airline crews were particularly besieged by secondhand smoke. Imagine working for hours in a tin can where dozens of people smoked. In those days, you could have a drink or a meal at a bar or restaurant and leave smelling like you smoked a pack of cigarettes, even if you didn't smoke.

Times have changed. Now more than half of all states ban cigarette smoking in public places. Restrictions at work, at shopping centers, and at most eating establishments make it more difficult for smokers to fit in as many cigarettes as they once could. Airlines universally prohibit smoking, and American airports do the same.

These restrictions and the changing perceptions of smoking have certainly led to the lowest smoking rates to date in the United States. Just changing rules governing where smoking is allowed delivered a powerful, implicit message: *Smoking is unacceptable and not welcome here.*

California is an example of a state that has put money and effort into dissuading people from smoking. Its model directly challenges the acceptability of tobacco use and exposure to secondhand smoke. the California Tobacco Control Program (CTCP) initiative includes the following efforts:

» Supporting smoke-free outdoor patios for dining

» Keeping parks and beaches free of smoke

» Campaigning against e-cigarettes

» Trying to prevent tobacco advertising from targeting vulnerable populations

» Providing educational materials to assist in quit efforts

TOBACCO 21: A PROPOSAL WITH STRANGE BEDFELLOWS

Legislation designed to raise the age for tobacco sales to 21 is being proposed at multiple levels of government. Most adult smokers begin as adolescents, which is a time of particular vulnerability to acquiring a nicotine addiction. The proposed laws (a few have already passed) hope to decrease teen tobacco use by making it more difficult for teens to buy tobacco and other related products.

Interestingly, many of the supporters of this legislation come from states that traditionally support Big Tobacco interests (think Virginia and Kentucky, both huge tobacco growers). Even more surprising, many of these proposals are supported by some of the largest tobacco and e-cigarette companies. What's going on here?

Some pundits cynically suggest that these laws will also prohibit future restrictions on tobacco marketing and sales that have also been proposed. In other words, the law will simply state that no one under the age of 21 can buy tobacco. But many of those laws will not include significant fines for store owners who break the law. Nor will they restrict tobacco flavorings that appeal to youth. Health advocates worry that the proposed laws will be meaningless and give tobacco companies exactly what they want.

This strategy has reduced smoking, helped people quit, and discouraged young people from starting. California reports that more than one million lives have been saved by the CTCP.

Australia has taken an additional approach to public health policy on cigarettes. In 2011, the Tobacco Plain Packaging Act required cigarette manufacturers to use plain packages for their cigarettes. Well, *plain* may not be an entirely accurate term. The companies are allowed a small company logo on the packages, but the rest of the package delivers a brief, powerful message (like "Smoking causes blindness," "Smoking kills," "Don't let your child breathe smoke," or "Quitting will improve your health"), often accompanied by a dramatic picture.

The proponents of the act hoped to reduce the appeal of cigarettes and other tobacco products using this simple, inexpensive strategy. Early studies are suggestive of the value of this approach. Given the low cost, it may ultimately hold promise for worldwide implementation with an excellent return on investment.

2

Clearing the Air about Vaping and E-Cigarettes

Chapter **5**

Grasping the Basics of Vaping

This book is intended to help people quit smoking cigarettes, chewing tobacco, or vaping nicotine or sometimes other substances. So, why are we giving you a whole chapter on vaping basics? Primarily because vaping has become a global phenomenon. In fact, although vaping devices have been on the market since only about 2007, almost half of all U.S. high school students have already tried vaping at some point in their lives and about a third report vaping regularly. And about 5 percent of adults currently vape. Those are astonishing figures given that vaping barely existed just over a decade ago.

The early vaping innovators were motivated to find safer alternatives to smoking tobacco. They claimed that they wanted to decrease the risks of regular cigarettes, which represent the leading cause of preventable deaths in the United States. And many smokers do, indeed, look to vaping as a potential way to help them quit smoking.

So, in this chapter, we give a brief overview of most of the major types of e-cigarettes (vaping devices) that you're likely to encounter. We also discuss the various liquids that are available for vaping. Both the devices and what goes into them are evolving rapidly.

A BRIEF HISTORY OF VAPING

The first patent for an electronic cigarette was granted to Joseph Robinson in 1930. It's unknown whether the device was ever actually constructed, but it was not marketed. In the 1960s, Herbert Gilbert created an e-cigarette device that was also never commercialized.

The first commercially successful e-cigarette was produced by a Chinese pharmacist and inventor named Hon Lik, a former heavy smoker whose father died of lung cancer. Since its introduction to the marketplace almost 20 years ago, vaping has become remarkably popular. The device developed by Hon Lik was called Ruyan, which means, "light smoke." Vaping nicotine was first introduced in the United States in 2007. Extremely rapid growth in e-cigarette use is reflected in sales numbers of 1.5 billion by 2014, which climbed to about 3.6 billion in 2018.

We provide information in this chapter about vaping devices and what goes into them for three major types of readers:

>> Concerned parents of teenagers who need to know something about the types of vaping devices and the contents of e-liquid that their kids may be using (see Chapter 7 for more information about teens and vaping).

>> People who have never vaped, but are smokers wanting to quit, who repeatedly have not been successful using other smoking cessation methods (see Chapter 12 for more information about this use of vaping).

WARNING

Health officials from various government agencies have warned against using e-cigarettes to stop smoking until more is known about the cause of serious pulmonary disease apparently following vaping.

>> Curious people who just want to know what this whole vaping craze is about.

WARNING

This chapter is not intended for people who do not smoke but want to start vaping. That seems like a really bad idea to us. See Chapter 6 for why we think so.

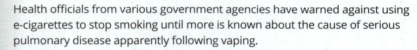
Vaping Devices: Basic Components

If you go to a vape shop, you can see vaping devices of all shapes, colors, and sizes. The materials used to make the device include wood, glass, plastic, and all sorts of metals. Some e-cigarettes look a lot like combustible cigarettes, others look like pens or highlighters and still others look like USB drives.

But there are similarities among vaping devices. Generally, vaping devices are composed of three basic elements: a battery, an atomizer, and e-liquid (or as it's also called, e-juice). See Figure 5-1 for an illustration of the main components of a basic vaping device.

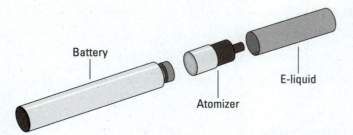

FIGURE 5-1: Components of a basic vaping device.

Batteries

Batteries for e-cigarettes come in three types:

» **Disposable:** Early devices such as the cig-a-likes (see the "Evolving Vaping Devices" section, later in this chapter) have limited lifespans and are meant to be thrown away when the device is used up. They are not rechargeable.

» **Integrated batteries:** These batteries are built into the device and are not meant to be replaced or removed. They have a finite number of rechargers after which the device needs to be disposed.

» **Removable batteries:** These batteries can be recharged. When they no longer recharge, they can be replaced. Removable and rechargeable batteries are typically found in more advanced devices.

WARNING

As discussed in detail in Chapter 6, batteries can explode or catch on fire. Many people find the devices a bit intimidating at first and they struggle to understand the potential dangers of them. Although explosions are relatively rare, they can be minimized, if not avoided, almost entirely by following a few basic procedures:

» Any damaged battery should be promptly disposed of. Damage can range from a torn, plastic sleeve surrounding the cells to indentations on the cell.

» All vaping device batteries should have a protective case while not in use.

» The battery should never come in contact with metals such as keys or coins.

» Batteries should be purchased from a reputable manufacturer.

» Batteries should be stored at temperatures between about 40 to 70 degrees Fahrenheit.

- » Keep batteries away from flammable materials.

- » Batteries should be removed from the device if not used for a long period of time.

- » Never overcharge a device by leaving it in the charger overnight.

- » If a battery gets hot or feels hot while recharging, it's time to dispose of it.

- » If a battery develops an unusual smell, it should be disposed of.

- » If a battery changes shape, it's time for a new one.

- » Never use chargers intended for other devices, such as phones.

Atomizers

The atomizer has a metal coil and a wick (usually made out of cotton). The battery heats the coil. E-juice is absorbed by the wick and heated. The heated e-liquid turns into vapor. There are three major kinds of atomizers:

- » **Disposable:** These atomizers are the simplest type because they require no refilling or replacement. When the e-liquid is depleted, users throw away the device.

- » **Cartomizers:** Cartomizers have joined the atomizer with a holder for the e-liquid. When the e-liquid begins to taste burned, it's usually replaced, although some people clean and refill them.

- » **Clearomizers:** A similar, but newer, design, clearomizers also contain the e-liquid and atomizer. E-liquid levels can be monitored because the material they're made of is — you guessed it — clear.

E-liquids or e-juices

Simply put, an e-liquid or e-juice is the solution that is in a vape device for the purpose of vaping. These liquids vary considerably depending on the concentrations of each substance mixed into the juice. See the "Knowing What You're Vaping" section, later in this chapter, for descriptions of the components of e-juice.

TECHNICAL STUFF

Vaping devices don't actually emit vapor. Technically, they emit an aerosol. An aerosol contains particles and liquid suspended in air. Vapor refers to the gas form of a substance that's normally a solid or a liquid. For example, water when it's evaporated becomes water vapor. Smoke is composed of many particles and is considered an aerosol. Very important stuff to remember for your sixth-grade science test.

Evolving Vaping Devices

E-cigarettes are often described as having come to market in a wave of either three or four generations. There is not a bright line demarcating one generation from the next, but technological advances give you an idea of where the field has gone and where it's headed. In general, over time, the devices have become more powerful, have more adjustable settings, and some now even track a user's vaping behavior. Figure 5-2 provides illustrations of the four generations of vaping devices.

Evolution of the E-cigarette

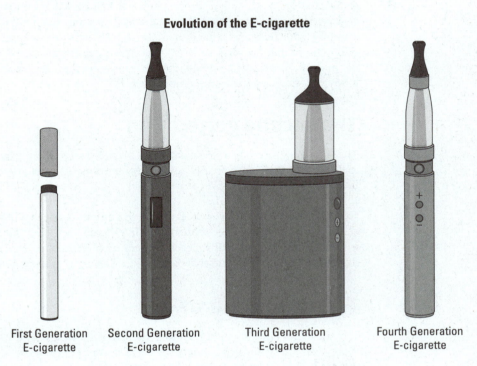

FIRST Generation E-cigarette   Second Generation E-cigarette   Third Generation E-cigarette   Fourth Generation E-cigarette

FIGURE 5-2: Four generations of e-cigarettes.

The first generation

The first generation of e-cigarettes were quite basic and consisted of a battery, an atomizer, and a cartridge of e-liquid. They're often referred to as *cig-a-likes.* They generally look much like a regular, combustible cigarette. They're also small and easy to conceal (see Chapter 7 for vaping info for parents). The experience of vaping with a cig-a-like is similar to smoking a regular cigarette and involves inhaling into the mouth first and then into the lungs.

Most of the first generation of e-cigarettes are not rechargeable or refillable. They're fairly cheap and extremely easy to use. Gas stations and drugstores often carry them. They're activated simply by inhaling, which turns the battery on and usually an LED lights up the end of the stick.

Later iterations of first-generation e-cigarettes include options for recharging the batteries and replacing the cartridges. Certain models have a button that you have to press in order to inhale. Some of these e-cigarettes come with a portable battery charger that is about the size of a package of regular cigarettes.

We talked informally to a number of vape shop customers who told us that they found first-generation e-cigarettes not very helpful when they were trying to quit regular smoking. They said these devices left them unsatisfied, still craving a regular cigarette. They claimed that later generations of e-cigarettes were considerably more helpful because later-generation devices delivered a higher amount of vape and nicotine. Obviously, these discussions can't be considered a scientific study, but they're interesting observations.

The second generation

The next generation of e-cigarettes is a bit more technologically advanced. They have more power and typically have on/off buttons. They usually look like pens or laser pointers.

Generally, batteries can be recharged and sometimes replaced. They have a cartridge called a *clearomizer* that's refillable with e-liquid (see the "Atomizers" section, earlier in this chapter). Most second-generation devices have an important safety device in the form of a chip that turns off the device to prevent overheating.

The third generation

The third-generation vaping devices are also sometimes called *advanced personal vaporizers.* These devices come in lots of different styles and don't look anything like traditional cigarettes. They tend to be much bigger than the older-generation products. They have more power and can heat the e-liquid to a higher temperature than older models, which may alter the toxicity profile of the vapor produced. Third-generation devices are rechargeable and refillable.

The power section of third-generation devices are called *mods.* Mods come in two major types:

>> **Mechanical:** These devices don't have a circuit board to control temperature or power. They're simple devices, but they're more dangerous than regulated mods because they run directly off the battery. The production of vapor declines over time as the battery discharges.

Enthusiasts sometimes like to make their own devices, but that can lead to a bad outcome if someone doesn't have advanced knowledge.

>> **Regulated:** These devices have a chip that controls temperature and power; they include safety features such as automatic shutoff. Some of these devices allow the chip software to be updated. They don't resemble combustible cigarettes or pens. There is usually a small screen that provides information about power.

WHAT DO OHMS HAVE TO DO WITH VAPING?

Talk to an avid vaper for a while and the discussion is likely to include electrical terms such as *ohms,* and sometimes the related terms *voltage, amps,* and *watts.* What in the world does this have to do with inhaling vapor from a device? It affects the individual experience of vaping and the desire for more or less vapor, flavoring, and heat.

Because our publisher wants us to make difficult subjects understandable to our readers, here goes. Instead of vaping, we're going to talk about water. Imagine you're really thirsty and all you had to drink with is a thin cocktail straw. It would be pretty hard to get enough water quickly to quench your thirst. So, how about a garden hose? Would that help? Sure, you could get more water more quickly. Okay, now consider a firehose turned on fully. Wow! Too much for you? Probably.

Now, let's go back to vaping and talk about ohms (you can learn more about voltage, amps, and watts in *Electronics For Dummies,* 3rd Edition, by Cathleen Shamieh [Wiley]). In vaping circles, most vapers focus on ohms and sub-ohm vaping. Ohms refer to the amount of resistance between two points in a conductor.

The conductor in a vaping device is called the *coil.* Coils that are thinner and longer create more resistance (think about a very long, thin straw) and, thus, transmit less electricity for heating the e-juice. Less heat results in less vapor produced. On the other hand, short, thick wires reduce resistance (more like a garden hose) and transmit more electricity and heat to produce a greater volume of vapor, flavors, and other possible additives such as nicotine. Many serious vapers prefer so-called sub-ohm devices that make lots of vapor (like a firehose allows lots of water flow). *Sub-ohm* refers to devices where the value of ohm is between 1.0 and 0.

Lower-resistance circuits allow for a greater range of power adjustments. Think about the firehose; it can be used with a full flow of water or a mere trickle. That gives vapers more options to adjust. But the converse is not true. High-resistance coils (like the thin straws) can't handle a large flow without risking failure or bursting. Well-made, safe vaping devices have the equivalent of a circuit breaker to prevent damage or bursting.

The fourth generation

Technological advances continually find their way into each new generation of e-cigarettes. The newest e-cigarettes are even more powerful and have more bells and whistles than those that came before. There are more options, allowing even finer adjustments in temperature and power. Fourth-generation e-cigarettes also have airflow slots, which allow adjustments to the flow of the vapor.

These devices are usually used by experienced vapers, some of whom participate in competitions involving blowing smoke into various shapes and sizes. See Chapter 7 for information about the uses of third- and fourth-generation devices in these competitions, which are referred to as *cloud chasing*.

WARNING

For new advanced devices, the cable that comes with the device is for attaching a device to a computer to download updates. A computer's USB port should not be used for recharging; instead, a standalone charger is preferable. If something goes wrong, you could lose not only a vaping device but a computer as well.

Pod systems

Pod systems are the newest wave of vaping devices. Pods are somewhat unique vaping devices and are not easily categorized. Some pods look strikingly like computer USB flash drives; others look like pens or cosmetic products. There's no assembly, and there are no adjustable buttons or switches. However, some devices have a single power button, whereas others are activated solely by taking a drag. Pods are easily recharged with the USB charger they come with. See Figure 5-3 for an idea of what some of these systems look like.

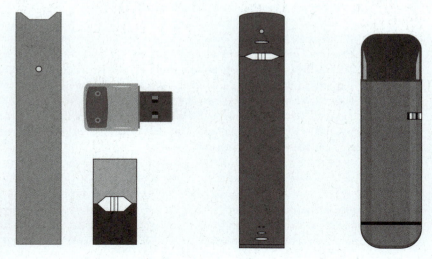

FIGURE 5-3: Examples of pod system vaping devices.

The devices were designed to be low hassle and easy to operate. They're small and discrete, lightweight, easy to carry, and produce a minimal cloud of vapor. Pod designers are trying to mimic the experience of smoking combustible cigarettes as closely as possible to make the transition away from regular cigarettes easier. The nicotine in a pod system is absorbed quickly, like that of a combustible cigarette.

Juul, one of the first pod system devices, was designed by a startup company which created several e-cigarettes prior to their Juul product. The founders, Adam Bowen and James Monsees, were former smokers and they ostensibly hoped to target the one billion smokers worldwide, most of whom want to quit. The Juul was launched in 2015 and in a few years, the product captured a substantial majority of the e-cigarette market.

Although the original market was allegedly for adults wanting to quit combustible tobacco, pod systems quickly became wildly popular with teenagers. (See Chapter 7 for more information about pod systems and teens.)

Knowing What You're Vaping

All vaping devices contain a liquid, which turns into aerosol (often referred to as *vapor*) when heated. Terms for this liquid include

>> E-liquid

>> E-juice

>> E-fluid

>> Vapor juice

>> Smoke juice

>> Vape oil

In this book, we use the terms *e-liquid* and/or *e-juice* for simplicity. It's important that consumers purchase their e-liquids from reputable sources because accuracy of ingredients listed on labels has been a problem. This problem should resolve in the near future; the U.S. Food and Drug Administration (FDA) is in the process of implementing more regulatory authority for e-cigarettes and their contents.

WARNING

Many of the ingredients found in e-liquids are, by themselves, probably of low toxicity. However, when they're mixed together and heated, new chemicals can emerge. We simply don't know how toxic these brews are or become when stored over time. Considerable research will be needed to answer these questions.

As a small beginning, ingredients should be listed on the label. Almost all e-liquids contain some combination of the following:

>> **Vegetable glycerin:** Vegetable glycerin is derived from plant oils. It's used in cosmetics, food, many pharmaceuticals, and toothpaste. Vegetable glycerin is colorless, has a slight sweet taste, and has the consistency of syrup. Using increased percentages of vegetable glycerin in vape juice promotes more cloud, which appeals to some users. Vegetable glycerin makes vaping smoother and easier on the throat.

>> **Propylene glycol:** Propylene glycol is a synthetic substance also used in cosmetics, food, and pharmaceuticals. It's odorless and also slightly sweet. Propylene glycol is somewhat thinner than vegetable glycerin, but slightly thicker than water. Propylene glycol in e-liquid enhances flavor and creates more of what users describe as a desired "throat hit."

TECHNICAL STUFF

Propylene glycol is sometimes used as an ingredient in antifreeze. That fact has frightened some people into believing that vaping propylene glycol could be highly dangerous. However, it isn't the propylene glycol that makes antifreeze toxic. Of note, propylene glycol is also used in asthma nebulizers.

Depending on individual tastes for flavor, throat hit, and amount of vapor, different proportions of vegetable glycerin and propylene glycol can be mixed for e-liquids.

Nicotine

When people quit smoking, they crave nicotine. They want a replacement for nicotine from smoking and in as similar a form as possible to their old smoking habits. Therefore, many e-liquids provide a jolt of nicotine.

REMEMBER

Nicotine gets a bad rap among much of the public. That's because it's so closely associated with the harm caused by smoking combustible cigarettes. However, as we've said more than once elsewhere, it's the inhalation of burning tobacco and its resulting tar that causes most of the problems from smoking. Nicotine is vastly less harmful, although it is *highly addictive.*

Most, but not all, e-liquids contain nicotine. Some contain only flavors. Nicotine concentrations vary widely among different e-liquid products. We've seen a range from 0 to 50 milligrams of nicotine per milliliter. Most smokers wanting to use vaping in order to quit cigarettes need to experiment with different concentrations of nicotine to find what works best to control cravings (see Chapter 12 for more information).

Nicotine salt (a form of natural nicotine) is sometimes combined with benzoic acid for vaping purposes. Nicotine salt absorbs more quickly into the bloodstream than so-called freebase nicotine found in most e-juice. It has a smoother hit, allowing users to increase the nicotine concentration they're consuming.

Nicotine salt requires its own type of vaping device such as the Juul or some type of other pod system or fourth-generation vaping device. Juul claims that its device using nicotine salt is absorbed 2.7 times faster than regular nicotine in other e-cigarettes (and similar to that of regular cigarettes). That absorption rate may cause Juul users to become addicted more quickly than those who use other vaping products. Anecdotal evidence supports this increased risk of addiction, although scientific research needs to confirm (or refute) this possibility.

Flavoring

One of the most seductive parts of vaping rituals is the variety of available flavors. Manufacturers are competing with regular tobacco companies and realize they can enhance the desirability of their product by infusing it with a variety of tantalizing flavors. Unfortunately, some of these flavors have been particularly tantalizing to teens (see Chapter 7).

Some flavors are derived from food extracts. Others are labeled simply as "natural and artificial flavorings." *Natural* refers to flavors derived from plants or animals. *Artificial* can refer to almost anything, and manufacturers rarely disclose specifics. There's no way to know exactly what's in those flavorings.

WARNING

Flavoring ingredients as well as many of the flavorings described in the following sections have been tested and approved for *ingestion* but *not* inhalation, which could present a quite different risk profile.

Currently, there are literally thousands of vape flavors available — everything from banana nut bread to bacon to menthol. Flavors like gummy bears or bubble gum have great appeal to teens and young adults (see Chapter 7); for that reason, many people have called for banning flavors from e-cigarettes. Under this pressure, Juul has recently (as of this writing) stopped selling vape cartridges containing any flavors other than tobacco or menthol. The U.S. federal government is actively considering whether to ban most vape flavors for other manufacturers as well.

WARNING

At the end of the day, we're pretty sure a person could find just about any flavor in the world and some that don't even exist. However, because of unknown risks of flavors and their highly varied ingredients, vapers would be on safer ground if they avoided them altogether.

Vaping CBD or THC

Cannabidiol (CBD) is an active component found in the cannabis plant. *Tetrahydro-cannabinol* (THC) is the active constituent in cannabis that gives people a sense of euphoria or what's called a high. Both come as an oil that can be vaped when mixed with vegetable glycerin and propylene glycol. (See Chapter 6 for important information about the risks of vaping CBD and THC.)

TECHNICAL STUFF

You may wonder what the difference is between cannabis, hemp, and marijuana. Hemp and marijuana are both cannabis plants. To be called hemp, it must contain less than 0.3 percent THC. Marijuana contains more than 0.3 percent THC. Sometimes the two plants crosspollinate and a hemp crop turns into a marijuana crop. Both CBD and THC are, thus, isolated components of two different types of cannabis plant.

Vaping CBD

CBD burst onto the scene quite recently. The 2018 Farm Bill changed everything. It legalized the production and sale of hemp that contains less than 0.3 percent THC. Today, you can find CBD derived from the hemp plant in everything from lotions to lollipops, water, tea, soft drinks, candy, and vape pens and other devices. You can buy these CBD products at your local drugstore, grocery store, CBD specialty store, smoke shop, vape store, online, and more.

You may wonder what made CBD so ubiquitous given that it doesn't make you high. CBD has numerous purported health benefits. Although the FDA has only approved CBD for the treatment of difficult-to-control epilepsy, claims of its efficacy for other problems abound. A *partial* list of these positive health assertions includes the treatment and/or amelioration of:

>> Alzheimer's

>> Anxiety

>> Arthritis

>> Brain injury

>> Cancer

>> Chronic pain

>> Depression

>> Inflammation

>> Inflammatory bowel disease (IBD)

>> Insomnia

>> Migraines

>> Nausea

>> Parkinson's disease

>> Post-traumatic stress disorder (PTSD)

>> Psychosis onset

>> Skin conditions

The value of CBD is recommended for more than humans. You can often buy it at your local veterinarian's office for your dog or cat. It's promoted for animals with arthritis, pain, seizures, separation anxiety, and more.

If the majority of these purported benefits prove to be valid, most of us will be able to empty our medicine cabinets and fill them with CBD products. Unlikely.

Vaping THC

California was the first state to legalize medical marijuana, in 1996, followed by over 30 states in the following two decades or so. Colorado and Washington led the way for legalization and/or decriminalization of recreational marijuana and THC in 2012, followed by another ten states and counting.

The major advantage of vaping THC over smoking marijuana is that vaping doesn't involve burning, which by itself produces a variety of additional chemicals of unknown risks. However, whether vaping THC is safer than smoking marijuana is an open question. One serious concern about vaping THC is that it has been implicated as a possible cause of some cases of serious lung damage, possibly due to ingredients mixed with it (see Chapter 6 for more information).

Health benefits of medical marijuana have been difficult to firmly establish because federal law made such studies exceptionally difficult to conduct for decades. However, there is substantial evidence that marijuana:

>> Helps with chronic pain

>> Works well to decrease chemotherapy-induced nausea

>> Helps decrease spasticity for people with multiple sclerosis (MS)

There is *moderate* evidence that marijuana improves the sleep of people with:

>> Chronic pain

>> Fibromyalgia

» MS

» Sleep apnea

There is *some* (limited) evidence that marijuana helps

» Decrease anxiety

» Increase appetite

» Decrease intraocular pressure associated with glaucoma

» Improve symptoms of PTSD

» Improve a few behavioral symptoms of dementia such as agitation and aggression

Finally, there is very *preliminary* evidence that marijuana may help people decrease or abstain from abusing alcohol or opioids and perhaps tobacco. Additional, preliminary evidence has provided hints that THC and possibly CBD may have a beneficial neuroprotective effect following traumatic brain injury. Considerably more research is needed to confirm or refute these exciting possibilities.

WARNING

Even in states where marijuana is legal, a robust black market offers THC for vaping, the safety of which is unknown. And vaping THC has been associated with serious cases of vaping–related lung damage (see Chapter 6). Never buy any vaping products from the street.

Chapter **6**

Recognizing the Risks of Vaping

We would love it if all humans enjoyed breathing clean, fresh air, devoid of any pollutants. But it would also be nice if everyone had a great diet of healthy food, never consumed too much alcohol, got plenty of exercise, got just the right amount of sleep, drove safely, never gambled to excess, never used illicit drugs, and abstained from risky sex.

As far as we can tell, our preferences are unrealistic for the vast majority of people. Some people live in polluted cities, others lack adequate nutritious food, too many don't get sufficient exercise or sleep. And about a billion people around the world use some form of tobacco.

Fewer people vape. But their numbers are climbing rapidly. In 2011, about seven million people reported vaping, and as of this writing, the number is approaching 50 million adults worldwide. This exponential growth explains the surge in interest about the health effects of vaping.

In this chapter, we explore the controversial debate about smoking versus vaping safety. Then we review what's known so far about specific health risks of vaping. (See Chapter 2 for more details concerning the risks of consuming tobacco in its various forms.)

We conclude with a discussion of the potential of vaping to lead people to pick up a combustible smoking habit. That concern is especially troubling, given that e-cigarette use is associated with higher rates of regular smoking by adolescents. (See Chapter 7 for more information about the implications of vaping among tweens and teens.)

Answering the Million-Dollar Question: Is Vaping Safer than Smoking?

Yes, probably — but with numerous caveats. In a head-to-head contest, smoking appears more dangerous than vaping. Think of smoking like playing professional football without a helmet or protective gear. Chances are, you're going to get hurt. Badly. You may even die. Half of all chronic smokers will eventually die from illness directly linked to smoking.

However, if you suit up in appropriate protective clothing and a helmet, you'll have a much better chance of surviving that football game. Nonetheless, you'll still be running substantial risks of getting hurt, especially over time. Consider all the serious brain injuries increasingly reported among former professional football players, even though they used helmets. For that matter, even in the short run, it's a rare NFL game that you don't see at least one player carried off on a stretcher. So, let's say that vaping is more like playing football for years with protective gear: safer but far from safe.

Yet, many in the public don't realize that vaping is probably safer than smoking. Surveys have found that increasingly, the public views e-cigarettes as equally, if not more, dangerous than regular, tobacco cigarettes. That may be because of frequent news articles about the dangers of vaping. Relatively few news articles appear that detail the dangers of cigarette smoking. That's because those dangers have been well known for decades and the topic is neither newsworthy nor controversial.

Scientists know that cigarette smoking kills, and the risks are well established. A lot of the damage from regular smoking is caused by the combustion of tobacco, which produces toxins that damage the cell linings of the lungs. That damage makes the cells more vulnerable to the effects of cancer-causing chemicals (some caused by the combustion itself) found in regular cigarettes.

Vaping appears safer, but many of the risks associated with vaping are not yet fully known. Long-term studies are sorely lacking because vaping is a relatively new phenomenon. Nevertheless, scientists have reached a reasonable consensus that vaping is safer than regular cigarettes.

TIP

Although vaping potentially exposes vapers to an array of toxic chemicals, there are fewer chemicals and the levels of those chemicals are much less toxic than those found in regular, combustible cigarettes.

You should know that conclusions about the safety of vaping are complicated because of the variety of devices and substances. In fact, there are literally *hundreds* of different types of vaping devices that produce variable levels of heat and amounts of vapor (see Chapter 5). There are almost an infinite variety of e-juice combinations. And the concentrations of these substances also fluctuate widely. For example, some e-liquid contains exceptionally high levels of nicotine. Other formulations contain no nicotine whatsoever. Still others deliver various flavors, tetrahydrocannabinol (THC), cannabidiol (CBD), and so on (see Chapter 5). Different risks likely depend on the actual device and specific ingredients in the e-liquid.

WARNING

Although most forms of vaping appear generally safer than smoking cigarettes, we want to be clear that we do *not* advocate starting vaping if you're not a smoker. Chapter 12 provides information on using vaping as one means of either quitting smoking or reducing overall harm from smoking — however, this use is *only* recommended for the small percentage of people who smoke heavily, have tried quitting by a number of other means, and are either unable or unwilling to quit smoking entirely.

WARNING

Because vaping in the United States is still lightly regulated, using e-cigarettes may confer greater risks than if purchased in the United Kingdom, where there are strict controls over the industry. So, for now, the U.S. Centers for Disease Control and Prevention (CDC) recommends against using vaping to quit smoking.

TECHNICAL
STUFF

The U.S. Food and Drug Administration (FDA) is often cited as having not found e-cigarettes to be a safe and effective method for smoking cessation efforts. One reason it hasn't reached this conclusion is that it hasn't yet studied e-cigarettes for this purpose. In the United Kingdom, the National Health Service (NHS) has assessed the issue and recommends e-cigarettes for the purpose of quitting smoking. More research is badly needed on vaping as a smoking cessation strategy because what we have now is both conflicting and controversial.

Examining the Dangers of Vaping

If you do decide to take up vaping, whether as an aid to quitting smoking or as a hobby or recreational activity, you should at least be aware of what's currently known about the risks. Again, our advice is to refrain from another, potentially addictive habit — a habit that will cost you time, money, and possibly your health. After all, this book is about quitting, not starting!

Ultimately, the choice of whether to vape is yours. The sections that follow lay out the major, known risks of vaping. Time will no doubt reveal more.

WARNING

When people smoked cigarettes during the Roaring Twenties, they had little concern about the health consequences of their new habit. Serious warnings didn't start appearing until around 1950. In part, that's because many of the diseases associated with cigarette smoking take decades to develop. Vaping today is much like smoking cigarettes in the 1920s. Yes, there are far fewer "known" toxins in e-cigarettes, but we just don't have long-term data to know for sure what the risks are over time.

Becoming addicted

Every morning we drink coffee. And we enjoy coffee. Any morning that our coffee routine is interrupted, we crave coffee. We both consider ourselves "mildly addicted" to caffeine. Not a big deal unless coffee is not available. And we have both had periods of time without caffeine. However, not all addictive drugs are as cheap and readily available and have as relatively high health/safety profile as caffeine. In addition, caffeine's downside risks are minimal.

Nicotine has many similar effects on the body as caffeine. So, why is it such a serious issue to be addicted to nicotine? Part of the concern has to do with the way nicotine is consumed. With cigarettes and vaping, people become *enslaved* by the routine of having to take numerous puffs all day long.

Most people generally drink coffee one, two, or at most, three times per day. That's partly because caffeine has a much longer half-life than nicotine, meaning that nicotine remains in the body a much shorter time than caffeine does. Thus, to maintain the good feeling, you must replenish nicotine much more frequently.

Then, of course, there's also the hassle factor of nicotine addiction. You don't see too many "no-coffee" zones out there, and no one else unwillingly consumes your coffee when you drink it. With smoking and vaping, severe limits are placed on where you can consume, and everyone around you inhales some of your nicotine, whether they want to or not.

One of the highest risks associated with vaping nicotine is that you'll become addicted to the substance. Nicotine is one of the most addictive drugs out there (and more so than caffeine). A major characteristic of becoming addicted is that you continue to seek out your drug of choice despite negative consequences.

Negative consequences of a nicotine addiction may include significant risks to health. Do you really want your life and the lives around you controlled so much by a drug?

Chemical concerns

If you visit a local vape shop and ask what chemicals are in the e-liquid, they're likely to tell you it comes down to just vegetable glycerin, propylene glycol, and whatever substance you're wanting added such as nicotine, CBD, or THC. They may inform you that various flavors are in the liquid, too. They'll likely assure you that the flavors are all safe and that many are FDA approved. (See Chapter 5 for more information about e-liquids or, as they're also called, e-juices.)

What they *won't* tell you is that these substances are mainly approved for human *ingestion,* not *inhalation.* For example, consider pepperoni pizza. It tastes great, and it's relatively safe. But what would happen if you liquified the pizza, heated it, and inhaled the vapor? We don't know the answer to that question, but just intuitively, it seems like it wouldn't be a good thing to do to your lungs.

In other words, most chemicals used in vaping have never been subjected to scrutiny for safety when inhaled. Because literally thousands of chemicals are used for flavoring in e-liquids, that leaves you quite uncertain as to the safety and nature of e-liquids used for vaping.

Furthermore, the chemicals that are put into e-liquids can break down and change when heated and vaporized. Just a few of the chemicals and toxicants your body may encounter when vaping include

>> Acetaldehyde

>> Acrolein

>> Acrylamide

>> Benzene

>> Diacetyl

>> Formaldehyde

>> Furfural

>> Nitrosamine

>> Phthalates

>> Various volatile organic compounds

And, as we said, these aren't the only chemicals you could be exposed to when vaping. Some of them are known carcinogens. Sometimes there are chemicals that are not listed on the labels of the e-liquids. Furthermore, toxic substances emitted from e-cigarettes vary with the device used and the contents of the specific e-liquid. At the same time, to be fair, you should know that your exposure to toxins from e-cigarettes is substantially lower than what you inhale from regular cigarettes.

Mining metals

Your local vape shop manager probably won't mention this, but there are studies indicating that e-cigarette aerosol contains metals. Metals are highly toxic and can affect multiple organs. However, this issue is still waiting for answers from good studies to address specific long-term health effects (or lack thereof) from vaping.

The levels of metals vary with the type of device in question. Most studies to date have focused on cig-a-like products and vape pens (see Chapter 5).

It's believed that heated coils and other components of the vaping device are the primary source of these metals, which are thought to leak into the aerosol. A few of the metals that have been found include

>> Aluminum

>> Chromium

>> Iron

>> Lead

>> Manganese

>> Nickel

>> Tin

The exact levels and concentrations vary among devices and, thus, long-term health effects are more difficult to definitively ascertain or predict. Cadmium is also found in e-cigarettes; however, at much lower levels than it's found in combustible cigarettes. Cadmium has high toxicity and causes lung and kidney disease.

Getting to the heart of the matter

Like combustible cigarettes, e-cigarettes carry nicotine into the lungs and circulate through the cardiovascular system. The nicotine is carried by microscopic particles in the aerosol. These ultra-fine pollutants have been linked to high blood pressure, coronary artery disease, and heart attacks.

In a large survey of close to 100,000 participants, researchers found that e-cigarette users had significantly higher risks of heart attack and coronary artery disease than non-smokers or non-vapers. The risk suggested a 34 percent increased chance of having a heart attack for e-cigarette users.

VAPING AND DIABETES

Diabetes affects millions of people in the United States. Those with the disease have an elevated risk for heart disease. Vaping also appears to increase hemoglobin A1C levels, which in turn make complications like diabetic eye disease, kidney disease, and heart disease more likely. So, it makes sense that people with diabetes should avoid smoking and vaping.

Alternatively, some doctors have suggested that if someone is both diabetic and a smoker of regular cigarettes, switching to vaping as a quit-smoking strategy may still have a payoff in spite of concern about A1C. Regular smoking is *that* bad for you. And consider the fact that tobacco smokers are more likely to get diabetes than nonsmokers.

The bottom line: Don't start smoking e-cigarettes if you have diabetes. The only value e-cigarettes would have for someone with diabetes is that they may help you quit. See Chapter 12 for more information about using e-cigarettes to quit smoking.

E-LIQUID AFFECTS HEART TISSUE IN THE LAB

A widely cited study led by researchers at Stanford University suggests that flavorings commonly found in e-liquid damage human blood vessel cells known as *endothelial cells*. These cells line the interior of blood vessels, lymphatic vessels, and the heart. Damage to this type of cell often precedes heart disease.

They found that cinnamon and menthol flavors were especially toxic. The study concludes that e-cigarettes are not heart healthy. However, it's important to note that the cells were studied in the laboratory, not the human body. For this reason, it's unclear what doses, concentrations, and duration of exposure is needed to create significant, actual heart disease. Again, considerable additional research is needed for us to make firm conclusions.

This type of study demonstrates a possible association, but it can't truly establish a causal relationship between vaping and heart disease. Furthermore, the authors acknowledged that regular smoking confers a much higher risk of cardiovascular disease than vaping. One preliminary study indicated an improvement in heart function when combustible cigarette smokers switched to vaping for a month. Once again, more data over long periods of time is needed.

Irritating lungs

E-cigarettes have been associated with increased risk of asthma, chronic bronchitis, and pulmonary inflammation. In addition, people who vape have decreased immunity and increased mucus secretion. There is concern that e-cigarette users may be predisposed to respiratory infections.

WARNING

Healthy adults and teenagers have been taken to emergency rooms with shortness of breath, chest pain, and fatigue. Some of them have ended up in intensive care with severe lung damage, and some have died. They all reported vaping prior to their illnesses. People have been vaping in large numbers for over a decade, and these cases have only recently emerged, so it seems likely that new contaminants have gotten into the supply chain.

Nonetheless, as of this writing, it appears that the only apparent common denominator for these lung damage cases is vaping. Those stricken reported using various devices with different e-liquids. A substantial majority (over 75 percent) admitted to vaping THC, some obtained legally and many others not. Vitamin E acetate is often used with THC to make a proper vaping consistency. Vitamin E, when inhaled, appears to cause a severe inflammatory reaction. Another possible culprit is contamination from using devices with bad e-liquid mixes and/or problematic flavorings of unknown toxicity. Careful reporting and study will be needed to track down the true source(s) of the problem. The bottom line is that the vaping industry is in dire need of robust study and regulation.

WARNING

While investigating a recent spike in pulmonary illnesses related to vaping, the CDC recently recommended the following:

>> Never buy e-cigarettes or e-liquids off the street.

>> Do not modify e-cigarette products on your own.

>> E-cigarettes should not be used by teens, young adults, pregnant women, or adults who do not currently use tobacco products.

>> If you vape and have concerns about your health, such as shortness of breath, cough, or chest pain, seek immediate medical care.

POPCORN LUNG

Much has been written about e-cigarettes and the flavoring agent called *diacetyl*. This chemical is used to give foods a buttery flavor and has been found in some e-liquids. Diacetyl is used in various food products such as popcorn, candy, and potato chips. It's that pleasant smell that hits your nose when you open a bag of freshly popped, microwave popcorn.

Breathing in diacetyl has been shown to cause a condition called *popcorn lung*. The condition was first diagnosed when a large group of factory workers at a microwave popcorn manufacturer came down with a respiratory condition that included symptoms such as:

- Dry cough
- Fatigue
- Rapid breathing
- Shortness of breath
- Unexplained wheezing

Popcorn lung cannot be reversed. There is no cure. Treatment can include steroids to decrease inflammation, antibiotics, and supplemental oxygen when needed.

The connection was made between diacetyl and popcorn lung. Precautions were taken in the factories. These workers had been exposed to daily, *extremely high* levels of the chemical.

When it was noted that some e-liquids contained diacetyl, there was understandable concern about popcorn lung. However, to date, there have been no studies linking popcorn lung and vaping. Nevertheless, it makes sense to limit exposure to a potentially dangerous, toxic chemical. That's why in the United Kingdom, a country with strict regulations of e-liquid, diacetyl is banned.

Although diacetyl is not banned in the United States, some e-liquid manufacturers claim that their products are diacetyl free. However, people who vape should have some concern about companies or shops that use bulk flavoring. That's because the labels on bulk flavoring often state that they contain a mix of natural and artificial ingredients, which could include diacetyl as an unlisted component.

(continued)

(continued)

All that said, the scare over this ingredient (and likely some others) has been overblown. The average regular cigarette package contains 6,718 micrograms of diacetyl compared to an average cartridge of an e-cigarette (roughly equivalent), which contains 9 micrograms of diacetyl. Furthermore, even smoking combustible cigarettes has not been connected to popcorn lung. Sometimes researchers wanting to prove a point leave out important information like this. Nonetheless, it's always a good idea to avoid inhaling potentially toxic materials, even when the risk is fairly low.

Getting burned

Are you someone whose money burns a hole in your pocket? We hope not. But we also hope that you're not someone whose vaping device burns a hole in your pocket or blows up in your face, hands, or groin. People have shown up at emergency rooms, after vaping devices have blown up, with broken facial bones, severe burns, and extensive lacerations.

Vaping devices exploding and burning is not a frequent occurrence, but it happens. In fact, there were over 2,000 emergency room visits due to vaping devices catching fire or exploding in the period from 2015 to 2017. It's believed that this statistic is an underestimate and that better surveillance procedures should be implemented to track this problem more accurately. You can see the whole exploding vaping device thing on YouTube. Just search for vaping explosions. Not a pretty sight.

Most vaping explosions happen due to problems with the lithium ion batteries and mechanical mod systems lacking regulators. See Chapter 5 for more information on devices, batteries, why these explosions happen, and what to do to prevent them.

WARNING

In the event that you do experience a vaping fire or explosion, you should seek immediate medical attention if the burn is more than 3 inches in diameter. Do so also if the burn affects your face, genitals, hands, feet, elbows, or knees and the skin is blackened or severely blistered.

WARNING

If your clothes catch fire when your vaping device explodes, stop, drop, and roll. And cover your face.

For minor burns, keep the area clean and cover it with a cool compress. Always watch for increasing symptoms of infection, such as redness, swelling, discharge, or fever, and seek medical attention if they occur.

Pregnancy and vaping

If you're planning on having a baby soon, our strong advice is to stay away from all nicotine products and vaping of any type. We discuss the hazards of smoking associated with pregnancy, as well as the effects on fertility, in Chapter 3. Although vaping may have a somewhat safer profile than smoking regular cigarettes, that does not make it safe — especially when you're pregnant.

Preliminary research on animals links the possibility of e-cigarette use as a cause of birth defects, especially to craniofacial development. It appears that flavors, especially complex mixtures of flavors, have the largest effect on this anomaly.

Early research suggests that fetuses exposed to nicotine and/or e-cigarette flavors, have a greater risk of brain or lung damage. Like other risk factors, much needs to be determined through further research. In the meantime, keep your baby safe and avoid all vaping.

Seeing seizures

A seizure occurs when there is a sudden surge of electrical activity in the brain, which can cause disturbances in movement, behavior, and consciousness. Signs of a seizure may include staring, confusion, or uncontrolled, jerking movements, as well as memory lapses. Most seizures last from a few seconds to minutes.

Some reports indicate the possibility of seizures having occurred after vaping with e-cigarettes. The FDA has had reports of seizures from people who just started to vape and regular users of vaping devices. It has been postulated that high doses of nicotine could be responsible for these seizures. And seizures are, indeed, one of the known side effects of nicotine poisoning. This effect would, thus, be in response to having overdosed on vaping if, indeed, vaping was the cause of the seizures. However, a causal link has not yet been established.

WARNING

Some e-cigarettes have very high levels of nicotine. In fact, one e-cigarette, Juul, popular with teenagers has as much nicotine as an entire pack of cigarettes in a single device.

Nicotine poisoning

Nicotine poisoning is relatively uncommon because most smokers and vapers self-regulate their consumption based in part on how they're feeling. However, emergency rooms and poison control centers have seen an uptick in nicotine poisoning over the past few years with the advent of vaping devices.

E-liquids can contain enough nicotine to kill a small child or pet. Many vapers refill their own devices and maintain a supply of premixed e-liquid formulations or the pure chemicals (including nicotine) that go into mixing the refills. Since 2016, nicotine bottles have been required to come in childproof containers.

WARNING

You can get nicotine poisoning simply by spilling or touching it while refilling your vaping devices. Always wear protective gloves when handling. It should also go without saying that nicotine products should be kept well out of the reach of children and pets.

Secondhand vapor

What about exposing other people to your vapor? Or what are the risks of being in a room with someone else who's vaping? The good news is that secondhand vapor is far less toxic than smoke from combustible cigarettes. The bad news is that vaping appears to make the air inside a room lower quality, with small amounts of nicotine and other particles. The health implications of this indoor pollution are unknown.

Encountering the Wild West

E-cigarettes first became commercially available in the United States in 2006. That's a short time span, and the FDA has been slow to catch up in terms of oversight and regulations. In other words, the industry has been largely on its own until quite recently. That means you don't have great assurances that products contain what they say and in the amounts that are stated. Furthermore, consumers can't assume that devices have been made with safe, reliable materials and designs.

New regulatory guidelines are set to come out soon and should provide consumers with more confidence in what they're purchasing. These directives should help reduce illegal, online sales of fake products as well. You can't fully assess a product's safety without knowing exactly what it contains or how it's manufactured.

Risks of Vaping CBD or THC

In this chapter, we focus on the health risks of vaping nicotine. That's because this book is intended for those struggling to quit using either tobacco or nicotine. Nicotine is the addictive substance used by vapers who may have the most trouble quitting. By comparison, THC and CBD are less addictive than nicotine. (See Chapter 5 for more information about vaping CBD and THC.)

Vaping CBD

We know of no evidence that vaping CBD has any risk of addiction. On the other hand, there are many claims of health benefits of CBD (see Chapter 5). Unfortunately, many of these claims appear a bit overblown and lack backing by research. At the same time, some benefits have been proven such as treating some severe seizure disorders.

WARNING

It seems likely to us that at least a few more of these claims will ultimately be proven to have substantiated value. Nonetheless, a risk of turning to CBD is that many of the products are quite expensive and may be less effective than more traditional treatment.

WARNING

Although CBD has a very low risk profile and is well tolerated at high doses, that doesn't translate into totally safe. The following problems can occur when vaping CBD:

>> Unreliable quality of the e-liquid, which can contain contaminants due to lack of regulations and oversight, which appears to be tightening.

>> Higher than allowable levels of THC, which is the component of cannabis that produces a high. Most CBD products contain small amounts of THC, but some CBD contains more than it should.

>> Devices that can release particles or metals with unknown risks.

>> Unsafe battery/device combinations that run the risk of fire or explosions.

TIP

You can avoid most of the risks associated with vaping by choosing CBD that comes in the form of edibles, lotions, or pills.

Vaping THC

THC produces a high or intoxicated state and can be addictive, though less so than nicotine. In addition to an addiction potential, there are side effects associated with THC, including the following:

>> Slowed reaction times

>> Problems with coordination

>> Feelings of paranoia

>> Red, irritated eyes and dry mouth

>> Memory loss with chronic use

Chronic users of marijuana, including those who vape THC, often have problems maintaining focus and motivation. These issues can have a deleterious effect on school or work. Especially in teens, large amounts of THC may also produce psychiatric problems, such as psychosis, depression, and anxiety. Due to problems with coordination and slowed reaction times, driving can become impaired.

TIP

Although THC is illegal at the federal level, it is legal in many states and medical marijuana is legal in even more states. Someone addicted to THC can use the same techniques to quit as discussed throughout this book.

WARNING

All the same risks cited in the preceding section on vaping CBD apply to vaping THC. Some people purchase THC on the black market. When you do that, you run a substantial risk of receiving a contaminated product. Many of the dramatic headlines in the news concerning vaping leading to serious lung problems and even death, may be due to such contamination (see the "Irritating lungs" section, earlier in this chapter, for more on this issue).

TIP

The good thing about THC is that it has an unusually low potential for overdose resulting in death. In fact, at this time, there is only one reported case of a death ostensibly caused by a THC overdose (from vaping). However, some scientists dispute whether THC caused the death.

On the other hand, you could die from an overdose of marijuana containing THC if you happen to be hit by a 400-pound bag of pot dropped on your head from 50 feet.

Evaluating Vaping as a Gateway to Regular Smoking

Numerous critics of e-cigarettes have cited the possibility that vaping may lead many of its adoptees to move on to combustible cigarette smoking. The data say otherwise. For most mature adults, vaping does not lead to the use of regular cigarettes. In fact, many adults are using vaping as a way to decrease or quit smoking entirely.

There are about two million adults who have never smoked but use e-cigarettes. Most of those are young males in their late teens to early 20s. It appears to be rare for them to graduate to regular cigarette smoking. Tweens and teens are another story entirely, and the story is more complicated. (See Chapter 7 for information about adolescents who vape and what happens to them.)

Chapter 7

What Parents Need to Know about Vaping

There is an epidemic of vaping among youth. In fact, a recent National Youth Tobacco Survey found a 78 percent increase in reported vaping among high school students from 2017 to 2018. The same survey revealed a 48 percent increase in vaping among middle school students. Today, at least one out of every five current high school students admit to vaping, compared with about one out of 20 middle school students.

The numbers continue to rise. In 2018, 3.6 million American youth reported vaping. In 2019, that number had risen to 5 million; of those 5 million, 1 million reported daily use and 1.6 million admitted to frequent use (20 or more days per month). This rise has occurred in spite of widely publicized incidents of serious lung damage associated with vaping.

It's important to point out that surveys depend on what's called *self-report data.* Lots of people fail to admit to potentially shameful behavior like vaping. That's particularly true of teenagers. So, actual percentages of teens vaping probably run *higher* than official survey data tell us.

E-cigarette use among adults is controversial — some consider it a godsend with the potential to help millions of regular cigarette smokers quit smoking and greatly reduce their health risks. Others see e-cigarettes as just as dangerous as regular cigarettes.

REMEMBER

However, there is no controversy about e-cigarette use by kids or teens. Any amount of vaping among kids has dangers and risks that exceed those incurred by adults who vape. *We need to do everything possible to prevent teenagers from vaping and help those who already vape to stop.*

In this chapter, we explain the reasons why the vaping craze has seduced kids. Then we take a look at the special risks vaping poses to youth development. We give parents strategies on how to reduce the risk of their own kids turning to vaping. We also provide parenting techniques for helping teens who have been caught in the vaping trap.

Hooking Up with Colors, Flavors, and Gadgets: Marketing to Kids

Kids like toys, colorful gadgets, and sweet flavors. So, it's no wonder that vaping, with its cool look and cute devices, is tempting to teens. The variety of scrumptious-sounding e-liquid flavors like grape or strawberry puts icing on the cake. As of this writing, the U.S. federal government is considering restricting vape flavors largely due to their appeal to kids.

There have been precipitous drops in regular cigarette smoking among both teens and adults in the past half-century. The tobacco industry is looking for new customers, so it wants to make the early experience of vaping appealing, smooth, and easy to indulge.

E-cigarettes have the potential to hook users quickly because they avoid much of the unpleasant harshness often associated with early smoking of regular cigarettes. And many have high levels of nicotine. Tragically, kids can graduate from casual e-cigarette users to confirmed nicotine addicts before they know it.

Stealth vaping

Teenagers know that their parents and teachers don't want them to vape. And vaping manufacturers have given teens a way to deal with this concern. Not surprisingly, many of the pod devices (see Chapter 5) are exceptionally easy to conceal. Even worse, if parents happen to encounter some vaping devices, they're highly likely to mistake them for something else, such as a USB drive.

Small sleek pod devices don't produce as much vapor as many other vaping devices. That makes stealth vaping at school pretty easy to accomplish. Some kids report actually vaping during classes. Others generally use the restrooms or vape out on the campus. Vapers hold devices in their fists and take surreptitious hits, then they slowly exhale in small amounts.

Schools have responded to the vaping crisis by installing vape detectors in the restrooms, but there have been some problems with detection:

> » Staff find it difficult to respond before the culprit escapes into the school hallways.

> » Some kids exhale the vapor into the toilet bowl as it's flushed, creating a suction that pulls the vapor away from the detector.

Taking kids to the market

Manufacturers have denied marketing specifically to adolescents. Whether their contention is true or not, it's hard not to see the youth appeal in their products and marketing. For example, almost one-third of kids report starting to vape so that they can enjoy flavors (such as cookies and cream or mango). And quite a few anecdotal reports by teens suggest that they'd have considerably less desire to vape if e-liquids didn't come in flavors.

The design elements of the pod system devices are also appealing to teens. They're attractive and can be personalized. Kids can purchase so-called *pod skins* online for less than $10. These skins come in all sorts of colorful, pleasing, and unique designs.

Evidence that the devices are appealing can be found in the fact that teens themselves are responsible for much of the marketing of e-cigarettes. Manufacturers don't even have to overtly market directly to kids. Teens and preteens post images and videos of vaping to Facebook, Instagram, Twitter, and YouTube in large numbers.

CHASING CLOUDS: WHEN VAPING BECOMES COMPETITIVE

Is cloud chasing an art, hobby, or sport? Cloud chasers would say all three. *Cloud chasing* involves producing the biggest, thickest plume from a vaping device. It can also entail blowing out various shapes and movements of vapor. There are cloud-chasing competitions throughout the United States and, increasingly, around the world. *Cloud gazers* (the audience) watch and cheer on competitors.

Imagine a giant ruler hung across a long wall. Two vapers stand back-to-back and exhale as large a cloud as they possibly can. The goal is to make the cloud large, wide, and dense. The winner can take home hundreds or even thousands of dollars at a large competition. Many cloud chasers practice long hours in order to increase lung capacity and finesse at blowing shapes.

Most cloud chasers don't use nicotine, but e-liquids with higher amounts of vegetable glycerin. Some vapers who don't engage in cloud chasing worry that the enterprise makes vaping seem like a video game rather than a serious way of giving up regular smoking. You can easily find videos on YouTube and see competitions for making the largest and most interesting clouds. Make up your own mind.

Recognizing the Special Risks to Kids

Adults own the responsibility for protecting kids from unnecessary risks. However, adolescence is often a time that kids experiment with risky behavior. Teens push the limits as they've done since the beginning of time. When it comes to vaping, most of them are unaware of the risks they're really taking. They're truly playing with fire (or, in this case, vapor).

Taking risks with addiction

Inhaled nicotine travels quickly to the brain. It produces an almost instant jolt of pleasurable and relaxing feelings simultaneously. That's bad enough for adults. But adolescent brains are not fully developed until around the age of 25. During adolescence, the brain is developing the ability to inhibit impulsive cravings or behavior; it's learning to put off short-term pleasure for long-term goals and acquiring the capacity to regulate emotions.

Until then, the brain has a limited capacity to put on the breaks and inhibit impulses. Therefore, teens more easily become addicted to almost any addictive substance like nicotine.

That's really bad news because early addictions prime the brain for later addictions. That's because an addicted brain before the age of 25 organizes itself differently than it would later, leading to problems with attention, impulse control, learning, and mood. That reorganized brain makes it harder for teens to change or quit vaping even when they reach adulthood. Of note, 90 percent of all adult smokers began smoking as teens.

Walking through the gates to other addictions

We're old enough to remember the '60s, when everyone worried about marijuana being a gateway drug into more seriously addicting drugs such as heroin and cocaine. The evidence for that concern was mixed, but not compelling. Most kids in the '60s who smoked pot did not graduate to harder drugs. That's not so true of vaping.

Teens who vape do often go on to smoke combustible cigarettes, which are at least as addicting and pose a much greater health risk (see Chapter 3 on health risks of tobacco). Therefore, vaping in this case, appears to be a gateway drug leading to regular smoking. This is especially true among the youngest vapers who go on to regular smoking in even greater numbers. And evidence suggests that among kids who vape, more of them go on to use marijuana or *tetrahydrocannabinol* (THC).

However, some argue that these data are simply correlational and do not prove causation. They say that kids who vape tend to be high risk takers to begin with and will engage in anything that gives them a thrill. One argument against that contention is that zip codes that previously had extremely low rates of regular smoking now appear to be turning to vaping in large numbers. And they then seem to seek out regular, combustible cigarettes in greater numbers, too.

Another worry about addicted kids is that they can't buy vaping devices and e-liquids as easily from legal sources. So, they turn to the local vape dealer for their fixes. Some of these dealers peddle counterfeit vaping supplies, which may be contaminated with dangerous substances.

WARNING

Teenagers and young adults are being hospitalized with serious lung damage with an unknown cause. They aren't responding to antibiotics, and their only common denominator appears to be a recent history of vaping. Vaping exactly what and with what devices, we don't know. However, a substantial majority of these people report having vaped THC products, often purchased on the black market. It's possible that contaminated e-liquids, the toxicity of some ingredients (such as vitamin E acetate), or contaminated devices could offer an explanation. However, at this time, the cause is not known, and investigations are underway. See Chapter 6 for more information about vaping and health risks.

WARNING

Because these risks are still unknown, the U.S. Centers for Disease Control and Prevention (CDC) has recently recommended that all teens, young adults, and pregnant women refrain from any e-cigarette use. They also tell vapers never to buy products on the street.

Catching Kids Before They Vape

More teens than ever report feeling worried, scared, and anxious. They worry about the future of their planet, they worry about getting shot in their classrooms, and they worry about finding a way to make a living in an ever-changing economy. Glued to their phones, they worry about how many likes they have. No wonder the rate of anxiety among adolescents continues to soar.

And anxious, scared kids are more susceptible to substances that temporarily quell their stirred-up emotions. A quick hit of nicotine can do that for them. So, what's a parent or other concerned adult to do?

TIP

If you're a parent of a younger kid, your task is to give your child the confidence and skill to say no to temptations. The job of protecting your kids from the temptations they'll face in their teenage years starts early. Start by doing the following:

>> **Make sure your kids have something in their lives that provides a sense of mastery or accomplishment.** If your kids aren't particularly good at school, find a sport, hobby, or activity in which they can experience success. Having something to be proud of helps kids stand up to peer pressure.

>> **Don't overprotect your kids.** Give them activities that they're likely to feel challenged by. That means allowing for minor failures and risks without overwhelming them. Praise them for hanging in with difficult tasks.

>> **Talk to your kids about vaping and other drugs early.** Kids are being exposed to vaping as early as late elementary school and certainly by middle school. Be factual in your descriptions. Understand that kids may be told by their peers that vaping is harmless. By providing facts early, you can inoculate them from the flawed information they're likely to get from their peers.

LISTENING TO A FAMILY DOCTOR

We wanted to understand how vaping has impacted the practice of family medicine, so we chatted with Susan Chiarito, MD. Dr. Chiarito is a family physician in Vicksburg, Mississippi, who's passionate about family health and serves on the Academy of American Family Physicians Health of the Public and Science Commission. Recently, Dr. Chiarito has become very concerned about the significant increase she has seen in teen vaping.

She especially worries about vaping devices that are almost impossible to detect, such as the ones that look like USB drives. She reports that about half of her teen patients have vaped in the last month. (We should note that if half of her patients admit to vaping, probably more actually *have* vaped, but just deny it when asked.) High levels of nicotine in vaping devices and the immature brain development make teens especially susceptible to addiction.

The doctor described a patient who started vaping to lose weight. Her chronic use led to heart palpitations. Teens who vape before bed can have sleep problems, as well as dry mouths. Dry mouths easily lead to gum disease, cavities, and down the road, increased risk of heart disease. An additional concern is that teens who begin with vaping are more likely to turn to combustible tobacco, with all the additional health risks.

Dr. Chiarito believes that early addiction to nicotine doesn't allow teens to reach their full potential. She advises parents worried about vaping to keep lines of communication open. And she wants parents to know that she doesn't think it's safe for children to inhale chemicals that can lead to byproducts that could cause long-term damage.

Whether you talked with them at a younger age or not, the conversation needs to continue with older teens. Even if you're feeling worry bordering on panic about vaping, be sure to keep your conversational style nonjudgmental. Stick to the facts. Threats will only push them away and make them more likely to rebel by vaping.

Knowing What to Look for in Your Kids

TIP

If you're a concerned parent or teacher, you probably want to know how to detect early signs of a nascent vaping habit. Early intervention has a better chance of helping prior to waiting for an addiction to gain a firm foothold. There are important red flags:

>> **Isolation:** It's pretty normal for teens to spend lots of time in their rooms. However, if your teen starts retreating far more than usual, it's cause for concern.

» **Sneakiness:** If you get a vague sense that something's going on with your teen, it probably is. Teens may start lying about where they're going or who they'll be with. If you catch one or two lies, there are more lurking in the background.

» **Smell:** Vaping does not smell like smoking. Sometimes there's little or no smell. Other times, the smell can be quite strong, but pleasant (like flowers or candy). Be suspicious if your teen puts an air freshener in his bedroom.

» **Frequent bathroom breaks:** Nicotine is highly addictive and requires frequent feeding. If your teen starts going to the bathroom more frequently than usual, suspect something.

» **Increased need for money:** Okay, all teens want money. But if your teen suddenly seems to be asking for it more often or even takes money from you surreptitiously, be concerned.

» **Unfamiliar battery chargers and excessive USB devices:** Vaping requires power, and most devices need recharging. Some devices look exactly like a flash drive or some other object. Others look like pens or highlighters. Also, look for discarded plastic e-liquid containers — they're generally small.

» **Increased thirst:** Vaping takes away moisture from the mouth and throat, causing increased need for water. It can also dry out the nose and increase risk of nosebleeds.

» **Vaper's tongue:** Some vapers experience a decrease in their sense of taste and compensate by increasing their use of salt and spices.

» **Irritability:** When addiction begins to take hold, many addicts demonstrate an uptick in irritability, especially when their urges are frustrated, such as during a long car trip.

» **Stopping or suddenly cutting back on caffeine consumption:** Nicotine is a stimulant, much like caffeine. If a teen stops or greatly cuts down on caffeine (for example, coffee, caffeinated energy drinks), pay attention and look for other signs.

» **Declining appetite and/or weight loss:** Nicotine pumps up metabolism and suppresses appetite. Weight loss often follows.

» **Declining grades and attitude problems:** Rebelliousness, disobedience, and not caring about school all indicate a higher potential for drug use, including nicotine through vaping.

» **Increasing chronic lung infections:** Vapers are at higher risk for bronchitis and pneumonia. Many vapers develop a chronic cough, and colds may tend to last longer.

If you see signs that your kid may be vaping, don't ignore it — and don't panic. We tell you how to talk to adolescents about vaping in the next section.

Talking with Kids about Vaping

Rebellion and defiance are a hallmark of adolescence. And there's no more sure-fire way to elicit that defiance than a harsh, confrontational style. It's tempting to get angry when you find out that your kid is vaping. You didn't raise a child to be so foolish!

EXAMPLE

So, imagine you're in that mind-set right after discovering that your kid has started to vape. You think to yourself that it's time to take charge, do something, and be a strong parent. Here's how we've seen that approach to parenting go in situations like this:

> Sam is 13 years old and began eighth grade six weeks ago. He has always had a little trouble making friends, but now seems more isolated than usual. He has also started to cop an attitude with his parents. His appetite has declined, and his grades have dropped. His parents wonder what's going on. Then they discover a small plastic pod in the trash that's labeled with "contains nicotine." His father decides it's time for a talk.
>
> "Sam, we need to talk," his father begins.
>
> "Yeah, well, I have homework now. How about tomorrow?" Sam retorts.
>
> "Now. I mean it, now," his father says, starting to feel annoyed.
>
> "Yeah, sure, so what do you want?"
>
> "What's this exactly, young man?"
>
> Sam replies, "I dunno. Some plastic thing, I guess."
>
> Growing more irritated, Sam's father firmly says, "You know darn well what this is. And so do I. Are you vaping?"
>
> "So, what if I am? Everybody at school does. It's no big deal," Sam retorts.
>
> "No big deal? Seriously? I'm not having any of this stuff in my house. And we didn't raise you to be some freaky vaper. What's next, tattoos and marijuana? Give me your phone. You're grounded for three months!"
>
> Sam picks up his phone and throws it violently across the room, narrowly missing his father's head. He then charges into his room and slams the door.

That didn't turn out so well, did it? No one wins. Sam is angry, now more likely to continue vaping, and his relationship with his parents is worse than before. His dad feels guilty, angry, ashamed, and confused. He has no idea what he could have done differently. (See "Supporting optimism," later in this chapter, for a revised, healthier way Sam and his dad could communicate.)

REMEMBER

It's important to realize that your teen can become addicted to nicotine very quickly. And anyone who's addicted will go to great lengths to continue using — that includes lying and stealing. Addicted kids also often feel anxious and scared.

Yelling will just send your kid away, to be alone to seek comfort from others. Your teen will probably not stop vaping after being yelled at. Plus, yelling brings on even more rebellion — probably not your goal.

However, a considerable body of research in the past decade or so has told us something very interesting about helping people change. These studies tell us that there is very little to gain and much to lose by confronting people head on about their problems. What works far better are liberal doses of empathy, support, concern, patience, and optimism.

Listening empathically with concern

If you suspect that your child is vaping, take a few minutes and put yourself in her shoes. Is she trying to fit in, under a lot of stress, struggling with school, or experiencing another set of problems? Recognize that her decision to vape probably has nothing to do with you. She's not vaping to make you mad or disrespect you. The ability to put yourself in someone else's shoes is called *empathy.*

But it's sort of hard to feel and express empathy when you're mad at someone — especially someone close and important to you. Nevertheless, if your goal is to help your child through a tough situation, empathy will take you further than anger or even irritation.

How do you become empathetic about vaping? For starters, do you know anyone who has ever struggled with addiction? Or have you heard stories of people who struggle with addiction? How about someone who struggled, but managed to get through it?

REMEMBER

No one *asks* for an addiction. But *everyone* struggles with something at some point in life, whether it be food, drugs, depression, anxiety, relationships, anger, money, gambling, or whatever. Your teen is no different.

Empathy starts with knowing that kids start vaping for many different reasons, but almost all continue to vape because they're addicted to nicotine. The following statements reflect an empathic response:

> » I understand that you may be vaping, and I'd like to hear more about what that's been like for you.

> » I hear that lots of kids at your school are vaping. It must be really hard to resist.

> » Sounds like you want to be accepted by your friends. Do I have that right?

> » So, I'm hearing you're at least a bit worried about what nicotine could do to your health. Is that sort of true?

> » I hear you saying that you really like the feeling you get from vaping. That must make thinking about quitting hard to imagine. Is that how you feel?

> » You seem to be thinking that vaping is harmless. Would you be okay with seeing a few articles about that?

> » I get the impression you're worried about how your new friends would react if you told them you're quitting vaping.

> » I want you to know that no matter what decision you make, I will always love you and care about you.

> » I'm wondering if you're not feeling up to talking about this right now. How about we figure out another time to try it again? Is that okay with you?

> » I know one of your goals is to lead a healthy life. Does it seem like vaping fits in with that?

TIP

It's critically important to have this conversation without feeling angry or frustrated. If such feelings start to emerge, suggest a break and return to the conversation another day. It's equally important to avoid sarcasm or a derisive tone. If your teen becomes hostile or confrontational, back down and go back to it later. You won't win by fighting and pulling harder.

TIP

It's also important not to worry about the outcome of the first talk. Don't even expect a quick resolution. Changes usually occur after a series of productive conversations, and not all attempts will go well. Keeping at it is what matters.

TIP

Teens are a lot like gorillas. They're strong but not always logical and reasonable. When you talk with teens (or gorillas), and you get into a verbal tug of war, logic and reasoning rarely prevail. So, how do you win a tug of war with a gorilla? You drop your end of the rope. Pulling harder simply will not work — and you may fall flat on your face.

Supporting optimism

The most productive talks with your kids will be laced with empathy and support an optimistic perspective. This combo lets your kids know you believe in them and stand on their side, come thick or thin. They may resist hearing that message for a while, especially if it's a new style for you as a parent. But keep at it. In time, this two-pronged approach can sometimes break through when nothing else has.

REMEMBER

Don't underestimate how difficult it is to give up an addiction. Teens become addicted to nicotine quickly. There is also the social component of vaping — peer pressure is hard to stand up to. The combination of peer pressure and addiction is formidable. It would be daunting to anyone. Combine that with a teen's immature brain, and the task is even more challenging.

You must become your teen's greatest cheerleader. Talk about all the things your teen has already achieved. For example, even walking, talking, riding a bike, learning to read all took considerable time and patience to master.

Point out to your teen that most challenging problems require lots of effort, mistakes, and mishaps along the way. It's normal to fail and then get up and try again. Remind your teen that you're confident he'll ultimately succeed.

Expect your teen to resist these messages for a while (or even longer than a while). Be patient and persistent. Never let your teen talk you into the hopeless mind-set that quitting is impossible. You have a good chance of breaking through if you continually express empathy and support an optimistic mind-set.

If, and hopefully, when a less rebellious attitude emerges from your teen, point out that this book was designed to help anyone stop smoking or vaping. Work together on developing a quit plan.

EXAMPLE

Remember the story about Sam and his father at the beginning of the "Talking with Kids about Vaping" section? Sam's father finds a plastic pod in the trash. Sam has become isolated, and his grades are falling. Let's take another look at a conversation between Sam and his father using a revised communication strategy based on empathy, patience, and supportive optimism.

"Sam, we need to talk," his father begins.

"Yeah, well, I have homework now, how about tomorrow?" Sam retorts.

His father feels a bit of annoyance but has practiced keeping a lid on it. He responds, "Sounds like you're busy, I understand, but this is important. I'd prefer talking now. Okay?"

Sam rolls his eyes and sighs, "Okay, fine. What's so important?"

His father responds, "I'm not angry with you — I'm just curious. I found this plastic pod thing with a *contains nicotine* label on it. I know lots of kids are vaping. Have you experimented with it?"

Sam says, "Yeah, what's it to you?"

Reaching deep for patience, Sam's dad says, "I wonder if you're feeling like I'm going to jump all over you. Is that how you feel?"

"Well, you always have in the past. Why would now be any different?" Sam says.

Sam's dad replies, "Fair enough. I *have* jumped on you, way too many times. I'd like to change that. Can you help me understand what vaping is all about?"

"Vaping is totally safe, all the kids are doing it. It's no big deal," Sam says.

"I trust you to make good decisions when you have all of the information," Sam's dad says. "You always have. Let's keep talking about this okay?"

Sam's father didn't resolve this issue then and there. But he did open the door to a productive dialogue. He and his son talked many times over a period of weeks before Sam was ready to discuss quitting his vaping habit. The bonus was that he and his son developed a much better relationship.

TIP

If you find this kind of communication beyond your ability to master, or if your relationship with your teen is just too contentious, consider getting professional help. Many people simply don't have the temperament to sustain communication like we've described. If you fall into this category, a mental health professional (like a counselor, social worker, or psychologist) can help you sort out options and improve your family's communications.

Getting Helpful Parenting Strategies

Preventing vaping before it begins is always better than intervening after it has already happened. As we explain earlier in this chapter, you can start that process by talking with your kids early about the dangers and allure of vaping. Another prevention strategy is to keep kids occupied and supervised.

Keeping kids busy

Make sure your kids have busy schedules with lots of healthy activities. That doesn't mean that you need to schedule every free minute for your teen. But teens tend to get in trouble when they have too much unsupervised free time.

For working parents, providing supervision can pose a challenge. If you do have to leave your adolescents alone for long periods of time, check in on them frequently in a nonintrusive, friendly manner. Try to find friends and family members who can take up some of the free time or check on the kids for you. Look into sports, clubs, and other after-school activities.

TIP

Keep a positive family environment by encouraging respectful, open communication like that described in the "Talking with Kids about Vaping" section. Teens like to talk, but they won't talk with their parents if the atmosphere is confrontational.

Setting limits

Hopefully, by the time children are teenagers, parents have instilled a basic set of values and morals that totally prevents any kind of misbehavior. Okay, that's magical thinking. So, how do you handle the inevitable misconduct a teen is likely to exhibit from time to time?

TIP

For younger teens or tweens, consequences set on their misbehavior usually work. So, it's important to have clear guidelines on what's expected in terms of school-work, chores, grades, attitude, and for that matter, vaping and other drugs. It's perfectly okay to take privileges such as the use of electronics, TV, time with friends, shopping, and allowances away for infractions of clear household rules. Here are some general rules for limit setting:

>> Don't make up rules along the way — have an explicit list.

>> Never say never!

>> Be specific with your plan.

>> Keep unpleasant consequences relatively short (usually a week or less). You can always reimpose a consequence if needed.

>> When taking away privileges, keep a calm, nonjudgmental stance (as emotionally neutral as possible).

>> Don't debate whether a transgression has really occurred. It comes down to your parenting instinct and if you think your teen messed up, assume you're right. Teens try, and often succeed, in creating "reasonable doubt," which works okay in court, but not in families.

>> Expect your child to try acting like consequences don't matter — that's a ruse you can safely ignore.

>> Be sure to criticize the misbehavior, not your adolescent. For example, if your tween brings home a bad test grade, criticize the lack of preparation and study; don't say, "You're lazy."

>> Avoid harshness but deliver consequences swiftly.

>> Balance negative consequences with praise for positive behaviors and occasional extra privileges or desired items.

We should note that setting limits with reasonable consequences becomes less effective as adolescents get closer to adulthood. They've largely formed their values by then and don't respond to removal of privileges with glee.

TIP

If you have an older teen, the focus needs to shift to talking and listening. Follow the guidelines in the "Talking with Kids about Vaping" section as well as you can, and you may still influence the outcome over time.

Accepting your limits as a parent

News flash: No matter how hard you try, you'll never be a perfect parent. We've looked around for decades and still haven't found one. You'll sometimes lose your temper. You won't always know what to do. You'll say or do something hurtful without needing or wanting to.

In addition, you don't have total control of anyone, especially your child. Other influences such as school, friends, relatives, health, genetics, and social conditions have a huge impact on how kids turn out. It's important to realize that child development is not solely up to you.

Rest assured, your kids will mess up. Every single one of them. All you can do is try your best to talk with your kids with as much empathy and supportive optimism as you can muster while setting reasonable limits.

3

Surveying Quitting Strategies

Leap over obstacles that keep you from quitting smoking or vaping.

Figure out if medication can help you quit.

Change the way you think about cravings.

Learn about the technical help available for your quit effort.

Decrease your risks if you're not ready to quit.

Know what doesn't work and why.

Chapter **8**

Overcoming Obstacles to Quitting

Whether you're wanting to give up cigarettes, smokeless tobacco, or vaping, the strategies for quitting are pretty much the same. That's because they all involve stopping an addiction. Giving up any addiction is difficult. But the data tells us it's doable, and millions of people succeed around the world. Many manage to quit without as much distress as they feared.

On the other hand, lots of people do have a significantly hard time quitting. And, alas, sometimes they struggle before they even *consider* trying to quit. Part of that struggle involves erroneous beliefs that interfere with the best of intentions.

The battle over quitting takes place primarily in your own head. Assumptions about yourself and smoking are what we call *quit-busting beliefs* (QBBs). These assumptions slam the breaks on attempts to quit.

This chapter explains the nature of QBBs. From lack of confidence to fears of failure, to thinking this is the wrong time in your life to quit, QBBs stand ready to sabotage your best efforts before you begin. This chapter lays out the most common QBBs and gives you the tools you need for challenging these surprisingly formidable obstacles to quitting.

Defining Quit-Busting Beliefs

QBBs are convictions that stand as roadblocks to implementing change, like quitting smoking or vaping. These beliefs pop up again and again in various situations. They powerfully influence your decision making, actions, and feelings.

REMEMBER

A QBB is an assumption that you believe without really thinking about it. For example, most people think that it's a given that the sun rises in the east and sets in the west. You don't really question that assumption. And there's no reason to most of the time. Your assumptions give you a generally reasonable guide to navigating life. However, if you were a resident of Venus, that belief wouldn't work out very well. On Venus, the sun actually rises in the west and sets in the east.

An inaccurate assumption about the direction of the sunrise and sunset is probably not going to interfere with quitting smoking or vaping or just about anything else in your life. However, some assumptions do become obstacles to quitting. For example, a common QBB that inaccurately guides you away from quitting is "I'm too weak." If you have that QBB about yourself and smoking, it's going to be hard to find the motivation for quitting because you believe that you aren't strong enough to do it.

REMEMBER

A QBB is more than a problematic thought. It's deeper and more ingrained than a thought, and it often operates unconsciously — as opposed to thoughts, which you're usually more aware of. (See Chapter 10 for more information about how distorted thoughts also influence smoking cessation attempts.)

Looking at the Main Quit-Busting Beliefs

There's no absolute, definitive list of QBBs that stand in the way of most smokers' attempts to quit. But here are some of the most common ones:

>> I'm too weak.

>> I'm afraid to fail.

>> I'm afraid of losing too much enjoyment.

>> It's the wrong time.

>> It shouldn't be so hard.

WHERE YOU GET YOUR BELIEFS

Why do people develop QBBs? We learn them through experiences, which often occur during childhood.

For example, someone with overly harsh, critical parents could develop a QBB centered around fearing failure. That fear developed because, when she failed or made mistakes, her parents yelled and screamed at her. No wonder she learned to fear failure! Years down the road, as an adult, that deep-seated fear could persist — even though her parents are no longer around to yell at her.

Or consider someone who was spoiled by his family as a kid. He never had to work for anything — he was born with a silver spoon in his mouth. His QBB theme might center around being overwhelmed by hard work. When faced with giving up vaping, he complains, "It's way too hard to do something like that."

TIP

QBBs can be identical or similar to problematic assumptions that invade other important parts of your life. For example, if your QBB centers around fearing failure, that QBB could easily prevent you from trying to quit smoking. But it could also keep you from taking on new challenges, learning new skills, or solving challenging problems in other areas of your life.

In the following sections, we focus on techniques for changing these QBBs or assumptions so you can prevent them from sabotaging your attempts to quit addictions like smoking. But you can use these same strategies in other areas of your life, too!

I'm too weak

One powerful saboteur to quitting is the QBB that you're too weak to face the challenge. Lacking confidence in yourself, you may not even be ready to start a quit plan.

The QBB that you're too weak takes many forms, such as the following:

>> **I'm just not tough enough to do something like quit smoking.** If this belief feels like something you could hear in your head, it's easy to see why you wouldn't bother to take on something as difficult as quitting smoking.

>> **I don't have any willpower.** With this belief, you tend to think that something requiring commitment and doggedness lies beyond your capacity.

>> **I've tried before and failed.** This thought assumes that one failure means more will surely follow.

>> **I can't stand feeling bad.** This belief assumes that you need to avoid anything that feels bad.

These variants of "I'm too weak" all involve feelings of powerlessness. Addictions often lead to that perception.

EXAMPLE

The following example demonstrates how someone's lack of confidence prevents her from even considering giving up vaping. She never expected to become addicted when she started experimenting with vaping. But that's what happened.

Leah, a 14-year-old high school freshman, started vaping nicotine (see Chapter 5) last summer at the park with her friends. It began as a lark. The kids experimented with devices containing nicotine and various flavors. After a few weeks of experimenting, Leah purchased her very own pink vaping pen. Soon, she found herself wanting to vape, even when she was alone. She keeps her stash hidden in her backpack, so her parents won't catch her. At night, she's often in her room, texting and taking a few hits.

Toward the spring of her freshman year, Leah's boyfriend tells her she needs to quit. Leah replies, "Yeah, I know, but I just don't think I can. I'm not very good at self-control. And it makes me feel good to vape. I love the rush it gives me. When I can't vape, I get edgy and nervous — I can't stand that."

You can see from Leah's story that she's very unlikely to have the motivation to stop. Not only does she feel too weak, but she believes that she won't be able to tolerate the unpleasant feelings that may come with quitting.

Does this lack of confidence mean Leah won't succeed at quitting vaping? Not at all. It does mean, however, that she has some work to do first. She needs to work on challenging her QBBs.

First, she said that she's not good at self-control. That belief is synonymous with "I don't have any willpower." She's predicting that she doesn't have the necessary fortitude to quit vaping. This prediction turns into a self-fulfilling prophecy if left unchallenged.

Leah also assumes that she can't stand having unpleasant feelings, such as edginess and nervousness. These assumptions virtually lock down failure if she moves ahead without confronting them. She's so sure she can't stand these feelings that she has little incentive to try. But a cost–benefit analysis may help her come up with the motivation to replace her QBBs.

Table 8-1 is what Leah came up with for her cost–benefit analysis for her QBB of "I'm too weak."

TABLE 8-1   **Leah's Cost–Benefit Analysis**

Benefits	Costs
I can keep indulging in whatever I want.	My boyfriend might break up with me if don't quit.
I don't have to do anything hard.	I'll never get anywhere in life if I don't do anything hard.
I can avoid feeling bad.	I feel terrible when I vape a lot.
I can keep on vaping.	Vaping is draining my whole allowance.
I can feel better more often.	I get really tense and nervous when I can't vape.
When my friends vape, I really want to be part of the group. Not quitting lets me do that.	

Leah reviews her cost–benefit analysis. She sees that her QBB is costing her more than it's worth. That surprises her because she'd been sure that it would support her assumption. Clearly, that's not what happened. Now Leah is far more ready to construct a more adaptive assumption.

Leah gets the point and you can too. Most of the time, QBBs represent gross over-generalizations that fail to hold up to the real evidence. Your mind will likely resist coming up with ideas and evidence that contradict your assumptions, but you can do this if you try. Really. You're not too weak. You just *believe* you are!

TIP

You can create new assumptions after looking at your assumptions and determining if they're worth holding onto or not. These new assumptions should be reasonable, logical, and balanced — evidence should support them.

In our example, Leah's new assumptions are

>> I have self-control when I work at it. And it can get better with practice.

>> I don't like feeling bad, but it's clear I can stand it. Sometimes you need to feel bad to feel better. Tolerating bad feelings is really just a skill, and like any other skill, it can be learned and improved on.

I'm afraid to fail

Another major disrupter of your good intentions to quit smoking is the QBB that you're afraid to fail. This overarching QBB has an array of variants that subtly differ from one another. You may discover one or more of these related beliefs lurking in your head when you look for them. Here are a few to consider:

>> **I'll disappoint my family if I fail.** Do you ever notice this thought clanging around in your mind? If so, you may prefer to sit on the sidelines rather than risk disappointing those who care the most about you.

>> **I don't want to look like a fool.** This belief puts a high importance on avoiding ridicule, criticism, and derision from others — so much so that it can cost you in ways you don't consider.

>> **It's better not to try than to try and fail.** Can you see how this belief keeps you sitting on the bench and out of the game?

All these variations of fearing failure keep people from putting out maximum effort on quitting smoking or vaping.

EXAMPLE

The following example is one of an addicted adolescent who was used to winning. But he wasn't so sure he could win the war against his tobacco habit.

Henry was only 12 years old when his cousin slipped him his first taste of chewing tobacco or dip. They were out on the ranch fixing fences on a hot, humid day, and Henry found the whole experience dangerously exciting. He thought it tasted awful, but he wanted to look cool in front of his cousin. He wasn't hooked that summer, but the memories of hanging out with his cousin and dipping were pleasant.

By the time he was in high school, Henry had become a regular dipper. Now in his senior year of high school, he has earned a scholarship to a prestigious East Coast university, but he doesn't want to take his dipping habit with him. He knows he won't fit in, suspecting that very few college kids on the East Coast dip.

So, Henry decides that he needs to quit. But his head immediately fills with doubts. Henry is a true perfectionist — he hates the idea of failing. That's just something he doesn't do. Henry doesn't mind taking on challenges, but he carefully calculates his odds of success before doing so. In other words, he rarely takes risks unless he's certain of success. Giving up dip feels like something he might not be able to do, so he remains stuck.

Henry felt conflicted and unsure whether to try to give up chewing tobacco. He had just one summer to succeed before going away to school. Henry's QBB centered around a fear of failure. Being a perfectionist, he decides to test the value of that QBB by constructing a cost–benefit analysis.

Henry doesn't want to face giving up dipping and the possibility of failing at it. He truly hates to start something he might not succeed at. He has two QBBs in this category that are interrelated:

>> It's better not to try than to try and fail.

>> I really fear shame and humiliation.

Table 8-2 shows what Henry came up with for his cost–benefit analysis of his two, related QBBs.

TABLE 8-2   **Henry's QBB Cost–Benefit Analysis**

Benefits	Costs
I can avoid failure by not trying.	I'm really not going to fit in at school if I bring dip with me. I'll be two steps behind before I even start trying to make friends.
I don't have to be frustrated by trying to quit.	This dip is expensive, and I'll need every cent I have at college.
No one can criticize me for being weak if they don't know I want to quit.	It's a messy, disgusting habit. A lot of girls hate it, especially out east, I'm pretty sure.
If I wait, I'll have more time to prepare everything for college.	I hate the feeling of being addicted to anything. This QBB keeps me stuck with an addiction.
Nicotine helps me focus better.	My breath stinks and it's a hassle trying to figure out where I can spit without being too gross.

After looking at his QBB cost–benefit analysis, Henry's ready to stop indulging in dip. He sees the disadvantages of his QBBs and he feels ready to develop a more reasonable, adaptive assumption.

Henry spends a bit of time pondering his cost–benefit analysis of his QBBs involving the theme of fearing failure. He realizes that he has missed out on several opportunities because he doesn't want to risk failing. If it hadn't been for a particularly caring and involved high school counselor, he probably wouldn't have even applied to the prestigious East Coast college that he was accepted by.

Henry decides to take an assertive run at quitting his dipping habit. He knows it will be good practice at dismantling problematic beliefs lurking in his mind. Who knows what successes may lie ahead for Henry after he succeeds at quitting his habit?

I'm afraid of losing too much enjoyment

The QBB that you're afraid of losing too much enjoyment is quite common for people facing giving up any addiction. They mistakenly believe that their lives would suffer massive losses if they gave up their substance of choice (whether nicotine, drugs, or alcohol). In other words, they see their substance as the source of amazing amounts of pleasure, happiness, identity, and even abilities.

In addition, with nicotine, there often is a real (although small) increase in focus. Plus, smokers burn more calories and experience a mild uptick in pleasurable feelings in the short run. So, it's understandable that folks addicted to nicotine have trouble seeing a positive future if they quit. Here's a list of common QBBs that belong under the theme of losing too much enjoyment:

>> **I'll never be happy again.** People with this belief assume that life without a cigarette will never be the same. They think they'll never enjoy coffee, work breaks, or even sex again.

>> **Who would I be without smoking?** Smoking often becomes part of a person's identity. Smokers often believe that giving up smoking will somehow diminish them.

>> **I would totally lose my sense of humor if I stopped smoking — I would be a crabby mess.** This belief is somewhat true in the short term due to withdrawal effects. However, symptoms go away after a few weeks or months.

>> **Smoking keeps me thin; I don't want to lose that advantage.** Many people continue to smoke in order to control their weight. With support to manage withdrawal symptoms and a good diet and exercise program, weight gains are often minimal.

For people who view the possibility of quitting as taking something valuable away from their lives, it's critical to reassess that belief.

EXAMPLE

The following example illustrates what happens when someone is afraid of losing too much.

Brooke began smoking when she was 13 years old. Almost 30 years later, she still smokes a pack and a half a day. Over the winter, she had a series of colds and a cough that never seemed to go away entirely. She made an appointment with her primary care provider, who told her, "Brooke, I have to tell you, cigarettes are causing your chronic bronchitis. Much worse is coming down the road for you if you don't quit. I know it's hard, but. . . ."

Brooke loves smoking. She feels smoking is a part of who she is. She sobs as she tells her doctor, "I can't quit. It's who I am. And I'll never be happy as a former smoker. I could never enjoy a cup of coffee again, and I couldn't keep my weight down. If I die a few years early, so be it!"

Her doctor suggests she carry out a cost–benefit analysis.

Brooke feels wobbly and threatened about the suggestion to take a hard look at one of her mind's core QBBs. But she feels she owes her doctor enough to at least give it a try. She knows that if she isn't convinced by the cost–benefit analysis, she can always just continue smoking, so what does she have to lose?

Table 8-3 shows what Brooke comes up with for her cost–benefit analysis of her QBBs related to the theme of losing too much.

TABLE 8-3   **Brooke's QBB Cost–Benefit Analysis**

Benefits	Costs
I can maintain my current weight if I don't quit.	This chronic bronchitis is really annoying. And my PCP said it will get much worse down the road.
I can continue to enjoy my favorite pastime: smoking!	I spend a lot of money on smoking; just think what I could use that money for if I quit.
I won't have to change who I am — and I like who I am.	I'd like to take dance lessons, but my cough starts up the minute I start moving.
	I read some material my doctor gave me about lung cancer. I really don't want to get that. The treatments are awful.

After spending time conducting her cost–benefit analysis, Brooke changes her mind about quitting. Her doctor gladly gives her a prescription for medication to help her quit (see Chapter 9 for more information about pharmaceutical treatments for smoking cessation).

Brooke concludes that smoking is costing her far more than quitting. She realizes that she will gain health and wealth by quitting. She'll also gain endurance for dancing. Her new, more adaptive assumption is "I'll lose some nice times by quitting but gain more in the long run."

It's the wrong time

We often hear smokers say, "Yes, I want to quit. But now isn't such a great time to do it. I'll wait until. . . ." The problem with that QBB is that the right time just never seems to arrive. There's *always* some stress, difficulty, or problem that stands in the way. Here are some common rationalizations for concluding it's just the wrong time:

>> **I have too much going on at work.** This QBB could refer to school, home projects, or just about anything. The addicted mind can be very creative.

>> **My relationships need more work first.** Another misguided QBB because relationships are never perfect — they always need work. Smoking really has nothing to do with it!

>> **I'll do it when. . . .** This could be after the new job, after the promotion, after getting a raise, after moving, after, after, always after.

If you wait for the perfect time, you'll probably never reach any goal you have. You can see where this thinking takes you. Procrastination simply postpones the task.

EXAMPLE

In the following example, the QBB of "It's the wrong time," keeps someone smoking even when the health costs begin to mount:

> Michael has been a procrastinator his entire life. And generally, he gets away with it. He's a bright and talented attorney. Although he has pulled many all-nighters, he always manages to get his briefs in by the deadline. But with smoking, there is no real deadline, other than the inconvenient fact that his doctor says he'll die of a heart attack if he continues to smoke. Now, in his mid-fifties, with high blood pressure barely controlled with medication, he realizes that the quit-smoking deadline might mean dead as in death. He goes to a quit-smoking group where the facilitator suggests a cost–benefit analysis of Michael's QBB.

Table 8-4 shows what Michael comes up with for his cost–benefit analysis of his QBBs related to the theme of it being the wrong time.

TABLE 8-4   ## Michael's QBB Cost–Benefit Analysis

Benefits	Costs
I can put off the discomfort of quitting for a while.	If I have a heart attack, I'll probably miss work for a few days. Hell, I could even die.
Smoking keeps me going when I work all night.	Procrastination is a bad habit that has cost me lots of stress and anguish.
I can accomplish more when I smoke. And there are times when I need to get a lot done in a hurry.	My doctor says that I need to add more medication to control my blood pressure; that's not a good sign.
I love getting together with my poker friends and smoking a cigar or two. It would be almost impossible to play cards without smoking.	I really don't want to die young and it's getting hard to deny that I will if I keep smoking.

Michael really doesn't want to quit smoking, at least not now. But he's an intelligent man and he realizes that the time has come. He can't ignore the health costs he has already incurred, and those costs will do nothing but get worse with more delay.

Michael surprises himself with his cost–benefit analysis. He realizes that he already knew what was contained in his analysis but putting it all down on paper makes it more real. He decides to rewrite his QBB with a more adaptive assumption: "If I wait for the perfect time, it will never happen. I need to set a quit date in the next week and jump on it. I plan to do the same with work, too, no more procrastinating there either."

TIP

If you find yourself procrastinating on setting a quit date, conduct your own cost–benefit analysis. Also consider reading Chapters 14 and 15 to assess and plan for quitting smoking or vaping.

It shouldn't be so hard

Let's face it: Quitting an addiction is hard to do. Many people rail at the idea of having to suffer. To avoid the short-term discomfort of quitting, they engage in a habit that will lead to a shortened life and considerable health consequences.

REMEMBER

When you look at the overwhelming evidence of the dangers of tobacco, you must marvel at the power of addiction — addiction so powerful that it keeps people smoking despite the inevitable harm that lurks for them in the future.

It's no wonder that lots of smokers don't quit because their QBBs tell them it's simply too hard to do. Here is a sampling of common QBBs related to the theme of quitting being too hard:

>> **It's unfair that I should have to quit something I like.** If you feel it's unfair that you should have to quit smoking, then it's unlikely that you'll feel the motivation necessary for such a tough job.

>> **Why should I have an addiction? I didn't do anything horrible, why me?** This belief makes people feel like helpless victims. Victimhood makes people feel weak and unable to move forward.

>> **I'll quit when I feel motivated.** This QBB is a road map to failure. People rarely want to stop something they enjoy. It could be a very long wait for motivation to come around.

These QBBs related to the theme of quitting being too hard interfere with designing and engaging with a plan to quit. In order to quit, you must be able to tolerate frustration. That's hard to do if you're mired in this QBB. But the bonus is that learning to tolerate frustration can help you in many other areas of your life as well.

EXAMPLE

The following example illustrates how the mind works when faced with work that seems too hard:

> Ashley is in her mid-forties and has smoked for over 20 years. She's a beautician who manages to squeeze in over a pack of cigarettes each day. She recently lost a few customers. Her colleague in the next booth tells her that she's aware of a couple of her customers who complained that Ashley stinks of tobacco smoke and takes too many smoke breaks.
>
> Ashley reacts to the news with defensive anger. Her irritation rises, and she tells her colleague that those customers are just too uptight. Years ago, no one seemed to care that she smoked. She briefly considers quitting but decides it is just too hard — she'll quit when she really has the motivation. Losing a few customers is no big deal.
>
> Ashley finds herself getting more and more crabby at work. She can't seem to get in enough cigarette breaks and her pack-a-day habit turns into two packs. She notices that she's not keeping new customers. She wonders if her smoking is getting out of control.

Ashley visits with her primary care provider about options for quitting smoking. Although her doctor says that she can help Ashley deal with some of her cravings, she doesn't promise it will be easy. She encourages Ashley to list all the costs and benefits of quitting smoking. Table 8-5 shows what Ashley comes up with for her cost–benefit analysis of her QBBs related to the theme of quitting being too hard.

TABLE 8-5   ## Ashley's QBB Cost–Benefit Analysis

Benefits	Costs
I enjoy almost every cigarette I smoke, and believing it's too hard keeps me from having to stop.	I can't afford to lose customers who don't like the smell of smoke. As much as I try to use mouthwash and mints, I guess my clothes still smell like smoke.
Smoking keeps me from feeling frustrated at work.	It seems that I suddenly need more cigarettes than I did before. It's costing more money.
I can avoid the awful cravings and urges by not even trying to quit.	I think that cigarettes keep me calm, but lately I've been more irritated even though I smoke more.
My fiancé smokes, and it might be hard on our relationship if I stop.	I might even start going to the gym if I quit smoking. I'm not as young as I used to be, and I notice I'm starting to sag a bit.

Ashley is not happy about her cost–benefit analysis. She sees that smoking is not in her best interest and it's no longer as satisfying as it used to be. She realizes that she's afraid to quit smoking. She's afraid that she won't be able to handle the frustration. She returns to her doctor for a follow-up appointment. She reports that she sees the problems with her habit but is not ready to give it up right now.

Well, it would be nice to say that Ashley sees that she needs to give up smoking with the help of her cost–benefit analysis. However, we want you to know that a cost–benefit analysis is not a magic cure that makes quitting smoking easy.

Sometimes people can see the problems but aren't yet ready to make the commitment. It might take more evidence or even a major health scare to push Ashley to quit. Or she could be one of the minority of smokers who smokes "till death do us part." Don't worry; that's not likely to be you. After all, you're already reading this book!

Chapter **9**

Finding Help at the Pharmacy

There are many different roads to quitting smoking or vaping. Some people try to do it cold turkey aided only by their own sheer stubbornness and willpower. Unfortunately, most quitters take this route. Without support from educational materials, brief counseling, or medication, only about 5 percent of those flying solo will remain smoke free in six months. The vast majority of cold-turkey, on-their-own quitters will relapse within a week.

Many resources are available to help people quit smoking, and we introduce you to these resources in this book. We outline practical ways of challenging thinking, getting through cravings, and changing activities that will help you quit in Chapter 10. Chapter 11 describes some of the various technological strategies that can support efforts at quitting.

In addition, we recommend that most people who are trying to quit consider talking to their healthcare providers about one of the options for replacing nicotine and managing cravings. That's because research clearly states that using prescription medications significantly increases the odds of successfully quitting smoking.

But taking medication is not for everyone. In this chapter, we describe the pharmacological options for quitting smoking now available. We give you the lowdown on side effects and success rates so that you can make an informed decision in consultation with your healthcare provider.

Replacing Nicotine

Nicotine makes most people feel good. It lights up the pleasure center in the brain and simultaneously relaxes and increases alertness. It's no wonder that nicotine is one of the most addicting of all drugs. But people who smoke, chew, or vape don't seem to get the same kind of euphoric high that other drugs like cocaine or heroin produce. So, why is nicotine so addictive?

The answer comes from the brain, which quickly learns to depend on nicotine. The fact that most users of nicotine use it repeatedly throughout the day increases this dependence. It has also been found that nicotine increases the pleasure of other activities, such as listening to music or watching videos. So, smokers or vapors who fear that life won't be as pleasurable without their crutch are sadly correct, but only to a point. That makes motivation even more difficult to maintain for those who want to quit. Replacing nicotine may help.

But if you don't replace the nicotine that your body craves, you'll probably experience nicotine withdrawal. That can be a rather unpleasant experience for many. Nicotine withdrawal symptoms often include the following:

>> Anxiety

>> Digestive distress

>> Headaches

>> Intense cravings

>> Irritability and frustration

>> Mood swings

>> Restlessness

>> Sore throat and increased coughing

>> Sweating

>> Tingling in the hands and feet

The good news is that you don't have to experience most of these symptoms if you turn to nicotine replacement therapy (NRT). Experts agree that NRT is one of the simplest and most successful aids to quitting smoking. In fact, NRT increases the rate of quitting by at least 50 percent. This finding has been replicated many times. NRT helps people manage the withdrawal symptoms so that they can concentrate on the emotional aspects of quitting. Those who are particularly dependent on nicotine (heavy smokers) are most likely to receive benefits from NRT.

NRT has been around for decades. For most healthy adults, it's safe to use. People with chronic diseases (such as heart disease), women who are pregnant or considering getting pregnant, and teens should talk to a healthcare provider before starting NRT. Keep in mind that, in almost all cases, NRT is far safer than continuing to use tobacco because nicotine doesn't contain most of the harmful chemicals found in tobacco.

Replacing nicotine from cigarettes with safer medications will probably help with physical withdrawal symptoms. However, it does not help with deeper psychological dependence. For help with your emotions, see Chapters 10 and 11. For more help with cravings, see Chapters 17 and 18.

Using nicotine replacement therapy

The day you toss your tobacco or vaping devices is the day you can start NRT. If you're still consuming tobacco or nicotine, it's often recommended that you not use any NRT product. However, some people do use NRT to help them cut down. If that's your plan, talk to your doctor. It's possible to overdose on nicotine, but under a doctor's direction, it's quite unlikely.

WARNING

UNDERSTANDING NICOTINE POISONING

Nicotine can be deadly. Although life-threatening overdoses are quite rare, they do happen. It's close to impossible to smoke enough cigarettes in a day to overdose on nicotine. However, nicotine can be deadly to children and pets when they consume it. Kids may be drawn to NRTs, which often look like candy or regular gum.

Even a teaspoon of pure, liquid nicotine can be fatal to small children or pets. In addition, liquid nicotine found in sprays, e-cigarettes (see Chapter 5), and inhalers can harm the skin or eyes if touched. Symptoms of nicotine poisoning include

- Nausea, vomiting, and diarrhea

- Agitation, confusion, and dizziness

- Fast or irregular heartbeat

- Seizures

- High blood pressure

- Death

If you even suspect nicotine poisoning, call 911 or the American Association of Poison Control Centers at 800-222-1222.

POSSIBLE POSITIVES OF NICOTINE?

Nicotine has a bad reputation for good reason. Nicotine addiction, because of its *association* with smoking tobacco, is still responsible for many cases of heart disease, cancer, and unnecessary deaths. This bad rep may be one reason that there is very little known about the beneficial aspects of nicotine — scientists may be more reluctant to study it and extoll its benefits. However, researchers have come to believe that cognitive performance may be enhanced for people with certain disorders including attention deficit hyperactivity disorder (ADHD) and schizophrenia. In addition, there are some links to improved attention and decision-making ability in those with cognitive impairments (pre-dementia). There's even some evidence that nicotine may serve as a partial protectant against the development of Parkinson's disease.

On the other hand, recent studies have indicated that nicotine may fuel the growth of certain tumors, possibly accelerating cancer or heart disease. So, the bottom line is that much more research is needed to know answers about nicotine's conceivable benefits. The deleterious effects of tar and the burning of numerous chemicals found in tobacco and possibly some vaping products are far better known (see Chapters 3 and 6). If you're not a smoker, it's not a good idea at this time to start consuming nicotine for its possible benefits.

TIP

Over-the-counter NRT is usually not covered by insurance. Typically, insurance will cover NRT when it's prescribed by a doctor. However, many states offer free or sharply reduced prices through their state-funded quit lines. To contact your state quit line, call 800-QUIT-NOW (800-784-8669). The National Network of Tobacco Cessation Quit lines will direct your call.

Surveying the drugstore shelves

The quickest and easiest way to find NRT is to drop by your local drugstore. Most of them have a good supply available for you to peruse. These do not require a doctor's prescription. All you need to do is walk in, look around, and buy the one you want! Nonetheless, your pharmacist will gladly discuss any concerns you may have. And if you have any health concerns, it's always best to check with your doctor. There are three major types of over-the-counter options: patches, gum, and lozenges.

TIP

The great news is that NRTs all work much better than trying to quit without extra help. Which one you decide to try is really a personal choice. We explain how they work, any special considerations, and side effects in the following sections.

WARNING

Keep all nicotine products such as lozenges and gum away from children and pets. Because of their lower bodyweight, overdoses can occur much more easily.

Nicotine patches

Nicotine patches have been well researched and found effective as an aid to quitting smoking. In a nutshell, they work! Patches work by continuously delivering a small amount of nicotine through the skin and into the bloodstream. You put a patch below the neck and above the waist (usually on the chest or upper arm) on a clean, dry, and *hopefully* hairless area!

TIP

Don't put the patch in the same area of the body every day. Move it around to minimize irritation.

Patches deliver nicotine over two different durations — 16 hours and 24 hours. The 16-hour patch usually has fewer side effects than the 24-hour version. However, some people find that they need the full-day, steady dose.

Nicotine patches also come in different strengths. If you're a heavy smoker, you're likely to want the higher-dosage regimen, generally starting with about 20 milligrams of nicotine per patch. Those who smoke somewhat less, are likely to find that the weaker starting strength of about 15 milligrams suffices. Typically, patches are used at the starting dose for four to six weeks; then a lower dose is used for two weeks, followed by a final two weeks at an even lower strength. Patches are approved for use for a total of five months; however, some people use them longer.

Side effects of nicotine patches include

>> Redness and itching at the application site

>> Strange dreams or problems sleeping

>> Racing heartbeat

>> Dizziness

>> Headache

>> Nausea

>> Muscle discomfort

These side effects can occur because the dosage is excessive for one's needs. Often, decreasing the dosage can help. Twenty-four-hour patches sometimes also cause sleep problems. Try switching to 16-hour patches if that happens. For skin irritation, trying another brand may alleviate the problem.

EXAMPLE

FINDING THE RIGHT FIT

Chris is a middle-aged man with a wife and four kids. He had smoked heavily since he was a teen. During the last few years, he suffered recurring coughs and bronchial infections. His boss complained about all the sick days, and his wife zeroed in on the mess, cost, and smell. His kids constantly got on his back about his smoking, too.

After Chris suffered one severe bout of bronchitis, his doctor diagnosed him with the beginning stages of chronic obstructive pulmonary disease (COPD). Chris decided it was time to quit. He picked out the strongest nicotine patch on the shelves. His side effects were terrible. He felt dizzy, headachy, and sweaty. He almost gave up, but his kids begged him not to.

So, he tried a patch at a lower dose of nicotine. It actually seemed to help with minimal side effects. He still had cravings four or five times a day, but not nearly as bad as when he tried to quit cold turkey. He credits the support of his family and nicotine patches for his ultimate success in quitting smoking for good.

Chris was able to adjust his dosage on his own, and it worked. If you have trouble with side effects, try decreasing your dose. Or try a different NRT. Talk to your pharmacist who may have some good suggestions. Some people do much better with one NRT than another, but you never know which one will work for you until you try it.

Feel free to experiment with different dosages and patch durations. Chris's story (see the nearby sidebar) illustrates a successful ex-smoker who thought he'd never succeed.

WARNING

If side effects, such as a racing heart, are disturbing, talk to your doctor about whether to lower the dose, change to another type of NRT, or stop it altogether.

WARNING

Do not use a heating pad or heat lamp on the skin area covered by the patch. Heat will speed up absorption of the nicotine and possibly result in an overdose.

TIP

It's easier to give up the patch than smoking cigarettes because you only put the patch on once per day rather than taking puffs off cigarettes hundreds of times per day.

Nicotine gum

Nicotine gum is used for a fast-acting nicotine replacement. It's absorbed through the mucous membrane of the mouth and acts faster than patches on the skin. Many smokers trying to quit use it for especially urgent cravings. It's also recommended for people who chew tobacco because it gives them a partial replacement for the sensations involved in chewing, which have become highly pleasurable over time.

Avoid eating or drinking for at least 15 minutes before and during use of nicotine gum. Chew the gum slowly until you feel a slight tingling sensation, similar to what pepper induces. Then keep the gum between your cheek and gums until the flavor and tingling fade. Then chew again until the sensation returns. Continue this pattern for about 20 or 30 minutes.

WARNING

Don't chew the gum continuously. Be sure to stop chewing when you first detect tingling or a burst of flavor. That way, the nicotine will be slowly absorbed into your mouth's mucous membrane. If chewed continuously, the nicotine will be delivered from your saliva directly into your stomach, resulting in an upset stomach.

Nicotine gum comes in two strengths — 2 milligrams and 4 milligrams. For those who are heavily dependent on nicotine, the stronger dose is usually recommended to start. The dose for the first six weeks is usually one piece every one to two hours, whether you're starting with the 2-milligram or 4-milligram regimen. The maximum recommended dose is never more than 24 pieces of nicotine gum a day. After six weeks, the frequency and strength are usually decreased gradually. A typical goal is to stop the use of gum after three months. Consider sugar-free, non-nicotine gum after that.

Nicotine gum sometimes produces a few side effects, including the following:

>> Bad taste

>> Mouth sores or throat irritation

>> Nausea

>> Jaw discomfort

>> Racing heartbeat

WARNING

If you have a racing or irregular heartbeat, stop using the product until you talk to your doctor.

Like nicotine patches, evidence is strong that nicotine gum provides a substantial aid to those trying to quit smoking, and there's every reason to believe that it will work equally well for quitting vaping nicotine or smokeless tobacco products.

Nicotine lozenges

A nicotine lozenge is like a hard candy that releases nicotine as it dissolves in the mouth. Lozenges should be sucked, not chewed or swallowed. It takes about 20 to

30 minutes for them to fully dissolve. While sucking them, it's best to move them around in your mouth and between your cheeks and gums. As with gum, do not eat or drink 15 minutes before or while using them.

TIP

As with the case for gum, people who are quitting smokeless tobacco may find lozenges particularly helpful for replacing pleasurable oral sensations.

Lozenges typically come in two strengths — 2 milligrams and 4 milligrams. Like nicotine gum, those with a heavier smoking history usually start with the higher dose. The maximum dose per day is 20 lozenges. The recommended schedule for the first six weeks is usually one every one to two hours. After six weeks, the dose is usually reduced, and the frequency is gradually tapered. You should not suck on more than one lozenge at a time, nor should you use them one right after another. Discontinue lozenges by around 12 weeks.

Possible side effects of nicotine lozenges include the following:

» Digestive distress

» Sore throat and coughing

» Headaches

» Insomnia

» Racing heart rate

WARNING

If you experience an irregular or racing heartbeat or other disturbing side effects, check with your doctor.

Checking for nicotine replacement therapies behind the counter

Nicotine nasal sprays and inhalers need a doctor's prescription. Drugs are prescribed because they're considered potentially harmful and their use needs to be supervised by a healthcare provider. In order to take a prescribed drug, you need to have a consultation with a healthcare provider, so if you're interested in one of these products, make an appointment with your doctor.

Nicotine nasal spray

Nicotine nasal sprays are like other nasal sprays in terms of how they're used. This type of NRT works faster than any other NRT.

An important caveat is that because nicotine nasal spray works so well and so quickly, it may be more addictive than other NRTs.

This product should be used as directed by your healthcare provider. Generally, a dose consists of two sprays, one in each nostril. The maximum dose per day is 40 doses of two sprays each. Nasal sprays should not be used for more than six months.

Side effects of nicotine nasal spray include those caused by other NRT's such as racing heart, headache, and stomach upset. In addition, they have the potential to cause

>> Irritation in the nose

>> Sneezing

>> Throat irritation

>> Coughing

>> Watery eyes

Some or all of these side effects may dissipate over a couple of weeks. However, you should contact your healthcare provider for any particularly disturbing side effects, such as racing heart rate, or if other side effects do not fade.

Because nasal spray bottles contain enough nicotine to harm children or pets, be sure to keep them out of reach. If skin contact occurs, the area should be thoroughly washed with plain water. Call the American Association of Poison Control Centers with any concerns at 800-222-1222.

Nicotine inhalers

Nicotine inhalers are the NRTs that are most like smoking a cigarette. Just like a cigarette, you inhale, and then nicotine is absorbed in the mouth and throat. Unlike a cigarette, there is no burning, and the nicotine does not go into the lungs. Former smokers like nicotine inhalers because they closely mimic the experience of smoking. Nicotine inhalers are also the most expensive of all the NRTs. However, insurance may cover some of the cost.

The nicotine inhaler is available in a kit that contains a thin tube and cartridges containing nicotine. You put the cartridge into the tube and inhale like a cigarette. Each cartridge supplies about 4 milligrams of nicotine, but only 2 milligrams are absorbed. That comes to about the amount delivered by a typical cigarette.

Cartridges last for about 20 minutes of inhaling. The maximum dose is 16 per day, but people generally use less than 10. You should stop after 12 weeks of use.

Stop smoking before you start using inhalers. Don't drink coffee, juices, or soda 15 minutes before and 15 minutes after using an inhaler. During the first week, you should use at least six cartridges per day. You may taper off over the course of treatment.

Side effects of nicotine inhalers include

>> Mouth and throat irritation

>> Coughing and runny nose

>> Upset stomach

As with other NRTs, excessive nicotine can cause headaches, rapid heart rate, or digestive distress. Talk to your doctor if you experience these symptoms and they fail to resolve.

The cartridges have enough nicotine to harm children and pets. Take special care to store and dispose of cartridges so they can't fall into the wrong hands — or, for that matter, paws.

Combining nicotine replacement therapies

We know at this point, that NRTs help people quit smoking. What about combining more than one NRT? For example, some people like the patch, but still experience sharp cravings from time to time during the day. Those people often turn to nicotine gum or lozenges to deal with those cravings.

Considerable research supports what these people intuitively figured out. Specifically, studies show that using the patch with "emergency" NRTs such as gum, lozenges, nasal sprays, or inhalers increases the odds for successful smoking cessation by up to a third.

If you choose to combine more than one type of NRT, be aware of the symptoms of excessive nicotine (such as headache, dizziness, rapid heart rate, or stomach upset). Decrease the amount of NRTs you're taking and consult your healthcare provider.

You may worry that depending on NRTs is just another form of addiction. After all, both smoking and NRT's deliver nicotine to your body and nicotine is truly addictive. Olivia struggled with this worry. Her story is in the nearby sidebar.

EXAMPLE

HOOKED ON NICOTINE REPLACEMENT THERAPIES?

Olivia, a navy veteran, started smoking when she was stationed overseas. When she returned, she tried to quit smoking and was shocked to find she just couldn't do it. She tried using patches as directed and thought she'd go crazy from her cravings. Someone suggested that she try using gum along with the patch. In desperation, she decided to try it. She immediately noticed a decrease in her worst cravings. She thought she might be able to handle quitting after all. But after six weeks, she still needed the patch and occasional gum just as much.

She had the thought, "I'm just as addicted as ever! I'm hopeless!"

A friend of hers told her to chill out — he'd been through a similar experience. He told her that he had used a few types of NRTs and even after six months, he sometimes pops a nicotine lozenge in his mouth when he feels especially stressed out. And he noted that NRTs are far less harmful than smoking tobacco. His story helped Olivia see things a little differently.

She decided to go easier on herself and take credit for the health gains she was already making. She noticed more stamina at the gym and more money in her bank account. After seven months, she realized she could go without her NRTs entirely.

REMEMBER

Few people find NRTs as fully satisfying or addictive as consuming tobacco. The more important point is that NRTs do not contain the literally *thousands* of chemicals found in tobacco and especially burned tobacco. They should be viewed as a temporary bridge to transition you from tobacco to nicotine to a full-blown ex-smoker. The timeline is up to you.

Prescribing Medications for Coping with Quitting

Way too many people still believe that addiction is a sign of weakness or some type of character flaw. Because of that belief, way too many people don't get the help and support that they need. They feel ashamed and weak, too embarrassed to admit they would like to quit, but can't. They think they should go it alone and, thus, avoid talking about it.

Yet, many tobacco users can find relief by talking to their healthcare providers honestly about their desire to quit. There are medications that can help some people give up tobacco and nicotine that comes in any form. Asking about the medication option doesn't label you as an addict.

When you talk to your healthcare provider about your desire to quit, be sure to discuss any medical conditions and allergies you have and any over-the-counter medications or supplements that you take. Also, be sure to tell your doctor if you're pregnant or planning to become pregnant. It's also imperative to come clean about any drug or alcohol use.

TIP

Your healthcare provider wants you to tell the truth. Providers have been trained in maintaining a nonjudgmental stance, and most have some of their own problems of one kind or another. There is no story they haven't heard. In the rare event that you do feel judged by a healthcare provider, try to talk about it. But if the conversation doesn't go well, find someone else to work with.

Turning to on-label prescriptions

There are currently two medications approved by the U.S. Food and Drug Administration (FDA) for helping people quit smoking. These medications work for some but not all people with nicotine addictions. Talk to your healthcare provider about whether you may benefit from one or the other.

Varenicline (Chantix)

Varenicline helps people stop smoking by decreasing the pleasure a smoker gets from smoking (some report that it makes cigarettes taste bad) and reducing withdrawal symptoms. It does this by interfering with the brain's nicotine receptors. Some studies have suggested that varenicline is at least as effective as NRTs and may for some people be more effective than bupropion (see the next section). This is particularly true for women smokers; however, the differences are relatively small.

You usually start taking varenicline about one to four weeks prior to quitting. Typically, the starting dosage is 0.5 milligram per day for the first four days. Then you take 0.5 milligram twice a day. Finally, it's increased to 1 milligram twice a day. Varenicline is most commonly given for about 12 weeks, and many people choose to continue taking it for 12 more weeks to help reduce the risk of relapse.

Side effects of varenicline can be significant for some people, and it should be reported to the prescribing healthcare provider. Side effects may include

>> Nausea, vomiting, and/or constipation

>> Disturbed sleep, unusually vivid dreams

- » Increases potency of alcohol

- » Headaches

- » Depressed mood

- » Agitation

- » Suicidal thoughts and behaviors

Although it's rare, if you have any increased depression or suicidal thoughts, you should immediately contact your healthcare provider. The story of Emma (see the nearby sidebar) illustrates a challenging side effect of varenicline.

Previously, the FDA issued a black-box warning about varenicline's potential to increase depression, agitation, and suicidal thoughts and behaviors. However, a large study convinced the FDA to remove the black box warning because it failed to find a statistically significant relationship between varenicline and adverse neuropsychiatric events. Some researchers feel that this cancellation was premature, because the study was not large enough to detect what they believe may be a valid concern.

EXAMPLE

BEWARE SUICIDAL THOUGHTS

Emma is a middle-aged software engineer. She's seeing a therapist because of anxiety and depression. Although she is a recovering alcoholic, she has been abstinent for almost 20 years. She has no history of suicidal thoughts.

She started to smoke when she gave up alcohol and attended AA meetings. Now she wants to quit because she knows the risks of smoking. Emma goes to her primary care provider and is given a prescription for varenicline. Emma has seen the medication advertised as a way to give up smoking by reducing her cravings and without having to stop smoking immediately.

After two weeks on the medication, she calls her therapist in a very agitated state. Her therapist is able to get her an appointment the same day. Emma reports having profound, powerful thoughts of running her car into a bridge at high speed. She feels terrified she may actually carry out these thoughts. The therapist calls the prescribing physician, and they agree on a plan to help Emma stop smoking without taking varenicline. Emma's thoughts of suicide abate quickly.

She eventually succeeds at stopping smoking. She uses the patch with occasional lozenges and supportive therapy. It takes her a while, but in the end she feels quite confident that she won't relapse.

If you or someone you care about is taking varenicline and begins to feel depressed, agitated, or suicidal, make sure to see a healthcare provider immediately.

Bupropion (Zyban)

It's less clear how exactly bupropion helps people stop smoking. Bupropion was first and continues to be used as an antidepressant (called Wellbutrin when used for depression). It was noticed that many depressed people taking bupropion basically lost interest in smoking, making it easier to quit.

Researchers studied the effects of bupropion and found that, indeed, it appeared to interfere with nicotine's addictive effects. Bupropion has been used successfully to help people quit smoking for decades. It appears to work best when combined with NRTs.

You should start bupropion one to two weeks before your quit day. Starting dosage is usually 150 milligrams for three days, increased to 150 milligrams twice a day. Treatment usually works within two months. If it doesn't work by then, bupropion is generally discontinued. Treatment lasts for about 12 weeks, but many people choose to take bupropion longer then that, sometimes as long as a year.

TIP

If you're depressed, bupropion may improve your mood. However, you don't have to be depressed to benefit from bupropion for smoking cessation. A benefit of bupropion is that it may lead to less cravings in other areas of your life, such as food or alcohol. However, there is little quality research to substantiate those claims.

WARNING

If you have a seizure disorder, a history of seizures, or bipolar disorder, bupropion is not likely for you. Talk to your doctor.

Bupropion, like almost all pharmaceuticals has a long list of side-effects. However only about 10 percent of those taking it need to discontinue bupropion because of these side effects. Most of these symptoms will decrease over the first couple of weeks. These side-effects include

>> Dizziness

>> Tremors

>> Insomnia

>> Jitteriness

>> Dry mouth

>> Concentration problems

>> Anxiety

>> Upset stomach and constipation

>> Rashes

>> Very small increased risk of seizures

Like varenicline, bupropion previously had a black-box warning that stated there may be an increased risk of suicidal thoughts and behavior, depression, and agitation. This was later removed based on the same study that prompted the FDA to remove it from varenicline (see the preceding section). Some researchers have questioned whether that study was robust enough to justify the removal of the warning.

WARNING

If while taking bupropion you experience increased depression, agitation, or suicidal thoughts or behaviors, immediately contact your healthcare provider. This may not be the medication for you.

Looking at off-label prescriptions

If you have health issues that prevent you from taking NRT or FDA-approved medication for smoking cessation or if other methods have failed, your doctor may consider another type of medication to help you quit. There are several drugs that have not been specifically approved by the FDA for smoking cessation but have been used and shown promise for individuals who have been unsuccessful with other methods.

There are two drugs that are used but have not been officially studied and approved by the FDA for this purpose. However, they are relatively safe and have been found to be reasonably effective in helping people quit smoking.

>> **Nortriptyline:** This drug is a much older antidepressant medication than bupropion. Limited research has found that it can be effective in helping smokers quit. Generally, people start using it for a few weeks prior to stopping smoking. Side effects include blurry vision, dry mouth, fast heart rate, constipation, orthostatic (low) blood pressure when standing up, and weight gain or loss.

>> **Clonidine:** This medication has been used to treat high blood pressure. Some studies have found it to be helpful for smoking cessation. It's usually started a few days before quitting. It can be given in a pill or patch form. Side effects include fatigue, dizziness, constipation, dry mouth, and weakness.

More promising medications are on the way. Quitting any addiction is highly individual and can take many different paths. Be patient. Don't give up. Work with your healthcare provider to explore options.

Thinking Medication Is Not an Option

There are a few reasons why certain medications are contraindicated for some people. For example, if you have a seizure disorder, some medications may not be good options. The same thing applies to pregnant or breastfeeding women, teens, and people with certain health problems.

But the more common contraindications occur in how people think and what they believe about medications. Here are some of the most common reasons that people cite for not wanting to take medications for smoking cessation and some answers to these concerns:

>> **I don't want to substitute one addiction for another.** Medications for smoking cessation are not particularly addictive. You can gradually taper off these medications with many fewer problems than trying to stop smoking. They also have *far less* negative health effects than smoking and vaping do.

>> **I prefer natural approaches to medication.** Tobacco is natural but it contains numerous harmful chemicals, which only multiply when smoked. The point is to get you off of smoking or vaping. If you can do that naturally, great. But if you can't, please consider medications or other techniques discussed in this book.

>> **I'm afraid of side-effects.** Smoking has side-effects, too — such as sore throat, cough, heart disease, and cancer. Side effects from medication pale in comparison. And many side-effects can be managed or go away on their own. Talk to your healthcare provider about your concerns.

>> **I'm worried about the expense.** You can call the National Network of Tobacco Cessation Quit Lines at 800-QUIT-NOW (800-784-8669) to obtain information about reduced-price and free options. Because most medications are a temporary bridge to quitting, the overall cost is much less than a lifetime of smoking.

Chapter **10**

Changing Thoughts and Actions

Many people think of addictions as purely a physical phenomenon. And it's true that addiction to nicotine is partially caused by a biological process in the brain. But if that were the whole story, the 70 percent of smokers who say they want to quit would stop by the drugstore, buy some nicotine replacements, and quit. End of story.

It's quite true that nicotine replacement therapy (NRT) helps people quit. But NRT does not suffice for most smokers. There must also be a change in the way smokers think, act, and feel for most quit attempts to succeed.

In this chapter, we explain the relationship between triggers, thoughts, feelings, and actions. Then we give you the tools you need to challenge and change the way you think and feel about quitting. Next, we look at smoking triggers and ways to handle those with avoidance when you can and actions when you can't. Finally, we show you new ways to relate to your feelings, so they don't continue to sabotage your efforts to quit smoking, smokeless tobacco, or vaping.

TIP

Throughout this chapter, we usually refer to smokers and smoking. That's for convenience. Most people addicted to nicotine smoke cigarettes. However, many are addicted to other forms of tobacco, such as chew or snuff, and some are struggling with a nicotine vaping habit. We want you to know that the same techniques we offer to smokers apply equally to people with other habits they want to break.

Exploring the Relationship between Triggers, Thoughts, Actions, and Feelings

Most smokers are aware of triggers that lead them to reaching for a smoke. For example, during the first cup of coffee in the morning, following an argument at work, while watching an exciting sports event—these could all serve as triggers for a smoker (see Chapter 2 for more examples of smoking triggers).

It's easy to think that triggers *cause* you to smoke. But there's far more involved. Triggers set off a cascade of thoughts, feelings, and actions. Let's take a deeper dive into the relationship between triggers and what follows them.

You may not realize that there are thoughts and feelings prior to your action of smoking. That's because these thoughts and feelings have become so automatic that you're probably not consciously aware of them. For example, if your smoking trigger is the first cup of coffee in the morning, you may reflexively reach for a cigarette without thinking and light up. You may have been aware of a small urge or feeling that you wanted that smoke. But because you had no intention of *not* lighting up, the awareness of the urge was weak.

Imagine what happens when you frustrate that trigger. That's when the thoughts and feelings tumble into your consciousness. "What, I can't have a cigarette? I *must* have a cigarette. I'll feel horrible without my first cigarette in the morning. I can't even enjoy a cup of coffee. Life is horrible. I'm deprived. *I can't stand it!*"

Sound familiar? And following these thoughts, you probably do feel even more intense urges and cravings and sadness and basically horrible. It's helpful to understand how this relationship plays out in addiction. But first, here's a quick review of terms:

>> **Triggers:** Situations, events, or occurrences that are connected with the action of smoking. Triggers are the result of associated experiences over time, such as smoking in the car, smoking after sex, or lighting up following a meal. Triggers can also be a particularly emotional event such as a stressful day at work or an argument.

>> **Thoughts:** The interpretations or perceptions that you have about the trigger. Examples include: "I have to have a smoke in this situation," "I can't enjoy a meal without the anticipation of smoking," and "I'm stressed out, so I have to smoke."

>> **Feelings:** The most common feelings associated with smoking are cravings and urges. But frustration, irritation, anxiety, sadness, aches, yearnings, and feelings of emptiness are also prevalent. In addition, positive feelings also

occur around smoking. For example, smokers often report contentment, relaxation, relief, and pleasure during or after smoking. Naturally, most smokers say they're reluctant to give these positive feelings up. Who can blame them?

>> **Behaviors:** Obviously, a cigarette is the first option most addicted smokers turn to. Quitters come up with *different* solutions such as chewing gum, spending time in the hot tub, going for a walk, or taking deep breaths.

TECHNICAL STUFF

USING COGNITIVE BEHAVIORAL THERAPY

Much of the material contained in this chapter comes from the principles found in cognitive behavior therapy (CBT). CBT is a type of psychotherapy that has been found to help with a wide variety of problems. A small sampling of these problems includes

- Addictions (including smoking)
- Anger
- Anxiety
- Chronic pain
- Depression
- Panic disorder
- Phobias
- Post-traumatic stress disorder (PTSD)

Numerous randomized, controlled research studies have supported the value of CBT for helping people deal with these problems. Core principles include the idea that the way people think about events greatly impacts how they feel about them. CBT also places importance on changing behaviors, which can also impact feelings and thoughts. CBT is optimistic in that it's assumed that people can learn new patterns of thinking and behaving in more satisfactory ways.

One reason we find CBT appealing is that it helps people learn to be their own therapist. CBT teaches people new ways of coping and behaving, more effective problem solving, and how to change their thinking in more adaptive ways. The influence of the past is acknowledged as important, but more emphasis is generally placed on recent events and the present.

You can probably list off major triggers you have for smoking. And behaviors are apparent as well — you light up or do something else. But many people confuse thoughts and feelings. For example, you may say to yourself, "I feel like I can't stand to not have a cigarette on my break at work."

That statement is not a feeling, it's a thought. A feeling is what occurs *after* you say, "I feel like I can't stand to not have a cigarette on my break at work," to yourself. After having that thought, you then feel strong cravings for a cigarette on your work break. The cravings are the feeling.

Another example is when you say to yourself, "I feel horrible when I don't smoke."

Again, that is a prediction, a thought about what will happen when you don't smoke. The feeling of "horrible" has not yet happened. But guess what, it probably will because you predicted it.

Thinking Differently about Triggers

People tend to believe that feelings occur as a direct result of situations or events that happen to them. In other words, events, occurrences, and triggers are responsible for how they feel. In terms of smoking, triggers are a type of smoking-related event, occurrence, or situation. How many times have you heard someone say the following?

>> My computer crashed, and I feel horrible.

>> I ran out of cigarettes, and feel desperate.

>> I broke my fingernail, and I'm totally stressed.

It's easy to say that the preceding events caused the feelings. But let's take another run at the same events and add the underlying thoughts. It's those thoughts about what happened that directly lead to your feelings. See Table 10-1 to further understand the relationship between events, thoughts, and feelings.

Maybe you think those feelings are inescapable. In other words, you think that your thoughts are a direct result of the event that occurred, and feelings follow naturally. Put that thought on hold for a moment.

Instead, consider how you would likely feel if you had different thoughts about what happened. The same event but viewed with a different thought or interpretation leads to strikingly different feelings. Table 10-2 shows how different thoughts lead to different feelings.

TABLE 10-1   **Connecting Events, Thoughts, and Feelings**

Events or Triggers	Thoughts	Feelings
My computer crashed.	It's going to cost me a fortune and I don't have time for this!	I feel horrible and angry.
I ran out of cigarettes.	I can't stand going another two hours before I can buy more.	Desperate cravings.
I broke my fingernail.	Everyone will notice; it looks terrible.	Totally stressed and irritated.

TABLE 10-2   **Connecting Events, New Thoughts, and New Feelings**

Events	Thoughts	Feelings
My computer crashed.	I've had computers crash before. It's a hassle, but not exactly the end of the world.	Mildly irritated.
I ran out of cigarettes.	This happens to me all the time. I'll be okay for a while.	Blasé.
I broke my fingernail.	Like, no one will care or notice.	Close to neutral.

You can see how different ways of looking at an event or trigger lead to altered, less upsetting feelings, including reduced cravings to smoke. You may be thinking, right now, "What does this have to do with me? I just want to quit smoking. I'm not really concerned about all these thoughts, feelings, and triggers. I want to cut to the chase, get rid of the awful cravings, and stop smoking!"

We hear you. But changing the way you think can help you get there. And we wish, like you, that it was easy to do.

REMEMBER

What makes it hard, is the fact that most people don't really think about what they think. They don't examine their thoughts. Instead, they interpret or perceive things automatically without a lot of attention to the process. Most folks simply assume that their thoughts are accurate.

TIP

Just because you have a thought doesn't make it true. Thoughts are merely thoughts, not facts. Consider putting a sign on your bulletin board or at least your mind, "Just because I think something doesn't make it true!"

In the following sections, we give you the tools for uncovering distortions in your thinking (we all have them), re-examining your thinking, and designing new, more adaptive thinking that can help you get to the finish line of quitting smoking, using smokeless products, or vaping.

Finding distortions in your thinking

The human brain is a thinking machine. Streaming thoughts churn constantly in response to daily life events. Some thoughts are accurate. But the brain likes to take shortcuts. And inaccurate thoughts are often simpler and come from past experiences that may no longer be relevant in your world today.

Inaccurate thoughts become habitual over time. For example, people with chronic pessimism tend to look at everything as having a negative outcome. They repeat pessimistic thoughts so often that they no longer notice a sunny day or a glass half-full. And they don't question their bleak predictions and perceptions.

The following sections describe the common ways thoughts can be distorted as related to urges, cravings, aches, and yearnings to smoke. Look for yourself in these thought distortions. Don't worry; we'll help you figure out how to challenge and replace them with more useful thinking.

Catastrophizing

One of the most common thought distortions is what's known as *catastrophizing*. This distortion habitually makes "much ado about nothing," as Shakespeare wrote. Others call it making mountains out of molehills. You may be resisting this interpretation. Quitting smoking is a big deal — it *is* a mountain!

You're right; quitting is a big deal. And no easy task. But it's not undoable. It's not impossible. If your thoughts are distorted by catastrophizing, you'll struggle all the more. The story of Isaiah (see the nearby sidebar) illustrates what catastrophizing can do to your quitting efforts.

TIP

If you hear these words or phrases rattling around in your head, it's a good indication that you're something of a catastrophizer:

>> Awful

>> Can't stand it

>> Dreadful

>> Hopeless

>> Horrible

>> Terrible

>> Worst thing in the world

Don't despair. If you're a catastrophizer, it's hardly the worst thing in the world. You can overcome this thinking. We show you how in this chapter. Recognition is the first step.

EXAMPLE

WHAT CATASTROPHIZING LOOKS LIKE

Isaiah goes to the dentist for a routine exam and cleaning. While there, his dentist tells him that he has some oral lesions in the lining of his mouth. He tells Isaiah that those lesions may be at risk for turning into cancer and that his tobacco chewing has likely caused them. At this point, Isaiah's dentist recommends a referral to a specialist to be on the safe side and states, "In most cases like yours, quitting tobacco chewing will probably keep the lesions from turning cancerous. It's good we caught this really early. But you do need to stop your tobacco consumption."

Isaiah leaves the dental office in a daze. He texts his girlfriend to call him immediately and tells her, "The dentist said I'll die of oral cancer if I don't stop chewing tobacco immediately. I can't do that! I'm so upset about the cancer; I'll never be able to deal with withdrawal symptoms. I can't believe I'm going to die before I'm 45. Life isn't fair."

You can imagine that Isaiah is not in good shape to handle depriving himself of tobacco. He's also in no shape to logically manage his current health issues. He is inadvertently making things much worse by wallowing in his catastrophic thinking style.

Fortune telling

People who engage in fortune telling predict the future. And guess what? As far as we know, no one can really do that with much accuracy. Some predictions are more likely true than others. For example, if all you eat every day is cake and ice cream, we can predict that you'll suffer from malnutrition and probably gain some weight. Or if you hop on a train traveling to Toronto, you're most likely to end up in Toronto.

However, when it comes to quitting smoking, fortune-telling predictions are usually negative and foretell bad outcomes. They don't do much to make quitting easier. Instead, by jacking up your emotions, fortune telling usually makes progress harder.

Common examples of fortune-telling phrases include

>> Without tobacco, I'll never be happy.

>> I'll never enjoy coffee again if I quit.

>> My cravings will never go away.

>> I couldn't ever enjoy time with my friends without vaping.

>> I'm too weak; I could never quit.

>> I could never find non-vaping friends to spend time with.

>> I'm so addicted; I'll always have to smoke to survive.

>> If I quit vaping nicotine, I'm certain to gain 30 pounds.

>> If I quit, everyone will hate me because I'll turn into a total crab.

>> My husband will leave me if I quit smoking — he'll never quit and he couldn't live with a nonsmoker.

TIP

Notice how the phrases include absolutist words such as *always*, *never*, *everyone*, *total*, and *couldn't*, without exceptions considered. That's always a clue that pernicious fortune telling is in play. Interestingly, after decades of work with clients trying to change troubling emotions and problematic behaviors, we've found that well over 95 percent of fortune-telling predictions end up not panning out. And the few times that they did, rarely did the predictions cause the expected degree of misery and distress.

EXAMPLE

THE FORTUNE TELLER

Mia is a graduate student in environmental engineering. She's a secret vaper, never vaping around her peers. Nonetheless, she has become quite addicted to nicotine. She vapes almost constantly when she's studying at home, believing that vaping improves her focus and concentration.

Mia is surviving on student loans, so the costs of her vape juice and vaping paraphernalia are of some concern to her even though they're cheaper than cigarettes. Mia is also a bit concerned about her addiction to nicotine and the risks of unknown chemicals in her e-liquid. Mia starts thinking about quitting and indulges in fortune telling, distorted thinking such as the following:

- I'll never be able to study without a nicotine hit.
- No doubt I'll gain tons of weight if I quit.
- I can't face life without vaping.
- I'm too addicted physically to handle quitting.

With fortune telling pervading her mind, Mia doesn't have the confidence to quit vaping. She also believes that her good grades are the result of studying under the influence of nicotine. She believes that without nicotine, she'd surely fail and face dismissal from graduate school. Predicting bad fortune ahead stops Mia from even trying to quit.

Predictions are powerful. They influence people's decisions about lots of things, including whether to quit smoking. Mia's story (in the nearby sidebar) shows how dire fortune telling leads to her giving up on quitting vaping.

Mental filtering

Mental filtering is another type of cognitive distortion. This distortion discounts and discards any data that does not fit with a preconceived notion. For example, if someone is quitting smoking, and fears that pleasure will plummet, the mind can make the data conform to that prediction with mental filtering. In other words, enjoyable times will be quickly forgotten, and unpleasant events well remembered.

EXAMPLE

FILTER ME THIS

Joshua quit smoking just ten days ago. He had planned his quit day and received lots of support from his family and friends for almost a week. Then things get a little tougher. Joshua's cravings are strong, and he begins to believe that he'll never be happy again. He tells his girlfriend that he doesn't think it's worth being so unhappy because of quitting. She asks why. Joshua says, "Since I quit smoking, I haven't laughed once, and I've been in constant misery. Nothing's fun anymore."

Joshua's girlfriend grins and says, "So, don't you think last night was a little fun? You sure seemed to enjoy it!"

Joshua allows himself a small smile and nods. He says, "Well, yeah, that was pretty nice. But we can't be doing that all day."

His girlfriend replies, "Yeah, but let's go over some of the good stuff that happened today alone. First, you told me this morning that you felt really good. Then you got that text from someone who wanted to interview you for that job you applied for. And you really seemed to enjoy that comedy show we watched together. Is it possible you're not letting yourself focus on the positive things that are going on in your life? I've heard that nicotine addiction can do that. It should get better, though. And meanwhile, how about we repeat last night's activity?"

Joshua feels a bit chagrined and puts his arm around his girlfriend. He realizes he has been zeroing in on negative events to the exclusion of some very nice positives. He knows he's lucky to have his girlfriend's support.

TECHNICAL STUFF

Nicotine activates the dopamine pathways in the brain, thus enhancing the experience of pleasure. Withdrawal involves a temporary depletion of available dopamine It's no wonder that many quitters addicted to nicotine can't see the possibility of a pleasurable life without it. However, given enough time, quitters usually re-establish a balanced life with both pleasure and pain.

Mental filtering caused Joshua (see the nearby sidebar) to ignore the pleasurable events in his current life and focus on his unpleasant cravings. His girlfriend helped him step back and look at events more objectively. It's easy to fall into the habit of mental filtering.

Addiction's aches and yearnings push you to filter out positives and dwell on negatives. Why? In order to suck you back into smoking. If things are as bad as mental filtering would have you believe, of course you'll want to smoke!

REMEMBER

The "Reevaluating your thoughts" section, later in this chapter, shows you how to overcome the mental filtering problem, as well as other types of thought distortions.

Black-and-white thinking

Black-and-white thinking is a surefire way to trip up your quit-smoking program. This distortion views the world and events as all or nothing, good or bad, wonderful or horrible, with little in between. It's an extreme way of thinking and extremes generate lots of emotion.

So, extreme thinking can cause cravings to become intolerable instead of uncomfortable. A single puff on a cigarette becomes a reason for a total relapse (see Chapter 19). The following list exemplifies black-and-white thinking.

>> I have no self-control at all.

>> I must be perfect.

>> There's a right way and a wrong way to do things with nothing in between.

>> I absolutely can't stop smoking even for a single day.

>> My partner won't give me any support at all.

>> I never succeed at difficult tasks.

>> I am completely addicted to smoking; it's hopeless.

You can see where black-and-white thinking goes. You don't have much hope for success if you engage in this type of thought distortion. But there is hope! You can change your thinking style.

Personalizing

Another popular thought distortion is known as *personalizing*. This distortion leads you to interpret everything that happens as related to you — whether it really is or not. For example, if a driver in the next lane cuts you off, personalizing will lead you to believe that the other driver did it intentionally to mess with you. This belief leads you to anger. However, it could be that the driver was on her way to the hospital to give birth to quintuplets! Or maybe the driver was inattentive and didn't even see you — not a good thing, but not about you personally.

So, what does personalizing have to do with quitting smoking? Personalizing leads to difficult emotions like anger, rage, or shame, which can be dealt with by what? Smoking, of course! Sarah's story (see the nearby sidebar) shows how personalizing makes her battle to quit smoking more difficult.

EXAMPLE

TAKING EVERYTHING PERSONALLY

Sarah is in her fourth week of abstinence from smoking. She's feeling pretty good about her progress. Downright confident, in fact. Sarah is the lead of her eight-person sales team. Her boss calls a meeting of the team. He provides statistics indicating that their last quarter wasn't as good as the previous two quarters. He asks for feedback and ideas about what happened.

Sarah feels awash with shame. She sees the boss looking straight at her when he's talking. She believes that her boss, obviously displeased with her performance, is likely to fire her. Her first instinct is to go outside for a smoke break. She desperately wants that smoke. But, instead, she pops in a nicotine lozenge and decides to stick it out.

Her colleague, Fred, interjects, "You know, I think all this seeming drop in sales is probably due to the fact that I was out for six weeks on family leave when I broke my leg. And Lucy is still out on maternity leave. If you calculate what both of us would have normally brought in, we're probably a bit ahead of expectations."

Her boss replies, "Yeah, I knew this team had been doing a fabulous job. And I particularly want to give a shout-out to Sarah for her amazing leadership and innovative ideas."

Sarah's habit of personalizing almost got the upper hand and caused her cravings to surge. She managed to resist the impulse and, luckily, her colleague stepped in to give a rational explanation. However, Sarah will remain at some risk if she doesn't get a grip on her tendency to personalize.

Unyielding obligations

This thought distortion causes you to think you should be doing something different from what you're doing currently. "I should," "I must," and "I have to" are prime examples of this thought distortion. The human mind likes to appraise, evaluate, and judge everything. This tendency adds additional, unnecessary pressure to any undertaking, including smoking or vaping cessation efforts. Review the following list to get a flavor of the pernicious effects of such thinking:

>> I must not get crabby.

>> I shouldn't have to suffer withdrawal symptoms.

>> I must quit smoking now.

>> I have to stay upbeat.

>> I should work at this harder.

You may be thinking all these statements are true. Why worry about them? Well, let's try a quick rewording of the statements and see if they feel a bit different and less harsh:

>> I'd like to work on being less crabby.

>> I'd prefer not to suffer withdrawal symptoms.

>> I'd like to quit smoking now.

>> I'd like to stay more upbeat.

>> It would be great if I could work a bit harder on this.

When your thinking includes distortions such as *should, must,* or *have to,* you're likely to believe you're coming up short. Most obligatory evaluations of yourself can be softened. The reason to do that is that the more you believe in *should, must,* and *have to,* the harder things get. Concepts like *it would be better, I'd like to,* and *I'd prefer* do the job with less emotional turmoil.

Reevaluating your thoughts

Having distortions in your thinking causes you to have more intense emotions, which are generally negative. In turn, when you already have cravings, those distortions can become more extreme. A vicious cycle ensues.

WHAT HAPPENS WHEN YOUR THOUGHTS ARE DISTORTED

EXAMPLE

Before quitting, Noah finds himself worrying about whether he can stand the withdrawal symptoms and feelings. He sees himself as weak and predicts that he won't be able to be successful. He thinks to himself, "Nicotine gets me through the day. I don't think I can stand quitting. But I absolutely must try."

And sure enough, the second day with cravings going up, he says, "I can't stand it. I knew I would fail. I've never been very good at sticking with anything hard. Maybe I'll try quitting again in a year or so. I just don't have the willpower now."

So, Noah gives up. But what if he challenges his thinking? Could there be a different outcome? The next sections will help Noah and you reevaluate your thoughts.

For example, someone who tends to catastrophize, filter out positive information, apply unyielding obligations to himself, and fortune tell, may begin the quitting process with considerable apprehension. That person would also lack the self-confidence necessary to take on quitting. Changing thinking will help build up that confidence. Noah decides to give up smoking. See what happens to his ready-to-fire thought distortions when the cravings strike (see the nearby sidebar).

TECHNICAL STUFF

We categorize thought distortions as catastrophizing, fortune telling, mental filtering, black-and-white thinking, personalizing, and unyielding obligations. Perhaps you noticed that the various types of thought distortions overlap. For example, the thought of "I won't be able to stand it" is a clear example of catastrophizing. However, it's also an example of fortune telling. In fact, most distorted thoughts contain two or more distortions simultaneously. Does this matter? Not really. The techniques for challenging thought distortions work pretty well for all types of distortions.

Examining the evidence

Not all of your thoughts are wrong, distorted, or erroneous. For example, if you have the thought "I'd really like to have a cigarette now," you're probably completely correct and honest. There's no distortion. Yes, you wish you could have a cigarette.

It's only when you add obvious distortions, such as "I absolutely must have a cigarette right this minute," that your thinking starts to look warped. And hopefully you can see, the later thought will evoke much greater emotionally driven urges and cravings.

TIP

Here are some evidence-gathering questions you can ask yourself about your smoking- and vaping-related thoughts in order to challenge them and come up with something more realistic.

>> Are my thoughts absolutely, 100 percent true all the time?

>> Is it possible that I'm exaggerating?

>> Have I ever handled anything challenging in the past and gotten through it?

>> Am I filtering out any important information?

>> Do I have experiences that would contradict this thought?

>> Have my dire predictions always come true?

In an earlier sidebar, "What happens when your thoughts are distorted," we present the story of Noah, a young man with multiple distorted thoughts. He believes that he must quit, predicts that he won't be able to stand the withdrawal, that he doesn't have willpower, and is too weak to face challenges. Not surprisingly, Noah's quit attempt fails after a couple of days. However, when he challenges his distorted thinking, he may be able to try again much sooner than he thought.

EXAMPLE

Take a look at Noah's answers to the evidence-gathering questions:

>> **Are my thoughts absolutely, 100 percent true all the time?** Well, I quit for a few weeks last year and it was starting to get a little easier. I was able to stand the withdrawal symptoms. I started smoking again at a party. That was stupid.

>> **Is it possible that I'm exaggerating?** Okay, I said I can't stand the withdrawal symptoms. It's not like I'm in horrible pain. They're sure uncomfortable — but I can manage if I don't talk myself out of it.

>> **Have I ever handled anything challenging in the past and gotten through it?** I've done some hard stuff in the past — like the time I flunked organic chemistry. I was devastated, but I took it a second time, studied like crazy, and passed. That was *so* hard, but I did it.

>> **Am I filtering out any important information?** I'm ignoring the facts that I could really use the extra money that not buying cigarettes would give me and that I would be quite a bit healthier without smoking.

>> **Do I have experiences that would contradict these thoughts?** I'm not actually weak. I'm very strong when it comes to being responsible in all other areas in my life. Smoking is hard to give up, but I can do it if I try.

>> **Have my dire predictions always come true?** I guess I predicted that I wouldn't be able to quit smoking. That does not have to be true. When I failed chemistry, I thought I'd never be able to pass. I proved myself wrong. I can do the same with smoking.

What do you think of Noah's chances of being successful will be after challenging his thinking? Have they improved? We think so (and *our* thoughts are certainly not distorted!).

Moderating extremist words

Thought distortions greatly aggravate negative emotions. Thus, they make you feel much worse than you would have without distortions. Thought distortions often involve extreme words such as the following:

>> Always

>> Awful

>> Devastating

>> Horrible

>> Impossible

>> Never

>> Unbearable

Imagine trying to quit using tobacco or nicotine and describing the process using extremist words. For example, a vaper might say, "Life without nicotine is unbearable. It's utterly impossible to get through the day. It would be horrible to quit and never have that nicotine buzz again. I'll always vape."

You can soften the impact of extremist words if you modify and replace them with flexible, less absolute words and phrases. Few things are totally impossible. Although some things are devasting, they aren't frequent and they're usually temporary. Rarely is life unbearable.

WARNING

If your life truly feels unbearable, that's probably a sign of significant emotional problems, such as depression. We strongly urge you to see a mental health professional as soon as possible. If you feel hopeless or like ending your life, another good option is to start by calling the National Suicide Prevention Lifeline available 24 hours a day at 800-273-8255. They also have an online chat available at www.suicidepreventionlifeline.org/chat. To get the text crisis line, text HOME to 741741.

Let's take each of the extremist words and come up with a more flexible, logical, and supportable word or phrase:

Extremist Words	More Flexible Words
Always	Most of the time
Awful	Distressing
Devastating	Upsetting
Horrible	Unpleasant
Impossible	Very difficult
Never	Not usually
Unbearable	Uncomfortable

TIP

It helps to think about your extremist language like saying your car never has any gas at all or it's always totally, completely full. Only once in a blue moon are those extreme thoughts accurate. The truth is your car could be quite low on gas, or pretty topped off, but most of the time, it's somewhere in the middle. So, when you're thinking about your thinking, consider using a moderate, balanced set of words. Such words will evoke less distressing emotions and feel easier to deal with. They're likely to be more supportable by evidence as well.

Sitting across from a friend

It's human nature to feel upset or distraught when you're going through a tough time. And quitting an addiction like smoking is definitely in the tough category. Sometimes it's particularly tough when urges unexpectedly surge. And when times are tough, it's often comforting and helpful to spend some time with a friend. But what if your friends are tied up or unavailable? Or perhaps you don't want to bother them or share your troubles. Or maybe they're still smokers.

We have a strategy that many people find helpful. It's called the two-chair technique. With this method, you can access a friend within yourself. Almost all people have a reasonable, logical part of their minds in addition to an emotionally driven side (see Chapter 2). When you quit smoking and urges emerge, the emotional side of your brain tries to take charge. Accessing your friend within yourself helps you fight back with reason, evidence, and logic.

In order to do that, we have an exercise for you to try. Okay, we know it sounds a little weird, but really in our many years of psychology practice (as well as a bunch of research studies), we've seen this work for lots of people. So, put your reservations aside for a moment and do the following:

1. **Set up two chairs facing each other only a foot or two apart.**

2. **Label one of the chairs, "My emotional mind."**

3. **Label the other chair, "My logical, reasonable mind."**

4. **Imagine two of you, one in each chair.**

5. **Now, the real you needs to sit in the emotional mind chair.**

6. **Tell the imagined logical, reasonable part of you why quitting smoking (or vaping or chewing) is utterly impossible, horrible, not worth it . . . you get the idea.**

   Conjure up every rationale you've ever used to justify continuing to smoke or cave into a craving.

7. **When you're out of emotionally based reasons, switch to the logical, reasonable mind chair and argue back.**

   Tell the emotional part of your mind why it's wrong and foolish to continue thinking like that. Talk about the numerous health concerns you're addressing by quitting and why it's all so important to you.

8. **When you run out of logical arguments, switch back to the emotionally driven chair.**

   Think of more reasons to dispute the logical part of your mind until you run out again.

9. **Keep switching chairs until you've run out of arguments.**

10. **Summarize what you've learned.**

11. **Repeat this exercise from time to time whenever you find the emotional side of you starting to take charge.**

REMEMBER

We're not suggesting that your emotions are always wrong. There are times your gut tells you something worth listening to. But when it comes to addictions, strong emotions usually lead you astray — they are not your friend.

The nearby sidebar shows how Miguel, a lifelong smoker, uses the two-chair technique to deal with strong urges and cravings.

TIP

Understanding how thoughts interfere with your smoking cessation attempts will help you quit. But there's an important side benefit — when you recognize distortions in your thinking about smoking, you can apply what you've learned to other aspects of your life. For example, if you have bouts of anxiety, sadness, or anger, reevaluating your thoughts can help you deal with these issues, too.

EXAMPLE

TALKING TO YOURSELF

Miguel quit smoking two months ago and has had only two cigarettes since then. Miguel is watching politics on TV and finds himself getting upset and a bit angry. His go-to reaction, of course, has always been to reach for a cigarette at times like this. Predictably, he feels a huge uptick in his cravings. His emotional mind is telling him that he can just have a couple of cigarettes and he'll feel better. He can then quit again.

Something tells him, however, that his impulse may not be such a good idea. He struggles for another half-hour and feels even stronger urges. Then he remembers the two-chair technique and decides to take a run at it. Here's what transpires when he sits in each chair.

Emotional chair: Those stupid politicians make me so mad — I need a cigarette to deal with this! I can smoke a couple and just go right back to quitting. I need it. It will help. Don't stand in my way. I can't stand the cravings.

Reasonable chair: Hold your horses there. Politicians all do that to you; you can't go running for a few smokes every time you hear one say something outrageous. Smoking even just one or two cigarettes won't change what politicians say. Remember the last couple of times you had a "cheat" cigarette? It made your cravings intensify. Is that what you want? That's not sensible.

Emotional chair: Yeah, well, I really want a damn cigarette! What's the big deal? I can handle it; I managed before when I cheated.

Reasonable chair: Maybe you'd call that handling it. You almost went nuts after you cheated. You spent three days with miserable cravings. You know, if you just wait this out, you'll feel better in just a couple of hours. Isn't it better to feel you accomplished something rather than cave into what cigarettes want you to do?

Emotional chair: Okay, already. I'm not happy about it, but I'll try what you're saying. Maybe I should go for a walk like my quit plan suggests.

Reasonable Chair: Good choice. And, I don't know, but maybe you should watch a bit less politics. You know it's one of your triggers. There's some great comedy on cable. Better to laugh than to get ticked off and smoke.

Miguel figured a few things out from this exercise. First, he doesn't have to cater to his cravings. His addicted mind doesn't have to stay in charge of him. He sees how the emotional part of his mind wants him to cheat and disregard consequences such as increased cravings and the possibility of a full-blown relapse.

The next time you find yourself captive to the messages coming from the emotional side of your mind, try the two-chair technique.

Relating to your thoughts in a new way

Problematic, distorted thoughts can be challenged through checking the evidence, replacing extreme words with flexible language, and using the two-chair technique (see the previous sections). If you've tried these strategies and they do the trick for you, you may not need to read this section. However, you may have made progress in challenging your distorted thoughts but want something more.

When you think about your thinking, it's so easy to believe that your thoughts are real and have great meaning and importance. And sometimes that's the case. For example, when you think you need to pay your bills, you probably do! Your thoughts are telling you an accurate, important piece of information.

But when your thoughts tell you "I can't stand it," "I must have a cigarette now," "I'll be miserable forever," or "Maybe I'll just have a couple of smokes," then they aren't giving you information with great meaning and importance. And they are not true!

Another way of dealing with problematic thoughts is not to replace them at all but relate to them in a new way. Try realizing that thoughts are just thoughts. You can hear them and refuse to engage with them. You can merely let them go.

TIP

We have three quick techniques for letting your thoughts go. They take a little whimsical use of imagination. But suspend your judgment of these until you've tried them.

>> **Leaves:** Imagine writing your thoughts on a large leaf. Look at the leaf and read your thought. A gentle wind picks it up and drops it into a stream. The leaf gradually floats downstream.

>> **Clouds:** Imagine you have a magic pen that can write on clouds. Write your problematic thought on one of those clouds. Read it and watch it slowly drift by.

>> **Train cars:** Imagine a very long freight train approaching. It has your thought written on each car as it slowly chugs along down the tracks. Wave goodbye as it passes.

You use these techniques to stop engaging, arguing, or evaluating your thoughts. Earlier techniques show how to rethink thoughts. This approach helps you merely let them go. You'll never stop having problematic thoughts from time to time, but you can choose to deal with them differently — just another part of life passing by.

As you let go of thoughts, your actions will change. For example, if you think, "I must have a cigarette," and you let that thought go, you may choose to do something different. In other words, you'll feel less compulsion to pick up another cigarette.

Listening to Feelings and Urges

Trying to avoid all unpleasant feelings, when you're battling an addiction, is a certain path to failure. But that's what many quitters desperately try to do. They turn to substitutes such as NRT or ask for medications to eliminate cravings (see Chapter 9). They go to hypnotherapists, dabble with acupuncture, or take supplements, all in a frantic effort to avoid the cravings that come with quitting.

There's nothing wrong with trying, and sometimes these endeavors work. In fact, NRT and prescribed medications can temper the bad feelings. However, for most people who are trying to quit, some bad feelings emerge, no matter what. But, the more you absolutely need to completely quash these feelings, the more likely they'll overwhelm you.

If cravings, urges, yearnings, aches, and feelings of emptiness derail your efforts, we have a different suggestion for your consideration. As counterintuitive as it may seem, open up space for these feelings.

The feelings we're interested in here include only those that tend to send you on a quest to find and consume tobacco or nicotine. Typical, problematic feelings that trigger lapses include

» Aches

» Anxiety

» Boredom

» Cravings

» Emptiness

» Loneliness

» Stress

» Urges

» Yearnings

TIP

Most common feelings or emotional triggers are distressing in nature. However, sometimes people find themselves triggered by positive emotions such as joy and excitement. The negative cravings and urges follow the initial positive feelings.

To handle these feelings in a different way, start by examining them closely. When they occur, jot down where you feel them in your body and how intense they are, and maybe rate them on a 1-to-10 scale of intensity. Time them, too — do they last a few minutes, an hour, or what? Look at them objectively like you have to write a science report on them. Allow them space to exist and realize they don't have to overwhelm you.

For this approach to feelings, you don't have to write down where they occurred or what caused them. We only want you to concentrate on feelings from an objective distance. The nearby sidebar offers an example.

OBSERVING YOUR OWN FEELINGS

EXAMPLE

Ella has tried to quit vaping five or six times to no avail. She has been using NRT but still has powerful urges to vape. Nonetheless, she is determined not to let nicotine control her life any longer. She tracks her feelings related to vaping. She writes:

> I notice I have a strong craving as soon as I get home from work. I feel anxious at a level of 5 or 6. Both of these feelings live in my throat. It feels uncomfortable, like I need more air.
>
> Okay, I'm going to wait this out. I want to make space for my feelings. I think I'll walk around as I study these emotions. The moment I decided not to succumb, the feelings jumped. They're a level of 7 or 8 now. Wow my throat feels tighter and I can even feel it in my chest.
>
> This may not be working, but I'm going to hang in there. I see I'm tensing my hands, too. My teeth are clenching as well. Kind of like I'd feel if I were giving a presentation at work. But now I'm feeling a slight improvement. It's almost as if my describing how I feel is helping just a bit. Now, it's almost ten minutes since I started this. I feel pretty okay. Maybe just a 2 or 3. I think I'll make it through without vaping.

Ella discovered that she doesn't need to totally eliminate difficult feelings and that she couldn't do so even if she tried. By opening up space and studying her feelings, she found a path toward acceptance. Acceptance helped soften the feelings and made them less overwhelming.

Become a scientist interested in the science of feeling and emotion. Study your own feelings in a detached and objective way. As you practice relating to your feelings in this new way, you'll likely find that you begin feeling differently. Not radically and not all at once. Just a bit less intense and a bit more manageable.

TIP

Opening up space and accepting feelings can help you in other aspects of your life as well. If you have anxiety or depression, acceptance of feelings can help. When you try to suppress or deny difficult feelings, that can cause greater emotional distress. That distress can lead to physical complications such as high blood pressure, digestive problems, tense muscles, and greater urges to smoke. Accepting emotions allows you to process them and let them go.

WARNING

If feelings of depression or anxiety or any other emotions are interfering with your everyday functioning or causing considerable distress, help is available. Consult a mental health professional or your primary care provider.

Taking New Actions

In the earlier sections of this chapter, we discuss how thoughts, feelings, and triggers can lead people to smoke or vape. In this section, we talk about how changing behaviors can help you keep your impulses to indulge at bay. It begins with avoiding triggers and doing something different when you can, making the triggers less potent when possible, and taking specific actions to handle smoking triggers when they can't be avoided.

Avoiding and minimizing triggers when you can

Realize that you can't avoid all smoking triggers all the time. But you can reduce the frequency and degree of your interactions with triggers that tempt you to smoke. Some exposure to triggers is necessary to break a habit, but you need to build up strength to be able to face the biggest challenges.

If at all possible, avoid the obvious, most problematic triggers. For example, if you play poker on Friday nights and the gang all smoke, take a breather, so to speak. Your buddies will understand. Don't think for a second that you'll be able to deal with such a loaded situation right out of the starting block.

That's even more true if alcohol is involved because alcohol reduces inhibitions and self-control. For that matter, watch out for that after-work drink or, even worse, drinks (plural). That's especially true if your drinking is associated with a relaxing cigarette. Alcohol is often a trigger for smoking.

If you can't easily stay away from alcohol, it could be that you have two addictions in play. Lots of people have difficulty with alcohol and function very well. They don't appear to be what most folks would consider an alcoholic. But if you drink more days than not and consume more than two drinks per day for men or more than one drink per day for women, you could experience health problems from your drinking eventually. You can check on the extent of your possible problem by going to www.checkupandchoices.com and take their confidential free screener for drinkers. It's been well researched as valid. If you do have a problem, they'll let you know about possible next steps.

For those who attempt to quit alcohol and other substances, there appears to be a better chance of sobriety when cigarettes are given up at the same time.

Another situation that you may be able to easily avoid is going outside with the smokers during your breaks at work. Take a walk instead and be sure to go out another door or avoid the smokers as you leave. Consider having a cup of relaxing tea at your desk. Avoid smokers as much as you can, for at least a few months, if possible.

Don't go into the store where you regularly buy your smokes or vapes. For that matter, don't go *near* the store — it's too tempting to stop and go in. If you can, go to another neighborhood or make a detour. The more triggers that you can flat out avoid, the better, especially in the early going.

On the other hand, some situations are hard to avoid. If you smoked in the car every day while driving to work, you have a challenge. You could possibly take public transportation to work for a while or use a ride share. Or maybe you could carpool.

Barring these possibilities, you may need to come up with a distraction. Possibly you could find an especially engrossing podcast or audiobook.

Quitting smoking is one of the best things you can do for your health. Be smart. Do everything you can do to be successful. Pamper yourself. Avoid temptations when you can and make a plan ahead of time for when you can't avoid triggers for smoking.

Having an action for every trigger you can't avoid

Some triggers you can't avoid. If you smoke after every meal, obviously you can't stop eating. If you smoke on the couch while you watch TV, we don't expect you to give up your favorite shows. After all, you're giving up something else you're extremely fond of, right?

Instead when you can't avoid a trigger, change it up. Don't sit still after a meal. Do something different. Be a hero and clean the kitchen or take a walk. During the first few weeks, moving away from the trigger spot may be the best way to deal with it. As for TV, change chairs or watch in a different room. Have some healthy snacks available that you can chew while you watch.

Some triggers may be difficult to change up. For example, it's tough to change up talking on the telephone. For cases like that, we encourage a brief burst of exercise. It can be done before or after the call. Obviously, clear this suggestion with your doctor first if you have any health issues. Do just enough exercise to get your heart rate up. A few minutes is usually all you need. By changing your body's in-the-moment metabolism, you change up the physical experience of urges and cravings.

Here are a few brief exercise bursts for your consideration:

- ❯❯ Jumping jacks
- ❯❯ Squats
- ❯❯ Pushups
- ❯❯ Quick-feet jogging in place

If you have arthritis, an injury, or another physical condition, there are lots of modifications you can find on the Internet. Or consider consulting a physical therapist or personal trainer.

None of these alternative or modified actions will work for everyone. Some people find movement of almost any kind helps. Others like to listen to podcasts or music. Do what works for you. We give you many more options in Part 4.

Confronting triggers head on

Don't make it your goal to avoid all triggers of urges and cravings. In fact, after you master the first month or so of quitting, we encourage you to consider *intentionally* exposing yourself to some smoking triggers. That's in order to build up your endurance and ability to handle inevitable encounters.

If you try this strategy and find it difficult, we encourage you to drop it. Some people find it enhances their quit attempts, but it's not for everyone. Not to worry — there are plenty more strategies in this and other chapters.

We're going to pretend that you're starting a light, free-weight training program. You start off easy — maybe 5 pounds. Then after you master 5 pounds, you advance to 8 pounds, and then on to 12 pounds and beyond (you can change up the weights in your mind to fit your own strength and fitness level).

This weight-training metaphor can help you understand how gradual exposure to tobacco or vaping triggers can build up your strength and resistance. Here's how to do that in a gradual, controlled way:

1. **Make a list of smoking triggers relevant to you.**

2. **Rate each one for intensity (easy, moderate, difficult).**

   Every trigger and rating will be different for every person.

3. **Pick one trigger for each category that you can plan to deal with.**

4. **Spend 5 minutes in the presence of an easy trigger.**

   Gradually increase the time to 10 minutes and then 15 minutes. Repeat until cravings decrease in response to that trigger.

5. **Do the same with a moderately difficult trigger followed by a difficult one.**

6. **Repeat until you feel greater mastery over your triggers.**

EXAMPLE

LIFTING WEIGHTS

Gavin has been smoke-free for six weeks. He has avoided lots of triggers, but now he feels ready to start dealing with them head on. He makes his initial list of triggers and chooses an easy, moderate, and difficult one. He calls his morning coffee trigger a 5-pound challenge, his work-break a 10-pound challenge, and watching a movie at home a 15-pound challenge.

Gavin starts with the morning coffee trigger. Up to now, he has been leaving for work before drinking his morning coffee to keep from experiencing cravings. Today, he sits at his kitchen table, coffee cup in front of him without a cigarette. He finds it mildly difficult, but a little harder than he thought it would be. He notices all the symptoms in his body — tightness in his chest, a feeling of anxiety, a strong craving in the pit of his stomach. He stays seated and continues to notice these sensations as he drinks his coffee. They ebb and flow and eventually decrease.

Gavin needs to continue this work, more morning coffee, more triggers, and longer duration. This work will gradually allow him to increase his sense of competence and help him deal with his cravings and urges.

For some people, exposure to triggers is an important part of recovery. If you can't build up the strength to resist triggers, you'll be at risk for relapse. The example of Gavin in the nearby sidebar illustrates a planned exposure to triggers.

Rewarding successes

You've had a smoking, chewing, or vaping habit long enough to be thoroughly engrained, or you wouldn't be reading this book! Each time you inhaled or chewed, you were rewarded.

Now you want to give up something that you enjoy doing and replace it with what? Well, yeah, you want to get healthier and spend less money. But those goals can feel a bit remote. You were getting rewarded instantly for indulging in your habit. You need to set up quicker, concrete rewards for your successes.

In the early stages of quitting, you need to do whatever you can in order to stay the course. Finding good self-rewards is a big part of that picture. It's even okay to indulge in ice cream every single day you don't smoke (that is, for a while). Gaining a little weight is much less dangerous than tobacco, and you can work on that issue a bit later (see Chapter 20 for information about dealing with weight).

Use your imagination and come up with a list of ideas for self-rewards. See Chapter 17 for ideas on how to pamper yourself during the first risky months.

TIP

You're saving a small fortune by not smoking. Right now, an average price for a pack of cigarettes hovers in the $6 to $8 range. In other words, most pack-a-day smokers will spend over $200 per month; vapers will incur somewhat less. For the first month or two, consider using a major portion of your savings to reward yourself. Doing so can reinforce your new, nonsmoking habit.

Chapter **11**

Tapping Technical Supports

Research on quitting smoking suggests that you should make a public statement of your intent to quit. By doing just that alone, you slightly increase your chances of success. However, some people are shy. They really don't want to share their business with other people. And they certainly don't want the public embarrassment of possible failure.

Now, we could reassure you that most of your friends, family, neighbors, or coworkers really want to support you in your efforts. But we don't blame you if you feel unsure and insecure. In fact, a few people in your world may have a tendency to be critical. Who needs that — especially when you're trying something excruciatingly hard, like quitting an addiction!

So, if you would like some support, but not from people you know, we have an app for that! Or anonymous help on the phone. This chapter reviews some of the best.

REMEMBER

The resources reviewed in this chapter are terrific. We think the more help and support you get the better. However, we did not find a product that we could endorse as a complete, stand-alone program for quitting smoking. The quitlines come the closest to a full-blown program, but you still get somewhat fragmented support. In almost all cases, you'll talk to someone different every time you call. So, yes, consider using apps on your phone, quitlines, text messaging, or Internet chat groups. Just don't expect them to be a complete solution to quitting smoking.

TIP

Chapter 24 covers reliable online sources of *information* about smoking and cessation and health effects. Here we're giving you sources of *support* for your efforts. In a few cases, the contact website is the same for both purposes.

Finding Help on Your Phone

The resources we review in this section are all free to download or access. You can get help without judgment. The quitline is welcoming and confidential. You don't have to tell the counselor your name. And you don't have to have stopped smoking when you call — you can just be considering the idea.

You can also sign up for an app. You may prefer this option if you'd rather not talk to an actual, live person. If you want text or email support, you'll need to provide your phone number or email address if you're comfortable doing so. Most important, lining up additional support through quitlines or apps can increase your chances of success.

WARNING

Be careful about the type of information you provide in order to access an app. They vary in their privacy policies, and the policies are not always made explicit. Never give your Social Security number or important passwords. If you're required to make up a password, make it unique to that app — don't use the same password you use to access other websites.

Turning to quitlines

If you live in the United States and you want personalized support and help for quitting tobacco or nicotine, there's no better place to start than 800-QUIT-NOW (800-784-8669). For Spanish speakers, call 855-DEJELO-YA (855-335-3569). Calling these numbers will automatically connect you with your local state quitline. Asian smokers can call 800-838-8917 for Mandarin and Cantonese, 800-556-5564 for Korean, or 800-778-8440 for Vietnamese. For more information, go to www.asiansmokersquitline.org. The Veteran's Administration also staffs a quitline especially for vets at 855-QUIT-VET (855-784-8838).

You'll be able to talk to a counselor with training in smoking cessation. Counselors are ready to give advice on medications, nicotine replacement therapy (NRT), and other strategies for stopping smoking or vaping. They can give you support through text messaging and email. This service is available 24/7 so you can call them when you're desperate, even at 2 a.m. We give this service our gold-star rating! It's the only line we feel is worthy of your attention. Sometimes there's something to be said about one-stop shopping.

TIP

Watch out for smoking cessation websites sponsored by commercial interests. Poke around in the fine print at the bottom of the page — you can usually figure the sponsor. Sometimes they disguise their sponsorship with initials. Google the initials when you aren't sure about a website. You don't have to pay for a quality quitline. And you want unbiased information rather than what some tobacco or pharmaceutical company may recommend.

Tapping out texts

Most phone assistance does not come in the form of texting, but through apps and quitlines. However, if you like to text, Smokefree.gov offers a free text messaging program that you can opt into or out of at any time. Here's how to sign up:

1. Go to www.smokefree.gov.

2. Click Tools & Tips.

3. Click Smokefree Texting Programs.

4. Under SmokefreeTXT, click Sign Up Now.

5. Enter the required information.

6. Click Submit.

TIP

Message and data rates may apply depending on your wireless provider's plan. Nowadays, many people have unlimited text messaging plans, but if you're not sure what your plan allows, check with your carrier.

You'll receive an instant welcoming text. The program checks in with you periodically. If you're having a tough moment, text "crave," "mood," or "slip," and you'll receive advice on getting through. The following are actual texts that we received when trying out this program:

>> **Crave:** "Take ten deep breaths in through your nose and out through your mouth. Appreciate your smoke-free lungs."

>> **Crave:** "We know the feeling. Think about what you're gaining and why you want to leave cigarettes behind. Stay focused — it will get easier."

>> **Mood:** "Like you thought this would be easy? Quitting sucks but the effects of smoking suck more. Yes, it's hard, but the rewards are huge."

>> **Mood:** "Surround yourself with supporters. Talk and do things with other people even if you don't feel like it, to boost your mood."

>> **Slip:** "Ditching your quit because of a slip is like slashing your other three tires because you got a flat. Focus on your successes and keep going."

>> **Slip:** "Quitting is tough and mistakes happen. The most important thing is to keep going! Learn from this. Forgive yourself. Now move on."

This program automatically terminates after six weeks. But if you haven't stopped yet, you can renew it. If you want to end it sooner, you simply reply, "Stop." It doesn't get any easier than that. By the way, when you text "Stop," you receive a friendly text telling you if you want to start again just text the word, "New" and you can change your mind.

REMEMBER

The prompts you receive from this text-messaging program can feel spot-on and personal. However, they're artificially generated and may sometimes miss the target. Don't take it personally. If you like texts, you may find this text-messaging program to be an additional support for your quit plan.

TIP

Young people (ages 13 to 24) who are interested in quitting vaping can access a free mobile program through the Truth Initiative that includes text messaging support. You can sign up at www.truthinitiative.org/thisisquitting.

Assessing apps for assistance

The bottom line for using apps to quit smoking is they're not enough by themselves to serve as tools or guides for quitting smoking. Formal studies on their effectiveness are too limited to make strong recommendations. However, our take is that most of what they provide is reasonable from a scientific basis. What they do best is help you with tracking your progress and bumps in the road. They are not robust in delivering advice on a full range of strategies. That doesn't mean they have no value; it's just that they should be combined with other approaches reviewed in this book.

Having said that, we should note that smoking-cessation apps are becoming better and more personalized over time. We suspect that with continued advances in artificial intelligence technologies, smoking-cessation apps will eventually become a mainstay approach to those wanting to quit smoking or vaping.

To get ready to write this section, we downloaded lots of apps. We wanted to not only read the reviews, check the stats, and dig into privacy, but also experience for ourselves what you do when downloading and accessing smoke apps that promise you help.

Before we get into specifics about the apps, we have some general observations:

>> Some of the apps start out free but pester you frequently to upgrade. Sometimes the cost of the upgrade is minimal, but it felt annoying to us.

>> Other apps offer products for sale. Again, mostly no hard sale tactics, but you may find that annoying, too. We point these out in our discussion.

>> A few apps are quite cute and engaging. That may sound superficial, but in terms of your likelihood of continuing with the app, design matters.

>> Privacy is an issue on any app. Many of the privacy statements are hard to find and even harder to decipher. Don't share financial information that could lead to someone getting into your personal bank account. Unless rules are made clear, visible, and explicit, you may be giving your information to a third party.

>> These apps should not need much personal information about you other than your approximate age, gender, phone number, email address, zip code, and sometimes your permission to track your location.

We confess that we gave the wrong birthdate when signing up for apps to sample. You can obscure your personal information, too. But don't make your information stray too far off from reality. For example, if you smoke a pack a day, say that — no one is going to be able to identify you with that small bit of information. And if you're 22 years old, don't say you're 65 or if you're 75 don't say you're 18 (even if you'd like that to be true). You're likely to get better advice.

Next, we review a few of the apps that have received significant attention from the public and/or professionals. We make no specific recommendations as these apps evolve over time. Again, these should all be considered as potentially useful adjuncts to your efforts.

QuitGuide

You can access this app from the Apple Store where users have rated it at 4.2. It's also available on Google Play, where it sports a rating of 4.0.

>> **Cost:** Completely free.

>> **What it does:** Tracks progress, cravings, moods, and slips. Identifies triggers, including time and location, and sends heads-up motivational messages as indicated. Also shows how much money you're saving.

>> **Bottom line:** Easy to use. The location feature is interesting. You can drop a pin in a location that sets off strong cravings — the app will remember and send you a tip whenever you return to that place. Good, explicit privacy standards. Simple, appealing, engaging design. Unbiased source (U.S. government).

QuitStart

QuitStart, developed by the U.S. National Cancer Institute and www.smokefree. gov, can be found at Google Play with a rating of 3.5. Apple users rate that version more highly at 4.5.

>> **Cost:** Completely free.

>> **What it does:** Tracks progress, cravings, slips, and moods. Offers simple distracting games for dealing with cravings, provides inspirational statements and challenges about diet and lifestyle. Sends tips three times per day for two weeks and more often if you choose that option.

>> **Bottom line:** Good app, easy to use. Some tips are a bit hokey and challenges for improving your mood (like wear something colorful today) seem to have no clear rationale. Some reviewers complained about inaccurate data collection. Privacy standards are good and easy to access. Unbiased source (U.S. government).

QuitNow!

QuitNow! is available at both Google Play with a rating of 4.4 and at the Apple Store where it's rated 4.6. It has more than 100,000 registered users and has been downloaded 1.5 million times.

>> **Cost:** The basic version is free. The pro version is $3.99.

>> **What it does:** Like most other apps for this purpose, it tracks progress (including days quit, cigarettes avoided, and money saved). It also alerts you to the health benefits you're accruing as the days pass without smoking. It has a chatroom available.

>> **Bottom line:** Easy to use but has an annoying tendency to bombard the user with prompts to upgrade to the Pro version. Free version has pop up ads. However, user popularity ratings are quite high. Available in multiple languages. Privacy policy is easy to access.

Kwit

Kwit is available at the Apple Store with a rating of 4.6. You can also find it at Google Play with a rating of 4.0.

- **» Cost:** Free to download, but it limits use and delivers frequent prompts to upgrade to a relatively expensive subscription. The current cost is over $7.49 per month or about $29.49 for six months and $89.99 for a lifetime.

- **» What it does:** Tracks your smoking and provides fun game-oriented design to help people stick to their quit-smoking plan. You compete to reach higher levels and rankings. Ostensibly, you can shake your phone and receive a large number of motivational messages, but the function didn't seem to work on the free download version.

- **» Bottom line:** Users report high satisfaction ratings. If you enjoy games and money is no issue, you may want to check it out. Just be aware that some available free apps appear to have similar ratings and a range of functions. Besides, they're well, free.

Smoke Free

Smoke Free can be downloaded for free at the Apple Store with a rating of 4.8. You can also find it at Google Play, rated at 4.7. Obviously, people like it. They also have a smoke–free baby app version for women who are pregnant and wanting to quit smoking.

- **» Cost:** Free download, but with limited functionality. There is a modest, $4.99 one-time fee or, if you're unsure that you want to stick with it, you can pay $0.99 weekly.

- **» What it does:** Keeps track of your cigarettes smoked, time you spend smoke free, and health improvements over time, and gives you so-called "missions" for dealing with cravings. You earn badges over smoke-free time. The app provides numerous stop-smoking tips.

- **» Bottom line:** The Quit Coach feature is automated but has a surprisingly personal feel. For example, we generated the following dialogue with the Quit Coach feature on the Smoke Free App:

  - **Smoker:** I feel like I won't ever be happy again.

  - **Quit Coach:** Hope you don't mind if I check, would you describe this as general craving to smoke?

  - **Smoker:** Nope

  - **Quit Coach:** Oops, sorry! I'm still very much in learning mode. Another go?

- **Smoker:** Sure.

- **Quit Coach:** What's triggering your desire to smoke?

- **Smoker:** Feeling empty.

- **Quit Coach:** Might seem a silly question, but does this fall into the general category of feeling down, depressed, low, etc.?

- **Smoker:** That's right.

- **Quit Coach:** Those cravings aren't easy to deal with. Hope this tip helps. . . . Know that this feeling will pass. That can be enough to make you feel better now. Let it be.

- **Smoker:** I'll try this.

- **Quit Coach:** Fantastic, I really hope it helps.

So, in our opinion, the Quit Coach doesn't exactly substitute for a live counselor or therapist. But it has the potential to help some folks who want a quick response — it's available 24/7, unlike a real person. The app is well designed and unusually easy to navigate. Smoke Free has some very preliminary research backing its efficacy. And techniques the app uses seem reasonably consistent with scientific approaches. For $4.99, it seems worth the investment if it helps you quit smoking.

Quitter's Circle

You can find Quitter's Circle at the Apple Store rated at 3.8 and on Google Play with a 2.9 rating. Both ratings are lower than most apps we reviewed.

» **Cost:** Completely free with no professional version.

» **What it does:** The most unique feature of this app is that it helps you connect with supportive family and friends to help you with your quit plan. Your supporters all need to sign into the app. They'll be notified of your progress, presumably so they can encourage and congratulate you. They'll also be notified of your slips. The effectiveness of this approach no doubt depends heavily on having a truly positive, nonjudgmental group of family and friends.

» **Bottom line:** Low ratings appear to be due to bugs and navigational difficulties. You can also make an appointment with a healthcare provider on another website called Doctor on Demand. It's unclear how Doctor on Demand is more effective than talking with your own doctor. This app is produced by Pfizer (a pharmaceutical company) and the American Lung Association.

All other apps for smoking cessation

Okay, we're tricking you with this heading. We're not about to review all or even most smoking-cessation apps. There are too many and not enough pages in this book to review them. Here, however, are a few parting thoughts on apps for your quit plan:

>> Don't spend much money. There are good apps available for free, and most others can be had for less than $5.

>> Beware of apps sponsored by commercial interests invested in selling products such as nicotine gum and lozenges.

>> Make sure you like the look and feel of any app you choose.

>> Read reviews on both the app store as well as independent sources when available.

>> Don't believe unreasonable promises like "stop smoking in ten minutes." If it sounds too good to be true. . . .

TECHNICAL STUFF

MindTools.io (www.mindtools.io) is a website hosted by a nonprofit group that hopes to give information to consumers of digital tools designed to improve quality of life and well-being, including quit-smoking apps. They use scientifically backed strategies to rate the potential of apps to deliver what they promise as opposed to rating merely on the basis of popularity. Although most of the apps we list have not been reviewed by MindTools.io, we think it's a great place to get useful information and validation. Hopefully, with time, they will expand their list of products reviewed.

Turning to the Internet for Support

You can also get support from others by joining a chat room or support group on the Internet. For example, there are hundreds of Facebook support groups. All you need is a Facebook account. Other types of social media also provide various options for connecting with others.

WARNING

As you know, social media has proven vulnerable to hacks and malicious imposters so be careful and a bit skeptical before plowing ahead. You may want to avoid giving identifiable information. And, of course, don't share any financial information.

TIP

A safer way to get support on social media is simply to share your struggles and accomplishments with your followers and friends. We assume you'll get support from them. If not, consider unfriending or unfollowing them.

Two more support groups available on the Internet include

>> **SMART Recovery (www.smartrecovery.org):** The acronym SMART refers to: Self-Management and Recovery Training. They have free support groups available to anyone wanting science-based addiction recovery. But they don't claim any particular success rate for smoking cessation. They have both in-person and online groups. You can join online using a pseudonym.

>> **Nicotine Anonymous (www.nicotine-anonymous.org):** Nicotine Anonymous is a 12-step program similar to Alcoholics Anonymous. They provide online chat groups, telephone support, and in-person groups. Some smokers may benefit from the sponsors that are also available. The efficacy of 12-step programs is controversial, but many people claim they've been helped by them. Many of the benefits of 12-step programs appear to come from the social support they provide.

Many other websites offer resources and basic information about health effects from smoking and vaping, as well as tips for quitting (see Chapter 24 for a list of online resources).

Chapter **12**

Reducing Harm from Cigarette Smoking

You already know the health risks associated with smoking. You know that smoking costs you a ton of money as well. You'd like to quit, but maybe you don't feel like you can face the battle right now. It would be nice if there were a perfect pill that would take away all your cravings or if you'd just wake up one morning as a nonsmoker. But there isn't a pill and you won't magically wake up a nonsmoker. You're simply not ready to give up what has become your best friend — a cigarette.

We want to be clear here: Quitting and complete abstinence from smoking represents your *absolutely best* bet at long-term good health. No question. But we're also realists. People vary in their tolerance and ability to fully quit smoking. And sometimes people just aren't ready or willing to completely stop.

TIP

If you're not ready to completely quit, at least keep the possibility of complete abstinence in your mind as your ultimate goal for the future.

In this chapter, we deal with, "in the meantime." Harm reduction is a concept in the addiction literature that has gained support over the past few decades. *Harm reduction* refers to the understanding that some people are going to smoke, vape, or consume tobacco in some form no matter what — at least for a while. Harm reduction approaches aim at reducing the harmful health effects of smoking or vaping until a person is willing to take a run at total abstinence. *Harm reduction can improve a cigarette smoker's quality of life and health.*

TIP

Here's a tricky point: If you're considering harm reduction as an approach instead of quitting, make sure that you're not kidding yourself. Are you doing it so that you can have an excuse to keep on smoking? There's a fine line between reducing the harm from smoking and simply making an excuse to keep on smoking.

REMEMBER

If you've tried quitting numerous times and you consider yourself a failure, you may want to rethink your conclusion. In reality, you've reduced harm and produced lots of nonsmoking days that do matter. For example, 30 attempts that average 20 days of nonsmoking means almost two years of nonsmoking! That reduces harm. Keep at it! Of course, the eventual and best goal is quitting, but you already know that.

Distinguishing Between Tobacco and Nicotine

People smoke cigarettes, consume smokeless tobacco in various ways, or vape, primarily to enjoy the effects of a sudden jolt of nicotine. Nicotine is a highly addictive drug.

REMEMBER

However, nicotine is *not* the primary source of increased risk of cancer, chronic obstructive pulmonary disease (COPD), heart disease, and other health maladies (see Chapter 3 for more information about the health risks of tobacco). This distinction is difficult for many people to keep in mind because smoking and nicotine are so frequently and closely associated. People smoke because they're addicted to nicotine, but they aren't addicted to the smoke or tar that ultimately makes them sick and kills them.

Rest assured, nicotine does not merit a totally clean bill of health. It is, indeed, a powerfully addictive drug. And it does have some negative health effects, including the following:

>> Increased heart rate

>> Increased blood pressure

>> Increased blood sugar

>> Gastrointestinal disorders

>> Decreased immune response

>> Links to cancer (mostly as a possible tumor promoter)

THE CONTROVERSY OF HARM REDUCTION

Complete abstinence is an almost universally favored outcome for dealing with smoking. But those who believe in harm reduction realize and accept the fact that 100 percent abstinence isn't going to happen for all smokers. They contend that reducing the number of cigarettes smoked or switching to safer, alternative products will ultimately save lives. Many in the total abstinence camp believe that anything short of total abstinence as a goal will result in promotion of unhealthy behaviors and products that will harm public health.

We maintain that both cessation and harm reduction can co-exist. Smokers who use safer tobacco products (or pure nicotine products) will experience reduced health problems such as lung cancer and heart disease. If public health officials only accept total abstinence as a goal, where does that leave those unwilling or unable to embrace that goal?

The severity and pervasiveness of these damaging effects are far less clear and less known than those for tobacco itself. In fact, the *relative* safety of nicotine is seen in the proliferation of nicotine replacement products available *without a prescription.* Clearly, the U.S. Food and Drug Administration (FDA) sees nicotine as far less harmful than tobacco. So, if you eliminate all tobacco and substitute pure nicotine, you'll greatly reduce your health risks from smoking and vaping.

TIP

Although nicotine replacement therapy (NRT) is generally not recommended for long-term use, many people continue with it far longer than initially prescribed or recommended. They're still reducing their health risks over those they would incur if they continued to smoke.

Trying to Reduce the Harm While Continuing to Smoke Cigarettes

Some smokers hoping to reduce harm, without totally giving up cigarettes, try various strategies that don't necessarily work. Sorry, you can't have your cake and eat it, too. Although these approaches make intuitive sense, research tells us something different:

>> **Cutting back the number of cigarettes smoked:** Smoking three packs of cigarettes a day is worse than smoking one pack a day. Duh. So, is smoking 15 cigarettes better than a pack and 10 better than 15? And is 5 better than 10? All things being equal, of course. But actually, it isn't always so equal, as you'll soon see.

>> **Smoking with a filter:** Filters came onto the smoking scene in the mid 1950s. Tobacco companies touted filters as a safer way to smoke. Unfortunately, their first attempt at filters included asbestos as an ingredient. You've probably heard that asbestos is a highly toxic carcinogenic. Later, asbestos was replaced with ostensibly safer ingredients. Today's cigarette filters do remove some tar and nicotine, and apparently, they *slightly* reduce the risk of lung cancer.

>> **Turning to light and ultra-light cigarettes:** The makers of these cigarettes claim that they contain decreased levels of tar. The labels have been banned by the government because tobacco company claims regarding safety convey a level of unwarranted protection. Smokers of light and ultra-light cigarettes have been found to be less addicted, but interestingly less likely to quit. That may be because these smokers believe they're smoking something relatively safe. Not true.

REMEMBER

Cutting back, using filters, and smoking light cigarettes are generally ineffective harm-reduction strategies. In part, that's because smokers who try to reduce their risks by smoking less or smoking ostensibly safer cigarettes end up smoking differently.

Numerous studies have shown that smokers who cut down the number of cigarettes smoked, smoke light cigarettes, or use filters:

>> Inhale more deeply

>> Hold the smoke longer

>> Inhale more often

Guess what these tactics do? They bring the level of nicotine, tar, and numerous carcinogens back up closer to the amount inhaled with regular cigarette smoking. In addition, filters make the smoke less irritating to the throat, which also encourages deeper inhalations.

WARNING

Many smokers are unaware that they're compensating for reduced nicotine by smoking differently. Cutting back by reducing the number of cigarettes smoked, often results in not cutting back at all — unless you're the rare smoker who can cut way back on quantity and not smoke differently. Therefore, these methods are usually a very bad choice for harm reduction. And if you're one of those extremely rare smokers who can smoke just a few each day, quitting surely seems to be a better option for you with significantly less grief overall.

Some people struggle with decisions about cutting back their smoking or going to a safer cigarette. Check out the nearby sidebar, "Cutting back," for a story of one woman's attempt to grapple with harm reduction.

CUTTING BACK

Ava started smoking when she was in high school. In the last ten years, she's tried to quit dozens of times. In her mind, she believes she'll probably smoke for the rest of her life. Her exasperated doctor suggests she at least cut down on her smoking and warns of the dangers of not doing so. Specifically, he's concerned with her frequent bouts of bronchitis.

Ava promises she'll find a way to do that and report back to him at her next visit. A couple of months later, Ava returns with another flare-up of bronchitis. She complains that she cut her smoking in half from one pack a day to a half a pack a day. Her doctor says, "That's better, but I'm also curious if there's any chance you could be inhaling more deeply and frequently with your lessened number of cigarettes?"

Ava says, "Hmm, I don't know. Maybe. I do seem to savor each cigarette more. So, it's quite possible I am inhaling more. Does that make a difference?"

Her doctor responds, "Well, yes, it can make a lot of difference. The reason you're inhaling more is that you're trying to make up for the nicotine lost by cutting back. So, you probably need to cut down a lot more to counteract that."

He continues, "But, let's see, here's a possibility for you. How about you cut down to five cigarettes a day. To get you through, I'm going to prescribe you a nicotine inhaler. Generally, we don't prescribe nicotine replacement therapy to people who are still smoking. But, in your case, because you're otherwise healthy, I'll monitor you closely for possible side-effects. Don't use the inhaler at the same time as you smoke. and make sure you smoke no more than five cigarettes per day."

After two months, Ava cut her risks significantly. And her doctor suggested she take another run at quitting, aided by NRT. She does so successfully.

Although NRT is not generally recommended as a way to cut back on smoking, a few studies have looked at using NRT in this manner. People who were not planning to quit smoking were provided NRT and told to smoke less. The group smoking while using NRT was compared to a group also told to smoke less but given an inert placebo instead of NRT. Results indicated that people using NRT and told to smoke less experienced a much greater likelihood of being able to cut their smoking in half. This finding may be good news for people not ready to stop smoking entirely, but at least wanting to cut down and reduce their risks.

Remember: If you choose to try NRT for cutting down on smoking, it won't do any good unless you avoid inhaling more deeply, longer, and more often. Also, NRT is not usually recommended for those still smoking. Check with your doctor before trying it to be sure it's safe for you.

Trying Smokeless Tobacco Products

Most people who try to quit smoking fail — not once or twice but multiple times. Some studies suggest that 30 attempts are not unusual. Most studies have used abstinence from tobacco and nicotine as the only long-term measure of success. But if you ask smokers why they want to quit, most will tell you that it's because of concerns about health.

So, if improved health is the primary goal of quitting, then reducing harm by using less toxic products makes sense. Smokeless tobacco would be one approach consistent with a harm reduction goal.

While *not* entirely safe, smokeless tobacco is much less harmful to health than burning tobacco and inhaling the smoke. Unfortunately, little effort has been devoted to studies of harm reduction with smokeless tobacco for those unwilling or unable to cease tobacco use entirely.

One reason for this reluctance is that smokeless tobacco does increase risks of oral cancer and likely the risk of premature death, although those risks appear quite small compared to those caused by regular smoking. The exact comparative risks are unknown because we need more studies to determine that. Of note, the FDA has recently granted permission to a Swedish company to market a smokeless form of chewing tobacco (known as *snus*) as a safer alternative to smoking combustible cigarettes.

Research indicates that smokeless tobacco has the potential to save lives compared to smoking (see the nearby sidebar, "Smoking rates and snus use in Sweden"). The appeal of this approach has gone up because products are now available that require little or no spitting and are easier to dispose. Users, increasingly including more women, report that some products can be consumed quite discretely, avoiding the considerable stigma once associated with smokeless tobacco.

TIP

Another important advantage of using smokeless tobacco products is that they don't produce smoke. So, they not only reduce harm to the smoker, but also eliminate secondhand and thirdhand smoke for the family, coworkers, and friends in the smoker's world.

TIP

Yet another advantage of smokeless tobacco is that some of the newer products are especially discrete and don't require spitting and awkward disposal — that allows for less possibility of young children detecting its use in adults and trying to model that behavior. On the other hand, this same discreteness makes the product more appealing to teenagers who are trying to hide their use of smokeless tobacco from their parents.

SMOKING RATES AND SNUS USE IN SWEDEN

Sweden has successfully cut the national smoking rate of its adult citizens to about 5 percent. That's the lowest rate in Europe and well below the U.S. rate of about 14 percent. How did they do that? Many experts attribute this phenomenal accomplishment to the Swedes' efforts to reduce smoking by introducing a less harmful tobacco product. Snus is a moist tobacco variant of snuff (see Chapter 2 for information about snuff and various tobacco products). It has been touted as having a lower concentration of the cancer-causing nitrosamines than the level found in other tobacco products.

Snus comes in an easily disposed pouch that's placed under the top lip and does not require spitting — thankfully for the rest of us. A long-term study from January 2003 to February 2011 found that both males and females who use snus were less likely to take up smoking. Therefore, snus does not appear to be a gateway drug to smoking.

In fact, smokers who started using snus were more likely to quit smoking entirely. Snus worked better than NRT at helping smokers quit. Although snus is associated with increased rates of oral cancer, that rate is much lower than the prevalence of lung cancer among smokers. Since introducing snus, Sweden has enjoyed the lowest male death rate from smoking in Europe.

WARNING

Smokeless tobacco products sometimes come in enticing flavors and colors, which makes them more desirable to children and pets. Be sure to keep them stored in a safe, unreachable location.

WARNING

Teens also find enticing flavors attractive. In fact, smokeless tobacco use among teens is growing. Teens are especially susceptible to nicotine addiction, so there's mounting concern over the issue of flavors and colors that could be used to lure them into the clutches of smokeless tobacco.

Veering to Vaping

The idea of using vaping as a path to smoking cessation is controversial (as is the use of smokeless tobacco). We want to assure you that we've done our homework. Some time ago, when we first began to study this issue, we thought that e-cigarettes' promise as a safer cigarette was a totally unsupportable ploy. We assumed that e-cigarette manufacturers were out to exploit an uninformed public for the purpose of profits.

In our search for the truth, we even visited various vape shops where seemingly sincere personnel did little to assuage our concerns. Nonetheless, we dove into the literature and discovered surprising support for the concept.

One of the benefits of e-cigarettes over NRT is that vaping mimics the act of smoking. Former smokers can enjoy both the act of inhaling with the absorption of nicotine without inhaling so many toxins. Yet, many countries have banned the sale of e-cigarettes.

In part, that's because numerous people believe that e-cigarettes are as dangerous or more dangerous than smoking tobacco. The basis for this line of thought likely rests upon various associations about vaping and smoking.

For example, nicotine (found in many vaping devices) has been repeatedly associated with the dangers of cigarette smoking for decades. In fact, many people use the terms *nicotine* and *tobacco* interchangeably. Indeed, nicotine is the addictive drug that keeps you smoking. But it's primarily the tar derived from burning tobacco in cigarettes that wreaks havoc on the body.

In addition, smoke is seen as unhealthy. And smoke from burning tobacco *is* unhealthy. The vapor from e-cigarettes *looks like* smoke while also being even more voluminous. Therefore, it's easy to assume that the vapor is highly toxic, even though the data don't support that idea.

Furthermore, vaping is associated with teenage use. This concern does have validity. Use by adolescents is surging and everything that can be done to keep the nicotine from e-cigarettes out of reach of teens is a good idea. No one wants teens to start a new addictive drug. But again, nicotine by itself, has a fraction of the health risks of tobacco. See Chapters 6 and 7 for more information about the risks of vaping and teen use.

WARNING

Finally, there's every reason to be concerned about the vaping-related crisis of serious lung damage, at times leading to death from e-cigarette or vaping product use-associated lung injury (now known as EVALI). Previously healthy vapers have been admitted to intensive care with life-threatening symptoms. The U.S. Centers for Disease Control and Prevention (CDC) is scrambling to determine the cause, although much of the focus has been on vaping products containing tetrahydrocannabinol (THC), especially those purchased on the black market. Particularly suspect are the ingredients (especially vitamin E acetate) used to make the THC liquid the correct consistency for vaping purposes. But as of this writing, the exact cause of EVALI remains elusive. Research continues and scientists believe that more than one cause could be involved.

WARNING

As discussed in greater detail in Chapter 6, a large part of the current risk associated with vaping can be found in the relative lack of regulations of the industry. You have no clear assurances of what ingredients are contained in the liquid you choose to vape. That's especially true if you purchase e-cigarettes or vaping devices through the black market. If you do decide to vape, be sure to purchase from a reputable shop. Of course, without clear regulatory guidelines you can't be sure of what's reputable. At least check the place out for length of time in business, Better Business Bureau (BBB) ratings, and Internet ratings. There are no guarantees, but do what you can to check.

EXAMPLE

USING E-CIGARETTES TO TRANSITION OFF REGULAR CIGARETTES

Bonnie, like many of her friends, began dabbling with cigarette smoking at parties during high school. By college, in the mid '70s, she was smoking a pack and a half per day. After college, she became a high school band teacher, which was hardly compatible with smoking, given her exposure to teens and high levels of physical activity associated with the marching band work. She tried to quit dozens of times, with marginal success. At best, she'd quit for a few months at a time, but she always relapsed.

In 2012, she heard about a new way to smoke through e-cigarettes. It was called vaping. What she found most appealing was the lack of smell. Over the years, she'd consumed tens of thousands of breath mints trying to cover up her smoker's breath.

As of today, Bonnie hasn't smoked a cigarette for seven years. She does continue to vape, but she has found she can get by with vaping only a few times per week. And, she has more energy and doesn't leave a trail of tobacco smell everywhere she goes.

Bonnie says, "Vaping may have saved my life. At least I hope it did. I know I smoked too long. When I first quit cigarettes by replacing some of them with e-cigarettes, I knew I had finally found something that could satisfy my cravings. That helped me to quickly decrease the number of cigarettes I smoked. After a few weeks, I stopped smoking cigarettes entirely. Now, I can go many days without thinking much about smoking or vaping. I feel like I got out of prison."

Bonnie's story is about someone who combined vaping and smoking for a while. But she found that doing so enabled her to give up cigarettes completely and gradually reduce her vaping. Bonnie has been smoke free for seven years. Her method wouldn't be considered ideal by many experts, but it seemingly worked for her.

Combining vaping and smoking

Although many people do continue to smoke and vape at the same time, it's probably not a great idea to engage in that practice over time. Why do some people do this? Most hope to taper off cigarettes and increase vaping. For some smokers, the tapering works to decrease cigarette consumption. But doing this involves some possible health risk.

Check out the nearby sidebar, "Using e-cigarettes to transition off regular cigarettes," for the story of a woman who continued vaping and smoking without the guidance of her physician as a means of cutting back on regular cigarettes.

WARNING

In a nonrandomized, non-controlled study, researchers found that people who smoked and vaped were at greater risk for heart attacks than people who only vaped or only smoked. More research is called for to confirm this finding. The bottom line is that the sooner you quit smoking and eventually quit vaping, the better.

Quitting smoking with vaping

Over time some studies have emerged with the tantalizing promise that e-cigarettes can help smokers quit smoking. In fact, more people in the United States and elsewhere trying to quit, turn to e-cigarettes for help than attempt to quit through NRT. Yet, as of this writing, the FDA has not approved the use of e-cigarettes as a sanctioned approach to smoking cessation.

On the other hand, the United Kingdom has a very different take than the FDA on vaping with e-cigarettes. They acknowledge that vaping is the number-one tool used by smokers to quit. Based on accumulated research, the Royal Academy of Physicians wrote an extensive report with the following conclusions, in which they contend that e-cigarettes:

>> Appear to help smokers quit smoking

>> Are only about 5 percent as dangerous as regular cigarettes

>> Allow former smokers to use nicotine without the risk associated with smoking

>> Are preferred by most smokers over NRT, so they're more likely to try quitting

The Royal Academy of Physicians further concluded that e-cigarettes should be promoted as a substitute for smoking and that most of the harm from smoking can be virtually eliminated.

Because vaping is a relatively new phenomenon, it may be premature for the Royal Academy of Physicians to go as far as they have in promoting the safety of e-cigarettes. Although e-cigarettes certainly appear to be safer than smoking tobacco, only longer-term research will enable us to reach firm conclusions about their precise degree of safety.

Current evidence from the *New England Journal of Medicine* indicates that abstinence from smoking at one year is twice as likely to occur with e-cigarettes than by using NRT. In addition, short-term health benefits (such as reduced wheezing, coughing, and phlegm) at one year are apparently greater when using e-cigarettes than NRT.

However, among successful smoking quitters at one year, those using e-cigarettes tended to continue vaping. Whereas, quitters who used NRT had pretty much dropped their use of NRT. This finding raises the importance of knowing more about the long-term health effects of continued e-cigarette usage, which is scant at this time.

WARNING

E-cigarette vapor has traces of toxins, but these appear to be at significantly lower levels than those found in regular cigarettes. Some preliminary research has suggested that e-cigarette vapor produces changes in the circulatory systems of mice, which over a period of years could lead to heart disease. This finding has been replicated in a single study on humans. But we simply don't know enough about how all this translates into long-term health effects of regular exposure to vapor for people. See Chapter 6 for a more complete discussion of the risks associated with vaping.

So, if you're interested in trying to quit smoking by using e-cigarettes as either a short-term option on the way to no nicotine or a long-term alternative to cigarettes, be aware that no clear guidelines exist for helping you from the government. That's because the FDA has yet to approve of e-cigarettes for smoking cessation purposes.

However, it's common sense, if you're a heavy smoker, to consider starting at a relatively satisfying amount of nicotine in your vaping devices. Stay at that level for several weeks. Then, if your goal is to become entirely nicotine free, gradually reduce your nicotine levels over a period of time.

Intriguingly, we've spent more time in vape shops than we ever thought we would in order to investigate the thoughts and perspectives of customers and employees — an admittedly biased group of folks! In spite of that bias, we noticed a consistent message from a variety of former cigarette smokers. The nearby sidebar, "Quitting by accident," illustrates that theme.

REMEMBER

The story on vaping with e-cigarettes to reduce harm from smoking is not over. More research is needed — especially about long-term effects. Stay tuned. And see Chapter 6 for more extensive information about the risks of vaping.

EXAMPLE

QUITTING BY ACCIDENT

Benjamin is a 35-year-old father of two. He had been a two-plus-pack-a-day smoker. One of his friends introduced him to vaping, and he found it surprisingly satisfying. He visited a vape shop and the owner set him up with a vaping device (see Chapter 5 for more information about vaping devices). The owner told him to start with a fairly high level of nicotine because he was such a heavy smoker and that he probably shouldn't smoke and vape at the same time.

Benjamin said, "Fine, but I've got no intention of quitting smoking. I just want to cut back a bit and try something new."

The owner told him, "Well, okay, but be careful that you don't overdo it. Too much nicotine can make you sick to your stomach and dizzy. I don't usually recommend doing both."

Benjamin said, "I got it. I'll go easy. I think I'll just use the vape at home, so I don't stink up the house and expose the kids to so much secondhand smoke."

Benjamin vaped while smoking for several weeks. He found himself down to a pack a day of cigarettes. Soon, he felt less desire for regular smoking. He even forgot to smoke on a few days. He went back to the vape shop for a refill and told the owner that he was shocked to discover he hadn't smoked in a week. The owner laughed and said, "You're becoming another accidental quitter, just like me and quite a few of my customers. It's weird, but true."

We're by no means suggesting you should expect the same results that Benjamin and other customers at the vape shop reported. This was hardly a controlled study! However, we heard a version of this story more than once. And we congratulate any accidental quitters. Bravo!

Chapter **13**

Searching for Help in All the Wrong Places

Everyone wants to discover the latest and greatest, best, easiest, and cheapest way to quit smoking. People who've tried a variety of approaches numerous times, but ultimately failed, are particularly motivated to search high and far for something new and easy. And almost anything will work for *some* people, sometimes, somewhere, somehow.

Why should we want to stop you from this quest even if it's a bit quixotic? Afterall, maybe you really can find something that works for you! Maybe you will and, if you do, that's great.

But we suggest that you pause first. It's all too easy to find new, interesting possibilities. But these can cost you both time and money (anywhere from a little to a lot). Sorry, for the vast majority of smokers, quitting isn't quick or easy. Throughout this book, we give you science-based, insurance-covered, free or usually low-cost methods of quitting. Try those first; then try them again. If none of the techniques we describe works, you may want to try an alternative approach — but please watch your wallet!

In this chapter, we review some of what are called *complementary* or *alternative* strategies for quitting smoking. We also throw in some of what we think are pretty kooky or downright scams. We tell you which are which and what to look out for when you're considering alternatives.

TIP

Some alternative strategies involve an element of helping you relax, whether that's with an herbal supplement or with hypnosis or massage. When you're really relaxed, you're unlikely to have an urge to smoke at a high intensity. So, for that moment, the alternative strategy may help you resist. However, the minute the relaxation goes away, the smoking urge returns. So, strategies that focus on relaxation alone are only temporary and incomplete. But as part of a quit-smoking package, they may have some value.

Surveying the Scene

This section covers a variety of quit-smoking approaches. These approaches range from interesting to wishful thinking to pure scams. You need to know how well strategies work so you can make informed judgments.

Taking dietary supplements

Eating the right foods and getting the right nutrients always make sense when addressing any health concerns. We're all for eating healthy, especially when you're stressed by trying to quit smoking. But, as of now, there's very limited evidence that any particular diet or supplement by itself will help you quit smoking. Here are some you may hear about and our thoughts on each:

>> **Sam-E** is a supplement that has sometimes been suggested as a way to treat depression, anxiety, pain, and smoking urges. It's formed naturally in the body. It has not been found to be effective in limited studies as a smoking cessation aid. It can also interact badly with some antidepressant medications. Never take Sam-E without talking to your doctor.

>> **St. John's Wort** is another supplement that's been recommended for smoking cessation but found to be ineffective. It can interact badly with antidepressants and a wide variety of other medications (including hormonal birth control). Because of these multiple interactions and lack of effectiveness, we recommend you *not* try St. John's Wort in your smoking cessation plan.

>> **Lobelia** is a plant used to produce medicine. It has been used for breathing disorders, bronchitis, asthma, shortness of breath, and relaxation. Although it has been used as a smoking-cessation aid, there is little evidence that it works. Furthermore, it can be toxic or even fatal at high doses. The U.S. Food and Drug Administration (FDA) prohibits the inclusion of lobelia in smoking cessation products.

>> **L-tryptophan** is an essential amino acid. It's commonly used for treating depression, anxiety, premenstrual syndrome, and insomnia. There is limited evidence that L-tryptophan can boost efficacy of conventional stop-smoking therapies and, other than drowsiness, there are very few side effects. There is insufficient evidence to support L-tryptophan as a stand-alone smoking-cessation treatment.

There is one exception: cytisine, which has been used in Eastern and Central Europe for many years for smoking cessation. This supplement is now nearing completion of drug trials in the United States. Preliminary evidence is promising.

Watch out for crazy claims about supplements touted as smoking-cessation aids. One company that advertised on television, radio, and the Internet had to pay over a million dollars in damages. It had claimed elimination of all cravings; the absence of any side effects; and effortless, permanent smoking cessation. This astounding outcome was allegedly accomplished with dietary supplements, vitamins, and herbs.

Promotions of various dietary supplements, herbs, and vitamin formulations abound on the Internet. Be skeptical.

Getting hypnotized

Hypnosis is rather difficult to define reliably, and it's hard to determine whether someone is truly in a hypnotized state. Nonetheless, hypnotherapists generally define *hypnosis* as involving an altered state of consciousness, an increased susceptibility to suggestion, and reduced awareness of surroundings. There is scant current literature on the effectiveness of hypnosis as an aid for smoking reduction.

The limited data that exists suggests that hypnosis is not an especially effective method for helping people to quit smoking. However, some people claim it has worked for them. For that matter, some people say that jumping up and down while clucking like a chicken helps.

To be fair, there is some limited, mixed data that supports a possible slight therapeutic effect from hypnosis, but that's it. If you want to try hypnosis, don't pay a lot of money for prolonged treatment. Ask your primary care provider for a recommendation of a licensed mental health or licensed hypnotherapy practitioner. The hypnotherapy field has sometimes attracted poorly trained charlatans, so be careful.

Even if your doctor doesn't recommend hypnotherapy and you've tried lots of other approaches, it may be worth taking a shot. David successfully quit with hypnosis after trying nicotine replacement, medication, and the cold-turkey approach (see the nearby sidebar).

EXAMPLE

HYPNOSIS: IT MAY HELP

David started smoking as a young adult when he transferred to Asia as a financial consultant. Practically everyone in his new office smoked. After six years, he was transferred back to the United States. Smoking wasn't even allowed in his New York office. He soon discovered that he was the lone smoker among his coworkers. It hit him that it was time for him to become a nonsmoker. Smoking wasn't worth the hassle, time, money, and social awkwardness.

David went to his healthcare provider after quitting cold turkey failed again for him. His doctor prescribed medication that made David sick to his stomach. The doctor then offered NRT, which David found unsatisfying.

David's friend suggested a hypnotherapist that he'd used with some success for weight control. David made an appointment and was surprised that the therapist seemed professional and competent. He found the session quite relaxing. After four sessions of hypnotherapy, David gave cold turkey another try. This time he had more success. He stopped for six months and then relapsed. However, he bought some nicotine gum and was able to quit again — this time for good.

So, what worked for David? Partly, he no doubt was more ready to quit than he had been before. He had an open mind-set. Who knows what forces were in play that enabled him to quit? Was it the hypnotherapy, the gum, his readiness, or his willpower? Does it really matter? The bottom line is he quit, relapsed, and at last quit for good.

REMEMBER

Hypnotherapy, in almost all cases should not be your first choice. What catches most people's attention is the promise of an easy, painless, fast method of quitting. If that really worked, there would be long waiting lines outside the local hypnotherapists' offices. There aren't.

TIP

Hypnosis, relaxation training, mindfulness, guided imagery, yoga, and meditation all share a few elements such as helping you learn to focus and relax. Therefore, they may help you deal with uncomfortable urges. These practices may have some value as part of an overall smoking-cessation intervention as opposed to stand-alone treatments.

Competing for dollars

A long, time-honored approach to increasing people's motivation is to set up competitive challenges. The Quit and Win program was developed in the 1980s by the Minnesota Heart Health Program. Competitions have taken place across local groups, college campuses, cities, states, and nations.

GETTING PAID TO QUIT

Smoking costs employers loads of dough. Some estimates run as high as $6,000 per year per smoker. Those costs come from lost productivity (think: smoke breaks and sick days), increased healthcare costs, disability costs, and increased absenteeism. That's why some employers are willing to fund quit-smoking programs for their employees — likely not out of altruism, but out of financial self-interest.

Early research on providing financial incentives to workers for participating in quit-smoking programs showed mixed results with small to no effects from receiving modest payments for successful quitting. Many smokers resumed smoking after receiving payments for stopping. That's one of the inherent problems with research on smoking — long-term follow-ups are needed to assess true success.

CVS participated in a large smoking cessation program for its employees, family members, and friends. This study included a generous financial incentive of approximately $800 paid for smoking cessation. The program also included information about smoking and quitting. Participants who received the $800 incentive were three times more likely to quit smoking than the group that received treatment as usual for smoking cessation. Do the math. CVS saved a lot of money and its employees profited as well.

We included this study in a sidebar because it's an interesting concept. Earlier studies using small financial incentives hadn't worked. We need more research to determine if the larger amounts used in this study hold up over time. We know the costs of smoking to society and employers alike are substantial. But we don't how willing they'll be to step up and offer incentives like these to more people. Time will tell.

The premise of Quit and Win is to sign up and pledge to quit smoking for a specified period of time in order to be eligible for prizes including cash. Although these Quit and Win contests continue to be held, the research on effectiveness for smoking cessation has been weak. This approach seems to result in slightly greater initial quit rates, but little is known about the long-term effectiveness. Less than one smoker out of 500 quits due to participation in such contests.

Study methodology has been poor, and relapse appears to be common. There were problems with people claiming to have quit so that they would have a chance of winning a prize. However, biochemical testing of their nonsmoking status often contraindicated their claims. In other words, some people tried to cheat.

These contests can be fun, and they can educate the public about the dangers of smoking and methods of quitting. Quit and Win contests can also provide opportunities for people to make their first attempt at quitting. We know that the more attempts people make, the greater the odds that they'll eventually quit smoking.

So, the bottom line is that Quit and Win contests are worth considering — just don't put a lot of faith in them. And we don't recommend voting for taxes to underwrite these contests because they're not cost-effective!

Magnetizing smoking urges

You probably understand by now that smokers who want to quit sometimes feel desperate. Wouldn't it be nice if you could just walk around with magnets in your ears, and your smoking urges would melt away?

That's what manufacturers of ear magnets claim. You simply put one small magnet on each side of your left ear (don't ask why the left). By the way, the magnets are 24-karat gold plated, though its unclear what the plating does other than to make the magnets more attractive. You're instructed to wear the magnets two to four hours per day and do nothing else to address your smoking.

You continue to smoke until your urges magically disappear, supposedly within seven days. After seven days, you quit and have no more smoking urges!

If an urge does happen to pop up after you've quit using them, you're instructed to put the magnets back in for a while. The manufacturer claims the magnets work due to acupressure principles, which cause a release of endorphins that squash urges.

Amazingly, the product website reports an 80 percent success rate. *That's far better than any other scientifically based smoking-cessation strategy available today.* Wow!

Unfortunately, there is absolutely no reasonable scientific evidence that this product does anything at all to help with smoking cessation. However, it does seem to be somewhat successful at pumping up profits for the manufacturer and costing desperate smokers their hard-earned cash. The bottom line: We do not recommend this product even as an experiment. Don't waste your money.

Analyzing acupuncture

Acupuncture is based on ancient Chinese therapy and typically involves inserting tiny needles into the skin at points thought to be critical for certain conditions. Modern procedures may use laser or electrical stimulation for the same purpose.

The theory suggests that the needles redirect imbalanced energy and blood flow through the body, which alleviates a wide variety of symptoms. Acupuncture has been purported to be effective for a wide variety of problems and disorders. The following list is just a sample of conditions that an acupuncturist might treat:

>> Hay fever

>> Low-back pain

>> Neck pain

>> Osteoarthritis

>> Tension headaches

>> Migraine headaches

>> Depression

>> Anxiety

>> Nausea and vomiting associated with chemotherapy

>> Menstrual cramps

>> Improved immune function

>> Neuropathy

>> Chronic fatigue syndrome

>> Various skin problems

>> Digestive disorders

>> Smoking cessation

TECHNICAL STUFF

Reviews of the literature on the effectiveness of acupuncture usually choose to assess studies that compare acupuncture to what's called "sham" acupuncture. Sham acupuncture involves inserting needles into positions that are theorized to have *no value* in redirecting energy and blood flow. That means that the research-ers compared normal acupuncture (inserting needles in their theorized ideal posi-tion for redirecting energy flows) with sham (or placebo) acupuncture.

Support for smoking cessation is weak. Smokers who choose acupuncture for their quit plan may have a decrease in urges in the short run. However, by six months, their rate of relapse is the same as those who get a placebo.

TIP

If you're someone who has had a particular problem with handling the first week or two of quitting, acupuncture may actually be something you could add to your quit plan. We don't recommend continuing with the approach over the long term, however.

Managing cravings with massage

When looking for promising smoking-cessation options on the Internet, you're likely to encounter positive messages about massage therapy. Massage certainly feels good and is relaxing. It makes intuitive sense that it would help for cravings. And it has been suggested that if your smoking is partly driven by anxiety, massage therapy can alleviate that part of the problem.

Like some other forms of relaxation, massage is a temporary, incomplete treatment for smoking or vaping. If you can find a really small massage therapist who fits in your pocket, you could probably pull the therapist out every time you have an urge to smoke. It's possible that would work. Could be a long search, though.

You Don't Always Get What You Pay For

Before writing this book, we knew almost all the strategies proven to be helpful for smoking cessation. However, we didn't know the complete set of commercial offerings found on the Internet. So, we poked around. Frankly, we found ourselves a bit disgusted by some of the promotions.

The promises were often excessive and research specific to the product being offered was completely lacking. Some of the offerings are products; others are programs with supporting CDs or video downloads. Here are a few miraculous smoking-cessation promises we found:

>> Quit smoking in hours or minutes.

>> Take brain boosters that crush smoking urges.

>> Take proprietary vitamin formulas to rebuild neurotransmitters that wipe out cravings.

>> Use aroma therapy for quitting smoking.

>> Use nicotine-free oral spray to combat urges.

>> Use a special filter modifier promising a natural way to quit and removal of almost all toxins.

>> Use vitamin and supplement inhalers.

We also found a few cases of seemingly science-backed smoking cessation programs. Claims tended to be excessive and the costs were often high. For example, after signing up for one information video, we were bombarded with "free offers." The program itself costs well over $500 and there were various supplemental products (for example, books, videos, and dietary suggestions complete with recipes) that ranged from $49 to $348.

We really have no idea how effective this program is. But the costs are higher than lots of available strategies. For example, we review free quit lines and apps in Chapter 11. And Chapter 9 reviews medications and their availability at subsidized costs. Chapter 24 lists website resources that can direct you to support groups and even professional counselors.

The point is, there's lots of snake oil out there being hawked by unscrupulous marketers. Be careful, especially if costs are high and claims seem questionable.

Putting on Your Smart Consumer Hat

Promoters of smoking and vaping cessation products and programs often make unwarranted claims of effectiveness based on scientific evidence. They sometimes even cite "studies" to support their claims. But, as consumers, we must adhere to the principle of *caveat emptor* (buyer beware), or we run the risk of falling victim to shams.

When you read or hear about a potential smoking-cessation product, program, or strategy, the following sections review some things to keep in mind to help you evaluate whether any given claim holds up to scrutiny.

REMEMBER

We tell you the scientific basis for most of the strategies we review in this book. When there's not much science to back something, we let you know. We want you to make informed decisions. We give you some of the most important scientific principles and guidelines in case you're especially curious about a particular study. If you're not so curious, feel free to skip these sections.

When things seem too good to be true, they usually are

You really can't effortlessly stop smoking in a few minutes. You'll probably have some uncomfortable urges no matter what product or program you use. So, when an advertisement or website promises much better, easier, and faster results than most, be skeptical. It's unlikely.

Maybe someday, a blockbuster product or program will come along that really blows everything else out of the water. But we're not holding our breath. You won't have to search around on the Internet for such a breakthrough. If and when a breakthrough really does come out, you'll see widespread news media coverage and lots of scientific support for it.

Using small groups limits conclusions

When scientists first become interested in studying the effectiveness of something, they often begin with a preliminary study. That's because they don't want to spend large amounts of time, effort, and money studying something that may not pan out.

So, they typically recruit a small group to participate in what they call a *pilot study* or *preliminary study*. These studies are great for looking at whether something has the potential or possibility of being effective. They aren't so great at looking for absolute conclusions.

For example, when researching the effectiveness of massage therapy, a study from 1999 took 20 smokers and trained half of them to give themselves hand or ear self-massages. At the end of the month, the self-massage group smoked fewer cigarettes than the other ten, who didn't get training in self-massage. That single study tells us very little about the effectiveness of self-massage for smoking or vaping cessation.

Studies using small numbers of participants can't tell us much. The results can too easily be caused by the chance results of just a couple of individuals. There are always a few people who have a great response to almost anything. If one group of ten has two or three of these people, the results can look better than they should for that group.

It's hard to make firm conclusions about effectiveness unless a study has large numbers of participants.

Lots of dropouts cause confusion

High dropout rates are rather common in smoking cessation studies because lots of people think they'd like to participate but discover it's too much work and discomfort. So, they return to smoking. Those dropouts need to be taken into account and not ignored. High dropout rates also often suggest that there may be something unpleasant about the treatment the participants are receiving, such as side effects from a medication, which causes them to drop out.

At the very least, look for what percentage of participants dropped out from the beginning to the conclusion (often called the *follow-up*).

Choosing not to choose

You've probably heard the term *randomized controlled study* (RCT). That term refers to a basic principle in scientific research. *Randomized* refers to the way that research participants are chosen.

Imagine a fifth-grade gym class. The coach designates two captains to choose players for a soccer team. One of the captains begins to choose his players. Someone says, "That's not fair; he's getting all the best players!" The coach decides to have the students count off by two's with the ones going to Team A and the twos going to Team B. That's not technically a fully random approach, but it's closer to fair than allowing one captain to choose.

Researchers want to give the same, fair shake to all groups so they can tell if the intervention was responsible for the results obtained.

Controlling for suggestion and expectancy

Researchers also want to know if a particular intervention, drug, strategy, or treatment works better than a placebo. Placebos lack any active treatment elements but look like they could be effective. For example, a placebo in a drug trial looks identical to the real, active drug, but does nothing. However, it induces as much expectation for effectiveness from the participants' perspective.

Placebos are important to include in a study because people are strongly influenced by their expectations of getting help. That expectation alone often produces significant effects or change. Having a placebo group for comparison allows conclusions about treatment effectiveness above and beyond the placebo effect.

TECHNICAL STUFF

Placebo comparison groups are sometimes tricky to design. But a good study will at least compare an active treatment group to a group called *treatment as usual*, or what's known as a *wait-list control group*. Without such a comparison, it's hard to draw firm conclusions about a study's findings.

Replication, replication, replication

Real estate agents are fond of saying that price and desirability of houses comes down to three words — location, location, location. Similarly, researchers greatly value three words — replication, replication, replication. Scientists don't put a great deal of stock in the findings from a single study.

There's always a decent possibility that a study's findings were due to a fluke, random chance, or a subtle flaw in the way the study was set up. Therefore, repeating the study with different participants, at a different time and place, and sometimes with small changes in methods, helps give confidence to what's being discovered. Replicating multiple times is even better.

Eating ice cream causes murder?

If you look at U.S. ice cream consumption in the months of May, June, and July, you'll see that ice cream sales skyrocket during those months. Murder rates also skyrocket during that time. If you put these results on a graph, you'll see that the lines showing ice cream sales and murder rates climb in tandem — what's called a high, positive correlation. So, does eating ice cream cause people to commit murder? Or, after murdering someone, are people driven to eat more ice cream?

EXAMPLE

A QUIT-SMOKING SCAM

Bella reads an ad about a free introductory smoking cessation group to be held near her home. She attends and is intrigued by the promises made by the group leader. He claims a 95 percent success rate of those who complete his five-week program. He shows her how much money she can save when she quits smoking by investing a mere $199, which she can charge to her credit card.

He also shows her a graph showing that the more sessions people attend, the more likely they are to quit. Those attending one or two classes after the introduction obtained a 10 percent cessation rate; those attending three sessions had a 12 percent success rate; those attending four had an 80 percent success rate; and those who completed the program had a 95 percent success rate. Bella gets out her credit card and signs up.

Did Bella make a rational, scientifically grounded decision? Probably not. Let's review the limitations of this so-called study:

- **Too good to be true.** Ninety-five percent success is phenomenally better than almost any good study you can find to date.

- **Possibly too small.** He doesn't tell how many participants he had, but as a private practitioner, it wasn't likely a large number. Dropouts are also not discussed in terms of percentages — for example, how many went to the introduction and never came back?

- **No attempts to randomize assignments to a comparison, placebo group.**

- **No data given on other studies similar to this one.**

- **Conclusions made on a correlation rather than comparing groups.** Most likely, those who attended all five sessions were more motivated than the dropouts were from the get-go. They very well may have quit on their own.

This analysis does not lead to any particular conclusions about whether his methods could work. It's just that his so-called study is seriously flawed. Other studies could address these deficiencies.

Um, well, neither. That's ridiculous. Scientists know that correlations do not indicate causation. Just because two things go together, doesn't mean something else is at play. With the example of increasing ice cream consumption and murder rates, it's thought that hot weather likely causes both.

What does this issue have to do with smoking? Some smoking cessation treatments declare their effectiveness based on correlational findings rather than randomized controlled research. The nearby sidebar illustrates how such findings can lead you astray.

4

Personalizing Your Quit Plan

Chapter **14**

Assessing Your Readiness and Motivation to Quit

You've made the decision that it's time to quit smoking, using smokeless tobacco, or vaping. Or you're at least curious and considering the possibility, or you wouldn't be reading this book. It's possible you're reading this book to help someone you care about — if so, that's great, too. This material can help you help your loved one.

In this chapter, we tell you about the stages of change. These stages have been identified and researched over a few decades. They help people understand where they are in the process of quitting and recovery from addictions. Next, we help you figure out where you stand and how to move through the stages. Finally, if you're ready, we move you to the step before quitting — declaring your intention, firmly — to yourself and most likely other people in your life.

Knowing How the Stages of Change Work

Sometimes ideas in psychology make such common sense or are so practical that they become a part of the popular narrative. The Stages of Change model is one of those theories that are currently applied to many aspects of behavior change, including smoking, weight control, drug abuse, and emotional problems ranging from anxiety to anger.

When people are faced with a challenging behavior or habit, such as smoking or vaping, they face a series of decisions about what to do. The Stages of Change model reflects the current thoughts, feelings and behaviors of a person's *readiness* to engage in changing behavior. The following sections describe the characteristics of people at each level in the Stages of Change model as it relates to smoking.

TECHNICAL STUFF

Initially proposed by Drs. James O. Prochaska and Carlo C. DiClemente, the model for Stages of Change has been updated and changed based on new research. For example, an addition of relapse has been proposed and the last stage, termination (the sixth stage), is often left off. For our purpose, we describe a six-stage model that includes termination, but not relapse — which we talk about in great detail in Chapter 19. This basic stage model has been rigorously studied and has remained robustly consistent.

TIP

Take as much time as you need in each stage of change. There's no need to rush moving ahead before you're ready.

REMEMBER

People do not necessarily start at the precontemplation stage and move smoothly up to the maintenance stage. It's perfectly normal to bounce around going up or down over time. That's especially true of smokers who normally have multiple quit attempts before succeeding.

Stage 1: Precontemplation

Smokers in the *precontemplation* stage are not even thinking about quitting smoking. They usually don't consider their behavior a problem. They have no intention of quitting in the near future. Smokers in this stage are pretty much not concerned about health risks, costs, secondhand smoke, or lost time from smoking. They're smokers, and that's the way they like it. Someone in the precontemplation stage would be likely to say or think things like the following:

>> I know someone who smoked for over 50 years and lived to be 92 — why can't that work for me?

>> I plan to smoke until the day I die.

>> Life without smoking isn't worth it.

>> I know my smoking is a problem, but I don't want to do anything about it.

>> I don't worry about my smoking — it's just not an issue.

Stage 2: Contemplation

Many smokers are in the *contemplation* stage. They haven't had their heads buried in ashtrays; they know that smoking is unhealthy. They see what they pay for cigarettes every week and how much time they waste on their habits. They have a sense that is growing over time that something may need to be done about their smoking but have no plan to accomplish it.

Contemplators feel ambivalent or unsure about quitting smoking. They know they should quit, but they don't really want to go through the discomfort. Quitting is hard; they may have tried and failed in the past. Smokers in this stage can definitely see themselves quitting in the future, and actually *hope to quit,* but the future is, well, down the road. They may plan on quitting in the next six months or so, but six months may just be a rolling timeline. Someone in the contemplation stage would be likely to say or think things like the following:

>> I often think about stopping smoking, but I haven't done much about it lately.

>> I enjoy smoking, but I do worry about what it will do to me.

>> Sometimes I think I really do have to stop smoking, but I don't know if I can.

>> I've come to realize my smoking hurts or at least bothers others.

Stage 3: Preparation

We imagine that quite a few readers of this book are in the *preparation* stage, starting to prepare for change — in other words, planning how to quit. You see that smoking is bad for your health and bad for your pocketbook, and the pain of quitting seems *almost* manageable. You're ready to take some steps to move forward with your own quit plan. You may even have cut back a few cigarettes or contemplated substituting something less dangerous (see Chapter 12).

You're getting ready to set a quit date (see Chapter 16). You may be giving thought to making an appointment with your primary care provider to talk about nicotine replacement therapy (NRT) or medication to help manage your cravings. You may be lining up people in your social sphere who could join with you to provide a support system. And perhaps you've been wondering what triggers will be most difficult for you to deal with — possibly even planning for how you'll manage them successfully.

In the preparation stage, you may be worried about taking a chance on changing and not being successful. What will others think? Don't worry, that's a typical part of this Stage of Change. It's good that you're a bit worried! It will help push you to make a complete plan before moving ahead to the next stage. Someone in the preparation stage would be likely to say or think things like the following:

>> Tomorrow I have an appointment with my doctor to review my options on quitting smoking.

>> I'm starting to read about how people manage to quit smoking.

>> I'm making a list of all my triggers for smoking.

>> I've decided that my quit date is going to be in two weeks — scary!

Stage 4: Action

The quit date is here. Now, the hard work begins. The *action* stage incorporates all the strategies necessary to get through the first day, month, and year of quitting. NRT or medication is already onboard to help with urges if it's part of the quit plan.

People in the action stage may have stopped or reduced smoking. They're learning to deal with smoking triggers by avoiding, changing, or handling them with new healthier strategies. They may have new concerns about gaining weight, irritability, or difficulty sleeping. These issues are additional problems that may need to be addressed.

During the action stage, there is considerable emotional energy spent handing the many urges and cravings that come with quitting. Vigilance is required because the worst urges are those that come by surprise. Temptations are still difficult, and the possibility of relapse always looms over the horizon.

REMEMBER

The early weeks of the action stage are the most difficult. That's evidenced by data indicating that most quitters relapse within a week of quitting.

Someone in the action stage would be likely to say or think things like the following:

>> I stopped drinking coffee at home in the morning because it's a trigger for me to smoke.

>> I cleaned my house with a fine-toothed comb and worked to get rid of the smoke smell.

>> I review my coping with triggers plan every single day.

>> I quit two weeks ago, but I think it's going to be really hard to hang out with my friends this weekend without smoking.

>> I made it through my first week of not smoking — yeah!

WARNING

Although most people who relapse do so early, the risk of relapse continues for weeks, months, and sometimes years for many smokers. It's doable, but constant attention is needed. In almost all cases, a single cigarette conveys a surprising degree of risk for relapse.

Step 5: Maintenance

Some people trying to quit don't make it to this stage and will need to try again. However, after about six months of nonsmoking, most of those who have succeeded in quitting enter the *maintenance* stage of change. These individuals have learned to adapt to a new, nonsmoking life. Urges and cravings have faded and occur relatively few and far between. New, healthier ways of dealing with what used to be smoking triggers have emerged as new, better habits. Someone in the maintenance stage would be likely to say or think things like the following:

>> Occasionally, I get tempted to smoke, but it's way better than it was.

>> I feel so much healthier since I stopped smoking.

>> It feels great to save the money I used to throw away on cigarettes.

>> I know I can't go back to smoking, although I get a few urges here and there.

>> Now that I don't smoke, I have lots of time to do other things I've wanted to do, like go to the gym.

The good news? Risk of relapse has decreased significantly in this stage of change. The bad news? The risk of relapse remains lurking for some time to come. More good news: Many people in the maintenance stage cope with a relapse by taking new actions to quit. That's because they have more confidence, knowing they've done it before and can do it again. But don't take that bit of information as permission to have only a few. If you do have a lapse, slam the brakes on as soon as you can.

Amir was a smoker for 20 years. He quit almost one year ago and firmly believed he was in the maintenance stage of change. However, one evening changed that. See the nearby sidebar for his story.

A FEW CIGARETTES DOESN'T MEAN IT'S OVER

Amir gets a text while waiting for his train home. It's from his sister-in-law, who rarely texts him. He reads the following about his wife: "Meet at ER. Aliya in car accident. Don't worry. Think she'll be okay."

Frightened, he texts back, "What do you mean you think she'll be okay? What happened?"

She replies, "Doc said possible concussion. Unconscious now. Needs CT scan."

Forty-five minutes later, Amir jumps from a cab racing into the ER waiting room. His sister-in-law greets him with a hug. "We're still waiting for the results," she says.

"Where is she? I want to see her now," he demands. The nurse at the desk explains that Aliya needs an MRI and that he can't go back yet. He paces around the room for 20 minutes and notices someone going outside for a cigarette. Amir follows him out and bums his first cigarette in almost a year.

Times of extreme stress, as seen in Amir's story, often lead to lapses. That's pretty understandable. Amir buys a pack of cigarettes at a corner drugstore and continues to smoke for the rest of the day. Then he realizes what he's doing and that Aliya won't be happy to hear he's smoking again. He recommits to his quit plan and throws the rest of the cigarettes in the trash.

Amir was lucky to see where he was headed. He was also lucky because his wife was fine. He went from the maintenance stage to the precontemplation stage in a short time (only a few hours). For those few hours, he had no desire to stop and wasn't thinking about pros or cons of smoking. However, he caught himself and flipped back into the action phase of quitting and soon moved back into the maintenance stage.

Stage 6: Termination

Stages of change models usually include a *termination* phase, but because relatively few people get there, it's sometimes dropped from the model. This stage refers to those fortunate people who've maintained their nonsmoking status for so long that they experience virtually no temptations any longer.

They feel confident that they'll never relapse, even under extreme stress. They no longer have any conscious desire to smoke. They don't pay much attention to cigarette ads or smoking triggers, both of which cause no trouble for these people. Someone in the termination stage would be likely to say or think things like the following:

>> Smoking feels like ancient history to me.

>> I would never consider smoking again and haven't thought about it for a year or more.

>> I can't imagine I ever used to smoke — I can barely remember what it felt like.

>> It doesn't bother me to be around smokers anymore, although I really kind of hate the smell.

WARNING

Relatively few smokers reach the termination stage of change. But that's okay, because they find life in the maintenance stage just fine. Yes, they still have some urges and cravings, but they know they can manage them. Yet they remain a bit vigilant for years. In other words, they're optimistic and hopeful, tempered with a bit of realism at the same time.

KNOWING HOW THE STAGES INTERACT

People don't always go through the stages in a straight-line manner from precontemplation to preparation to action, to maintenance, and finally, termination.

For example, someone could be in the precontemplation stage, not even thinking about quitting. Then, boom, a longtime friend is diagnosed with lung cancer. The smoker immediately jumps into the action stage and quits. The quit decision lasts for three days; then, boom, the person goes back to the precontemplation stage. The plan didn't work because there were no contemplation and preparation phases to smooth the path.

In another example, imagine someone who smoothly moves from precontemplation to contemplation to preparation and then to action, getting to the maintenance phase. Then the attempted quitter loses focus and decides she's done with smoking forever. She thinks she doesn't need to worry about triggers. But she falls off the wagon and goes back to square one, precontemplation. That's because she ignored a previous serious trigger and went back to a bar to meet some friends. She had a few drinks, her friends lit up, and she had no plan for dealing with that major set of triggers. So, she started smoking again. See Chapter 19 for more information about lapses and relapses.

Other relapsers go from the action stage to preparation when they relapse for a while. Other people who relapse go from action to contemplation, intending to take a break from quitting for a while.

Remember: There's no precise right way to go through the stages of change. But it's usually a good idea to spend enough time in each stage to properly prepare for the next.

Identifying What Stage of Change You're in Right Now

You can probably guess that it wouldn't hurt to know what stage you're in currently. You're right! You may already know. If not, read over our descriptions of each stage (earlier in this chapter) and ask yourself which one fits you the best at this time. Realize, your status could change, and you may even feel a bit of two stages at once.

After you've decided which stage you're in, you can concentrate on moving up one level at a time to combat your smoking or vaping addiction. Each stage can be thought of as a springboard to progress onto your next step. Start at the stage you're currently in and answer the questions listed for that particular stage. Be thoughtful and thorough. Take your time:

>> **Precontemplation:** How do you feel about smoking? Have you ever wondered about your health and smoking? What do you think other people around you think about smoking and health? Was there ever a time in your life when you didn't smoke? If so, what was that like for you? What could get you to think about quitting smoking?

>> **Contemplation:** What do you think is getting in your way of quitting smoking? Are there things you could do to make it easier for you to stop? If so, what? Have you ever experimented with cutting back or stopping for a short time? If so, what did you do? If you were a smoker a year from now, what would that look like?

>> **Preparation:** Do you feel you know enough about the best ways to quit smoking? If not, where can you get that information? When (if) you've quit in the past, what got in your way? What plans have you made to manage triggers and cravings? Who could support you in your quit effort? What are your most problematic triggers for smoking?

>> **Action:** How have you gotten through your first day? Week? Month? What are the best things you've done to manage your cravings? How much money have you saved so far? Do you know that after a day of not smoking, you're already getting health benefits? Do you know what those benefits are? What's working for you and what's been more difficult?

>> **Maintenance:** Congratulations! How are you feeling about smoking and not smoking today? How are you handling occasional triggers? Are you adding up the health benefits as the months go by? What are they? What helped you get where you are today?

>> **Termination:** What advice would you give to other smokers who are struggling with addiction? Do you think you're in a better place without cigarettes? Do you feel that your cravings have become almost nonexistent? What's the best thing about being a nonsmoker?

Spend some time reflecting on the answers to the questions in the stage that you're in currently. Now, how do you feel about moving on to the next stage? Do you feel there's light at the end of the tunnel?

TIP

Millions of people move successfully through the Stages of Change to become nonsmokers. You can also use the model to help you meet other life challenges.

DECIDING WHAT TO DO IF YOU'RE JUST NOT READY

What happens if you've read through the Stages of Change and you decide that you're not ready to give up smoking, using smokeless tobacco, or vaping? Maybe you're reading this material because someone who cares about you suggested it (or nagged you until you agreed to give it a try). And now that you're reading it, you still don't want to change.

Well, guess what? That's okay. Because we'd like all our friends and readers to be healthy, we're a bit sad. But somewhere along the road, we've learned that you can lead a horse to water . . . you know the rest.

If you aren't ready, give yourself a big pat on the back for getting this far. You obviously feel that, for right now, the positives you get from smoking outweigh the negatives. But that may change. You probably wouldn't be reading this unless you had at least a *little* doubt, a small feeling somewhere in the back of your head that you're going to have to face this battle one way or another.

So, when and if that time comes — that the negatives of smoking are beginning to outweigh the positives for you — remember that there are resources, like this book. And all the tools we present here can make your challenge just a bit easier. Good luck, and don't forget that you can always change your mind!

Oh, and one more thing: Just for fun, try going back and skimming through Chapter 8. Or, review the next section — you've got nothing to lose by taking a glance. And it won't take too long. Something there just may catch your attention. Really, it's totally up to you.

Deciding Your Intent

Perhaps you're still not sure what stage you're in. Or maybe you know, but you're not sure you're ready for the next stage. We have an exercise to help clarify your own intentions. After completing it, you may find yourself closer to a decision about what comes next for you. We mostly recommend this exercise for those who think they're in the precontemplation or contemplation stages of change. Here's how you can illuminate what your current stand on your smoking decision is with the Smoking/Quitting Clarifier:

1. Take a piece of paper and divide it into a box with four quadrants.

2. Label the upper-left quadrant "Why I Like to Smoke."

3. In the upper-left quadrant, list every idea you can come up with.

When you're done, leave it for a while and go back again — see if you can come up with more reasons you like to smoke.

4. Label the upper-right quadrant "Why I Really Don't Want to Smoke."

5. In the upper-right quadrant, list every idea you can come up with, no matter how small.

When you're done, leave it for a while and go back again — see if you can come up with more reasons you don't want to smoke.

6. Label the lower-left quadrant "Things That Make Quitting Hard."

7. In the lower-left quadrant, list every idea you can come up with.

When you're done, leave it for a while and go back again — see if you can come up with more things that make quitting hard.

8. Label the lower-right quadrant "Reasons I'd Like to Quit."

9. In the lower-right quadrant, list every idea you can come up with.

When you're done, leave it for a while and go back again — see if you can come up with more reasons you'd like to quit.

10. When you finish, read what you've written.

Consider reading it out loud with some emotion — as though you're talking to someone else. Read it out loud again while checking in on how you *feel* when arguing each side. Your feelings will inform you about where you're headed for now.

TIP

You may find this exercise a bit redundant. That's okay. We want you to come up with *all* the reasons on both sides of the argument. There's a subtle difference between wanting to smoke and not wanting to quit. Don't worry if many of your responses overlap.

GETTING CLEAR ON YOUR FEELINGS

EXAMPLE

Nicholas had mixed feelings about quitting his smoking habit. Several years ago, he'd decreased his smoking from two and a half packs per day to one pack per day. He felt good about that but wasn't sure he was ready to quit completely. He now knows he's at the contemplation stage of change. Now he uses the Smoking/Quitting Clarifier to figure out what's next. Here's what he came up with:

Why I Like to Smoke	Why I Really Don't Want to Smoke
I love the taste.	It's bad for my health.
It helps me relax.	It costs too much.
It keeps my weight down.	It smells.
It helps me focus and think better.	My wife hates it.

Things That Make Quitting Hard	Reasons I'd Like to Quit
Urges and cravings are tough.	It would make my wife happy.
I'll just gain weight.	I could save money a whole lot easier.
I'll be tense all the time.	I wouldn't have to worry about what others think.
My thinking will get fuzzy.	I'd prevent my secondhand smoke from hurting my family.
I don't know who I'd be as a nonsmoker.	

Nicholas carefully ponders his Smoking/Quitting Clarifier. Later, he even goes back and adds more items. He tries reading the Smoking/Quitting Clarifier out loud to his wife. She's thrilled!

Nicholas decides that he's ready to start making plans for his quit day after reading his responses. He's always known logically that he should quit, but now he senses that his feelings are in line with his logic. He concludes that he's ready to move from the contemplation stage of change to the preparation phase.

It's not just about the *number* of reasons in each quadrant, but the actual *importance* of these reasons to you. Highlight the most important items.

Writing down what's been rattling around in your head may feel a bit silly or unnecessary. But our decades of practice have informed us that getting thoughts and perspectives on paper increases the power of commitment. It really works. Try it! What have you got to lose?

The decision about quitting or continuing with smoking, vaping, or smokeless tobacco is yours and yours alone. The information in this chapter is designed to help you know what *you* want at this moment, and to show you that what you want may change over time.

Chapter **15**

Preparing Your Plan

Because you're reading this chapter, we're going to make a giant leap and assume that you're serious about quitting and you want to know what steps you should take. This is a big book, full of lots of ideas on ways to quit smoking, using smokeless tobacco, or vaping. Very few people will want to use every single strategy contained in these pages.

TIP

The ideas and techniques in this book are like a menu at a restaurant. You're not going to order every single item on the menu (of course, if you do, you probably need help with weight control!). But you can pick and choose what looks good to you. And if you don't like what you select, in this restaurant, you can send it back and try something else.

In this chapter, we help you find and choose the best methods for your individual, personal quit plan. These methods will be the ones that fit your history and interests. But, again, don't worry about choosing the exact, perfect plan. If one set of strategies doesn't work, there are lots of others to try. So, if plan A doesn't work, give plan B a shot, and possibly plan C.

REMEMBER

Every time you take a run at quitting, you've cut down on your addiction and improved your health at least a bit. Every cigarette you smoke hurts your health. Every cigarette you *don't* smoke improves your health. More important, by trying to quit, you've given yourself more data on what may finally work for you. *Don't quit quitting!* The vast majority of successful, long-term quitters have a rich history of attempts.

Monitoring Your Problem Before You Quit

Your odds of success at quitting will increase if you identify your personal smoking patterns. A good first step for quitting almost any kind of habit is to keep track of the whens, wheres, and whys. You can do that with our Personal Pattern Tracker (see Table 15-1).

TABLE 15-1   **Personal Pattern Tracker**

When	Where	Why	Additional Notes

Keeping track of smoking may seem like unnecessary work, but it can provide useful information. Many programs suggest a two-week data collection/monitoring plan before you determine a quit date. We're a tad more flexible.

TIP If you're not sure that you're ready to prepare your plan, check out Chapter 14 to see what stage of change you're in. You may need to do more preparation for quitting first. On the other hand, if it looks like you're prepared to quit, let's go.

TIP Simply monitoring your smoking increases your knowledge and awareness of what you're doing. It often leads to reduced smoking all by itself and improves your odds of successful quitting.

Some people already know when, where, and why they smoke. Keeping formal track may be superfluous for those folks. If you're not learning anything new from your monitoring, why do it?

However, most folks will find a week or two of tracking useful. It's really up to you to decide if it looks worth the effort and may give you useful information. If you're not sure, try tracking for a least a day and see for yourself. Here are a few things you could learn about your smoking from this exercise:

>> You smoke more at home than elsewhere.

>> You smoke when you're unhappy.

>> You smoke when you're stressed.

>> You smoke when something unexpectedly pleasant happens.

>> You smoke more around certain people.

>> You smoke when you're bored.

>> You smoke more when you have a drink.

>> There's hardly a time you go more than an hour without smoking.

Here's how you go about it. Every time you light up (or chew or vape), write down the approximate time, place, and situation. Time and place should be obvious. Situation can refer to how you were feeling, as well as any relevant observations, thoughts, or insights.

You can record the information on a 3-x-5 card, on a piece of notebook paper, on your smartphone — whatever is easiest for you. If you want to track on your phone, check out Chapter 11 for information about apps that have trackers. The bottom line is having the information somewhere that you can turn to for review. Keep the log going for at least 24 hours. Then decide whether to continue with it.

EXAMPLE

Table 15-2 shows a typical Personal Pattern Tracker for use with smoking, vaping, or smokeless tobacco cessation. Wendy is a pack-a-day smoker wanting to quit smoking in the next month or so. She starts by keeping track of her habit for a day and decides to go ahead and track for a week. This tracker just contains a few of her first cigarettes for the day.

TABLE 15-2   **An Example Personal Pattern Tracker**

When	Where	Why	Additional Notes
6:45 a.m., right after I got up	My bedroom	I always do it then.	
7:30 a.m.	Kitchen	With my coffee.	I can't stand the thought of drinking coffee without a cigarette.
7:45 a.m.	In the car on the way to work	To calm my nerves.	Traffic gives me fits.
8:25 a.m.	Walking from the parking lot to work	My last one for two hours.	I'm glad they don't let me smoke at work. That helps.
10:30 a.m.	Outside the building on my smoke break	I feel like I really need it.	It sucks we have to go outside, but at least they let us do it.

Wendy hadn't thought about the fact that she smokes when she first gets up in the morning. That information may help her in devising her personal quit plan. She'll also be able to make use of the information about traffic serving as a trigger for her urges (see the "Personalizing Your Quit Strategies" section, later in this chapter).

EXAMPLE

Table 15-3 shows a typical Personal Pattern Tracker for use with smokeless tobacco cessation. Owen started out as a smoker and began chewing during times he couldn't smoke cigarettes. Eventually, he managed to quit smoking cigarettes, but found himself still addicted to smokeless tobacco in the form of snus. This tracker contains a limited selection of Owen's day with smokeless tobacco.

TABLE 15-3   **An Example Personal Pattern Tracker**

When	Where	Why	Additional Notes
8:30 a.m.	At work	I always enjoy snus when I'm working on a car. It relaxes and focuses me.	I didn't realize how much I use tobacco to relax.
9:30 a.m.	Still at work	The buzz wore off from my first pouch. I love that buzz feeling.	I'm really addicted to this snus stuff. It feels great.
11:00 a.m.	Taking a car out for a test run	I enjoy driving, and I like feeling good.	I never thought about how much or often I use snus.
11:45 a.m.	Back at the shop, finishing the paperwork for the car	I hate doing paperwork. Snus helps me get through it.	Wow. I rely on snus to do a lot for me.

Owen had been using snus mindlessly, without thought. Tracking helps him connect what he's been using snus for — to help him focus, relax, and feel good. He realizes that he'll need quit strategies that help him take care of these issues, or he's not likely to succeed. The good news is that he may also be able to quit with a manageable number of techniques — he doesn't need to use them all.

Reviewing Your Quit History

Another source of information for use in developing your personal quit plan can be found in looking back at your previous attempts to quit smoking, vaping, or consuming smokeless tobacco. No doubt, a few things you tried in the past worked at least for a while, until you relapsed, whereas other strategies may have done nothing helpful or you may have even found them to be counterproductive.

TIP

Jot down as much information as you can recall about your previous quit history. Include the following:

>> When did you quit?

>> Did you plan to quit but gave up before starting?

>> How long did you quit?

>> What worked?

>> What didn't work?

>> What do you think caused your relapse?

For example, if you tried quitting cold turkey and it didn't work, you may want to consider using a bridge strategy that includes nicotine replacement therapy (NRT) or possibly even vaping with just nicotine and no tobacco (see Chapter 12 for more information about using vaping in this manner).

Or perhaps your history tells you that you tend to relapse during the holiday season. Well, obviously, you'll need to quit well before the holiday season or come up with extra supports during that time. You may also want to change the way you celebrate the holidays, at least during the first year of quitting.

Many people find alcohol to be a daunting trigger for smoking. You may consider abstaining from drinking during your first months of quitting. Think of this time as an opportunity for starting a new healthy lifestyle.

WARNING

If you find it almost impossible to consider giving up alcohol temporarily, you may have another problem. Be sure to talk to your healthcare provider about your current use of alcohol or any other substances.

REMEMBER

We can't say this enough: Every attempt at quitting smoking is a success because it gives you information and practice that will serve you well in case you need to make another attempt.

Personalizing Your Quit Strategies

The next sections give you a brief reminder about the major techniques found in this book. Then we give you some thoughts about why you may or may not consider each approach as part of your personalized quit strategy. Don't worry about making the perfect selection; you can always change it up later. You can add one strategy or stop using another. It's totally up to you.

Challenging obstacles to change

Perhaps your personal history tells you that you often have thoughts about quitting, but something gets in the way. You may think that you don't have the willpower or it's the wrong time in your life to quit. You may believe that smoking is part of who you are or that your friends or family members cause you to smoke.

Beliefs like these often keep people from attempting or cause them to give up prematurely. If that's the case for you, review Chapter 8. Consider doing this task first, before you go any further.

Alternatively, if you don't have these sorts of thoughts, and you're pretty sure that you want to quit now, you may not need this approach. This is also true if you've had previous quit attempts that lasted for several months or more. You wouldn't have been able to quit for that long if you harbored beliefs such as "It's too hard" or "I'm too weak" or "It's the wrong time."

Trying nicotine replacement therapy

Almost everyone with a long-term history of using smokeless tobacco, vaping, or smoking cigarettes is addicted to nicotine. Yet the nicotine, by itself, is much less harmful than actual tobacco. Therefore, for many people, replacing nicotine through nicotine replacement therapy (NRT) makes sense.

In fact, you increase your chances for success if you use NRT. Most people who use NRT are able to decrease and discontinue it after a few months (see Chapter 9 to decide which form of NRT is best for you).

However, some people may not like the feeling they get when using NRT. Or some people, without great effort, can give up cigarettes for weeks or months without major cravings. For those people, nicotine addiction may not be what is causing them to relapse. Other strategies may make more sense than NRT if nicotine doesn't appear to be a core part of the problem.

Starting medications

The U.S. Food and Drug Administration (FDA) has approved two medications for helping with smoking cessation efforts. Many people find them to be a useful part of their quit plan. Both of them are prescription medications, and you'll need to talk with your doctor before starting them (see Chapter 9 for more information about this approach).

One of the medications, Chantix, allows you to taper rather than quit cold turkey. If cold turkey has given you fits in the past, that property of Chantix could be useful for you. In addition, you may find one or the other of these medications appealing if you've used medications for emotional issues (for example, depression or anxiety) successfully in the past. Another positive indication would be that you've rarely experienced problematic side effects with most medications you've taken before.

Some people get nauseous at the very thought of taking almost any medication. Both medications do have side effects such as upset stomach, disturbed sleep, and jitteriness. Some people who take one of these medications discontinue due to uncomfortable side effects. If you tend to be particularly sensitive to side effects such as these, medications may not be your best option. In that case, leave the pill approach on the shelf, at least for now.

Other people already take medications that may interact with smoking cessation medications — be sure to ask your pharmacist or healthcare provider. Finally, some people just hate taking pills for whatever reason. If that's you, consider trying other things first. You can always go back to this one later.

Rethinking thoughts

If you're someone who spends a lot of time in your head, that's great. Thoughts can help you navigate all kinds of problems. However, some thoughts can get in your way of accomplishing what you want. For example, do you tend to exaggerate, dwell on catastrophes, try to predict the future, worry constantly, or take things personally? Or do you find yourself obsessively tangled up in your thoughts, unable to find a way out?

If so, you're probably a good candidate for challenging your thinking. See Chapter 10 for lots of ideas about challenging and smoothing out your problematic thinking.

We think that most people could profit from spending at least a little time working on their thoughts. However, you may find yourself resisting tackling this issue. It may feel like a hassle or seem silly to you. So, if you choose to bypass this approach, that's okay. Just remember: Challenging your thinking is an option if other efforts fail you. You decide — this is *your* personalized quit plan after all.

Doing something different

We really hope you have no trouble quitting smoking. We also hope that a million-dollar check will show up in our mailbox today. Unfortunately, we're not getting that check, and you'll probably have some difficulty with quitting.

One of the most important pieces in most people's personalized quit plan is doing something different in response to triggers. *Triggers* are anything that you associate with smoking.

The power that triggers exert can be considerable. Frankly, it's hard to imagine designing an effective smoking-cessation program without doing something about your triggers. This is one strategy you just don't want to leave out of your plan.

See Chapter 10 for a variety of ways to take action for avoiding, minimizing, and/ or confronting triggers.

Managing feelings and urges

There's nothing that smokers fear more than being overwhelmed by strong feelings and urges. Some say they'll do almost anything to avoid them. But you can't really avoid all bad feelings when you give up an addiction. Instead, it's important to manage, cope, and deal with unpleasant feelings. See Chapter 10 for ideas about relating to difficult feelings differently. You can also review Chapters 18 and 21 for a variety of methods for learning to relax and manage feelings.

Then again, you could be one of those rare people who take medications and quit smoking without problematic, strong feelings remaining to trip you up. If so, fabulous! Otherwise, ignore this strategy at your own peril.

Getting tech support

Quitting smoking usually takes lots of support. But support can come in many forms. Nowadays, technology has rushed to the rescue. There are some really good, free or low-cost apps to help you. Most of them warn you about problematic locations, give advice on managing urges and cravings, keep track of your progress, send you tips, and more. You're likely to find them helpful or at least sort of fun.

Some people just plain hate tech or don't own a smartphone or similar device. Those people may want to turn to online support (see Chapter 24 for useful websites). Others prefer speaking to a real live counselor at a free quit line — if that's you, call 800-QUIT-NOW (800-784-8669).

Alternatively, you could be a highly independent person who hates asking for help or support on almost anything. Okay, but remember that the cost is typically either free or low. Why not give one of these options a shot?

Soliciting social support

Humans are social beings. Numerous studies tell us that having a good social support system helps with almost everything, including overall health, emotional well-being, success, and more. Overcoming addictions of almost any kind is no exception to the rule. We talk about formal social support in the form of Nicotine Anonymous and SMART Recovery in Chapter 11. And there may be other options in your local area — call the quit line number in the preceding section for more sources.

You can also cobble together your own, informal support by asking trusted friends and family to help you. See the "Declaring Your Intent" section, later in this chapter, for information about what to say to them.

Alternatively, you could be a certifiable loner. Maybe you find opening up to other people difficult, to say the least. Still, you can consider anonymous tech help lines. If that's still too much, skip this strategy, at least for now. It's available if and when you want it.

Choosing Your Quit Day

Gulp! Relax, you don't have to quit today. It's just a good idea to actively choose your quit day ahead of time. Give yourself enough time to complete your pre-quit plan (see the "Creating a Pre-Quit-Day Game Plan" section, later in this chapter). And give yourself time to go through our quit strategies for determining which ones you'll put into your plan. But don't push your quit date out so far that it becomes an excuse to keep smoking — that could even lead you to change your mind.

TIP

You also may want to consider the following ideas for coming up with your personal quit date:

>> **Consider your work and life schedules.** Choose a day that's busy, but not overly stressful, if possible.

>> **Reconsider quitting while on vacation.** Although a vacation may seem like a good time to quit, it's not always a good idea because when you return to work, the old triggers and stressors will be facing you again. Your success on vacation may possibly evaporate when you return to your "real" life.

>> **Consider selecting a personally meaningful date.** Some possibilities may be a birthday, a holiday, a Great American Smokeout date (sponsored by the American Cancer Society), or an anniversary.

If all else fails, throw a dart at a one-month calendar! The point is, just set a date. And don't make it more than a few weeks in the future. Don't change your mind. *There is no perfect time.*

Declaring Your Intent

You've made a decision: You're going to quit. Now you can devise a personal quit plan. Making a written commitment to yourself and others reinforces your resolve and improves your odds of quitting. That's because most of us take contracts seriously. Let's get to it!

Writing out a personal quit plan

You can write your quit plan on a notepad or type it into your computer or smartphone. It's pretty simple. Figure 15-1 shows a sample template for your personal quit plan.

EXAMPLE

We introduced you to Wendy, a pack-a-day smoker, earlier in this chapter (see "Monitoring Your Problem Before You Quit"). After considering her smoking pattern and her quit history, she chooses the strategies she's going to use and her quit day. She designs the personal quit plan shown in Figure 15-2.

Wendy's personal quit plan spells out her commitment and some of the major strategies that she plans to use. Over time, she may delete a few items or add some.

REMEMBER

Think of your plan as a flexible work in progress. Keep what works, toss what doesn't, and add what could work. Keep your personal quit plan in a convenient place, and review it often.

Telling friends and family what you're up to

Assuming you have a supportive family, you may want to make your intentions known to them. Share your plan with them and ask for their support. Tell them you're determined to quit and why.

Not everyone is fortunate enough to have an unconditionally supportive family. Maybe your parents are highly critical or your siblings pounce on your every mistake. In that case, you'll probably want to hold off telling them for a while. No sense in adding to your stress.

Hopefully, you have some friends who are less judgmental. If so, tell them all about your game plan. Acknowledge that you may not make it successfully and you want their support anyway. That's because you're going to keep on trying until you succeed.

I, _____, have committed to stop smoking on this date:_____.

The top five reasons I'm quitting smoking are:

1.

2.

3.

4.

5.

I'm going to use the following strategies to help me quit (for example, NRT, medication, challenging obstacles, rethinking thoughts, tech support):

I'm going to avoid (and later confront) the following triggers by these actions:

I've lined up the following people to help support me:

Signed: _____

Date: _____

FIGURE 15-1:
A personal quit
plan template.

I, Wendy have committed to stop smoking on this date: July 4.

The top five reasons I'm quitting smoking are:

1. I worry about my long-term health.

2. My smoking makes my allergies way worse.

3. I can't afford cigarettes.

4. My family will be really happy if I finally quit.

5. My clothes won't smell anymore.

I'm going to use the following strategies to help me quit (for example, NRT, medication, challenging obstacles, rethinking thoughts, tech support):

* I'm going to use NRT because I realize I have intense cravings in the morning.

* I've already downloaded a great app.

* I need to work on my thoughts a little.

* I plan to join the gym.

* Every week I don't smoke, I'm going to buy myself something new to wear.

I'll consider other strategies as I go.

I'm going to avoid (and later confront) the following triggers by these actions:

* I'm going to drink coffee at work rather than at home where it's too easy to smoke.

* I'll take a new route to work with less traffic because that's a huge trigger for me.

* I'll take that afternoon yoga class at the gym because afternoon is when my willpower goes down.

* I'll walk around the block a few times if my urges get really tough.

I've lined up the following people to help support me:

* My sister agreed to talk with me on the phone when I get terrible urges.

* A quit-smoking group is getting together at work — I'll join them.

* My doctor said to come in anytime to discuss my progress; I think I will.

Signed: Wendy

Date: June 20

FIGURE 15-2:
An example
of a personal
quit plan.

TIP

If you don't have supportive friends or family, consider calling 800-QUIT NOW (800-784-8669) and chat with a friendly staff person who's trained in being nonjudgmental and supportive.

Creating a Pre-Quit-Day Game Plan

Before you actually quit smoking, there are a couple of things you can do on your pre-quit days. The first is to change components of your smoking habit in any way you can to make smoking less rewarding. The second is getting your house, car, office, and environment ready to be smoke-free.

Changing things up

Smoking is not just an addiction; it's a habit. Like any habit, it's tough to change because of all the associations you have that trigger your habit. Therefore, you may find it useful to change a number of your smoking associations. These changes are designed to make your smoking less automatic and less enjoyable. For example:

>> If you love your cigarette with your morning coffee, try smoking it before that first cup in the morning.

>> Change the position of your cigarette between your lips. Most people who smoke tend to have a habitual way of placing the cigarette in their mouths. Move it to the other side.

>> Hold the cigarette in a different hand. Be careful not to drop it and burn yourself!

>> Use a brand of cigarettes (or other tobacco product) that you don't like as much. But don't try to reduce tar or nicotine at this point.

>> If you smoke outside your office, go somewhere else to smoke. Look for places that feel less comfortable for you.

>> Use different ashtrays in different locations.

You get the idea. Use your imagination with the goal of coming up with ways of making your smoking habit less habitual — in other words, less automatic and comfortable. You're not actually depriving yourself of nicotine yet, but you are breaking down pesky associations.

WARNING

Cutting down on the overall number of cigarettes you smoke prior to quitting works for some people. However, you need to be careful not to inhale more deeply and take more frequent puffs.

Cleaning out your smoking environment

Before your quit day, survey your home. Look for all the ashtrays. Clean all of them and put them away — except for one (you can get rid of it after you actually quit). Then clean your house from top to bottom, especially rooms you typically use for smoking.

TIP

This is a great time to get your carpets and drapes cleaned. Don't forget to take clothing like winter coats in for a cleaning — they collect smoke and smell. And do your car a favor: Get it washed on the day before your quit day.

Chapter **16**

Celebrating Your Quit Day

In earlier chapters, we describe and explain the *major* techniques for quitting smoking — trying nicotine replacement therapy (NRT), taking medication, changing thinking, dealing with triggers, getting social support, managing emotions, getting technical support, and challenging mental obstacles.

In this chapter, as well as the next two, we delve into the moment-to-moment challenges of quitting and how to get through the worst cravings using tiny targeted tips. By turning to major techniques, as well as tiny targeted tips, you can get through your quit plan, one day at a time.

Prepping for Your Quit Day

TIP

You've made a contract with yourself, and tomorrow is the day to implement your quit plan. The day or days before your quit day is the time to get some supplies, meals, and entertainment plans ready. Here are a few tiny targeted tips:

» Break up and throw away all remaining cigarettes in your home. That means all of them. No time to cheat now.

» Put away all ashtrays or throw them out.

» Get rid of lighters and matches.

» Prepare a smattering of easy, great menus for several days, and buy the ingredients.

» Buy a few packs of gum or hard candy.

» Buy or find things to fiddle with, like toothpicks, a stress ball, a fidget spinner, or rubber bands.

» Make sure you have a good supply of NRT if it's a part of your plan.

» Reread your personal quit plan (see Chapter 15), and review the reasons you're quitting; it will help you focus.

We have one more task for you before the Big Day hits. Doing this after you've completed your personal quit plan, but before you quit will give you a big boost of motivation right when you need it. Furthermore, the activity is kind of fun!

Make a set of cue cards (any format) for yourself as reminders — write something meaningful on each one, including the reasons for quitting you wrote on your quit plan and other messages such as the following:

» I will save tons of money — about $10 today alone!

» I can get through this.

» My blood pressure and pulse will drop after 20 minutes without a smoke.

» My oxygen levels will return to normal after just eight hours.

» I've done even harder things in my life.

» Watch out for unexpected urges.

» Urges will decrease over time.

» After 48 hours, my sense of smell and taste will improve.

» No more yellow fingers and smoky, smelly clothes.

» I love the idea of being an ex-smoker.

» Keep active — don't sit around moping.

» Remember to check my app for more tips.

» Wow, time to get an appointment to have my teeth whitened.

>> No more social ostracizing from others because of my smoking.

>> I will succeed.

You get the idea. Put these messages and more on notecards or sticky notes. Carry them with you. Pull one out whenever you have an urge. Pull one out even if you don't have an urge. Repetition, repetition, repetition.

After your last cigarette, tell yourself that what you're doing will be hard but worth it in the long run. Get a good night's sleep.

Waking Up as an Ex-Smoker

Good morning! It's a great day! Take a deep breath, and enjoy your smoke-free air. Appreciate that you'll be breathing clean air from now on, for the rest of your life. This first day as an ex-smoker (that's you) can be tough, but it's only one day. You can do it!

Now, *get moving!* This is no morning to dawdle. If you have the time, take a walk or work out. If not, at least spend a few moments reviewing your day's schedule. If you see any significant gaps in your schedule, find something to do during those periods.

Then throw yourself into a shower right away. Take time to enjoy the shower. Imagine the soap and steam are starting to clean out your lungs.

If morning is a time you normally smoke (and it probably is), change your routine. If you usually linger over a cup of coffee while you smoke, consider skipping the coffee at home and stopping at a coffee shop on the way to work. If you smoke while reading the news on your computer, don't read it today — believe us, the news won't go away or change because you're not reading it.

TIP

Pull out those cue cards that you wrote last night. Read them. Now read them again. Take a few deep breaths and get on with your day. When you have an urge, pull the cue cards out and read them again. If you're by yourself (or with someone on your support team), read them out loud.

THE POWER OF A PLAN

EXAMPLE

Jonathan is a 32-year-old I.T. manager for a local startup. He started smoking in grad school and has tried to quit almost every year since. It has become his usual New Year's resolution. His friends are supportive but tease him about his revolving quit door. This time, he realizes that his previous attempts have failed to include nearly enough preparation and planning. This time he has prepared.

The alarm rings and Jonathan jumps out of bed. This is his official quit day, his first day as an ex-smoker. Normally, he heads straight to the coffee pot and lights his first cigarette. But not today. Instead, he shaves, takes a hot shower, and gets ready for work. He remembers to apply his nicotine patch; then he looks for a pack of sugarless gum to stash in his backpack. He grabs his cue cards and puts them in his shirt pocket for easy access.

Instead of having breakfast at home, Jonathan stops at a local coffee shop and orders a latte and a breakfast sandwich. He checks his email while eating his breakfast. He notices he's doing pretty good so far. He's proud of the fact that he has changed his routine and hasn't had any severe cravings.

He doesn't think he needs to, but he pulls out his cue cards anyway. He particularly focuses on the one that says, "Watch out for unexpected urges — they don't mean you have to smoke." He realizes that the day is young and he's likely to have more trouble later. Right now, he feels confident.

Jonathan has prepared carefully for this day. He realizes that his past quit attempts have taught him a lot about quitting. They weren't failures, just golden opportunities for learning. He has a complete personal quit plan and his chances of permanent success have increased.

Managing Food and Drink: You're Not Giving Up Everything

First, don't let yourself get hungry, even if you're concerned about weight — you can deal with that issue later. Hunger is often reported to feel quite similar to cravings or urges for cigarettes. So, be sure to eat three meals today along with a couple of modest snacks in between.

Everyone says to have celery sticks and carrot sticks to chew on in place of smoking. Well, we don't know about you, but after a couple of chews, it just doesn't do much to satisfy a craving. Try crunchy veggies with a little dip (it helps) or a handful of popcorn here and there.

Equally useful is to drink lots of water — tap, bottled, carbonated, or lightly flavored. Treat yourself to a cold glass of ice water with a slice of lemon or lime. Every time you feel a craving coming on, drink some water. When drinking water, imagine that your body is cleansing itself of toxins.

As you know, nicotine is a stimulant even though it can relax you, too. Caffeine in coffee is also a stimulant. However, for some people, coffee is a powerful trigger for smoking. If that describes you, consider switching to tea or possibly a form of coffee you don't normally drink. Iced coffee may have little or no association with smoking for you; if so, try it out.

Additional treats for dealing with cravings include fresh fruit (such as grapes, strawberries, and orange slices), nuts, and a few small whole-grain crackers. (See the "Opening a Pack of Pleasures Instead of a Pack of Smokes" section, later in this chapter, for some additional food alternatives for cravings that may surprise you.)

Keeping Busy at Work and Play

Today is a day to keep busy. If you're working, try to avoid too much stress or conflict. Also avoid, if you can, making big decisions or taking on new, complicated projects. Admit it; you're not going to be at your best.

Don't underestimate the difficulty of giving up an addiction. Your thinking may not be as clear as usual. Cravings and urges take energy. Give yourself a break today, and just get through what needs to be done.

If you've told your colleagues what you're doing (we usually think it's a good idea to), talk with them about how it's going. Most people are very understanding and want to help, particularly in the early stages of quitting. Reread your cue cards.

After work, it's play time. Don't bring any work home if you can possibly avoid it! We strongly encourage you to be active and busy tonight. Here are some possibilities:

>> Go out to a movie (where you obviously can't smoke).

>> Stroll through a shopping mall.

>> Take a walk with a nonsmoking friend.

>> Play with your kids or dog.

>> If you're a member of a gym, go for a workout. While you're there, listen to your favorite music or podcast.

>> If you're not a member of a gym, consider joining one.

>> Maybe it sounds silly, but try going roller skating or ice skating.

>> Catch a baseball game if it's a smoke-free stadium.

>> Take your car to the car wash if you haven't done so in preparation for quitting.

>> Do something nice for a neighbor or friend.

Be creative. Ask your support people for other ideas. The bottom line is that the more engaged you get with activity, the less room you'll have for uncomfortable urges.

Avoiding Triggers for Now

The first smoke-free day is a day to plough through. No drama, don't climb any mountains or ford any streams. And stay away from your smoking triggers as much as you can. So, if you normally take a smoke break at work, find some other way to fill that time. Call a friend or send a couple of emails to update your support team. Surf the web for quit tips or for some things to buy after you save your cigarette money.

Other smokers whether friends, coworkers, or family members can be extremely difficult to be around at first. Ask them not to smoke in front of you for at least the first week or two — longer if they're agreeable. It's better for you and for them (they'll be smoking less). If you live with a smoker, you may have made an agreement that, for now, your partner or roommate will mostly smoke outside or in a specific room that you can avoid. The smell of smoke can trigger urges or cravings.

Commuting can also serve as tough triggers for many people. Cigarettes often go along for the ride as part of a long commute. Change up your mode of transportation for a while, even if it's a hassle (and sometimes a bit more inconvenient or expensive). It will be well worth the cost in the long run if it helps you quit.

Maybe you're a TV aficionado and you watch it from your favorite smoking chair. Tonight, go to a movie instead. See the "Keeping Busy at Work and Play" section for more ideas.

If you're struggling with cravings today, call 800-QUIT NOW (800-784-8669) to talk with a quit-smoking counselor. You can even do that if it wasn't part of your personal quit plan. *Remember:* Your plan can be continuously updated as needed.

Ultimately, you'll have to encounter and deal with smoking triggers. You'll get a sense of empowerment when you can pull that off. We discuss how in Chapter 10. And we give you more ideas in Chapter 18. But that's for another day. Today, your goal boils down to not smoking and getting through the day.

Opening a Pack of Pleasures Instead of a Pack of Smokes

Now we're going to go against all the rules. In our book, when you're initiating your quit day, carrots and celery sticks just don't do the trick. Your urges are strong — they want more than that!

Just as NRT can serve as a temporary bridge from smoking to a smoke-free life, guilty pleasures can do the same. So, we're going to give you permission *for a while* to have your cake and eat it, too. That goes for ice cream, brownies, candy, chocolate, or spoonfuls of peanut butter right out of the jar. Seriously, you ask? Yes. If it gets you through for a little while, why not? But you protest, "I'll gain weight!" You're right. You probably will a bit. We help you out with that issue in Chapter 20.

If you're diabetic, prediabetic, or morbidly obese, this advice is not for you. Think about other indulgent pleasures like buying something special for yourself.

What's good for you in the short run isn't so great in the long run. The core concern is that you quit smoking. Yes, being overweight is not healthy and can certainly impact your health. However, the risks of smoking are generally much greater.

Besides, we're not talking about eating this junk forever. We're talking about indulging this way for a week or two and possibly *on occasion* for the first month or so. That's it. You won't gain an insufferable amount of weight doing that unless you go over the top (four scoops are, duh, too much).

Plan to reward yourself at the end of your first smoke-free day. You did it. Congratulations! We'll deal with your ice-cream addiction soon enough!

Going to Bed

You spent the day in survival mode. Your body has been used to a steady stream of nicotine via smoking. It's a big shift even if you're taking NRT. A few lucky people have no issues with sleeping the first night after quitting smoking. Other people feel excessively tired and fall asleep early — that's totally okay.

Unfortunately, still others feel revved up from dealing with quitting and physiological rebound effects whether they're using NRT or not. If you have trouble sleeping tonight, realize it's normal and temporary. Tell yourself:

>> I've had other nights when I didn't sleep, and I lived through all of them.

>> I may struggle tonight, but it's likely to get better soon.

>> Quitting smoking is worth the aggravation of a couple nights of bad sleep.

>> Maybe I'll read a trashy novel until I get sleepy.

WARNING

If you can't sleep, it's a good idea to stay away from screen time. Read a real book (remember those?) or a magazine. Light emanating from screens messes up your brain's circadian rhythm. See Chapter 17 for more help with sleep problems if they continue for more than two or three nights. Insomnia can derail your efforts if you don't address it.

WARNING

Medications that are used to help with cravings can sometimes lead to strange dreams or nightmares. See Chapter 9 for more information about medications and side effects.

Chapter **17**

Getting through the Risky First Month

Y ou got through the first day. Yeah! In the first week of quitting, you mostly want to do what you did for the first day. Treat yourself like royalty. However, as the days pass, life re-emerges. You can't avoid every trigger, and early enthusiasm fades a bit. This first month represents your greatest relapse risk (see Chapter 19).

In this chapter, we give you some tips and strategies for making it through the difficult first month. The good news is that withdrawal symptoms from nicotine usually peak within a few days and come down further within two to four weeks. These symptoms will be milder if you're using nicotine replacement therapy (NRT).

WARNING

Your withdrawal symptoms may abate during the first month. However, you will probably continue to experience urges and cravings for some time. These are due to the numerous triggers you encounter in daily living. These triggers set off powerful urges, sometimes quite unexpectedly. These associations take time to lose their power.

Managing Your Inner Curmudgeon

Okay, let's get real here. You're not going to be the best version of yourself during the first few weeks of quitting, especially if you're doing it cold turkey without NRT or medication. In fact, you may find yourself:

>> Snapping at your spouse or partner over virtually nothing

>> Lacking patience with others

>> Feeling cranky

>> Experiencing nervousness

>> Wanting to lash out with road rage

>> Feeling easily frustrated

>> Feeling on edge for no apparent reason

>> Experiencing frequent sensations of restlessness

>> Flying off the handle once in a while

WARNING

There is a common myth that it's best to express your anger, that left inside, anger will build and eventually explode from the pressure. Nothing could be further from the truth. Numerous studies of this issue have shown that expressing anger (such as screaming or hitting a pillow) leads to more anger. It's important to learn to control anger and express it in an effective, healthy manner (see Chapter 22). When, and if necessary, expressing anger very carefully and mildly is usually your best course of action. If anger is a significant problem for you, consider checking out *Anger Management For Dummies*, 2nd Edition, by Charles Elliott and Laura Smith (yes, that's us).

The next two sections show you various ways of managing your irritability. These strategies keep the temperature down for you and those around you.

Taking a time-out

Much like urges and cravings, difficult feelings of prickliness or touchiness pass after a little time. Try one or more of the following delay tips when you feel edgy (it's better than smoking or vaping):

>> **Take slow, deep breaths.** Inhale slowly while you count to three and then exhale as slowly as you can. Repeat at least three times or until your feelings quell.

>> **Slowly count to ten.** This really works. You may have to count as high as 100, but keep at it until you calm down.

>> **Repeat a mantra.** Say to yourself, "Calm down," "Give it time," "Peace," or "Chill." Repeat one or more of these words slowly or choose your own word or phrase. Keep repeating until you feel better.

>> **Close your mouth.** Don't let any words escape! They're likely to make things worse, no matter how careful you try to be. If you actually talk, the odds of your saying something useful while you're upset are about one in 28 billion.

>> **Let it go.** Remember that your emotions are transient and will pass. Remind yourself that time is on your side.

One of the most compelling reasons for delaying the expression of your irritability is that withdrawal from nicotine is very likely causing you to perceive things and people around you in twisted, negative ways. Ponder that probability!

Not only are you likely overreacting, but if you do become irritable with others, you'll likely make things worse not better. You could even annoy the people you're counting on for support. So, do yourself a favor and take a time-out. Breathe.

Taking anti-curmudgeon actions

We also have a list of actions you can take in order to curtail your inner curmudgeon. Try whichever ones appeal to you. If your first choice doesn't work, try another one.

>> **Suck on hard candy or a mint.** Don't chew! Take the time to slowly dissolve the mint in your mouth. By having something in your mouth, it's harder to talk and get yourself in more trouble.

>> **Go for a walk.** Take a brisk five-minute walk. It will give you time to burn off some excess adrenaline. Consider taking your dog with you.

>> **Clean up the kitchen counter.** Do any brief housekeeping task that can distract you for a few minutes. It will also give you a sense of accomplishment.

>> **Try splashing your face with ice water.** You can also submerge your hands in ice water for 30 seconds. Or rub ice on your wrists or face. When you're done, you won't feel quite so uptight. Maybe a bit chilly, but. . . .

>> **Put on a happy face.** This tip is also called "acting as if" — in other words, acting as if you're not irritated. You can put on a Mona Lisa face — sublime and serene. Your feelings will follow.

>> **Play a quick game on your phone.** This is another distraction that works pretty well to diminish upsetting feelings. Make sure it's a game that engages your attention.

>> **Apologize and mean it.** If you're the kind of person who finds it difficult to apologize, get over it!

REMEMBER

Realize that it's almost inevitable that you'll mess up a few times during the first month of quitting. You'll say some things you don't mean or you'll snap at someone without good cause. After you calm down, apologize genuinely. You can then explain what's causing your irritability. Most people will understand.

TIP

Take a few minutes to review your personal quit plan at least weekly during this first month. If any of the strategies mentioned in this chapter work for you, consider adding them to your personal quit plan (see Chapter 15). When distressing emotions or cravings break through, also read your cue cards out loud (see Chapter 16).

Sleeping Through the Night

We know you're cranky because you gave up one of your favorite companions, smoking. Poor sleep can add to the crankiness. Stopping nicotine often disturbs sleep. And smokers who quit and experience sleep disturbance are more likely to relapse — especially during the first month. Furthermore, exhaustion leads to more irritability.

The good news is that there are ways for helping sleep and indications are that those methods will reduce that relapse problem. But first, we'll give you the reasons why sleep is important in your quitting efforts. Sleep deprivation leads to:

>> Emotional outbursts

>> Impaired memory

>> Difficulty concentrating

>> Suppressed immune function

>> Weight gain

>> Inefficiency

>> Decreased frustration tolerance

>> Pessimism

>> Impaired moods

>> Impaired ability to cope

>> Inflexible thinking (the inability to see both sides of an issue)

>> Being accident-prone

>> Lack of stamina

>> Road rage

And with all that going on, you're supposed to quit smoking and resist urges, right? No wonder people trying to quit who experience sleep problems, relapse more often than those without sleep impairment. Sleep problems are important to deal with in the first weeks of quitting — don't wait.

Even though it's true that the very act of quitting can mess up your sleep, there are things you can do to address that problem. It's usually preferable that you don't start sleep medications as your first strategy. That's because sleep medications typically should only be used for the short term.

Why just for the short term? Simple. All too often, they lead to:

>> Long-term problems with thinking and memory

>> Addiction and additional sleep problems if you stop them

>> Daytime drowsiness

>> Bizarre wandering at night, including driving without awareness

>> Increased anxiety

So, for now, look at how to improve your sleep quality in other ways. But if you do want to check out sleep medications either now or later, be sure to talk with your doctor and carefully weigh the pluses and minuses of them for yourself.

TIP

Melatonin is a hormone that your body produces naturally. Many people find melatonin supplements to be a useful sleep aid. It's safer than prescription sleep medications, so you may want to start with melatonin.

Getting ready for bed

If you ever had a baby, you probably remember a bedtime routine. You may have had story time, a bath, and a last feeding before putting the infant down for the night with a goodnight kiss. When the routine was followed, for the most part, things usually went as planned. But when a bedtime routine gets disrupted, chaos can occur. That's why you probably tried to keep to the routine as closely as possible.

If you want to sleep like a baby, set up a bedtime routine for yourself. Start a few hours before bed. Here are some easy things you can do (and a few *not* to do) to wind down your day before going to bed:

>> Don't do aerobic exercise within a couple of hours of bed.

>> Exercise earlier in the day — it can help sleep later.

>> Drink chamomile tea or another herbal or decaffeinated tea with relaxing properties.

>> Don't talk about a highly conflicted issue with your family.

>> Don't eat a big meal a few hours before bed. Instead, eat a small snack, such as a handful of nuts or some yogurt.

>> Consider a warm bath or shower if you like them.

>> Don't watch violent, scary, or suspenseful movies or TV shows if they rev you up.

>> Do consider reading a book as long as the themes are not upsetting.

>> Don't use screens an hour before bed because they can alter your circadian rhythm, although some people find that screens don't bother their sleep.

After you've designed your sleep routine, try to stick with it. Don't vary it much, especially in the first month of quitting. Your body gets used to it and starts to drop off more quickly.

Making your room rest ready

Your immediate environment matters when it comes to sleep. Once again, associations are key. Here are some of the most important points for associating your bedroom with a restful sleep:

>> Turn the thermostat down. Most people do better in a cool room.

>> Make your room as dark as possible. Consider including new, room-darkening blinds if necessary.

>> If noise is a problem, think about using a sound machine app to generate soothing sounds in the background.

>> Have comfortable sheets. Get some new ones if you're ready for them.

>> Turn notifications off on your cellphone at night. And above all, don't get up to look at your screen.

>> Clean and organize your bedroom. Don't leave stuff lying around you could trip on in the middle of the night. Besides, messiness doesn't associate with peaceful sleep.

REMEMBER

These suggestions could seem trivial to you. But they add up to a more restful setting, and that's what your mind and body want.

Associating your bed with sleep

You need to associate your bed with sleep. Beds have two major purposes — sleep and sex. Both associations are fine. But if you have a sleep problem, be careful about other associations. Avoid the following:

>> Doing work in bed

>> Watching much TV in bed (a few minutes to wind down could be okay)

>> Reading for an extended period of time in bed (again, that's if you have a sleep problem)

>> Listening to loud music in bed

If you can't fall off to sleep within about 20 minutes, it's best to get up out of bed and do something else. That's to avoid associating your bed with tossing, turning, and ruminating. Your choice of something else to do should be nonstrenuous and, ideally, a bit boring. Don't try going back to bed until you feel significantly more fatigued. Get up again if you don't fall asleep within about 20 minutes.

It's a pain to keep getting up if you don't drop off to sleep quickly. But if you put up with a few sleep-deprived nights, you'll likely get a big payoff.

TIP

Sometimes you're snuggled up in bed, totally relaxed and peaceful, for longer than 20 minutes. We don't expect you to jump out of bed and do something else in that case. It's when you're fully awake and thinking about a long to-do list or worried about something that it's best to get up. Otherwise, enjoy the peace and quiet.

Avoiding alcohol and other drugs

It's often tempting to have a nightcap just before bed — and it may help you drop off. Unfortunately, alcohol interferes with normal sleep patterns, and you're more likely to wake up in the middle of the night, unable to go back to sleep.

The same advice goes for a variety of other medications and over-the-counter drugs — check carefully before taking them to avoid sleep problems. Common cold or allergy medications often contain stimulating ingredients. Finally, avoid caffeine and other foods with caffeine such as chocolate.

TIP

Some people even have a problem with decaffeinated coffee before bed — that's probably due to the association between regular coffee and feeling stimulated. Your brain sometimes reacts to the association and responds as if the decaf coffee actually contained caffeine. If you think that has happened to you, consider dropping that decaf at night.

Making your mind rest ready

Just as your bedroom environment matters, so do the contents in your mind. If you're stewing about a work problem, sorting out a difficult relationship, or figuring out your monthly budget, you're not likely to drop off to sleep easily.

TIP

Put off your worries until tomorrow. Consider having a notepad and pen to jot down your concerns so you can leave them alone. You may want to spend 15 minutes problem solving on paper, and then set it aside. Ideally, do this several hours before bed. Bedtime itself should be sacred — people rarely come up with brilliant solutions to issues while tossing and turning anyway.

TIP

Some people find mindfulness a useful approach to aiding sleep. See Chapter 21 for information on meditation techniques.

TIP

If sleep continues to elude you, try to realize that, while not ideal, it's something you've probably coped with before. The more you obsess about your sleep, the worse it will get. If you continue to struggle past the first month or so, read Chapter 18 to see if you have problems with depression or anxiety. Those moods often cause sleep problems. Depression and anxiety after quitting smoking are common but often abate, and when they don't, they're fortunately treatable.

WARNING

You may be tempted to try to make up for lost sleep by staying in bed more hours. That's a big mistake. Stick to your regular sleep schedule. You'll sleep better in the long run.

TIP

If you try all these sleep suggestions and continue to have prolonged insomnia, talk to your primary care provider about seeing a sleep specialist, particularly a psychologist trained in cognitive behavior therapy for insomnia. Sleep is an important problem to address early.

Tolerating Withdrawal in the First Month

TIP

We discuss withdrawal from smoking, vaping, and chewing throughout this book. Your worst problems with this issue will occur during the first month. Be prepared to experience one or more of the following symptoms:

» **Increased cough:** Wait a minute, didn't you quit smoking to get rid of your smokers' cough? Yes, but when you stop poisoning your lungs, they begin to start cleaning themselves out. So, it's kind of a good sign that your coughing increases. Expect it to diminish within a couple of weeks — check with your primary care doctor if it doesn't.

» **Tightness in chest:** This could be from coughing too much or having strong cravings. This symptom usually fades within days.

» **Fatigue:** Well, we did already mention sleep problems in the previous sections. But fatigue can come on even if you're sleeping all right. It happens because your body is adjusting to having no stimulation from nicotine, though less if you're on NRT. This, too, shall pass.

» **Minor sore throat:** The nerve endings in your throat start to regenerate and can cause minor irritation for a while. Drink lots of water and suck on lozenges often.

» **Concentration problems:** You've probably used nicotine to help you focus and concentrate. It takes some adjustment to learn how to pay attention without a cigarette, but your focus will improve.

» **Strong cravings:** Hang onto your hat and wait it out. Distract yourself especially with exercise. Unfortunately, this side effect can linger for a while.

» **Dizziness:** This symptom usually fades within a few days. It occurs because your body is not accustomed to the increased oxygen that comes from stopping smoking.

» **Increased hunger:** You may feel more hungry than usual because cravings feel much like hunger and nicotine suppresses appetite. Try drinking lots of water, chewing gum, and/or having a variety of low-calorie snacks.

» **Constipation:** During the first month of quitting, a certain percentage of people experience constipation. It's important to drink lots of water and increase fiber in your diet.

REMEMBER

Withdrawal symptoms are common and expected. So, expect them! Most of these will reduce and disappear before the end of your first month. Things do get better.

Talking Back to First-Month Excuses

The mind is an amazing thinking machine. It solves complex problems and helps you navigate a byzantine world. It's also quite dexterous in the art of lying and deception. It feeds you false information in a quest to make you feel better in the short run.

In Chapter 2, we explain that you can think of the mind as consisting of two parts. The first is like an elephant that responds to whatever the elephant wants at any given moment, such as food, water, and sex. The elephant tries to avoid danger, pain, or discomfort as well. The second part of your mind is more like an elephant rider that wants to do the right thing in both the short and long term. The rider is more logical and reasonable, but the elephant is more powerful.

In the first month of quitting, the rider is supporting your quit efforts. But the elephant wants nicotine. He's going to try to get it any way that he can. And he's strong. His tactic in this case is to convince you that it's okay to have just a puff, or a couple of puffs, or give up entirely.

Here are some of the things the elephant part of your mind is trying to tell you:

>> I've been good this week, just one cigarette can't hurt anything.

>> I'll just smoke at this party and get right back on the wagon tomorrow.

>> This isn't a great time for me to quit; I'll do it in another month or two.

REMEMBER

You can't have one cigarette and not increase your urges and struggles. Maybe you'll get away with it, but your odds go down. Tell your elephant that:

>> Cheating does nothing but make it harder.

>> There's always an excuse not to quit — many excuses, in fact.

>> Stop trying to convince me to do the wrong thing.

The elephant lies. So, decide it's time to get your elephant under control. Take charge and read your cue cards again (see Chapter 16).

EXAMPLE

THE ELEPHANT RUN AMOK

Jessica quit smoking three weeks ago. She's having trouble sleeping and feels overwhelmed by withdrawal symptoms. When she looks back at the last few weeks, she can't believe that she's made it through without cheating. It's Friday night, and she's tired and cranky after a long week of working. Her phone buzzes, and she sees a text message inviting her to happy hour. She hesitates because she's been avoiding going out since she quit smoking, but her bad mood and lack of sleep wear her down.

"Just this once," she thinks.

She types back, "I'll be there, but only for a while."

It's a mild summer evening and her group of friends are sitting out on a patio having drinks. Jessica joins them and orders a beer. She feels instant relief. The friends, the cool breeze, and the cold, crisp beer — nice. She hasn't felt this good since three weeks ago, when she had her last cigarette.

Joe, an acquaintance from work, lights up. Jessica didn't know that you could smoke on the bar's patio. She finds herself unthinkingly staring longingly at the glow of the cigarette.

"Do you want one?" Joe asks.

"Um, no, I've quit. But thanks, it looks really good," she says. The elephant part of her mind decides to have some fun and entice her with some thoughts. At the direction of the elephant, she begins thinking, "I've been really good for three weeks, I could have just one tonight and get right back on track. I deserve a reward for getting through some super-tough times. It's a beautiful night, and a cigarette would taste so good. Just one. That's all."

She turns to Joe and says, "Well, maybe just one. That would be great. Thanks." He smiles, gives her a cigarette, and lights it for her. She inhales and relaxes, thinking, "I can't believe how great this feels. Maybe I can stop smoking next month."

After three weeks of struggle, Jessica's elephant mind led her to an eight-month relapse. She tried again successfully, but she knew not to listen to her elephant. She didn't fall for those lies again.

Remember: The elephant is not your friend. He's lying to you because he wants something right now! Stop listening to your elephant and pay attention to the elephant rider.

Appreciating Your Payoffs

The average price of a pack of cigarettes is approaching $7 in the United States. If you're a pack-a-day smoker, by the end of your first month, you've saved about $210. Not bad.

But that amount does not take into account the gas money you spend by having to stop at the store, the costs of frequent cleaning of your clothes, and extra visits to your doctor because of your increased susceptibility to various viruses and ailments. Smokers miss work more often and are less productive. Long term, you save at least double the price of the actual cigarettes, probably much more.

And you can't put a price tag on health. After one month of not smoking, coughing, congestion, fatigue, and shortness of breath will get better. Your sense of taste and smell will begin to return to normal. You're on the way to decreasing your risk of a heart attack, your circulation improves, and you're already getting more air into your lungs. Your physical endurance starts improving — you can walk faster or run longer. Physical withdrawal symptoms largely fade by the end of that first month.

WARNING

All these great physical improvements are something to savor and appreciate. However, don't let them fool you into thinking that urges and cravings won't crop up and try to beguile you. You've made it through the hardest month! Don't drop your guard now. Remain vigilant. You'll be glad you did.

Celebrating the New You

As this first month of nonsmoking goes by, life as a nonsmoker really starts to become new and different. Your world no longer has to revolve around where, when, and how to get your next fix of nicotine. Contrast this new life with your old one by observing other, current smokers.

Watch them gather outside at break time or at someone's wedding and see how they slink off to sneak a smoke outside. Watch them purchasing their cigarettes at the store. Notice the hassle and the money, and remember the smelly clothes and the stinky breath. Notice the disdainful looks nonsmokers give to smokers, vapers, and those chewing tobacco. Remember and feel the ostracism.

Now, it's time for the new you. Embrace the joy of knowing that you're:

>> No longer dependent on finding the right place to indulge your cravings

>> Feeling increased confidence

>> Making the environment better for your loved ones

>> Experiencing a release from the bondage of addiction

>> Feeling proud and accomplished

Let that pride express itself in the way you stand. Walk with greater power and assertiveness. You're a former smoker now! Give yourself two thumbs up! You've met a great challenge head on, and you're winning!

Chapter **18**

Staying the Course for the Next Five Months and Beyond

We're going to assume here that one way or another, you made it through the first month with the help of your personal quit plan (see Chapter 15) and that, if you did slip, you managed to crawl back and get onboard the quit ship again. By now, your body is free of nicotine and the physical withdrawal symptoms are, for the most part, over.

The remaining uneasy feelings of quitting are likely more closely caused by the powerful psychological addiction of smoking. Therefore, in this chapter, we're going to focus on how to deal with the emotional and psychological aspects of addiction.

First, we give you more tools to confront difficult triggers. Then we delve into the concept of willpower — what it is, how it gets depleted, and how to build it up again. We also discuss potentially disruptive emotional issues that could get in your way — specifically, anxiety and depression.

Next, we help you form an exercise plan to fit your lifestyle and boost your mood. We also look at discontinuing nicotine replacement therapy (NRT) over the next few months so that withdrawal symptoms won't disrupt your quit plan. Finally, we suggest that you look back at your reasons for quitting to help solidify your resolve going forward.

As you progress through these months, we recommend rereading your personal quit plan from time to time. Also review your cue cards (see Chapter 16). Repetition may seem a bit silly, but it works. *Remember:* You're learning a new skill.

Boosting Your Plan for Problematic Triggers

During the first month, we strongly suggest that you avoid smoking, vaping, or chewing triggers as much as possible. We recommend that you stay away from people who smoke and avoid the places where you would normally smoke.

Avoidance usually works for a while. However, as the months go by, no matter how hard you try, you're going to run into smoking triggers. Be prepared for using more active coping strategies to successfully get through problematic triggers.

Avoiding avoidance

Now it's time to actively confront what you've been avoiding. Instead of allowing triggers to find you, you go after the triggers with this approach. Start small and pick an activity that you feel you can probably handle with minimal effort. For example, if you switched to tea because coffee sets off smoking urges, you may be able to try a cup of coffee again. Use the strategies in the following sections to prepare. Slowly work up to handling somewhat more powerful triggers. Go slow and easy.

Then again, you may not be quite ready to confront your most problematic triggers. For example, if everyone at the poker game smokes and drinks, that activity may remain outside your comfort zone — the temptation may be insurmountable. Stay away from the poker game if you think you may slip up and smoke.

In fact, a few highly charged situations, like the poker game example, may be best avoided for the rest of your life, or at least until some of the other players quit smoking, too (it's bound to happen). The decision about confronting the worst of the worst triggers ultimately is up to you. By the way, we hear that competitive Scrabble is extremely exciting, and most Scrabble players don't smoke. Okay, Scrabble isn't exactly poker, but you never know — maybe you could learn to love it!

Breathing through urges

Breathing is automatic. You spend your whole life breathing, and yet you probably don't think about it much. Under stress, breathing typically becomes shallow and rapid. Controlled, paced breathing slows things down and reduces tension.

TECHNICAL STUFF

Slow, controlled breathing can slow nerve activity in the sympathetic nervous system, which is aroused under conditions of stress or physical activity. This breathing also increases the influence of the parasympathetic system, which is needed for relaxation.

A good way to get through a craving is to simply pay attention to your breathing. You should practice one or both of these techniques *before* you're experiencing an urge so that the breathing pattern becomes an easy response to a smoking trigger. Focusing on your breathing takes your attention away from your urges.

TIP

If either of the following breathing techniques work especially well for you, consider adding one or both to your personal quit plan.

Urge-busting belly breathing

This breathing technique is a good distraction from triggers because it takes concentration; it's not what you're used to. Follow these steps:

1. **Sit in a chair or lie on the floor.**

2. **Place your hand on your belly slightly below your rib cage.**

3. **Exhale slowly to a count of 5 and tighten your abdominal muscles.**

4. **Pause and hold for a few seconds.**

5. **Now, breathe in fully while expanding your belly and chest.**

6. **Pause and hold for a few seconds.**

7. **Repeat ten times.**

TIP

Make sure you can see if your belly is expanding and contracting while you do this exercise. You may experiment by putting a book on your stomach (if you're lying down) and watching it rise and fall.

Breathing to counteract big bad triggers

Occasionally, you may encounter a very, very strong craving set off by one of your triggers. You really want to smoke, but you've come so far, you really don't want to slip. This breathing technique is for situations like that. Take the following steps:

1. **Inhale through your nose, deeply and slowly to a count of four.**

2. **Hold your breath and count slowly to four again.**

3. **Exhale through your mouth, to a slow count of five.**

4. **While exhaling, make a soft hissing sound.**

    You can make it so quiet that no one around you can hear it.

5. **Repeat until your urge passes.**

REMEMBER

With practice, controlled breathing has been shown to decrease anxiety, reduce blood pressure, and improve mental acuity. Controlled breathing may sound simple, but it has a lot to offer your quitting efforts and more.

Giving yourself a pep talk

Perhaps you've heard of the term *daily affirmations,* in which you're asked to write down a series of brief supportive self-statements focused on your strengths, abilities, and positive outcomes. When we first heard of daily affirmations, they were the subject of Al Franken's Stuart Smalley comedy routine on *Saturday Night Live.* We thought they were as silly as they sounded. The routine went something like "I'm good enough, I'm smart enough, and doggone it, people like me."

However, as time has gone on, there are reasons for thinking that Stuart Smalley was on to something. Such daily affirmations may have value for a range of goals. There isn't strong evidence yet, but why not give them a try? Affirmations are easy to do, don't cost anything, and just may help. Try a few of the following, or make up your own:

>> I'm happy to breathe fresh air.

>> The more I practice, the more in control I can be.

>> I am capable, and I will succeed.

>> Healthy living is my priority.

>> I can do this.

>> I have a lot to look forward to as a nonsmoker.

>> I am proud of my growing willpower.

If you like this idea, write a few affirmations down and include them in your stack of cue cards. Repeat them as often as you like. Can't hurt.

Rehearsing what to do

As you can see, we encourage engagement with your triggers — engagement accompanied by coping actions. One coping strategy is to anticipate a future situation that may trigger an urge for smoking and plan how you're going to handle it before it happens.

PLANNING AHEAD

Since quitting smoking two months ago, Louise, a 35-year pack-a-day smoker, has been avoiding phoning her son who lives out of town. She knows that conversations with her son trigger thoughts and feelings about smoking. Before quitting, she always smoked when she talked to her son on the phone. Now, he's going through a tough time, and she knows she'll likely get stressed while she talks to him. That will certainly trigger her smoking urges.

Sunday is usually the day they talk. She thinks about what will help her get through the call without smoking and decides that having something close by to eat and drink will help. So, she decides to have a cold glass of water with lemon and a few crackers and cheese out before she taps in his number. She'll also talk at the kitchen table instead of her usual place in the living room.

While talking, he brings up that he's having lots of stress related to work. He's worried about hiring a chief financial officer who can help guide the company through an expansion. Louise struggles to control her suddenly surging impulse to smoke. Instead, she puts her hand on her belly and takes several slow measured breaths. She takes a sip of water and pops a cracker into her mouth.

She tries to listen rather than solve his problem, which gives her a chance to do some more controlled breathing. Her son explains that his situation is far from dire and that he has no major worries about his own job security or the viability of the company. As they finish the conversation, Louise proudly tells him that she has quit smoking for good.

By anticipating her problematic trigger before it occurs, Louise resists the temptation to smoke. Her concrete plan with two strategies (controlled breathing and eating a snack) gives her more confidence that she'll be able to keep her commitment to herself and her family to quit smoking.

Think about situations that trigger your smoking urges. Plan to take an action or two to counter the craving. You may want to have something to do with your hands or something like gum to chew on. You could do some breathing techniques, or you may have some coping statements or affirmations. It's not a bad idea to have two or three actions ready to go.

Keeping Your Confidence Level in Check

WARNING

You got through a month smoke-free, but there's a lifetime of quitting to go. Fortunately, in the long run, it's a much-improved life. However, watch out for feeling overconfident. Unrealistic, overly optimistic expectations do many people in during this phase of quitting. You may believe that you've won the battle and start to let down your guard.

Think of confidence as a balloon. Not enough confidence is like a deflated balloon. Pretty useless. Without enough confidence, you're unlikely to gather up the strength to carry on. You need confidence to be able to get through these next months.

The right amount of confidence is like a properly inflated balloon. It's resilient. An inflated balloon can bounce and fly. That amount of confidence will serve you well. You know that you're up to the task of quitting — even though it's hard.

Too much confidence, however, is like an overly inflated balloon — highly vulnerable to popping at the slightest touch. If you're overly confident, you may just burst at the touch of a trigger. That's because your overconfidence has made you feel *invulnerable.* When you start to struggle, overconfidence leads you to feel shocked and surprised. Such inflated expectations could even make you feel you could get away with cheating — just a few puffs or a cigarette or two should be no problem for you!

REMEMBER

So, keep your confidence in check. Of course, you want to feel proud and capable — just not immune to urges, slips, and desires to cheat. Stay the course. You've done great so far, but remain realistic and prepared for more tussles with triggers.

Knowing What to Do When Your Willpower Wanes

Think of willpower (or self-control) as a muscle. You can exercise your willpower regularly and build it up. You can also carelessly deplete it if you don't manage willpower carefully. Willpower becomes exhausted, like a fatigued muscle when you don't get enough sleep or experience excessive stress. Willpower also needs to be fed a healthy, balanced diet to keep working. A hungry, tired body results in weakened willpower.

REMEMBER

Willpower is required to resist temptations like smoking. Willpower helps you manage your emotions and thoughts about almost everything, including smoking cessation. It can also focus your energy on seeing an arduous task to completion, such as the gargantuan undertaking of giving up an addiction.

Also, realize that people tend to run low on willpower at certain times of the day. Late mornings and late afternoons are especially problematic because the body's glucose levels tend to be at a low ebb as the length of time since eating increases. Therefore, gird yourself for those times and be prepared to deal with increased urges. Consider a small snack at those times as well.

TIP

In other words, it's important to respect willpower. Everyone has some, and no one has it in unlimited amounts. Because it's not unlimited, you must decide to manage or parcel out your willpower throughout your day.

Recharging willpower

TIP

If you habitually run out of willpower when you need it, there are a few things you can do to rebuild your willpower muscles. The following suggestions will help you maximize your willpower reserves:

>> **Don't do everything at once.** If you're quitting smoking, don't go on a difficult diet regimen at the same time — save that for later.

>> **Make sure you give yourself enough time for sleep.** A tired body is a willpower-depleted body. (See Chapter 17 for ideas.)

>> **Eat small, healthy meals and healthy snacks throughout your day.** Your body's glucose supply provides fuel for your willpower reserves. Keep those levels as even as you can.

>> **Start making regular use of to-do lists.** These take important tasks off of your mind — what psychologists call *decreasing cognitive load.* When tasks are put on paper, you no longer have to spend so much time worrying about them.

>> **Organize your work and personal spaces.** Studies have shown that self-control or willpower *increase when clutter decreases.* Good organization wastes less time and takes less brain power to manage. If you're a flat-out terrible organizer, ask a friend for help or hire a professional organizer. Work hard to keep it up — it will cost you far less in the long run if you do.

>> **Keep track of your success.** Count how many cigarettes you didn't smoke each day and tabulate how much you're saving. Even if you slip up, you'll be able to see the progress you've made and feel inspired to get back on track.

>> **Take time to relax and have fun.** Watch a comedy show, go for a short hike in a park, take up a hobby, or stroll outside on a nice day. Recharge your batteries frequently.

Rewarding willpower

You can also increase your willpower reserves by rewarding yourself regularly for exerting good self-control. You don't want willpower to be a drudgery in which you constantly deny yourself. Willpower needs to be rewarded for a job well done, just like you do.

TIP

Steadily reward your willpower for achieving smoke-free days. Then plan for larger rewards for smoke-free weeks and, finally, months. Have a party after a smoke-free year. Don't be cheap! You're saving a fortune in the long run, not to mention saving your life.

Recognizing Problematic Emotions

Some smokers who want to quit have a history of emotional difficulties such as anxiety or depression. These problems may worsen with the additional stress of quitting. That doesn't mean you shouldn't try to quit! But it does mean that you have something extra to attend to.

TIP

In the long run, quitting smoking will improve your mental health.

Other smokers have no history of anxiety or depression, but they acquire one or both problems when they try to quit. It's kind of like a side effect of quitting for them.

Studies tell us that if you have a problem with anxiety or depression when you're trying to quit smoking, your risk of relapse rises. That's why, in the next two sections, we provide you an overview of what anxiety and depression look like so you can recognize them. Then we give you an idea of what sorts of treatments are available to help with these problems.

All human beings experience anxiety or depressed feelings now and again. That's completely normal. What makes these disorders problematic is when they reach the level that they persistently interfere significantly with your day-to-day living (at work, home, and play).

Analyzing anxiety

Many people report that smoking, vaping nicotine, or chewing tobacco, relaxes them. So, when they feel tense or anxious, they indulge and feel better. And most people who quit smoking feel increased tension, stress, and anxiety, at least for some period of time after quitting. That's because nicotine withdrawal increases anxiety in the short run. Those feelings are normal and usually improve over the first couple of months of quitting.

But, for some, anxiety lingers and interferes with sustained smoking cessation success. Not only can anxiety mess up your quitting efforts, but it can also get in the way of daily life. If that happens to you, it's entirely possible that you're suffering from an anxiety disorder. About one in four people experience a full-blown anxiety disorder at one point or another in their lives.

There are various types of anxiety disorders. In this section, we cover some of the most common along with a brief description.

These brief descriptions of anxiety disorders are not intended for you to diagnose yourself. However, if you think you may suffer from one or more of these problems, start by seeing your primary care doctor who may recommend that you see a psychologist, psychiatrist, counselor, or social worker.

Review the following list of anxiety problems to see if you think any may apply to you:

» **Generalized anxiety disorder (GAD):** GAD is considered the common cold of anxiety. It's characterized by excessive worry and apprehension that interferes with your life. It occurs more days than not. People with GAD have problems concentrating, feel restless, and on edge.

» **Social anxiety disorder:** People with social anxiety disorder are fearful about rejection and negative evaluations from other people. They may avoid social situations, even when those situations may be important. Former smokers often report that social anxiety increases when they're unable to reach for a cigarette.

>> **Panic disorder:** Panic disorder involves an eruption of intense, unexpected fear and discomfort. This fear and discomfort frequently involves a pounding heart, shortness of breath, chest pain, dizziness, and other symptoms that mimic a heart attack. People with panic attacks should work closely with their physician and therapist to learn how to manage their symptoms without making excessive, unnecessary trips to the emergency room. The good news is that panic attacks are highly treatable.

>> **Agoraphobia:** Agoraphobia is characterized by intense fear or anxiety about situations that involve being in open spaces, being trapped in places with no easy exit (theaters, shops, and so on), being in crowds, and having to be outside the home. Frequently these people fear not being able to escape, being embarrassed, or being unable to find help. Panic disorder often accompanies agoraphobia.

>> **Specific phobias:** These involve extreme fear or anxiety about an object or situation such as flying, traffic, seeing blood, snakes, spiders, heights, or certain diseases. People with phobias go to great lengths to avoid coming into contact with their feared object or situation. Their fear is way out of proportion to the actual danger.

If you think that you may have one or more of these problems with anxiety, refer to the section "Treating anxiety and depression," later in this chapter.

Detecting depression

Depression disorders, like those of anxiety, come in a variety of categories. But these different types are more difficult to sort through for the average layperson. What really matters to you are the symptoms of depression in general. These symptoms include the following feelings:

>> Sadness

>> Emptiness

>> Hopelessness

>> Worthlessness

>> Lack of purpose

>> Inability to feel pleasure

In addition, depression may be in play if you

>> Have a sudden, unexplained weight loss or gain

>> Have trouble sleeping too little or too much

- » Feel very agitated
- » Have a lack of energy
- » Have unwarranted guilt
- » Experience changes in appetite
- » Have problems thinking and concentrating
- » Experience lowered interest in pleasurable activities
- » Have recurrent thoughts of death

WARNING

If you have any suspicion that you could be depressed, especially if you have thoughts of suicide, please seek help immediately. Call 911 or the national suicide prevention lifeline at 800-273-8255. Depression can be a serious, deadly disorder. Fortunately, it's also treatable.

Treating anxiety and depression

Your odds of succeeding at smoking cessation are greatly enhanced if you get help for your anxiety and/or depression. These disorders are highly treatable, often without medications.

There are two major treatment types to inquire about. These are the most heavily researched and supportable as effective at this time. Other therapies may also be beneficial, but not as common and widely available. If you're offered a different type of therapy, ask what the evidence says about its efficacy. You're far better off in most cases to seek empirically supported treatments.

The two approaches we suggest you inquire about are

- » **Cognitive behavioral therapy (CBT):** CBT involves teaching you new ways of thinking about events, which, in turn, usually improves how you feel and lifts your moods. It also entails changing behaviors in a systematic way. CBT has been widely studied and supported as highly effective in treating both anxiety and depression. (Chapter 10 is largely based on CBT principles and strategies, both in terms of thinking and behaving.)

- » **Medications:** Some medications have been studied and found to be effective in treating both anxiety and depression. We usually recommend trying CBT first because it will teach you lifelong skills that can help prevent relapse. If you choose to try medication first, consider seeking therapy at the same time. Talk to your healthcare provider. (Chapter 9 covers medications designed to help specifically with smoking cessation efforts.)

Quitting smoking increases stress for most people. Increased stress can lead to a greater susceptibility to emotional problems such as anxiety and/or depression. Don't ignore an uptick in difficult emotions. Early treatment works better and more quickly. Ignoring difficult feelings could lead to a relapse. You have too much to lose. For more help and information consider reading *Overcoming Anxiety For Dummies* or *Depression For Dummies*, both complements of yours truly (and published by Wiley).

Pumping Up Exercise

During your first weeks of quitting smoking, we encourage you to, well, baby yourself. Basically, do whatever you need, whether it's eating a bit too much, binge-watching television, or getting daily massages, just get through this time without smoking, vaping, or chewing.

But now, as the strongest urges and cravings pass, it's time to get moving. You know the benefits of exercise, but just in case you don't, read Chapter 3, which summarizes them for you. With smoking cessation, exercise improves your health, gives you a nice strategy for battling urges, and helps keep your weight under control (see Chapter 20 for more information about controlling weight when stopping smoking).

The key is to start slowly. Respect that your willpower reserves are limited. Begin with a short, ten-minute walking routine. Gradually increase the duration and pace of your walks. If you watch TV, get up during commercials and walk around your living room. We highly recommend getting an activity tracker to give you feedback on how you're doing — they're amazingly motivating.

TIP

Consider surveying all your exercise options to find a type you especially enjoy — including walks, weight lifting, yoga, dance classes, aerobic classes, or running. Find a partner to team up with if you can.

Looking Forward to Fading Nicotine Replacement Therapy

Too many people quit NRT prematurely. Most people should stay on NRT for 12 weeks or more. As your urges decrease, simply decrease your use of NRT very gradually. If urges increase with decreased NRT, consider upping your dose of NRT for a while. (See Chapter 9 for more information about NRT and medications.)

Although NRT has been established as a safe and effective way to increase smoking cessation success, many people don't use it correctly, thereby decreasing its effectiveness. People have erroneous beliefs and worries about NRT, including the following:

>> **I don't want to get addicted to NRT — what's the point?** Studies tell us that NRT is much less addictive than smoking, for a variety of reasons, and it's easier to discontinue, too.

>> **It's just not working for me — I still have urges.** You may be taking too little NRT; many people do. Consult with your physician about dosage possibilities but realize that most people can take fairly high doses of NRT without excessive side effects. You can probably add an additional piece of gum or two or even another patch. You also may be relying too heavily on NRT for your quit plan. Strongly consider turning to your support system and reviewing your quit plan for strategies that you haven't used enough. If you continue to struggle, consider adding an additional medication, such as varenicline or bupropion.

>> **The side effects are too uncomfortable.** Side effects from NRT usually soften with time. If your sleep is impaired, consider removing the patch at night. Take care to slightly reduce your use of oral products. Are you greatly exceeding the recommended doses? If so, pull back a bit. Sometimes people chew the gum too forcefully and long; if that's you, be sure to follow instructions that come with gum and lozenges. You can also consider changing brands of NRT; that seems to help some people who experience side effects.

>> **I prefer to do things without help from chemicals.** Well, that sounds okay. But you need to appreciate that nicotine is a chemical, and most forms of smoking tobacco contain nicotine and upwards of thousands of other chemicals. Even vaping comes along with flavorings and sometimes unknown additives that may cause yet-to-be determined amounts of harm.

>> **It costs too much.** We hate to say it, but there's some intense rationalization going on here. As costly as NRT is, it's more affordable than cigarettes, especially over the long term. However, you can get help with the finances by calling 800-QUIT-NOW (800-784-8669), which can sometimes refer you to sources of subsidized help for purchasing NRT. In addition, generic brands from big box stores or drugstores are another option. Many insurance plans will cover NRT with a prescription. Some states also provide free NRT through Medicaid or the health department.

>> **I caved and smoked a cigarette, so I stopped my NRT.** You can still use NRT after a lapse. In fact, keeping up NRT may help you keep your lapse from becoming a relapse (see Chapter 19 for more information about lapses and relapses).

>> **I'll never get off it if I start.** Even in the very unlikely event that you never get off NRT, your health will improve greatly as compared to what it would be if you continue to consume tobacco.

>> **I read that you should stop at 12 weeks and that's now.** Use NRT until you're able to handle smoking triggers without intense cravings. Many people continue to use gum or lozenges for urges long after the recommended 12 weeks. If you're concerned, ask your doctor for advice.

TECHNICAL STUFF

You may wonder why NRT works. A small part of the equation is that NRT literally replaces some of the nicotine you were addicted to. But it's not trading one addiction for another. We've already covered the greater safety profile of NRT, but there's more. NRT also helps your brain disconnect the associations it has formed between various actions and events and smoking — things that trigger smoking like a cup of coffee, a beer, driving, you know the story. The nicotine is already in your system when you confront these situations. Over time, your brain disconnects the association of smoking with those events. It takes a while for this disconnection to happen, though, so give it time. Don't discontinue prematurely.

Staying Vigilant Beyond Six Months

After six months of not consuming tobacco, you have every right to feel you've overcome your addiction. Good for you! Unfortunately, that's not quite the case for many people. Studies tell us that the risk of relapse lingers on past a year for some. In fact, the potential for relapse never completely disappears.

That's not cause for terrible concern, however. It's not as though cravings continue to feel frequent and intense. It's just that it's easy to let down your guard. When you do that, your risk of relapse shoots up.

No one knows for sure how to prevent such long-term relapses, but we have a few thoughts on the subject. See Chapter 19 for information on bouncing back from relapse. And for building personal reserves, see Chapters 21 and 22 for strategies we believe you may find helpful over time. Meanwhile, keep up the fight! Good luck!

Chapter 19

Recovering from Lapses and Relapses

With a good bit of luck, you'll be able to skip this chapter. That's assuming you manage to quit smoking, vaping, or chewing and never slip up. You succeed at quitting and never look back.

But we're realists. The truth of the matter is, most quitters slip and slide a bit along the way. How you deal with those slips makes all the difference in the world. One way to deal with your slip is to transform it into a temporary lapse. After that short lapse, you get right back on the path to quitting and recovery.

WARNING

Too many times, a lapse evolves into a relapse. That's the danger of lapsing. One puff quickly causes urges and cravings to surge and, suddenly, you're smoking again.

In this chapter, we help you deal with possible lapses and give you the tools for preventing the slip from sliding into a full-blown relapse. But, if a relapse occurs despite your efforts, we show you how to recover and move on from that and get back to quitting again.

Deciding to Lapse

Lapses are shorter and less serious than full-blown relapses. Knowing the subtle differences between these two concepts helps quitters quickly get back on track. A *lapse* may involve taking a few puffs off someone else's cigarette or vape pen, or even bumming a couple of smokes at a party. By contrast, a *relapse* occurs when the smoking behavior returns to a regular pattern similar (but often somewhat decreased at first) to the pattern that existed prior to the quit attempt.

Lapses often occur in situations in which you've unexpectedly or inadvertently lost focus and dropped your guard. Quitting smoking is not in the front part of your brain for some reason. Lapses often occur when you're around other smokers or when drugs or alcohol decrease your inhibitions. Another lapse-triggering situation is when you experience an uptick in strong emotions such as joy or despair. The emotions distract you from the rational part of your mind and — *voilà!* — a lapse occurs.

REMEMBER

Much as this description sounds like something overtakes you in an automatic, unconscious way, it's also important to realize that all lapses actually involve *decisions.* You're only fooling yourself by having thoughts like the following:

>> I couldn't help it.

>> I did the only thing I could.

>> I did what anyone would've done.

The truth is, you made a quick calculus of your situation and decided it would be acceptable to smoke. At that point, you're not considering the alternative and the implications of your choice. Understandable to be sure. But it helps to realize it's always a *willful, active, conscious* decision to smoke. That's because viewing lapses as conscious decisions helps you recognize that you have more control in these situations than you think you do.

TIP

If you feel a sudden, quick urge or craving to smoke, grab hold of yourself and pause the process. Ask yourself if this is the decision that you truly want to make. If you do decide to go ahead and indulge, at least you know you controlled that decision. That makes you realize that you can control other situations by deciding *not* to cave into your urges.

TIP

If you lapse, consider what circumstance set things off. Whether it was a stressful event, a party, or something else from your trigger list, take note of it. Decide how to manage the trigger in a better way the next time it happens. Review what has worked for you to manage that trigger successfully in the past.

REMEMBER

In the future, instead of automatically giving in to an unexpected trigger, remember to hit the pause button. Think, think, think.

Profiting from a Lapse

Now you know what a lapse is and its more serious cousin, a relapse. Although lapses and relapses happen, they aren't desirable. But, as they say, you can always make lemonade from lemons. In other words, use lapses or relapses as opportunities to improve your coping skills.

Two lessons you can learn from a lapse are how to deal with rationalizations and how to dispute common faulty myths about smoking urges. Rationalizations give you permission to lapse in response to specific situations. Myths are more general beliefs about the nature of urges.

Rationalizations and myths are both dangerous and set the stage for lapsing and relapsing. By disputing them and using logic and rational thinking, you can regain momentum for your quit efforts.

Rationalizing and excuse making

Lapses involve rationalizations that move you toward saying yes to a temptation. Your thoughts try to justify a brief lapse. If you've had a lapse by now, you no doubt contended with one or more of these rationalizations, whether you thought about it or not.

The following rationalizations are common excuses for a lapse. When you believe these rationalizations, they lead to more lapses that will undoubtedly lead you to a relapse. Then you must start over. Instead, use your logical mind to answer your rationalizations.

Next, we give you some samples to consider, accompanied by a logical, rational perspective for each. Feel free to think of additional rational thoughts you can use to counter your most common rationalizations. When you come up with your own rational thoughts in response to a smoking trigger, write them on paper or a device.

>> **I couldn't say no when my friend offered me a vape.** The truth is, you can tell your friend, "No, thanks." It's not like you're obligated to do everything a friend asks you to do. If you were horribly allergic to peanuts and your friend offered you a peanut butter cookie, would you eat it? Try explaining that you're working hard to quit vaping and you want to keep with your game plan.

If your friend pushes you, stick to your guns. You don't want your life to be dictated by peer pressure, do you? The point is to take charge of your own life — don't be obligated to substances or other people.

>> **I just wanted to feel good for a little while; I've given up so much.** Yes, you *have* given up a lot. It's natural to want to feel good for a while. The problem with this sort of thinking is that short, temporary pleasure will come to an end. You'll be left feeling guilty and having increased urges and cravings.

What are some other things you could do to feel good? How about watching a movie, taking a long hike, or eating an ice cream cone? Experiment and find out what works for you.

>> **It was my birthday (or other celebration).** Yes, and, in a sense, you do "deserve" a cigarette on special occasions. But is that truly what will make you feel better? Will it only be just one? Will your cravings go up or down after a lapse like this? You know the answers. You're going to experience stronger urges. You're only kidding yourself with this justification.

Celebrations of all sorts feel like times to indulge. But if you do, you're likely to feel worse. On the other hand, if you don't give in, you have even more to celebrate! Another success.

>> **It was a horrible day.** True. No one is going to deny that you have horrible days from time to time (we all do). The more horrible the day, the more you want to indulge.

Think carefully about where that goes. How will you feel if you cap off that horrible day with cheating? And now, think how you'll feel if you end the day with a success.

>> **I got sick.** Sorry to hear you came down with something. There's no time like being sick that makes you want to find comfort however you can. That desire

goes back to when you were a kid. It's a tough habit to break. But one of the main reasons you're quitting is to get healthy and not be sick so often. Adding more toxins to your already sick body doesn't really work out too well, does it?

>> **I was involved in an accident.** Gosh, that's horrible. Accidents can really shake a person up. And when you're shook up, it's so tempting to turn to your old friend — tobacco. It calms you down. Gives you something else to focus on. We get it. But instead of reaching for a smoke, try some deep breathing or even that emergency stash of NRT gum you keep around.

>> **The traffic this morning was unbearable; I couldn't take it.** Yes, heavy traffic can send the strongest people over the edge. Sometimes it feels like you're navigating a minefield with explosions ready to go off without warning. Have you ever managed to get through a stressful time without lighting up or vaping? How did you do that?

Remember that you've learned a few tricks on how to manage cravings already, such as calling a friend or chewing a piece of gum. And by the way, caving to temptation won't make the traffic go away.

>> **I found an old cigarette in my drawer at work; how could I not smoke it?** Sure. How do you pass up something free that's right in front of your face? It would only be one after all.

Are you having thoughts like these? Once again, how will you feel later? Better about yourself and with fewer cravings or just the opposite? You know the answer. Take that cigarette and squash it as hard as you can. Toss it in the garbage can. Then pat yourself on the back.

When you're dealing with rationalizations like these, recognize that they truly are illogical. The rationalizations are just trying to clear the path for you to return to your old behaviors. You've been working hard to quit. Don't let rationalizations derail your efforts. Use them productively instead. Listen for rationalizations and prepare to use logical answers to refute them.

TIP

You have enough willpower to quit successfully. You have the skills to work through urges. If you want more information on how to manage willpower, see Chapter 18.

Rethinking myths about urges

Many people believe faulty myths about their own ability to withstand the inevitable frustration of quitting smoking. These myths can make it easier to lapse and then, when the frustration increases, relapse. Therefore, it's important to explore the deeply flawed ways of thinking about urges and rigorously dispute them. Then you'll want to replace these myths with rational, reasonable perspectives.

>> **Urges are unbearable — I can't stand it.** Humans love to say they can't stand things that they really can. You've handled numerous urges in the past. For example, we're pretty sure you don't eat every dessert you're offered. You also don't hit everyone you're mad at (we hope). And you've given up your addiction at least for a while. And you're still alive — evidence says you did and can stand it, unpleasant though it may be. Besides, most serious cravings don't last for more than a few minutes.

>> **I must use when I have an urge.** Obviously, this belief also belies reality. Can you imagine a world in which everyone acted on every urge and the resulting chaos that would ensue? People routinely running red lights, having sex with anyone they found attractive, eating and drinking with abandon . . . you get the idea. Living in a civilized society requires a reasonable amount of self-control. You have more than you think.

>> **Unsatisfied urges are the worst thing anyone ever has to deal with.** In reality, as hard as it is, there are many more exquisitely difficult challenges to deal with compared to holding off urges. Think about what it's like to deal with the unexpected loss of a loved one, serious chronic pain, or the loss of a home to a natural disaster. The next time you think how horrible your urge is, consider comparing it to some of life's truly difficult challenges.

>> **The urge will never go away unless I cave into it.** The urge will go away whether you cave into it or not. Next time you think an urge will never go away, try rating its severity on a scale from 1 to 10 every 30 minutes. You're likely to see significant variability and, eventually, a big reduction if you resist it.

>> **I don't have enough willpower to deal with my urges.** As discussed in Chapter 18, willpower is much like a muscle. You can gradually strengthen your reserves if you routinely work out. That means the more you successfully use your willpower, the stronger it will get.

Challenging myths about urges and rationalizations help you stand up to lapses or the inevitable temptations following a lapse. The good news is that lapses do not always lead to relapses. That doesn't make them okay — it's the extremely rare person who can occasionally lapse, smoke a few cigarettes once in a while, and not eventually relapse.

REMEMBER

Most people who lapse struggle with increased urges for a while. That's how addictions work. If you're one of those extremely rare people who can indulge now and then, you probably wouldn't have become addicted in the first place. However, we don't recommend giving into urges in order to determine if you're one of those rare folks who can get away with occasional lapses.

Realizing When a Lapse Is a Relapse

Alas, sometimes, despite your best efforts, lapses, indeed, turn into relapses. You lapsed, cheated once, then started to use more — the beginning of a relapse. So, is there a way to determine whether you can quickly climb out of that emerging relapse and return to your quit plan?

We have two concepts to consider in the following sections. The first one, drifting, involves catching subtle changes in your quitting action plan. The second concept shows you how to snuff out smoke before it bursts into flames.

Drifting from a lapse into a relapse

Your personal quit plan (see Chapter 15) probably has a series of activities that you use to avoid triggers and fill up your time without smoking or using. Your plan may have included increasing healthy activities such as exercising, exploring new types of recreation, relaxing regularly, spending time with a support group (online or in person), or engaging in social activities that don't involve smoking.

Frequently, it's those activities designed to support change that begin to fade away before lapsing turns into a habit itself. This tendency to lose focus on activities that you put into place to help support your quit plan can be called *drifting.*

Drifting starts slowly. You may find looking at your quit-smoking app less interesting and start ignoring it. Or you may find more reasons not to go to the gym — like all that annoying traffic, you need the time for other things, or you just don't feel like it.

Excuses pile up and you end up having more time on your hands. What better way to deal with that time than by smoking just for tonight? Then, tomorrow, you say yes to an invitation to happy hour, which you know will involve your former smoking friends. You're drifting into a relapse.

REMEMBER

You can catch the lapse turning into relapse cycle if you pay attention to drifting. It's the loss of quit-supporting activities that serves as your best warning sign. Review your quit plan regularly. Don't forget that quitting requires vigilance for many months and sometimes years. You'll be glad you did.

Just because there's smoke, doesn't always mean there's fire

Even after months of quitting, former smokers are at risk for relapse. A brief lapse is usually what precedes a relapse. The smoker who lapses feels guilt, self-doubt, and a reduced sense of confidence. Those feelings can lead the lapsed smoker into the jaws of relapse. That happens because the smoker has the belief that he messed up and might as well forget the whole thing and go back to smoking.

TECHNICAL STUFF

Psychologists love coming up with names for phenomena that mean something to them, but hardly anyone else. In the addictions field, they created what they call the abstinence violation effect (AVE). What does that mean anyway? We prefer to call it the "I blew it effect." The "I blew it effect" takes what could be a learning opportunity and turns it into a self-fulfilling prophecy; in other words, it becomes true because you think it will. A few thoughts indicative of an "I blew it effect" include the following:

>> I might as well keep on smoking because I've already cheated.

>> I blew it this morning, so I might as well consider this a relapse day.

>> This failure means I don't have the willpower to quit.

>> It's horrible to cheat; I can't do this.

So, if you find yourself ensnared in the clutches of an "I blew it effect," it's important to view a lapse merely as a mistake, a mistake to be learned from. It's not a good reason to give up. And it doesn't mean that you're a failure. Instead, lapses make you human. So, instead of considering a lapse an "I blew it effect," think about it as an unwanted experience to grow from. Ask yourself the following questions if you have a lapse and begin to think of it as an "I blew it effect":

>> What can this lapse teach me?

>> What new coping strategies can I bring into play?

>> How will I react differently if I happen to have another lapse?

>> What's a better way to respond to the trigger that caused my lapse?

Many people fall prey to the "I blew it" effect, but few realize that it's happening at the time. Jack's story (see the nearby sidebar) illustrates what commonly happens and how to change an "I blew it effect" into an opportunity for strengthening resolve.

FOCUSING ON PROGRESS, NOT PERFECTION

EXAMPLE

Jack started vaping when he tried to quit smoking cigarettes. He knows vaping is probably healthier than smoking, but too much of his world is revolving around vaping. He actually vapes quite a bit more frequently than he smoked. He realizes that he's totally addicted to the high levels of nicotine in his device. He decides to stop vaping and goes cold turkey. His cravings and urges surge to incredibly high levels for a week.

Jack is miserable, cranky, and can't focus. His work suffers some, and he forgets to finish a report that was due. His boss gets on his case about it. Jack can't take it; he gives into his craving and vapes. Then he says to himself, "I blew it. I don't have the willpower to quit. I'll vape this weekend and take another shot at it on Monday."

Monday arrives, and he has no desire to quit at all. His lapse has quickly morphed into a relapse. Several weeks later, Jack talks to his counselor, who explains the abstinence violation effect (which we call the "I blew it effect"). His counselor helps Jack figure out how to move forward without allowing the situation to derail his quitting effort.

After talking more about quitting techniques, Jack decides to give quitting another try. This time, he plans to include NRT on his personal quit plan to help him with his urges. He also understands that he needs to pay more attention to the triggers that have, in the past, led him back to using nicotine.

He decides to let his boss know about his new quit plan and hopes that he can be a bit more patient for a few weeks. His boss enthusiastically agrees. Jack appreciates the fact that he's just like everyone else and can learn from a lapse rather than call himself a failure.

Jack made a mistake and gave in to an urge. That's perfectly understandable. He's quite capable of evaluating his mistake and adjusting his course of action. This adjustment involved taking another look at his earlier quit attempt and realizing that he needed a more sophisticated plan that included help for his nicotine addiction.

Moving on from a Relapse

The good news about starting a fresh new attempt at quitting after a relapse is that you already have skills and strategies from your previous quit attempts that you can use again. But this time, you know what worked and what didn't. Go back to your personal quit plan and tune it up based on that knowledge.

REMEMBER

It's totally unhelpful to dwell on your relapse. Don't engage in self-abuse or criticism. Like millions of smokers, you had a slip-up. And like millions of smokers, you can try again. Maybe this time you'll be successful. Meanwhile, remember that every cigarette that you didn't smoke during the time you quit is a healthy victory.

Your odds of success do nothing but increase if you let the relapse instruct you. Table 19-1 gives you some examples of how your relapses can lead to specific changes in your personal quit plan for the next quit. Review our sample examples, and then do your own.

In the first column, jot down your best ideas for what may have caused you to relapse. Anything at all qualifies, including motivational issues, symptoms you found problematic, and triggers. In the second column, put down changes to your personal quit plan that could address these problematic issues. (See Chapter 15 for ideas to include in your plan.)

TABLE 19-1   **Learning from Relapses**

Reason for Relapse	Changes to Your Quit Plan
Intense restlessness, poor focus, headache from nicotine withdrawal.	Consider adding NRT or increasing your dose.
Running into unanticipated triggers and now knowing what to do.	Ask your support team for ideas about other possible triggers you haven't thought of. Add these new triggers to your plan and come up with strategies to deal with them, such as breathing techniques, rehearsal, or avoiding them.
Talking yourself into caving in.	See Chapter 10 for examples on challenging irrational thinking.
Finding your motivation diminishing.	Conduct a cost–benefit analysis of smoking (see Chapter 8). Note the importance of the costs and the benefits more than the actual number of each. If the costs outweigh the benefits, consider beefing up your personal quit plan, especially your plan for rewarding yourself for not smoking.
Feeling overwhelmed by strong emotions like anxiety or sadness.	You may need more help from a mental health professional. See Chapter 18 for information about anxiety and depression and treatment.
Noticing a weight gain of 9 pounds in three weeks.	Review your reasons for quitting. Consider adding strategies for exercising more and gaining control over diet and eating. Appreciate that you're in this for your long-term health, and the weight gain can be mostly a short-term issue. See Chapter 20 for ideas on controlling weight issues.

Consider this exercise as a foundational piece of your recovery. After you figure out what went wrong, consider what went right; in other words, decide what strategies you want to retain or strengthen.

Getting Some Final Tools for Battling Lapses and Relapses

Earlier in this chapter, in the "Deciding to Lapse" section, we discuss the fact that lapses (and the relapses they too often lead to) are active, conscious decisions. As much as you'd like to blame something or someone else, the ultimate responsibility of lapsing resides within you — not that we're recommending harsh self-criticism (everyone makes mistakes), but taking ownership of mistakes gives you more control to fight off impulses.

The following questions may help you pause and make better, more rational decisions. Consider writing them on a card or in an app on your phone and carrying them around. Take a look and answer them before you decide to cheat or lapse. Again, the goal is to make your decisions more considered, conscious, and deliberative.

>> How will this decision affect me in good or bad ways?

>> If I decide to take this short-lived few minutes of pleasure, what's the long-range future effect on my health?

>> Will this brief pleasure justify the feelings I'll have later?

>> How will I feel about this in a few hours? Tomorrow? Next week?

>> Will this transgression interfere with my long-term life goals? If so, how?

>> How long will it take for me to feel bad about this decision if I decide to vape or smoke?

TIP

The temptation of smoking is extremely difficult to resist. The war can be won, but you may lose some battles along the way. Be strong. Fight. Be smart. Win by owning your decisions. Start today!

5

Living after Smoking

Chapter **20**

Dealing with Weight Gain

Lots of smokers say they smoke to keep off weight. Nicotine increases metabolism and helps burn more calories. In fact, for most people, the increased metabolism due to nicotine burns about 200 extra calories a day. That's the equivalent of a glazed donut every day. Smoking also decreases appetite and provides something to do with your hands and mouth that doesn't involve eating food. Thus, current smokers weigh about ten pounds less than nonsmokers.

Those who quit smoking generally gain up to ten pounds, mostly in the first six months. This gain varies, and smokers who start out either underweight or overweight tend to gain the most. People who quit smoking often reward themselves with a bit of extra food. We endorse that. Go for it, that is, for the first couple of months after quitting. After that, it's time to turn your attention to healthy eating.

REMEMBER

Don't lose sight of the fact that smoking is absolutely more harmful to your health than carrying around some extra weight. At the same time, in the interest of honesty, you should know that weight gain following smoking cessation does erode some of the health benefits of quitting.

In this chapter, we help you consider your priorities and set realistic goals regarding weight gain associated with smoking cessation. We stress the importance of monitoring what you eat. Then we lay out a plan for how to rethink your relationship with food and food cravings. Next, we give you some basic tips on nutrition. Finally, we discuss how to boost your metabolism and maintain your motivation.

Prioritizing Health First and Setting Realistic Goals

This book's priority is to help you quit smoking first and foremost. Hopefully, you're reading this chapter because you've accomplished that goal. Now, you're appropriately concerned about putting on too many pounds. We're glad you're here.

You probably already know how to lose weight: Eat less and exercise more. If it were that easy, there wouldn't be a multi-billion-dollar weight-loss industry, and everyone would fit into their skinny jeans.

Start by making a commitment to lose weight. Decide how much you want to lose, but don't get excessively ambitious here. Don't consult a chart of your "ideal" weight and make that your goal if you've never been close to that your entire life. Consider changes as small as 5 percent of your body weight — losing that amount can improve your health significantly.

After you've decided on your goal, give it plenty of time and go slow. Don't go on a starvation diet — they sometimes work for a short spurt, but rarely over the long haul. That's because starvation diets actually slow down your metabolism so you burn less calories. Most people should not attempt to lose more than a pound or two a week, and a little less can be a reasonable goal as well.

REMEMBER

If your new eating plan stalls, vow to stay away from smoking or vaping. You've already proven that you've got what it takes to do something quite difficult. But just as quitting smoking often takes people multiple attempts, the same goes for adjusting entrenched eating patterns. Keep at it, try new things, and don't give up.

Keeping Track of What You Eat

Monitoring your intake of the foods you eat and your weight doubles your chances of successful weight loss. That means that you create a food journal and write down what and how much you eat of everything. We mean *everything*. If you cheat and don't write down a few items, you're only cheating yourself.

Keeping track of food intake alone helps you lose weight — without even trying to reduce calories. But it helps only if you're totally honest. That means every piece of chocolate, every drop of soda, and every stick of gum. The reason that monitoring works is that people do less *mindless* eating when they realize that they must write down every bite.

 You probably want to monitor a few other things like body measurements, weight, and amount of exercise. Weigh yourself every day at the same time. Remember that a few fluctuations will occur due to water retention and other variables, but it's the trend that matters over time.

 Start monitoring before you change your eating habits. You can take your time before implementing a calorie-cutting plan. But there's every reason to start monitoring right away. Tracking sets the stage for everything else, and it subtly starts changes in eating all by itself.

 If you also choose to calculate your caloric intake, there are apps for helping you make that task less of a chore than it used to be. Those apps also include strategies for keeping a food diary.

 If you engage in what's known as *binge eating,* you'll have a lower chance of success with quitting smoking, as well as managing your weight. If you frequently eat especially large quantities of food to the point of distress and shame, this problem may apply to you. We suggest you consult with your primary care physician or a mental health professional about the possibility of a binge-eating disorder.

Rethinking Food and Dieting

The change strategies throughout this book are based on cognitive behavioral therapy (CBT). That holds for our approach to food and eating as well. An especially important component of CBT involves helping people understand that the way they think about things greatly affects how they feel and react.

In this case, the way you think about triggers for food cravings affects how you'll respond to them. You have many choices for the ways you respond; this approach nudges you to consider alternative thoughts and behaviors. Distorted thinking about food quickly leads to making poor, self-defeating choices.

 Distorted thinking is the mind's way of trying to get what it wants by convincing you to take a path that's based on emotions, inaccurate perceptions, and short-term desires over reason, logic, and what's best for you. Most people have a long habit of basing their responses and actions on such distorted thinking. When you're aware that many of your thoughts are distorted, you have the option of changing your thoughts, and your actions will follow.

Table 20-1 displays ten particularly common distorted thoughts about food and weight management followed by more rational, logical, and evidence-based thoughts. Consider writing down any of these distorted thoughts that resonate with you along with their more rational responses on a 3-x-5 card to carry around with you. Read them over whenever you hear them in your head.

TABLE 20-1   **Ten Distorted Tempting Thoughts and Rational Alternatives**

Distorted Tempting Food Thought	Rational Alternative Thought
I ate a donut, so I've blown it and I might as well eat whatever I want today.	I ate a donut, that's all. That doesn't mean I have to double down and blow the whole day.
I've never succeeded at dieting. Why would this be any different now?	I never succeeded at quitting smoking until now. So, I guess you're never too late to learn something new.
I'm overwhelmed. I'll eat now and deal with the consequences later.	Yes, I'm feeling overwhelmed, and I'll feel even worse if I eat. I'll try a walk instead.
It's my birthday, and I can eat whatever I want to.	Sure, it's my birthday. My gift to myself will be to have a small slice of cake and stick to my plan for the rest of the day.
I can't go on a vacation. I always gain weight because I always overeat.	Yes, I usually overeat on vacations. On this vacation, I'm going to keep my exercise up so I can eat just a bit more. It's not all or nothing.
I'm so lonely/angry/stressed/bored that I need something comforting to eat.	I'll feel even worse if I always cave into difficult feelings. It's time to try something different, like reading that great book I have.
I'll get back to my plan when I feel like it, probably in a couple of days.	It won't be easier in a couple of days. I'm just making excuses for eating what I want.
I can't turn down a food sample at the grocery store. It's *free* for gosh sake!	Free doesn't mean calorie-free. Every little bit counts.
If I don't eat these cookies, my friend will feel insulted.	How about I take these cookies down to the local fire department? They always want food. I can let my friend know how much they enjoyed them, and why I didn't eat them.
I can't stand the cravings. I have no self-control. It's horrible.	I thought I couldn't stand smoking cravings, but I've learned to. I can do the same with food and gradually improve my tolerance.

We're guessing you found several (or more) distorted thoughts that feel familiar to you. And you probably have various other distorted thoughts that get in the way of sticking with your eating plan. For dealing with those, we have a list of questions to consider subjecting your distorted thoughts to:

» Can I think of evidence that would contradict this thought?

» If my friend told me this thought, what advice would I give?

» Has this thought ever not been true in the past?

» Are there any more balanced alternatives to this thought?

» How will I feel if I act on this thought as opposed to a different thought?

» Am I just kidding myself with this thought?

» Is this a temporary, fleeting thought that may go away if I just wait it out?

» Would I think about this thought differently if I were in a better mood?

» Is there a way to test out this thought with an experiment?

EXAMPLE

COMBATTING DISTORTED THOUGHTS

Stan gave up smoking three months ago and has gained 15 pounds. He's discouraged about his weight gain but feels like losing weight is too hard. Someone brings brownies to the office. Stan's distorted thought is: "I have no willpower left after quitting smoking, so I can't go on a diet and I can't resist this brownie."

Stan uses three questions to challenge his distorted thought and comes up with answers for each.

- **Can I think of evidence that would contradict this thought?** Yes, I can. Obviously, I have some willpower left. I get up every morning and go to work. I pay my bills. And I'm still not smoking. I'm building my willpower day by day.

- **Would I think about this thought differently if I were in a better mood?** I can see that I'm actually feeling sort of sorry for myself. I just don't feel like going on a diet. But if I don't do something about my weight, I'm going to do nothing but feel worse.

- **If my friend told me this thought, what advice would I give?** I'd tell him to start slow and easy. Don't try to lose a lot all at once. Any small change is better than none. You can do it; I've seen you do lots of tougher things before.

After subjecting his distorted thought to these questions, Stan realizes he's got more rational thinking options to guide him. His new rational, alternative thought is, "I do have willpower. I'll take my time and go slowly. This time, I won't cave into my distorted thought."

TIP

You don't have to provide full answers to all these questions — two or three is usually enough. Just use them to confront your distorted thinking. Consider writing a new, more rational alternative thought based on this confrontation. You can also write your distorted thoughts on one side of a 3-x-5 card with your rational, alternative thought on the other side for easy reference.

In order to show you how to do this, follow the process with Stan (see the nearby sidebar).

REMEMBER

Thoughts are just thoughts. They can be accurate or not. Just because you think something, doesn't mean it's true. Start a brand-new habit of questioning your thoughts and developing rational, alternative thoughts to guide your behavior.

Figuring Out What to Put on the Table

After years of putting a cigarette in your mouth, it's understandable that you've been putting a bit too much food in your mouth to replace the cigarette. We didn't try to dissuade you; in fact, we gave you permission to indulge in a bit of ice cream during the early stages. So, now you have a few extra pounds to deal with. Don't worry, we're here to help. Read what we have to say next, and then slowly implement changes in your eating habits. At least it's not cold turkey — you can still eat!

TIP

The good news is, we don't want you to start cutting calories right away. First, focus on making your food healthy. Sometimes, that alone starts a slow, easy weight loss. If not, we recommend a variety of simple, small cuts for you to choose from. It won't be as bad as you think.

Starting with nutrient-dense food

Managing weight starts with improving the *quality* of what you eat more than the *quantity*. The goal is not to deprive yourself and walk around hungry all day! Healthy eating will give you more energy, improve your looks, and keep your weight under better control. A healthy diet is rich in nutrient-dense food. Nutrient-dense foods have these characteristics:

>> Lots of vitamins and minerals

>> Little or no added sugar

>> Little or no added salt

>> Relatively few calories

It's important to prepare nutrient-dense foods with minimal use of extra salt, sugar, and fats. You can phase in these changes slowly over a period of weeks or months. Examples of nutrient-dense foods include the following:

>> Vegetables of all different colors

>> Fruits, especially berries

>> Whole grains

>> Unsalted nuts and seeds

>> Fat-free or low-fat dairy products

>> Seafood

>> Eggs

>> Beans and peas

>> Lean meat (minimal red meat) and poultry

In addition, pay attention to seeking unprocessed foods whenever possible. Many experts strongly suspect that a heavy reliance on processed foods has contributed to rising obesity rates in countries all over the world. That means cutting back on chips, packaged crackers, processed cheese, lunch meats, white bread, soft drinks, packaged bake goods — you get the idea. Look at the labels — just the sheer number of ingredients gives you some idea of how processed the food is that you're buying.

Filling up on fiber

Fiber is the part of food that the body does not digest. Fiber passes through your system and leads to better digestive health. A diet high in fiber supports weight loss by creating feelings of fullness. Fiber also reduces cholesterol, lowers blood sugar, and lowers risk of cardiovascular diseases. Most Americans fail to get much more than half the fiber that's generally called for. The American Heart Association recommends women consume about 21 to 25 grams of fiber daily and men 30 to 38 grams.

TIP

To add more fiber to your diet, eat whole fruits instead of drinking juice, eat whole grains instead of white breads and pasta, and try to eat some of the following high-fiber foods:

>> Apples

>> Artichokes

- Avocados
- Bananas
- Beans
- Broccoli
- Brussels sprouts
- Chia seeds
- Flaxseeds
- Oatmeal (steel-cut is especially good)
- Pears
- Quinoa
- Raspberries
- Spinach
- Strawberries

TIP

Get in the habit of looking at food labels for the amount of fiber per serving. Whole foods are almost always higher in fiber than processed foods.

Cutting out calories

Here's where going slow matters. Cutting out 500 calories a day amounts to about 1 pound per week if your weight is currently stable. One way to get there is to make swaps of current high-calorie foods you eat for lower-calorie alternatives. Examples include the following:

Instead of this . . .	Try this . . .
Latte	Black coffee
Whole milk	Skim milk
Soda	Sparkling water
Ice cream	A bowl of berries with 1 tablespoon of whipped cream
Potato chips and dip	Vegetable sticks with hummus

TIP

You can also get there by looking for easy 100-calorie cuts to make from your usual diet. Some good examples include the following:

>> Using cooking spray instead of a tablespoon of oil

>> Cutting out one glass of wine or a beer

>> Leaving one slice of cheese off your burger

>> Cutting out one slice of bread

>> Dropping the bacon from your sandwich

>> Having some fruit instead of cookies

>> Ordering veggie pizza instead of pepperoni

Still, 500 calories less per day may feel like a lot. You can cut a little less if you elongate the time for reaching your goal. You can also cut a little less if you increase the amount of exercise you're getting (see the "Boosting Metabolism" section, later in this chapter).

REMEMBER

Make your cuts tolerable. Going too fast likely won't work even though it can be more rewarding in the short run to see pounds drop off. Slower is better when it comes to weight loss.

TIP

Additional tips for cutting calories include the following:

>> Use small plates and servings. You can always go back for more if you're truly hungry.

>> Eat slowly and chew thoroughly. Your brain needs about 20 minutes to detect and send out signals for fullness.

>> Don't eat in front of the TV or while reading. Distractions allow you to eat too much mindlessly.

>> Put all food on your plate. Never eat out of a box or a bag where you can't see how much you've consumed.

>> Avoid buying junk food. If it's in your kitchen, you'll end up eating it!

REMEMBER

There is no such thing as a totally forbidden food. Making something forbidden merely increases its desirability. You can still eat chocolate, pie, or ice cream. Just have it less often and in smaller portions.

Planning for holidays and eating out

Unfortunately (from a weight management perspective), holidays and eating out at restaurants are still likely to occur in your life. Let's consider dining out first. In order to manage your eating at restaurants, consider the following:

>> Choose what you're going to eat before you arrive from the restaurant's online menu. Most places have them!

>> Order one or two appetizers instead of an entrée.

>> Consider ordering entrées that are baked or broiled instead of fried.

>> Drink lots of water during your meal.

>> Be the first to order so as not to be influenced by what others order.

>> Have a cup of tea or coffee instead of dessert.

>> Switch out vegetables instead of fries or pasta.

>> Ask for salad dressing on the side.

>> Consider having a small, modest dessert that you share with the table.

TIP

A particularly good idea is to ask for a to-go box at the beginning of your meal. Box up about half of your meal when it arrives, and have it the next day.

Holidays are often stressful. Adding a strict diet regimen may only add to the stress. Our advice: Try to maintain your weight during the holidays instead of sticking with austerity. That means keeping portions small, avoiding drinking too much, staying away from too much sugar, and remaining focused on healthy food choices as much as possible. Get through the season without a major setback.

A couple of the best diets to follow

Surf the Internet a while, and you can find every sort of diet imaginable. New ones pop up regularly. But even the term *diet* is problematic because it sounds so restrictive to most people. The best diet is one you can use as a guide to lifelong, healthy eating.

But if you want to use a particular diet for guidance, we have two to recommend:

>> **Dietary Approaches to Stop Hypertension (DASH):** This diet includes six to eight servings of grains daily, along with four to five servings of vegetables,

four to five servings of fruit, two to three servings of low-fat dairy, and one serving of lean meat, poultry, or fish. In addition, the plan calls for four to five servings of nuts or beans weekly, two to three servings of fats per day (a serving of fat can be as little as a teaspoon of oil), and five or fewer servings of sweets weekly. Check out *DASH Diet For Dummies,* by Sarah Samaan, Rosanne Rust, and Cynthia Kleckner (Wiley), for more information about this food plan. Numerous studies have shown it's effective for weight loss and reducing cardiovascular disease.

>> **Mediterranean Diet:** The core message of the Mediterranean Diet emphasizes eating plants more than meat. It includes seven to ten servings of fruits and vegetables per day, combined with whole grains and healthy fats from olive oil. Small portions of fish, poultry, eggs, and beans provide protein. A bit of dairy is included, as well as modest intake of red wine, if desired. Occasional red meat is allowable. Processed foods (such as, hot dogs, sausages, lunch meats, packaged baked goods, and white breads) are to be avoided as much as possible. Check out *Mediterranean Diet For Dummies,* by Rachel Berman (Wiley), and *Mediterranean Diet Cookbook For Dummies,* 2nd Edition, by Meri Raffetto and Wendy Jo Peterson (Wiley), for more information about the Mediterranean Diet approach.

Boosting Metabolism

You have to deal with the fact that nicotine previously revved your metabolism, and now you'll have to adjust to that change by increasing your metabolism in other ways. You can find lots of reputed ways of revving up your metabolism on the Internet, and these suggestions may help a little. Here are a few of them:

>> Eat more protein.

>> Drink cold water.

>> Drink green tea.

>> Eat more spicy foods.

>> Drink coffee.

But the *real key* to boosting your metabolism is found in three words: *move, move, move*. We don't need to tell you again that exercise is healthy. But you don't have to become a gym rat to benefit from exercise. The federal government recommends the following guidelines for adults:

» Sit less.

» Exercise at least 150 minutes a week with moderate intensity. Even more exercise is better; more intense is good too.

» Engage in strength training twice a week with weightlifting involving all major muscle groups.

Additionally, older adults should include activities that improve balance. If you're unable to engage in moderate intensity exercise, you should do as much as you're able to.

If these exercise guidelines sound overwhelming to you, figure out what you do right now and find a way to do more. For example, if you haven't seen the inside of a gym or even exercised moderately in years, you're not hopeless! Start with where you're at right now.

Invest in a fitness tracker. Don't try to do anything except track how many steps you take in a day. If you're averaging as little as 1,500 steps per day, that's where you are. Start by making a goal of 1,750. Stay there for a week and move up to 2,000. Slowly increase your goal week by week. You can also gradually pick up your pace.

Some fitness trackers also nudge you with a vibration to remind you to walk a certain minimum number of steps each hour in addition to your daily goal. All your walking doesn't have to occur in a single, long walk; you can break it into segments. Keep your metabolism revved with frequent walks.

You can add more steps by taking the stairs instead of the elevator, parking farther away from where you're headed, walking instead of driving, and taking walk breaks at work rather than planting yourself in a break room. Walking after meals may offer even more benefit.

The human body is meant to move. The farther you go and the more frequently you do it, the better. Plus, walking is a great way to quell cravings to smoke, chew, or vape. Other than nicotine, exercise (including walking) is the only thing we know of that also stimulates and relaxes at the same time.

Your fitness tracker also stands ready to monitor your more intense exercise if and when you decide to include it in your regular life routine. It's rewarding to see the exercise numbers pile up throughout the day and week.

You can add more bits of exercise daily by standing at work, on the bus, or on the train rather than sitting. In addition, you can make a plan to do simple exercise during TV commercials. You don't have to exhaust yourself — just move!

There are lots of good, short exercise routines on the Internet. Try a few and see if they work for you. No fancy equipment is needed for most of them. We've both benefitted from these in-home, short routines to break up hours of sitting during writing days.

Staying Motivated

The less concern you have over controlling your weight, the easier time you'll have in controlling your weight. Paradoxical, but true. In other words, stress less and don't sweat about some extra pounds. You've done the hardest work — quitting smoking or vaping. You can lose a few pounds slowly but surely. There's no rush.

That's because the more you absolutely, positively, *must* do something (like lose weight), the less likely you are to find yourself able to do it. The pressure builds, and your resolve collapses. See Chapter 22 for more information about developing self-compassion and how you can benefit from lightening up on yourself.

If quitting smoking or vaping has depleted you, back off for a while on your attempt to control your weight. Take a look through Chapter 14 and see what stage of change you're in specifically regarding weight management. Don't get ahead of yourself. Accept where you are, and move ahead when you're ready.

Smoking, vaping, or chewing was likely a very rewarding companion for you. You probably turned to food as your new rewarding chum. That's understandable. Now it's time to find another buddy or two — ones that aren't deadly or unhealthy for you.

For starters, you may want to connect with a quit-smoking support group in person or online. You could also check out local or online support groups for weight issues. Check out Chapter 21 for information about developing a more rewarding lifestyle.

Chapter **21**

Strengthening Resilience

L ife would have less meaning and purpose without adversity. If everything you ever needed or wanted dropped down from the sky whenever you asked for it, what would the point be? What would success or accomplishments mean if they were achieved without effort?

People who bravely face obstacles or adversity reap positive benefits such as a greater appreciation of life, better connections with others, and an enhanced sense of well-being. *Resilience* is the ability to push forward and carry on in the face of adversity. Resilient people manage to persist even after multiple setbacks and failures. They bounce back when life dishes out the most difficult challenges.

When you quit smoking or vaping, you prove that you can handle a good measure of difficulty and distress. And, for some, the struggle against relapse may continue for a while. But if you've made it for six months to a year, your odds of permanently quitting are pretty good.

An important and common risk factor of relapse is having something extremely stressful happen, such as losing a relationship, experiencing a natural disaster, or facing a major financial setback. The odds of maintaining recovery can improve significantly if you work on increasing your overall resilience.

Resilient people learn from mistakes and carry on without wallowing in self-pity. They bravely go forward after bad things happen yet are not immune from suffering. Instead, by working through suffering, they get stronger, find renewal, and feel more capable.

In this chapter, we discuss the concept of resilience and how to strengthen it. We note the importance of building a sense of competence and the confidence in improving a resilient person's ability to set goals and see them through. We also discuss the value of being connected with others.

We give you skills for handling difficult emotions when they threaten to overwhelm you through acceptance and mindfulness. Finally, we offer a few tips on uncovering the purpose and meaning of your life. Armed with this information, you'll be able to face most of the toughest times you're likely to face. Fortifying resilience is all a matter of practice, patience, and persistence.

Enhancing Competence and Confidence

Resilient people choose to work on projects or tasks that they can actually accomplish. For example, only a few powerful people can make a dent in reducing world hunger. A resilient person would find another way to help fight hunger, such as donating to a homeless shelter or food bank — not reducing world hunger, but successfully feeding a small group of people and making a difference.

If you're reading this chapter, you've already made a decision to quit smoking (we hope). You set a goal, worked on a plan, and succeeded. Now, you can use your skills in other areas of your life.

TIP

If you haven't quit yet, it's possible that strengthening your resilience will help get you there.

Making wise choices for where to make a difference enhances confidence and a sense of competence — core components of resilience. The first step is learning how to set and evaluate the right goals, whether it's smoking cessation or anything else in your life.

Setting goals

TIP

People with resilience know how to choose achievable goals. You know that goals are achievable when

>> **Your goals feel important to you.** Why would you want to bother with goals that have little significance to you? That doesn't mean your goals should be huge in scope or meaning. Maybe you want to lose 5 pounds or take better care of your lawn.

» **Your goals are specific and measurable.** Losing 5 pounds is more specific (and, therefore, achievable) than a goal of "losing weight." Fertilizing and mowing your lawn is a better goal than "taking better care of it."

» **Your goals have a timetable.** Losing 5 pounds in five weeks is a better goal than losing 5 pounds someday. Cutting the grass weekly and fertilizing it in the spring and fall works better than just saying you'll fertilize and mow.

» **Your goals are attainable.** There's nothing wrong with one or two very long-term goals. But it's important to break them down into segments that can be attained within a shorter time span. For example, "I'd like to save $2 million for retirement" is great but setting yearly goals along the way makes more sense. Focusing only on the long-term outcome at retirement age makes it easier to ignore along the way.

In setting goals, it's also useful to keep in mind a few key principles:

» **Reduce your focus on competition with others.** Achieving goals is about increasing your sense of competence and confidence in yourself. It's not about beating someone else. It's about moving forward on your own, personal path to resilience.

» **Avoid perfectionism.** Perfection as a goal won't work because no one's perfect all the time. Stressing perfection leads to frustration and inevitable loss of confidence.

» **Embrace mistakes.** Mistakes have a lot to offer. You can learn valuable lessons from mistakes. Let them teach you!

» **Push back on procrastination.** The number-one cause of failure to reach your goals is chronically putting off your efforts to get there. Ask any writer about procrastination — we know exactly what it does. Combatting procrastination requires making the goal more specific and as small as needed to feel achievable. Some days, we vow to write just one page, but we usually end up writing much more after we get started. You're likely to experience the same result.

REMEMBER

Almost every accomplishment worth achieving involves setting goals and striving to reach them. The decision to quit smoking is an important goal that is specific, involves a certain time period, and is attainable. In order to achieve that goal, it's useful to learn from mistakes and focus on yourself rather than beating others. If you do slip up, don't allow perfectionism to turn your slip into a full-blown relapse. Start your efforts anew without delay.

Problem solving

Resilient people are great at solving problems. The risk of relapse increases when life stressors become overwhelming to former smokers, smokeless tobacco users, and vapers. In order to inoculate you from becoming overwhelmed, it's useful to learn how to problem solve.

The following problem–solving strategy has been found to help people with almost anything that stands in their way. With practice, you'll see that problems start feeling less crushing and more solvable. You'll become more resilient. Take these steps for dealing with the next problem that comes your way:

1. Identify the problem.

Describe the problem as objectively and clearly as possible. If the problem involves lots of issues, try to focus on one issue to deal with at a time. Describe the problem without emotions and as concretely as you can.

EXAMPLE

For example, Anthony works for a manufacturer of medical equipment. He and 200 of his coworkers are laid off. Anthony quit smoking eight months ago and worries that he'll go back to smoking in order to cope with the stress of losing his job. He defines his problem as needing to find a new job without going back to smoking. He decides to focus on the job first. Hopefully, he won't have to worry about smoking if he gets a new job.

2. Brainstorm solutions.

Consider every imaginable solution and write them all down. Don't try too hard to come up with a perfect solution. For now, anything goes.

EXAMPLE

Anthony knows that he has a few options:

- He could transfer with his current company to a new location about 1,500 miles away.

- His cousin offers him a part-time job at his restaurant that could possibly develop into full-time work.

- He could take unemployment and go back to school for retraining in computer coding paid by his former employer.

- He could simply take unemployment and look for whatever job he can find.

3. Examining consequences.

Each brainstormed option has various consequences with different levels of likelihood. Write down the consequence for each of the brainstormed options and include your thoughts on the likelihood of each outcome.

EXAMPLE

Anthony looks at his first option of moving 1,500 miles. He immediately discards this solution because it includes leaving his aging parents, something he definitely doesn't want to do. He discarded the second option because he doesn't get along with his cousin that well and feels uncomfortable working for him. His third option sounds great in terms of potential, but Anthony fears he doesn't have the ability. But he doesn't know much about this type of work either, so he decides to get more information by talking to a vocational counselor provided by his former company. Anthony takes a look at his fourth option and realizes he can try the third option without sacrificing the ability to look for other jobs.

4. Taking action.

After you've examined the consequences and likelihood of each option, it's time to choose and act. Don't delay; do something. If it turns out badly, you can always examine other options again.

EXAMPLE

Anthony takes action by talking to the vocational counselor and, after taking a brief test, discovers he has an aptitude for coding. He jumps in with both feet and starts going to school.

5. Evaluating the outcome.

After you select an option and take action, the job isn't finished. You want to evaluate whether the problem solving worked. Was it the outcome you hoped for? Was it a "good enough" solution? Or do you want to take another look at other options?

EXAMPLE

Anthony stepped back after six weeks of training in coding. It was harder than he expected. He realizes his money could run out almost at the time he finishes school. He decides to work for his cousin a couple of nights a week in order to make it through. It isn't as bad as he feared.

This simple, five-step problem-solving technique is easy to put into practice. Research shows that people who use this strategy routinely are more capable of getting what they want and have less emotional distress.

Taking care of yourself

Resilience building requires paying attention to your own needs. That includes taking care of your health and finding sources of pleasure to recharge your batteries as often as necessary.

Staying healthy

You can find lots of information about living a healthy life throughout this book. It basically comes down to eating right (see Chapter 20), routinely exercising (see Chapter 20), and getting enough sleep (see Chapter 17).

In addition, it helps if you go outside, stay active, drink plenty of water, stay away from tobacco products of any kind, and have regular checkups with your health-care provider. No problem is too large to handle if you take care of yourself, but you'll quickly become overwhelmed if you don't.

WARNING

If you're feeling overwhelmed and like you can't handle things, or take care of yourself, you need to seek help with a mental health professional. Check with your primary care provider or your health insurance company for a referral.

Having fun

You may think that "having fun" has little to do with a healthy, vibrant lifestyle, but you'd be wrong. Studies show us that people who routinely put pleasure into their lives tend to be more joyful, healthier, more energetic, and more resilient. You've already experienced unhealthy pleasure from tobacco or nicotine.

TIP

Now let's turn to seeking healthy pleasures. Make a list of things you find possibly pleasurable or fun, and make sure you engage in some of these routinely. If you need inspiration, here are a few ideas to get you started:

>> Treat yourself to a movie.

>> Take a day trip.

>> Pick up a new hobby or craft.

>> Sign up for season tickets to a local theater.

>> Read some great novels.

>> Listen to music.

>> Go on hikes.

>> Go to an interesting museum.

>> Go to the zoo.

>> Sit outside in a park.

>> People-watch at a shopping center.

>> If your town has tourists, go where they go!

>> Take a hot bath.

>> Get a massage.

>> Eat a great meal somewhere new.

>> Play with your pet. If you don't have one, watch animals at a dog park.

You get the idea. We're sure you can dig down deep and get creative in order to come up with your own possibilities.

REMEMBER

Prioritizing pleasure is important. When inevitable troubles come your way, you'll have more in reserve to work through them.

Improving Relationships

Humans are social beings. Literally, thousands of studies have shown that people with good social support networks are happier and healthier and live longer lives. Sometimes that consists of a spouse or live-in partner; other times it's a variety of friends or family members. Some people find social connections in their neighborhoods or in their workplaces.

We have a few thoughts for improving relationships. In this section, we focus on improving intimate relationships. However, you can use some of these techniques to help you get along better with almost anyone in your social circle.

Trying the Daily News Report

The essence of any good relationship involves sharing. That means sharing mundane events that occur during the day, as well as hopes, dreams, and ambitions. Frustrations, angst, joys, and struggles form part of the mix, too.

Have you ever come home from work and your partner asked, "How was your day?"

You think about all the miserable things that happened that day and are about to respond, but your partner is already asking whether you want to go out to eat. You may quash your feelings and go along with the plan — but there's a part of you that wishes your partner would pay attention and listen.

TIP

The Daily News Report is a structured exercise that helps. Make a deal with your partner or friend to abide by the following:

1. **Agree to spend a set amount of time (even as short as 15 minutes daily) on most days to discuss what's happened and how things are going.**

2. **Choose one of you to start the conversation.**

3. **Listen.**

    That means asking questions for clarification. It also means looking at the person and not at your phone.

4. **Express *empathy* (your thoughts on how your partner may be feeling).**

5. **Don't try to fix problems right away or give advice unless you're asked.**

   Even then, tread carefully. You don't want to sound like a know it all.

6. **Take turns, but don't do so until the first news person is finished.**

   It's great to take longer than 15 minutes — that's just a low target.

TIP

If you're doing the Daily News Report right, you won't have any conflict. This is a time of support and connection. No judgment allowed.

TIP

If you're doing this with a friend, it can become the Weekly News Report and take a little longer than just 15 minutes a day. It can also be a Monthly News Report for friends you see less frequently.

REMEMBER

Everyone benefits from having supportive relationships. Good relationships build resilience and keep relapse away. The Daily News Report supports and enhances relationships.

Disclosing vulnerability

Have you ever had friends who seem to have a perfect life? People who know all the answers all the time? People who never need advice but can dole it out liberally? They apparently have perfect families, including perfect children, perfect cars, perfect houses, and perfect jobs. If so, do you have warm, close feelings for them? Or do you feel a little distant and removed from them?

Our guess is that you probably feel a little detached from these friends. Maybe you're not jealous of them and their perfect lives — you just find them too good to be true. Relationships with so-called "perfect" people, don't usually feel satisfying. That's because those people feel false and unrealistic. Life is never perfect.

You probably can't change people who pretend to be perfect. However, you can vow not to come across as perfect with your true friends. The solution is simple: Learn the value of honest self-disclosure with trusted friends. The expression of vulnerability with each other brings people closer. People with good, close relationships are more resilient.

WARNING

Take some care in deciding who you can trust enough to disclose personal, vulnerable details of your life with. Unfortunately, there are a few people out there who will use such information to gossip about you. The remedy is to listen to your feelings and disclose a few less vulnerable details first and see how it goes.

Giving help and caring

Solid relationships require attention and nurturance. All too many people forget this fundamental principle. Friends and couples drift apart when they overlook caring for one another. Stop that process before it starts.

Too many times, friends forget to give each other compliments, offer to help each other out, or do nice things. It's not that they don't care about their friends or partners, it's that they don't show specific acts of caring for their friends or partners. In other words, there is a difference between care and actual behaviors that demonstrate caring.

TIP

Review the following list of caring and/or helpful behaviors. Try expressing these more often — one or two daily isn't overdoing it for someone who lives with you; less often works for friends you spend less time with. Try out the following actions:

>> Express thanks or gratitude for something you appreciate about your friend or partner.

>> Give flowers.

>> Hug often.

>> Send a "thinking of you" text message.

>> Offer to run an errand or simply run it without even offering.

>> Offer a backrub.

>> Prepare a special meal.

>> Tell your friend or partner how much you care.

>> Do a household task (the more disagreeable, the better) without being asked.

>> Make an effort to learn something new about your friend.

>> Give compliments often — just be sure they're sincere.

Add to this list. Be creative! These are not random acts of kindness — they're planned, thoughtful, and targeted acts of kindness. And they fertilize and rejuvenate relationships.

REMEMBER

Sometimes people are nicer to strangers than the ones they love and care about. That's sad because it's easy to give help and caring. Caring behaviors make resilient relationships.

WARNING

When there's lots of conflict in a close relationship, it's important to get professional help from a mental health provider skilled in relationship therapy. When you're involved in a relationship, it's hard to sort out what's really causing the conflict and how to resolve it.

Acquiring Mindfulness

Mindfulness involves becoming aware, connected, and engaged with the *present moment* without judgment. Mindfulness allows people to accept and tolerate difficult thoughts and emotions in a healthier way.

Humans are unique among species in the ability to think both about the future and the past. Reminiscing can be a pleasant activity. However, it can also result in memories that cause guilt, resentment, sadness, and pain. Thoughts about the future can also feel pleasant. Yet, many times looking ahead can engender distress, worry, fear, anxiety, and dread.

When connected to the present moment, you don't get bogged down by guilt and shame over the past or worries about the future. Acquiring the ability to go into a mindful state when you want has many benefits.

Benefiting from mindfulness

Mindfulness can be thought of as a skill. The skill of mindfulness involves a willingness or acceptance to cope with life, both the good and the bad. It's a skill that bestows many advantages to those who acquire it.

Managing emotional distress

Acquiring the skill of mindfulness helps people manage strong feelings more productively. Mindfulness practice improves moods and reduces anxiety and stress. Mindfulness helps people with depression. Depressed people who practice mindfulness techniques are less likely to experience relapses of their depression. That's because the skill helps people react to difficulty with calm, composed, detached, cool emotions rather than driven, boiling, hot feelings.

Reaping health rewards

Mindfulness, usually practiced as meditation (see the "Looking at meditation techniques" section, later in this chapter), has been shown to

- >> Reduce high blood pressure
- >> Improve sleep
- >> Decrease discomfort from chronic pain
- >> Improve colitis symptoms
- >> Help with addiction recovery
- >> Improve immune function
- >> Reduce stress hormones

TIP

In addition, there is limited research suggesting that mindfulness may help people stop smoking. However, it's likely that the strategy is maximally beneficial when included in an overall package of strategies such as those found in this book.

Making brain gains

Mindfulness also trains your brain to function more efficiently. It improves people's ability to focus and concentrate. It decreases the tendency to think negative thoughts over and over again — a pattern called *rumination.* Instead, with mindfulness, you pay attention to the present moment. Mindfulness skills also improve the ability to think of multiple things at once and make decisions flexibly.

Looking at meditation techniques

Meditation complements and supports a mindful life philosophy of connection to the present. *Meditation* describes a mental state of focused attention. In meditation, there is an awareness of the present moment and a hope to achieve mental clarity and emotional calmness.

There are a multitude of meditation techniques and strategies. However, a few of the most common types include the following:

- >> **Breath awareness:** This technique consists of attending to your breathing. Those practicing this approach are told to notice how air feels as it flows in and out of the body. Many practitioners suggest breathing in through the nose and out through the mouth, although this suggestion may not make a great deal of difference. Some people find it useful to count the breathing, but the main point is to notice the sensation of breathing.

- >> **Body scan:** This strategy is particularly good for people with chronic pain. Attention is given to each part of the body while sitting or lying down. A body scan can begin at the feet, slowly going up to the head, or the other way, from head to toe. Bodily sensations are noticed and accepted for whatever they are without judgment.

>> **Moving meditation:** With this approach, you are, well, moving. Focused attention is paid to the body and the breath while in motion. Basic slow walking can serve quite well for this purpose. T'ai Chi is a type of slow-moving meditation. Yoga sometimes can serve as an additional form of moving meditation.

>> **Mantra-focused meditation:** This technique begins with a word, sound, or phrase that is repeated over and over. When attention drifts, the practitioner is instructed to refocus on the mantra. The sound or phrase can have personal or spiritual meaning or be totally meaningless. Mantras are some-times said out loud, whispered, or repeated inside the head.

TIP

A meditation practice is easy to begin. All you need is 10 or 15 minutes and a place to do it. Longer sessions have their place, too, but aren't always necessary. Daily practice is great, but you can profit from less often, too. Most people find that regular practice improves their skill and gives them more benefits.

The following instructions can be thought of as generic in nature; that is, they can be applied to many slightly varying forms of meditation:

>> **Turn off devices.** When you're meditating, you can be disturbed by the vibration of your phone. No need for that.

>> **Find a peaceful place.** You can meditate just about anywhere. But it's nice to have somewhere that feels serene and peaceful. That's especially true when you're first starting. Later, when your brain is accustomed to meditating, you can turn off the outside world at will.

>> **Sit on a chair, cushion, couch, floor, or wherever.** It really doesn't matter where you choose. Some types of meditation require specific (sometimes uncomfortable) positions, but those can take a lot of practice to achieve. You can still benefit from meditation with less austere approaches.

>> **Close your eyes.** Though not always required, most people find that closing their eyes helps them focus.

>> **Choose something to direct your attention to.** You may want to concentrate on your rhythmic breath, your body (one part at a time), a mantra you repeat to yourself or in your mind, or nothing at all.

TIP

>> **When thoughts intrude, refocus.** Thoughts will pop into your mind. It's important to realize that these intrusions are inevitable. Accept those thoughts and let them drift on. Return your attention to your mantra or other target.

>> **Accept your meditation practice however it goes.** Some days will induce a blissful feeling of acceptance and relaxation. Others will feel like more of a struggle. Meditation takes practice. Be patient with yourself — after all, one of the elements of meditation is to learn acceptance and nonjudgment.

TIP

You can find apps that give you good-quality, guided meditation instructions. Many of them can be tailored to a desired duration. Many are free. If you decide to pay for one, be sure to take advantage of the free trial many of them offer.

WARNING

Be careful in parting with your money for meditation instruction. Use your common sense. Fees should be reasonable. There are a few unscrupulous, cultlike groups promoting unbelievable benefits from extended meditation programs. Don't be fooled by a free introductory session unless you're immune to any high-pressure sales pitches.

Finding Meaning and Purpose

You may wonder why a book on quitting smoking and vaping would have a section on finding meaning and purpose. Well, people who profess to having a more meaningful, purposeful life also appear to be more resilient. Resilient people work through all kinds of adversities, and giving up addictions is tough work.

Purpose provides motivation and helps people make decisions and set meaningful aspirations. Some people believe the purpose of life is to be happy. Others want to lead an honorable life while somehow making a difference in the world. We're not so sure these goals are mutually exclusive, but too many people neglect to balance them.

We've already discussed the importance of pursuing pleasures (see "Taking care of yourself," earlier in this chapter). Now, we suggest you look at the "making a difference" part of the equation.

Social connections lead to a multitude of positive outcomes, including better health, longer life, improved mood, and resilience. Certain activities provide meaning and purpose in life while also facilitating social connections. Specifically, we're talking about volunteering and community involvement. Here are some examples:

>> **Get involved in your neighborhood watch program or organize one if it doesn't exist.** Go to www.nnw.org for information about this program.

- » **Support your local community theater.** Buy season tickets and/or volunteer to serve as an usher or try out for a part!

- » **Deliver meals to the shut-in seniors in your area.** Go to www.mealsonwheels america.org for information about this program. It exists in almost every community across the country.

- » **Volunteer for neighborhood cleanups.**

- » **If you're so inclined, consider getting involved in a religious or spiritual organization that fits your beliefs.**

- » **Volunteer at your local animal shelter.**

- » **Take a class that interests you.** Many low-cost or free classes are available online or through adult education centers at local universities and colleges.

- » **Volunteer at a food bank.**

- » **Be a volunteer tutor.** Ask your local school for more information.

- » **Get involved in local politics.** Participate in get-out-the-vote campaigns for your favorite candidate or work on behalf of a cause you support.

This list is just to get you started thinking. You can easily look around and find many more. If you do, you'll find many like-minded people that could readily become close friends.

Finally, one more thought for enhancing your sense of purpose and meaning as well as resilience: Look around. Savor your good fortune. Ask yourself what's around you that you appreciate and feel a sense of gratitude about. People who feel grateful and express it have better connections with others, are more optimistic, and experience greater well-being.

TIP

Your sense of gratitude will increase even more if you develop a gratitude habit. You can do that by journaling about every trivial to important thing you feel grateful for each day. Call it your gratitude journal, and make a goal of finding three to five items to list each day.

Chapter **22**

Developing Self-Compassion

Have you ever watched a news story about a scam victim losing a big chunk of money to a fraudulent investment scheme? If so, you probably found it easy to feel compassion for the victim. You felt that way, even if the victim wasn't very sophisticated and failed to detect that something fishy was going on. You never thought that the victim was primarily at fault. The blame was on the perpetrator.

However, if you were the victim of the same scam and lost a bunch of money, you'd undoubtedly call yourself stupid for having been such a fool. You'd likely feel ashamed and guilty. Your confidence in yourself might be shaken badly. You would blame yourself rather than the conman that stole your money.

Most people can easily feel compassion for others, but they don't even think about having compassion for themselves. Yet, there is another way: It's called *self-compassion*. Self-compassion confers many benefits for those who manage to acquire it, including the following:

» Greater life satisfaction

» Better relationships

>> Increased happiness

>> Optimism

Self-compassion encompasses four somewhat related, overlapping concepts:

>> Being kind to yourself

>> Asserting yourself

>> Forgiving yourself

>> Accepting yourself

If you've battled an addiction such as smoking or vaping, you probably experienced a number of lapses or even relapses along the path toward eventually quitting.

If you have little self-compassion, you probably blamed yourself for relapsing, thought of yourself as weak, and stayed stuck longer than necessary. Self-compassion allows you to push forward through setbacks and, as such, is a great companion of resilience (see Chapter 21).

In this chapter, we discuss how to recognize the four related concepts of self-compassion. We also describe methods for enhancing each of these components.

Being Kind to Yourself

Being kind to yourself doesn't come so easily for most people. But it's a habit much like any other — something that can be strengthened and developed by repeated practice. It's easy to imagine being kind to others. For example, when someone is sick, you immediately feel empathy and concern. You ask what you can do to help.

Now it's time to start treating yourself the same way. When you're in pain, find ways to comfort and soothe yourself. The pain could be from craving a cigarette. Or the discomfort could be from a physical ailment. Or perhaps you've lost someone important to you, and you're suffering. Ask what you'd do or say to someone else and do it for you at such times. For example, you might do or say the following to yourself:

» Get more rest.

» Order food in tonight.

» Go out and see a movie if you're up to it.

» Hire a temporary cleaning person.

» Ask a friend for help.

» Take a mini vacation from work.

» Get yourself some chicken soup!

REMEMBER

Don't think that self-kindness is self-indulgent. When you treat yourself with kindness, you have more stamina in reserve for facing challenges. Realize that it takes time to develop the self-kindness habit. Consider putting a note on your refrigerator saying, "Be kind to yourself today."

Asserting Yourself

Part of showing self-compassion requires practicing standing up for yourself with others and learning to say no. That skill is called *assertiveness*. Assertiveness is an effective, middle-ground way of communicating wants and needs. It's positioned between overly passive and excessively aggressive communication styles.

Passive people acquiesce to the demands of others. When you acquiesce and simply do what others want, you end up neglecting your own wants and needs and show more compassion for others than for yourself. You may be too passive in dealing with others if you agree with many of the following statements:

» I'm afraid to disagree with others.

» I let other people have their own way.

» I apologize even when things aren't my fault.

» I hate it whenever someone is mad at me.

» I want everyone to like me.

» I give in to avoid any conflict.

» I say yes even when I want to say no.

Aggressive people dominate and attempt to crush those who oppose what they want. They show little regard for other people's desires even when others have a good point. You may be overly aggressive in communicating with other people if you agree with many of the following statements:

>> I have to win every disagreement.

>> I don't care if I have to step on someone to get my way.

>> I want to be in control at all times.

>> I never see the point in apologizing for anything.

>> If someone crosses me, I push back ten times harder.

>> It's my way or the highway.

>> I never walk away from a good fight.

Assertion, by contrast, is neither passive nor aggressive. To be assertive, you listen to others, evaluate any differences from your own views, and look for compromise positions. You don't automatically agree or reflexively disagree with others. You listen carefully and expect others to listen to you. Sometimes you may have conflict, but that's okay because conflict is inevitable in human interactions.

You probably have an attitude of assertiveness (and self-compassion) if you agree with many of the following statements:

>> I have the right to express my opinions if I'm respectful of others.

>> If someone asks me to do something, I have the fundamental right to say no.

>> An important key to asking for what I want is to do so without anger or rancor.

>> When people try to take advantage of me, it's my responsibility to stop them. I don't have to let it happen.

>> I respect others, and I respect myself and my needs.

>> If someone is unkind to me, I can choose to leave or say, "Stop being unkind."

>> When I'm irritated, I will express it constructively.

>> When a contentious issue arises and does not resolve, I can agree to disagree.

>> When someone mistreats me, I can set a boundary without getting angry.

If you feel your assertiveness skills are up to snuff (no pun regarding tobacco intended), that's great. If not, it's probably something for you to work on. Being assertive is treating yourself with compassion and respect. You believe you're equal to others — no better no worse.

Consider reading *Your Perfect Right: Assertiveness and Equality in Your Life and Relationships*, 10th Edition, by Robert Alberti and Michael Emmons (Impact), for detailed instructions on becoming more assertive.

If you have trouble with assertiveness, you may want to consider talking with a mental health professional who can help you learn this skill. It can make a difference in your life.

If you're a teenager or young adult, realize that considerable difficulty with assertiveness is common. However, it's a necessary ingredient in resisting peer pressure to smoke or vape. Here's a look at how the three styles of communicating would look when a friend pushes you to try a new vaping device and you've never vaped:

>> **Passive style:** "Oh, um, sure I guess."

>> **Aggressive style:** "Screw you, dude! Get the hell out of my face."

>> **Assertive:** "I know you'd like me to try it, but it's just not my thing. No, thanks."

Forgiving Yourself

If a little boy fell down in the mud, right in front of you and you were the only adult around, what would you do? Would you tell the kid to buck up and stop crying? Or would you help him to his feet, make sure that he's not seriously hurt, dry him off, and maybe give him a hug?

When you fall down in the mud, what do you say to yourself? Do you scold yourself for being a klutz? Or do you get back up, tell yourself that it'll be okay, take a warm bath, and treat yourself to some hot tea? Far too many people take the self-critical approach.

When people criticize themselves, they often think that the self-condemnation will somehow motivate them to do better in the future. But self-criticism actually has a paradoxical effect. Instead of motivating people, it usually drains them of initiative.

Think of a teacher who berates and humiliates his students whenever they fall short of his expectations. Students who misbehave get their knuckles rapped with a ruler. By contrast, the teacher down the hall, praises students for their efforts and encourages cooperation, creativity, and even the willingness to take a few risks and make a few mistakes. Which classroom would you want to be in? Which students do you think would perform the best? As you would probably guess, most students achieve more and perform better with the teacher down the hall.

Train your brain to be the teacher down the hall for yourself. When you mess up, make a mistake, or forget to do something, treat yourself with kindness and compassion. We give you more ideas for creating self-forgiveness in the sections that follow.

Saying no to perfectionism

One of the most common issues experienced by people with emotional problems is that of perfectionism. They adhere to a life credo of striving for ultimate flawlessness and a refusal to accept anything else. Examples of a perfectionistic attitude include the following:

>> I cannot accept mistakes.

>> I can't relax until my work is done.

>> Work always comes before pleasure.

>> I have extraordinarily high standards.

>> I push myself relentlessly.

>> I hate for my work to be interrupted.

>> Play is for foolish people.

>> Mistakes are unforgiveable.

REMEMBER

Perfectionism explains part of the power of nicotine for many smokers. People who work all the time don't give themselves permission to play or do anything but toil. Nicotine delivers badly needed feelings of pleasure without interrupting the ever-constant striving of perfectionists.

Perfectionists do literally millions of things very well. But they dwell on their mistakes. One way to battle perfectionism is to start valuing and appreciating mistakes. Mistakes have much to teach you if you let them. Savor your mistakes!

TIP

Let's say that a perfectionistic man has stopped vaping for over a year. He ends up lapsing after getting a traffic ticket. He's so upset about the ticket (a mistake on his part) that he self-sabotages by vaping. He made one mistake, but he failed to learn from it and he made another (vaping). Ideally, he can embrace his mistakes and stop a continued cycle of mistakes by forgiving himself and moving on.

One last example of the absurdity inherent within a perfectionist's perspective: Imagine a painting of a landscape. The grass is cut evenly, the sky is blue with no clouds, flowers are all in full bloom, and the sun is shining. No weeds in sight. Trees have perfect, unbent branches. Everything is in order. Would you feel drawn to this scene? Or would it seem artificial and unreal? Would it feel like it's missing something? Would the painting seem uninteresting and flat? Imperfections give us richness and true beauty. The painting begs for life, flaws included. That's what giving up perfectionism gives you.

Not turning guilt into shame

Simply put, guilt is a reaction people often have when they've done something wrong or inappropriate. Guilt can be a useful emotion in that it tells you to pay attention to your behavior. If you've violated one of your own personal moral guidelines, guilt can alert you to that and make you more sensitive to the issue in the future.

On the other hand, many people respond to personal transgressions by feeling a deep sense of shame. Shame represents a personal evaluation of the entire self. It's a global, painful, humiliating feeling of unworthiness and disrepute. Unlike guilt, shame erodes the belief that change is even possible. It repudiates the soul. Such self-repudiation hardly paves the way for moving to a better place. Instead, it keeps you stuck, mired in self-loathing.

REMEMBER

Guilt tells you that you *did* something bad. Shame tries to tell you that *you're* bad.

Shame has a variety of toxic effects on those who experience it, including:

WARNING

>> Increasingly engaging in self-destructive behaviors, such as a relapse in smoking

>> Self-sabotaging by getting into unnecessary arguments

>> Neglecting yourself

>> Believing you're undeserving of good outcomes

If you've acquired the shame habit, it's time to do something about it. With shame, it's like you're stuck in a muddy pothole in your road of life. It's time to fill that hole in with sand rather than more water. To fill up that hole of shame try the following:

>> Admit that you have these powerful feelings of shame and share them with someone you trust. If you don't have the right person in your life, consider seeing a therapist.

>> Ask yourself if your actions are more appropriate for the feeling of guilt, which is a normal response to misbehavior. Is shame possibly an overreaction?

>> Appreciate that guilt is an emotion that pushes you to change your ways. Shame stops change cold.

REMEMBER

Quite a few smokers feel ashamed of their habit. They feel humiliated and weak — not a good place to be if the goal is quitting. Instead, realize that no smoker starts smoking with the intention of becoming addicted. So, give up shame and understand that smoking does not define you. Self-forgiveness is a better path.

Enhancing self-forgiveness

The road to finding self-forgiveness can be a rocky one. It takes time, perseverance, and patience. We offer the following strategies to stimulate your endeavor.

Figuring out what's responsible: Taking a look at the blame game

When people feel guilty about something, they often assume the complete blame or responsibility about what they did. That's rarely true. Let's take smoking, for instance. Smokers think that they are entirely responsible for their habit. In some ways, that's true.

Indeed, smokers are the only ones who can stop smoking. But if you take a wider lens, many other factors are likely responsible for a smoking habit. For example:

>> **Heredity:** There is an inherited tendency to become addicted to nicotine and other drugs. This inherited tendency is out of the smoker's control.

- » **Upbringing:** The way smokers are raised has a lot to do with whether she develops self-control, has models who smoke, or has opportunities to smoke at a young age.

- » **Exposure to secondhand smoke:** This appears to seed the nicotine addiction in many cases by altering brain development.

- » **Exposure to advertising:** Tobacco companies spend millions of dollars trying to influence especially vulnerable populations such as young people to become smokers (and vapers). They have decades of experience and are quite good at what they do.

- » **Peer influences:** When a teen's best friends smoke or vape, he's more likely to start. If peer groups exert pressure or simply provide multiple models for smoking or vaping, it can prove to be an irresistible force.

Ponder this list of sources of blame for acquiring the smoking habit. Consider which of these may have influenced you and to what degree. Ultimately, there is no definitive answer. But what is clear is that no one deserves 100 percent of the blame. We suspect these factors account for a majority of the influences that lead people to nicotine addiction.

Realizing that the past is the past

Many people carry their past throughout their adulthood. It's important to understand that you can't change what's already happened in your life. Focus on the present and the future because that's where you can make changes. Use your past mistakes only as a guide to improve your present and future decisions.

Accept that you're human. You, like every other person in the world, have hurt others and made dreadful mistakes. You, also like everyone else, need to take responsibility for what you've done. However, being truly human means you can't be perfect. So, strive to feel compassion for yourself.

Writing yourself a compassionate letter

TIP

Think about what makes you feel guilty or ashamed. Imagine all the details. Now, pretend that you're someone else. You're a loving, kind, and forgiving friend of yourself. As that friend, write a letter to your ashamed self. Offer comforting words and ideas to your ashamed self. We recommend you write one. See Figure 22-1 for an example of such a letter.

We realize writing such a letter could feel a little silly. However, techniques like this have been found to be effective. Give it a try. And feel free to add to your letter over time. Carry the letter with you for a while and review it often.

Dear Ashamed Self,

I'm writing this to you today because I've been watching you beat yourself up for being a human being. You've called yourself weak, lacking in willpower, pathetic, and stupid for vaping. Well, guess what? Nicotine is one of the most addictive drugs you can find. It's not your fault you got addicted. You started out vaping in an attempt to quit smoking; you didn't expect to get addicted.

By the way, you're a great friend to so many people. You drop everything to help out whenever someone needs it. You love your family and give them everything they need. You're a great son and stay in touch with your parents. People like and respect you. Your boss recently gave you a promotion. Give yourself a break! The last time you quit, you stayed away from vaping for three months. You can do it again. Good luck!

Warmest regards,

Your best friend on the sidelines

FIGURE 22-1:
A sample letter to my ashamed self.

Accepting Yourself

Accepting yourself takes the idea of forgiving yourself one step further. With this approach, you drop the entire notion that there's even something to forgive. In other words, you quit judging, evaluating, and critiquing. Doing so frees up emotional energy to be directed toward whatever you want.

Letting go of self-evaluations

Rating or grading yourself is a foolish endeavor. The process almost never produces anything useful. So, let us explain why the practice of judging and evaluating yourself is a bad way to go:

>> **Evaluating yourself takes up valuable time.** You could spend that time fishing or going to a movie. Why waste it on self-evaluation?

>> **Evaluating yourself takes away your attention from problems at hand.** Studies show us that people focused on how they're doing actually perform worse because they're concentrating on their self-judgments rather than working on a problem or task.

>> **Self-evaluation promotes thinking in terms of all good or bad.** Most actions we take involve a complex mix of outcomes.

>> **It's impossible to rate your overall worth.** For example, say you're a model citizen who volunteers, helps your neighbors, participates in neighborhood cleanups, and donates to charity. One day, you're texting while driving and accidently hit another vehicle, causing minor injuries. Are you a good person or a bad person? Neither. The very idea of evaluating you as a totality is absurd.

Accepting yourself is another facet of acquiring a mindful lifestyle as described in Chapter 21. Mindfulness involves awareness of present moments without judgment. Similarly, accepting yourself means letting go of the need to judge or evaluate yourself as a person, which can interfere with living a fulfilling life. Instead, you can explore yourself with curiosity and detachment and learn a lot in the process.

Exploring accepting affirmations

An additional avenue toward self-acceptance can be found by exploring accepting affirmations. We have a sample list for you. But feel free to add to it or make your own.

>> I am today and not my past.

>> Living matters more than judging.

>> I am open to all possibilities and potentials.

>> I don't need to fear failure if I just open myself to greater understanding.

>> My experiences matter more than my accomplishments.

>> I don't need to say I'm sorry for being who I am.

>> I accept who I am unconditionally.

>> I am grateful for my life.

>> I feel comfortable with myself.

>> I matter.

>> I am neither perfect nor flawed.

>> I accept my body and embrace it.

TIP

Research tells us that familiar things are more believable, so we recommend that you repeat these affirmations often. They'll slowly begin to feel part of you. Consider making flashcards with a few of your favorite affirmations.

REMEMBER

These affirmations can help you avoid dropping into a hole when negative events occur. Instead of berating yourself, you can give yourself true self-compassion. You can refocus on your goals and stop negative, self-defeating beliefs. And affirmations as part of self-compassion can help you stay nicotine-free for the long run.

6

The Part of Tens

IN THIS PART . . .

Discover ways to help someone else quit.

Find help on the web.

Uncover messages that can help teens or young adults.

Chapter **23**

Ten Ways to Help Someone You Care about Quit

Quitting smoking is one of the toughest challenges a person can face. It takes the ability to handle frustration, manage intense cravings, break strong associations, and ignore frequent temptations. Having support from family members and friends can improve a person's chances of success.

Being around someone who's trying to quit smoking presents its own challenges. The smoker may start showing disagreeable behaviors, reactions, and emotions that you've rarely seen before. This chapter helps you anticipate these possibilities and deal with the person you care about during an especially difficult time.

TIP

Although this chapter describes helping someone you care about stop smoking, the advice applies equally to those trying to stop vaping, chewing, or other related addictions.

Making Your Home a No-Smoking Zone

The fewer places a smoker has available to smoke in, the better. For smokers, part of the problem is the numerous associations they have between certain environments and their smoking habits. For example, if they always smoke at the dining room table, that location in and of itself tends to trigger strong urges and cravings to smoke.

TIP

Make your house a no-smoking zone. While you're at it, make your car a no-smoking zone, too. Eliminating the opportunity to smoke in the house or the car cuts down on the number of available triggers. By doing this, realize that you're not telling the smoker that he or she can never smoke again (which could lead to unproductive rebellion). Mutually agreeing to a no-smoking zone merely sets the stage for quitting. This action can happen prior to actually setting a quit date.

TIP

You can help make the case for declaring your home and car smoke-free by explaining that you're also trying to improve your own health by reducing the amount of secondhand smoke you and your family are exposed to.

Cleaning Up the Smokey Mess

Over time, your home has no doubt taken a hit from all the tobacco exhaled into the air over years of smoking by the person you're helping. Tobacco smell, as well as toxins, permeate the carpet, walls, curtains, furniture, bedding, and clothes throughout the home. Consider the quit date a time for massive spring cleaning, no matter what time of year it is.

Removing the odors will also cut down on the associations that trigger smoking. Smokers will hesitate before lighting up in a newly decontaminated environment. Consider opening all the windows and doors in the house to a day or two of completely fresh air. And if you want to really go all out, have your duct work cleaned as well.

TIP

Don't forget to thoroughly clean the car. This is a great time to get your car professionally detailed.

REMEMBER

Remove all ashtrays, lighters, and other paraphernalia from the home. If you can't stand to throw away your great-great-grandfather's ashtray, clean it up and store it in a drawer out of sight for a while. Maybe someday, you can use it as a place to put paper clips. But that'll come well down the road, after months of smoke-free living.

Remaining Positive

Helping someone quit smoking, chewing, or vaping can feel like a burden. Plus, when you're around someone who's unusually irritable, it's easy to become crabby yourself. It's important to work at staying as upbeat as you can. Think about a future when cigarettes and such are no longer a part of your lives.

REMEMBER

Remaining positive doesn't mean you put on a sickeningly sweet persona. It doesn't mean you give in or capitulate to honest disagreements. However, this probably isn't such a great time to have deep talks about long-term relationship issues or chronically difficult subjects. Postpone arguments if possible. Be sincere in your effort to stay positive.

Depersonalizing Crabbiness

It's hard not to take irritability and cantankerousness personally. But when someone is trying to quit smoking, his or her crabbiness is *not* about you. Withdrawal from tobacco sets off moodiness and discomfort in most quitters. The person you're helping probably feels like lashing out at the world and you're the part of the world that's most available. This isn't fair, but the withdrawal symptoms — including the crabbiness — won't last forever.

REMEMBER

When you feel like striking back, take a deep breath. Ask yourself what your goal is. Will you really achieve something useful by counterattacking? Probably not. And you're only likely to make things worse. What you really want, down deep, is a nonsmoker. Play the game for the long haul.

Keeping Judgment at Bay

We can't say this enough times. Look for ways to express empathy with your family member or friend who's trying to quit smoking, chewing, or vaping. Empathy is all about putting yourself in someone else's shoes. If you're a smoker or a former smoker, that's probably pretty easy to do — you've likely had the same struggle with trying to quit.

But if you have never smoked or struggled with an addiction, it can be more difficult to feel empathy. Imagine a time in your life when you were especially hungry, yet you were hours from being able to eat. That's the kind of feeling quitters face every day. The difference is that you were ultimately able to satisfy your hunger.

If a quitter tries to satisfy his or her hunger by smoking or vaping, the battle could be lost — or at least made more difficult.

Also, we'll go out on a limb here and suggest that, because you're human, you probably have a few of your own flaws. Maybe you eat too much, spend too much, have a quick temper, forget birthdays and anniversaries, leave your house a mess, are late to pay bills — you get the idea. No one's perfect.

So, try to avoid nagging and criticizing. Instead, try empathizing by saying something like the following:

>> I know this is a really hard time for you. Let me know if I can help.

>> I get it that you're crabby. I would be, too.

>> Quitting is probably the hardest thing you've ever done, isn't it?

>> You look like you're struggling. How about we go over our list of positive actions?

>> It probably feels like things will never get easier, but from everything I know and have read, you'll likely feel better in a couple of weeks. Thanks for working so hard at this!

Planning Distractions

It's likely that your friend or loved one has a list of things to do instead of smoking. That may include chewing hard candy, going to the gym, riding a bike, or going for a walk instead of heading into the breakroom at work, among other things. But it's also good to develop a list of alternative distractions that the two of you can do together. These could include going to a movie, going to the beach, taking a hike, playing fetch with your dog, or eating out. Get creative! Plan your list together, and make sure to identify distractions that don't serve as triggers for the person trying to quit. If eating out makes him or her want to reach for a cigarette, skip that and throw a ball for the dog instead.

Reducing Stress

Hopefully, your friend or loved one who's quitting hasn't chosen a highly stressful quit date — you know, like the week before income tax forms are due or when you're putting your house on the market. But no time is stress-free — and you can help. Offer to take on a bit more responsibility for a few weeks. For example, you can help with childcare, meal prep, or the laundry.

We're not giving the quitter an excuse to be lazy, but it takes a lot of energy to stay focused on quitting. Give your friend or loved one all the support you can.

REMEMBER

This is not a free ride. After a month or so, things should gradually go back to normal. Be clear about what you're willing to do and for how long.

Encouraging All Attempts

Slips or lapses are normal and expected. Try not to catastrophize if your partner slips and has one or more cigarettes. We're not saying that slipping is good — slips pretty much always make things tougher. But they don't mean that failure looms on the immediate horizon.

So, if the person you're helping slips, remind him or her that slips can serve as learning opportunities. If he or she wants to talk about why the slip happened, by all means talk and search for reasons together. You can talk about how long he or she was able to go without smoking and all the good reasons for quitting. But don't criticize, blame, induce guilt, nag, shame, or harass!

Even if the slip turns into a *total* relapse, it's still important to encourage more attempts when the time seems right. Remind your friend or loved one that most smokers try to quit as many as 30 or more times before finally succeeding. You both need to be patient and positive. Repeated runs at it still have a good chance of working eventually.

See Chapter 19 for information about lapses and relapses.

Checking In

Some people trying to quit think they should go it alone. They don't talk about what they're doing or how they're feeling. Generally, that's not such a good idea. Check in regularly with your friend or loved one. Ask about how it's going. Encourage a discussion about what's working and what's not, as well as how you can help.

In other words, ask questions about how you can help make quitting easier. Be sure to stay positive and encouraging when discussing the struggles of quitting. Checking in lets the person know that you appreciate what he or she is going through and that you care.

Celebrating Success

Whether the smoker has gone for one hour, one day, one week, or one year, celebrate every successful day without smoking. Here are some ideas:

» Plan fun activities.

» Bake a cake.

» Give a small gift.

» Send a congratulatory card.

» Go to a movie.

Recognize success even if your smoker relapses. Each smoke-free day benefits health, and getting back on a successful track is always possible.

TIP

Sometimes after quitting, even after quite a while, cravings come up. So, be sure to continue to notice and celebrate regularly!

Chapter 24

Ten (Or So) Reliable Resources for More Information

Surf the web, and you'll find that information abounds when it comes to smoking and vaping. But, as you know, the web is filled with accurate information, misleading information, and downright false information. Scratch the surface of many websites, and you'll see they're nothing more than thinly disguised marketing ploys designed to sell products or gather subscriptions.

In this chapter, we give you ten (or so) reliable web-based resources. There are no promises of easy ways to quit or completely safe and satisfying alternatives to smoking and vaping. But there is solid information you can obtain from the following sites.

TIP

If you're looking for more information online, keep in mind that the most reliable sources of information on quitting smoking are typically federal, state, and locally funded agencies, as well as trusted medical centers and institutions (like the Mayo Clinic), and nonprofit organizations. Beware of any site that tells you that vaping is completely safe, that promises a quick or easy way to quit, or that's trying to sell you something or give you something for free in exchange for your email address.

The American Cancer Society

The American Cancer Society offers lots of resources on quitting smoking at `www.cancer.org/healthy/stay-away-from-tobacco.html`. The American Cancer Society also sponsors the Great American Smokeout on the third Thursday in November of every year. It's a great day to quit smoking! Find out more at `www.cancer.org/healthy/stay-away-from-tobacco/great-american-smokeout.html`.

The American Lung Association

The American Lung Association (`www.lung.org`) offers lots of reliable information about lung cancer and smoking. It also has a quiz on its website designed to determine if you're eligible to receive a lung cancer CT scan. Just go to `www.lung.org/our-initiatives/saved-by-the-scan/`. The quiz takes less than a minute and could save your life.

TIP

If you've been a long-term smoker, and you're suffering from chronic lung problems, the American Lung Association is *the* place for you to find out more important information.

Cochrane Reviews

You can look up the latest information about smoking, vaping, tobacco, addiction, and health at `www.cochrane.org`. Cochrane is an organization that promotes evidence-informed health decision-making by looking at published research and rigorously evaluating its quality. It attempts to be unbiased and objective, and it doesn't accept donations from commercial sources or sources that have conflicts of interest. Although the articles contain some sophisticated statistics, you don't have to be a full-fledged scientist to read its reviews — you can understand the gist of the conclusions even without an advanced degree. Better still — the reviews are free!

The U.S. Centers for Disease Control and Prevention

The U.S. Centers for Disease Control and Prevention (CDC) has a large section on its website dedicated to smoking and tobacco use, including tips from former smokers on how to quit. Go to www.cdc.gov/tobacco/. In addition, the CDC has an extensive library of information about heart disease, cancer, and chronic obstructive pulmonary disease (COPD).

The American Psychological Association

The American Psychological Association's website has journal articles and policy statements from the world's largest organized group of psychologists. To access this information, just go to www.apa.org and, in the Search box at the top of the page, search for terms like *vaping, addiction, smoking,* or *tobacco.*

The National Institute on Drug Abuse

Go to www.drugabuse.gov to find scientific information about addiction and drugs. The National Institute on Drug Abuse has screening tools for adults and adolescents. You can even find articles written in both English and Spanish, as well as easy-to-read drug facts.

Smokefree.gov

Smokefree.gov is a fabulous, user-friendly, and federally sponsored website that has specific information for veterans, women, teens, adults over 60, and Spanish speakers. In addition, it offers 24/7 support from your smartphone.

Your State Quitline

Each state maintains a phone quitline and website for helping smokers quit. Their advice is sound and generally well researched. Simply search the web for your state's name and the word *quitline.* It will pop up immediately.

The American Heart Association

You can find tips for quitting smoking and vaping on the American Heart Association's website at www.heart.org/en/healthy-living/healthy-lifestyle/quit-smoking-tobacco. There are also articles with ideas for helping teens refrain from vaping and smoking.

The UK's National Health Service

The United Kingdom's National Health Service (NHS) has tips on quitting smoking at www.nhs.uk/smokefree. The UK has long demonstrated a keen interest in helping its citizens quit smoking and vaping due to the profound health consequences. You can also read success stories and watch videos of people who managed to quit.

MedlinePlus

At www.medlineplus.gov, you can find health information from the U.S. National Library of Medicine. Use the Search box at the top of the page to find reliable, scientifically sound articles about any kind of health topic, including smoking and vaping. MedlinePlus also has extensive resources for learning about medications, both prescription and over the counter, for helping people quit smoking and vaping.

Truth Initiative

The Truth Initiative is a nonprofit, public health organization committed to achieving a culture that rejects tobacco. It has tons of reliable information on vaping and quitting smoking of all types. You can find the Truth Initiative at www.truthinitiative.org.

Chapter 25

Ten Messages for Teens and Young Adults Who Vape

Vaping is a relatively new pastime that has become increasingly popular with young people. In the early years, vaping went largely unnoticed and unstudied. But as more and more teens experiment with vaping, there are mounting concerns. We're concerned, too. And we have some messages for those who are considering trying it out or who have already started to vape.

If you're a parent or caring adult, and you have concerns that a young person in your life may be vaping or thinking about vaping, see if you can get that person to read this chapter. And if you're really lucky, your young person may agree to also read Chapters 5, 6, and 7. If all else fails, use these messages as talking points. Keep the communication door open!

Your Lungs Love Air

We know your peers (and maybe a dude at the vape shop) have told you that vaping is safe. Many people think that. And it's true that vaping is "probably" quite a bit safer than regular cigarettes that emit burned tobacco smoke.

But that does *not* make vaping safe. Even the CEO of JUUL recently announced that people who have never smoked or vaped before shouldn't take up the habit due to the risks involved, which are not yet completely known.

REMEMBER

Lungs were meant to breath air — not smoke, not pollution, and not aerosol from your vaping device. Sure, most of those delicious flavors are natural and many are approved by the U.S. Food and Drug Administration (FDA). But unless you're drinking your e-liquids (and we advise against that, too) those flavorings were approved for *ingestion* not *inhalation*. The safety of all possible flavoring ingredients has not been established. And the FDA is now moving to restrict flavors. In the meantime, beware.

Stay Away from Street Products

You can buy fake Rolex watches off the street that look exactly like the real deal to the untrained eye. They're pretty cheap, too. On the other hand, the gold finish is fake, and the innards are made of cheap materials with questionable reliability.

You can buy e-liquids, vaping devices, and chemicals off the street as well. You can also get vaping paraphernalia at unlicensed shops that move often and escape regulatory oversight; they're no more reliable than street vendors.

Contaminated street products and their ingredients are the most likely culprits (there may be others) in the recent uptick of serious lung damage (sometimes resulting in death) showing up among teens and young adult vapers. Kids who started out as athletes are ending up in intensive care or the morgue after using some of these products.

TIP

We don't advise you to vape, but if you do, buy your e-liquid and devices at a reputable store — somewhere that has been around a while, has accumulated positive ratings on the Internet, and has no complaints from the Better Business Bureau (BBB). It's no guarantee, but it's a start and most likely safer than the street.

Your Brain Is Still Changing

You're not going to want to hear this, but your brain is still developing and changing as it processes new information and encounters various chemicals and substances. Given that your brain is the only one you'll ever get, you need to take really good care of it. Substances like nicotine can permanently affect your memory and concentration, as well as raise your future risk of addiction.

Getting Addicted Is No Fun

More bad news: Teens' brains get addicted faster than the brains of adults. With vaping, a nicotine addiction can happen very quickly. Although loading up on an addictive substance often feels really good at first, the long-term effect isn't so great. It's easy for your mind and body to focus obsessively on the need for continual buzzes. That crowds out a lot of brain space that could be used for listening to music, watching movies, hanging out with friends, or even acing your exams in school.

If you're addicted, you likely have less interest in pursuing other goals and accomplishments in your life. You become consumed with obtaining what you crave, getting that buzz, and then finding a way to repeat the process again. Addiction can cost you a lot of time and money, not to mention your health.

It's Not Your Parents' Marijuana

Vape pens are a new way to smoke marijuana that has very little smell and can be extremely discreet. However, the market is virtually unregulated right now, and the safety of these devices is highly questionable. In fact, the vast majority of the emerging lung damage crisis from vaping has been associated with vaping THC. Although marijuana is legal in some states, tetrahydrocannabinol (THC) is still often purchased from black markets, which adds to the concern.

The potency of THC in many vaping devices is many times greater than what your parents may have inhaled back in the day. Experts worry about the unknown effects of long-term use of excessive THC levels. Concerns have also been expressed about the pesticides used by marijuana cultivators, which are known to kill brain cells and increase the risk of some cancers. We're not trying to scare you — we just want to give you something to think about.

Nicotine Levels May Be Higher than You Think

It's virtually impossible to calculate how much nicotine your body absorbs from a combustible cigarette or from a vaping device — that is, unless you're in a medical laboratory with sophisticated equipment. Cigarettes vary in their nicotine levels, and smokers vary in how long they hold a puff in their lungs. Vaping devices and the e-liquids they contain vary greatly in terms of the nicotine levels produced. You can easily be getting more than you think. That possibility is especially true with some of the new pod devices that are particularly popular with young people.

Don't Let Frustration Ruin Your Life

Psychologists have found that the ability to tolerate frustration is one of the most important skills to acquire during adolescence and young adulthood. It's a great predictor of future earnings, success, and happiness. Unfortunately, the ability to tolerate frustration is likely to be impaired when you become seriously addicted. So, if you want money, success, and happiness, stay away from vaping.

What Would You Tell Your Little Brother or Sister to Do?

We know you most likely have an imperfect relationship with your little brother or sister (if you have one). But, on balance, we bet you'd want what's best for the kid. Would you advise your little bro or sis to take up vaping? Probably not. Why not? You know exactly why not: unknown risks, addiction potential, money, and more. So, if you wouldn't advise it for your brother or sister, why are *you* doing it? By the way, your younger siblings look up to you, and you're serving as a role model — whether you want to or not.

Choosing What's Cool rather than What's Good for You

Teens want to be accepted by their friends. Part of being accepted is doing what the rest of the crowd is doing. Standing up to peer pressure is a struggle that some kids find overwhelming. Many teens succumb and do things like vaping, in order to be cool, knowing deep down that it's not the right thing to do — maybe not even what they really *want* to do.

Most adults can understand the temptations of following the crowd. Your parents may not know that you vape. Those devices that look like USB drives are pretty easy to conceal. But you probably know that.

TIP

If you want to quit, consider telling your parents about your desire to quit and you may be surprised by how helpful and supportive they are. If not your parents, talk about your concerns with a school counselor, school nurse, or a coach or teacher you trust. Be smart and do what you know is best.

Thinking about the Long-Term Game

At your age, it's really hard to think about next *year*, let alone the next decade or two. But use your imagination and consider what you want to look like in the future. Do you see yourself blowing smoke from a vaping device around your future family, your kids, or at your workplace?

By then, what do you think the science will say about the long-term effects of vaping? No problem? Really? Do you truly think that regularly inhaling chemicals won't cause a few health issues? It's your call.

Index

Numbers

decreasing cognitive load, 253

depression, 137, 149, 156. *See also* emotions

  causing insomnia, 240

  medications for, 184–185

  overview, 256–257

  as side-effect, 254

  treatment for, 257–258

diabetes, 50, 79

diacetyl, 77, 81, 82

DiClemente, Carlo C., 200

diet

  choosing, 280–285

  distorted thinking and, 277–280

  eating out and, 284

  fiber in, 281–282

  nutrients in, 280–281

  on quit day, changing, 228–229

  recommended, 284–285

  reducing calories from, 282–283

  tracking food intake, 276–277

Dietary Approaches to Stop Hypertension (DASH), 284–285

dietary supplements, 184–185

discarding cigarettes, 225

dissolvable tobacco, 33

distorted thinking, 280. *See also* feelings; triggers

  catastrophizing in, 140, 141

  challenging

    evidence-based questions, 147, 148, 149

    moderating extremism, 149

    self-talk, 150, 151, 152

  extremes in, 144

  feelings and, 138

  letting go of, 153, 154

  mental filtering in, 143, 144

  negative predictions in, 141, 142, 143

  obligatory evaluations in, 146

  overlapping in, 147

  overview, 22, 140

  personalizing in, 145

  psychological role of, 136–137

distractions

  cleaning as distraction, 235

  controlling anger with, 236

  planning with smoker, 320

dizziness

  in panic disorder, 256

  as withdrawal symptom, 241

Doctor on Demand, 168

dopamine, 20, 144

drinks

  alcohol, 239

  tea, 238

  as triggers, 229

dropout rate, 192

E

ear infections, 52, 53

eating out, 284

e-cigarettes. *See* vaping

Electronics for Dummies (Shamieh), 65

e-liquids. *See also* vaping; vaping devices

  chemicals in, 75, 76, 77, 78, 79

  contaminated, 80, 85, 91

  defined, 62, 67

  diacetyl in, 81, 82

  flavoring of, 69, 75, 79

  nicotine in, 68, 75

  overview, 10, 31, 75

  regulation of, 67

  toxicity of, 83, 84, 121

  types, 68, 69

emotions. *See also* distorted thinking; triggers

  anger, 234–236

  controlling

    with breathing exercises, 249–250

    confidence, 252

    with daily affirmations, 250–251

  distorted thinking and, 146, 147

  empathy

    defined, 296

    towards smoker, showing, 319–320

  frustration, 330

  guilt, 309–310

  invulnerability, 252

  negative

    anxiety, 255–256

    causing relapses, 258

    depression, 256–257

World Anti-Doping Agency (WADA), 39
writing
    cue cards, 226–227, 250
    distorted thinking, 280
    in food journal, 276
    in gratitude journal, 302
    increasing chance of commitment to quit, 210
    letter of self-compassion, 311–312
    plan for quitting, 220
    Smoking/Quitting Clarifier, 208

Y

young people. *See also* parenting
  experimentation by, 1, 59
  modeling by, 24, 25, 26

nicotine replacement therapy (NRT) and, 121
pod systems and, 67
secretiveness of, 89, 108
vaping and, 327–331
    addiction, 90, 91, 92
    contaminated supplies, 91
    statistics, 87, 88
    targeted marketing, 88, 89

Z

Zyban (bupropion), 132, 133

About the Authors

Laura L. Smith, PhD: Dr. Smith is a clinical psychologist. She is past-president of the New Mexico Psychological Association. She has considerable experience in school and clinical settings dealing with children and adults who have emotional disorders, frequently accompanied by substance abuse problems, including smoking and vaping. She presents workshops and classes to the University of New Mexico adult continuing education program. Dr. Smith is a widely published author of articles and books to the profession and the public.

Charles H. Elliott, PhD: Dr. Elliott is a clinical psychologist and currently president of the New Mexico Psychological Association. He is also a professor emeritus at Fielding Graduate University and has served on the faculty of two medical schools. He has extensive experience in the treatment of children, adolescents, and adults with emotional disorders, especially disorders that interact with health, such as smoking and vaping. Dr. Elliott has authored many professional articles, book chapters, and books in the area of health psychology and cognitive behavior therapies, including *Why Can't I Get What I Want?: How to Stop Making the Same Old Mistakes and Start Living a Life You Can Love* (Davis-Black).

Drs. Smith and Elliott have worked on numerous publications together. They are coauthors of: *Anger Management For Dummies* (Wiley); *Borderline Personality Disorder For Dummies* (Wiley); *Child Psychology & Development For Dummies* (Wiley); *Overcoming Anxiety For Dummies,* 2nd Edition (Wiley); *Obsessive Compulsive Disorder For Dummies* (Wiley); *Seasonal Affective Disorder For Dummies* (Wiley); *Anxiety & Depression Workbook For Dummies* (Wiley); *Depression For Dummies* (Wiley); *Hollow Kids: Recapturing the Soul of a Generation Lost to the Self-Esteem Myth* (Prima Lifestyles); and *Why Can't I Be the Parent I Want to Be?* (New Harbinger). Their work has been featured in various media including *Family Circle, Parents, Child,* and *Better Homes & Gardens,* as well as popular publications like the *New York Post, Washington Times, Daily Telegraph* (London), NPR, CNN, Canada AM, and various Sirius Satellite radio shows. They have committed their professional lives to making the science of psychology relevant and accessible to the public. You can contact the authors at www.quittingsmokingandvaping.com.

Dedication

We dedicate this book to all the people who struggle with addiction to smoking or vaping. We also dedicate this book to our grandchildren — Lauren, Cade, Alaina, Carter, and Viktoria — whom we fervently hope never turn to vaping or smoking.

Author's Acknowledgments

We want to thank our outstanding team at Wiley. As usual, their expertise, support, and guidance was of immeasurable help. From the beginning, our acquisition editor, Tracy Boggier, helped us formulate and execute a plan for developing this book on quitting smoking, as well as the new phenomenon of vaping. Elizabeth Kuball, development and copy editor, ensured that our text stayed on point and error-free. We also thank Alicia Wiprovnick, our technical editor, for her contributions.

We would also like to acknowledge Jackson Gantzer for offering advice and information about the technical aspects of vaping devices. Thanks to Lauren Rodriguez for her help with understanding the teen vaping culture. Others also provided us with invaluable feedback and ideas: Kitty Tynan, Scott Bucholtz, Brian Elliott, Nancy Handmaker, Sarah Pastore, Allison Wolfe, Kate Wolfe, Trevor Wolfe, and Janice Guerin.

Publisher's Acknowledgments

Senior Acquisitions Editor: Tracy Boggier
Project Editor: Elizabeth Kuball
Copy Editor: Elizabeth Kuball
Technical Editor: Alicia Wiprovnick

Production Editor: Mohammed Zafar Ali
Cover Photos: © Carpe89/Getty Images

Leverage the power

Dummies is the global leader in the reference category and one of the most trusted and highly regarded brands in the world. No longer just focused on books, customers now have access to the dummies content they need in the format they want. Together we'll craft a solution that engages your customers, stands out from the competition, and helps you meet your goals.

Advertising & Sponsorships

Connect with an engaged audience on a powerful multimedia site, and position your message alongside expert how-to content. Dummies.com is a one-stop shop for free, online information and know-how curated by a team of experts.

- Targeted ads
- Video
- Email Marketing

- Microsites
- Sweepstakes sponsorship

20 MILLION PAGE VIEWS EVERY SINGLE MONTH

15 MILLION UNIQUE VISITORS PER MONTH

43% OF ALL VISITORS ACCESS THE SITE VIA THEIR MOBILE DEVICES

700,000 NEWSLETTER SUBSCRIPTIONS TO THE INBOXES OF *300,000* UNIQUE INDIVIDUALS EVERY WEEK

Custom Publishing

Reach a global audience in any language by creating a solution that will differentiate you from competitors, amplify your message, and encourage customers to make a buying decision.

- Apps
- Books
- eBooks
- Video
- Audio
- Webinars

Brand Licensing & Content

Leverage the strength of the world's most popular reference brand to reach new audiences and channels of distribution.

For more information, visit **dummies.com/biz**

PERSONAL ENRICHMENT

Staying Sharp
9781119187790
USA $26.00
CAN $31.99
UK £19.99

Facebook
9781119179030
USA $21.99
CAN $25.99
UK £16.99

Guitar
9781119293354
USA $24.99
CAN $29.99
UK £17.99

Investing
9781119293347
USA $22.99
CAN $27.99
UK £16.99

Beekeeping
9781119310068
USA $22.99
CAN $27.99
UK £16.99

Digital Photography
9781119235606
USA $24.99
CAN $29.99
UK £17.99

Meditation
9781119251163
USA $24.99
CAN $29.99
UK £17.99

Pregnancy
9781119235491
USA $26.99
CAN $31.99
UK £19.99

Samsung Galaxy S7
9781119279952
USA $24.99
CAN $29.99
UK £17.99

iPhone
9781119283133
USA $24.99
CAN $29.99
UK £17.99

Crocheting
9781119287117
USA $24.99
CAN $29.99
UK £16.99

Nutrition
9781119130246
USA $22.99
CAN $27.99
UK £16.99

PROFESSIONAL DEVELOPMENT

Windows 10
9781119311041
USA $24.99
CAN $29.99
UK £17.99

AutoCAD
9781119255796
USA $39.99
CAN $47.99
UK £27.99

Excel 2016
9781119293439
USA $26.99
CAN $31.99
UK £19.99

QuickBooks 2017
9781119281467
USA $26.99
CAN $31.99
UK £19.99

macOS Sierra
9781119280651
USA $29.99
CAN $35.99
UK £21.99

LinkedIn
9781119251132
USA $24.99
CAN $29.99
UK £17.99

Windows 10 All-in-One
9781119310563
USA $34.00
CAN $41.99
UK £24.99

SharePoint 2016
9781119181705
USA $29.99
CAN $35.99
UK £21.99

Fundamental Analysis
9781119263593
USA $26.99
CAN $31.99
UK £19.99

Networking
9781119257769
USA $29.99
CAN $35.99
UK £21.99

Office 2016
9781119293477
USA $26.99
CAN $31.99
UK £19.99

Office 365
9781119265313
USA $24.99
CAN $29.99
UK £17.99

Salesforce.com
9781119239314
USA $29.99
CAN $35.99
UK £21.99

Coding
9781119293323
USA $29.99
CAN $35.99
UK £21.99

dummies.com

dummies®
A Wiley Brand